MICROCOMPUTER-BASED DESIGN

MICROCOMPUTER-BASED DESIGN

JOHN B. PEATMAN

Professor of Electrical Engineering
The Georgia Institute of Technology

McGRAW-HILL BOOK COMPANY

New York   St. Louis   San Francisco   Auckland   Bogotá   Düsseldorf
Johannesburg   London   Madrid   Mexico   Montreal   New Delhi   Panama   Paris
São Paulo   Singapore   Sydney   Tokyo   Toronto

MICROCOMPUTER-BASED DESIGN

34567890 **FGFG** 783210987

This book was set in Melior by Progressive Typographers.
The editors were Peter D. Nalle and Matthew Cahill;
the copy editor was Susan Sexton;
the proofreader was Mary Ann Rosenberg;
the designer was Anne Canevari Green;
the production supervisor was Charles Hess.
The drawings were done by J & R Services, Inc.
Kingsport Press, Inc., was printer and binder.

Library of Congress Cataloging in Publication Data

Peatman, John B
Microcomputer-based design.

Includes bibliographical references.
1. Miniature computers.   I.   Title.
TK7888.3.P37   001.6′4′04   76-29345
ISBN 0-07-049138-0

To
Marilyn and
Lisa, Katie, and Bob

CONTENTS

PREFACE

This book is directed toward the engineer interested in obtaining an integrated understanding of the design of "smart" microcomputer-based instruments and devices. It opens the door to the many applications of microcomputers. It differs from many books in that it develops fundamental design capability while keeping this breadth of application in mind.

An effective digital designer requires at least three distinct capabilities. First, the designer must have a fundamental understanding of available components. This begins with the microprocessor chips, memory chips, and I/O chips which make up a microcomputer. It extends to the keyboards and switches for setting up an instrument or device, transducers for sensing inputs, actuators for control, devices for communicating with computers and other instruments, devices providing extensive storage capability, and printers and displays for informing the user of results. Furthermore, for a designer to be effective, this understanding must extend beyond the framework of only simplified and idealized devices. For example, since the proper use of a printer requires careful observance of timing considerations, the designer is aided by having systematic ways to design with microcomputers so as to maintain control over these timing considerations.

Second, the designer must thoroughly understand the algorithmic processes required by each aspect of the design and be able to translate these into the language of the microcomputer. For example, an instrument which automatically carries out several measurements and then must fit the resulting data with a sinusoid requires the designer to develop a Fourier analysis algorithm and then be able to implement it as a sequence of microcomputer instructions.

Third, the designer must understand how the extensive requirements of an instrument or device can be broken down into manageable parts. The hardware must be selected and configured. Where tradeoffs occur between hardware and software, these will usually be resolved so as to minimize hardware. The software requirements of each aspect of the design must then be met, be they the reading and interpreting of a keyboard, the development of a data-averaging algorithm, or the control of a stepper motor. Finally, the software parts must be put together into a coordinated whole so that the overall goals of the instrument are met.

This book attempts to organize and unify the development of these three capabilities: to understand and use components, to exploit powerful algorithmic processes, and to realize an effective organization of hardware and software so as to meet the specifications for an instrument or device.

From another point of view, this book is directed toward a specific goal of engineering studies—the development of creative design capability. With the development of microcomputers, design capability has centered upon the understanding and use of a limited number of complex but well-defined microcomputer chips. The various requirements of an instrument or device have largely become translated into software. Thus, the development of creative design capability has largely been translated into the domain of microcomputer instructions and is measured by the simplicity and clarity of algorithms. This evolution of digital technology provides a beautiful opportunity to develop design capability under rather ideal conditions: the specifications for each aspect of a design can be made both real and unambiguous; only a few microcomputer chips need be understood to meet the hardware needs of these design goals; and the amount of read-only memory required to hold the microcomputer instructions used by the student to carry out each aspect of a design provides a specific, real, cost criterion for measuring the quality of a design. To take advantage of this opportunity, most chapters close with a broad variety of problems having a design flavor.

This book will typically be used in a one-semester or two-quarter course in introductory microcomputer-based design at the senior level. It may be used at the junior level if it is deemed worthwhile to trade off the increased engineering experience of seniors for the opportunity to follow this course with other design-oriented courses. Because the design process is so dependent upon the characteristics and use of the specific microcomputer selected for its implementation, this book is dependent upon a parallel study of the characteristics of at least one specific microcomputer. To support such a study, appendixes are included on each of six microcomputers. Furthermore, any one of the appendixes can be used as a guide for culling through the manufacturer's information on some other microcomputer so as to pick out the data most immediately important for design purposes.

Although the content of the book is electrical, each component is sufficiently explained to permit the book to be used in a variety of curricula as an introduction to microcomputer-based design. The incentive to so use the book lies in the diverse applications of microcomputers, many of which are described in the first chapter.

An attempt has been made to make many of the parts of the book self-contained. Consequently, one way in which the book might be used is to study the "bare bones" of each chapter in order to obtain an accelerated route toward the overall instrument or device design picture. The remaining sections of each chapter can be studied at a later time as the need arises or in a subsequent course. Such an accelerated route through the study of *microcomputer software* might begin with Sections 2-1 to 2-9, perhaps using examples from Sections 7-6 and 7-7. At the same time, the register and data manipulation viewpoint of a specific microcomputer might be studied, using one of the appendixes. This might include the conventions inherent in the assembly language for the microcomputer, as presented in the manufacturer's assembly language user's manual. An accelerated study of *microcomputer hardware* might begin with Sections 3-1, 3-4, 3-6, 3-7, 3-9, 4-1, 4-2, 5-1, and 5-2. With this as a basis, the interactions between hardware and software are best exemplified by a study of the specific I/O devices of Sections 5-4 to 5-8. Chapter 6 then provides an overview of a variety of alternatives for actually carrying out the hardware and software development of an instrument.

It has been my good fortune to become involved with instrument design and the use of microcomputers through my work with some of the outstanding engineers of Hewlett-Packard Company, particularly with Ed Donn during two summers in Colorado Springs and David Dack during a year in Scotland. I am deeply indebted to my students at Georgia Tech who, through their design problem work, have also been my teachers.

My learnings and my activities have been fostered by several able administrators. Dr. Demetrius Paris has been instrumental in his support of my microcomputer-based design course and laboratory at Georgia Tech, while Dar Howard, Chuck House, and Bob Coackley have each in their own way opened new vistas for me within Hewlett-Packard. Finally, I am grateful to my wife, Marilyn, for sharing herself and her own career with her devotion to me and my career, and for typing the manuscript.

John B. Peatman

MICROCOMPUTER-BASED DESIGN

1

THE ROLE
OF THE
mICROCOMPUTER

1-1   MERITS OF MICROCOMPUTER-BASED DESIGN

The creation of the microcomputer is revolutionizing instrument* design.
Not only are traditional instruments becoming "smart," but entirely new
kinds of instruments are appearing.   With their extensive computing capability contained in a very few small integrated circuits, microcomputers
have invaded the minds of design engineers, as in Fig. 1-1. In this section,
we will consider ways in which this computing capability is enhancing instrument capability.

   Simplified data entry is exemplified by the marked-sense card reader
built into the point-of-sale terminal shown in Fig. 1-2. Each row of the card
lists one of the items sold. Each column lists a quantity (1 to 9). Thus, to
total an order requires only the filling in of appropriate marks for the quantity of each item purchased. The card reader senses these pencil marks and
computes the total cost. In this way, pricing is handled automatically.

   Sophisticated transduction permits a sales clerk to enter product-

---

* We will use the term *instrument* in a general sense. We will mean a self-contained, stand-
  alone device, not a rack full of equipment.

Figure 1-1. . . . , 6797, 6798, 6799, . . . (Rand
Renfroe.)

description information for each item sold into a point-of-sale terminal
using the laser scanner shown in Fig. 1-3. As the laser beam scans the light
and dark bands making up the Universal Product Code (UPC) symbol* on
the item, the time durations for the succession of bands are normalized and
converted into a UPC number. The terminal then looks this up in a table to
convert it to a price for the product.

A microcomputer-based measuring instrument may achieve *high accuracy via repetitive measurements plus averaging of the results.* Thus the
distance meter shown in Fig. 1-4 determines the distance to a passive re-
flector with an infrared light beam. It maintains an error of less than 1 in. in
measurements up to 1 mile by taking 2000 measurements and comparing the
standard deviation of these measurements against a preprogrammed limit.
If the standard deviation is acceptable, it computes and displays the average
distance. If it is not acceptable, it doubles the total number of measurements and checks the standard deviation against a new limit suitable for this
number of measurements in order to meet the accuracy specification of the
instrument. The instrument keeps trying for an acceptable standard by repeatedly doubling the number of measurements, up to a maximum of 32,000
(which takes less than 21 s). If an acceptable standard deviation is not attained after 32,000 measurements, an average is computed anyway, but it is
flashed on the display.

As can be seen from the rear view of this distance meter, the microcom-

---

* Described in Sec. 5-5.

(a)

(b)

Figure 1-2. Data entry with a marked-sense card reader.
(a) Card reader; (b) pencil-marked order card. (Doc-
umentor Division, Addressograph Multigraph Corp.)

*Figure 1-3. Laser-scanner entry
of product information. (NCR
Corp.)*

puter permits *simplicity of use.* It has only four switches (power off/on/self-
test; feet/meters; signal strength for aiming/signal strength for measuring; set
up/begin measurement), two knobs (correction for temperature and pressure;
adjustment of signal strength), a meter (signal strength), and a display (distance). One of the challenges of "smart" instrument design is forestalling
requests for "extra features" and maintaining the vision of a simple-to-use
device, as was done for this distance meter.

An instrument can employ a microcomputer to *obtain a desired measurement indirectly by combining the measurements of several different
parameters.* For example, a distance-measuring instrument for sporting
events like discus throwing would be more convenient to use if it could measure the distance between two points from a third point. By combining a
shaft-angle encoder with the distance meter of Fig. 1-4, a measurement of
both distance D1 and angular position (relative to an arbitrary reference) $\theta 1$
can be made for one of the points P1 and stored in the instrument. Then a
measurement is made for the other point P2, providing new values D2 and
$\theta 2$. These are then combined using the "law of cosines," as in Fig. 1-5, to
obtain the desired distance D3.

The Dioptron® automatic objective refractor of Fig. 1-6 helps determine
the eyeglass prescription for a patient indirectly. As can be seen from the
figure, it also provides the ultimate in simplicity of use, with only two push
buttons. Pressing one illuminates the patient's eye for accurate alignment.
Pressing the other initiates the measurement. The instrument detects blinks
and interrupts the measurement for the duration of each blink. At the completion of the measurement, the refraction is printed out.

To understand how the instrument works, consider the simplified
optical-system diagram of Fig. 1-7*a*. The image source can be thought of as

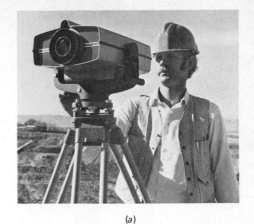

(a)

Figure 1-4. Distance meter. (a) Front view;
(b) rear view. (Hewlett-Packard Co.)

(b)

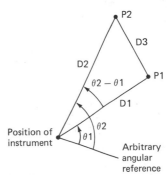

Figure 1-5. Indirect measurement of distance.

Law of cosines:
$$D3^2 = D2^2 + D1^2 - 2(D2D1)\cos(\theta2 - \theta1)$$

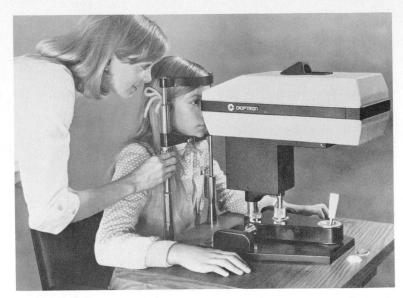

Figure 1-6. Dioptron® automatic objective refractor. (Coherent Radiation.)

having the shape of an arrow. It is bounced off a semitransparent mirror to form an image on the patient's retina. A motor-driven lens compensates for the patient's nearsightedness or farsightedness to form as sharp an image as possible on the retina as determined by the focus detector. The position of this lens yields the amount of correction needed, measured in "diopters." If the patient's eye is completely free of astigmatism, the number of diopters of correction will be independent of whether the arrow-shaped image on the patient's retina is horizontal or vertical or anywhere in between. This is illustrated in Fig. 1-7b, where six measurements have been made, one for each of six orientations, 30° apart. The required correction consists solely of the "spherical equivalent" component shown.

An astigmatic eye magnifies differently for different orientations of the arrow. A cylindrical lens produces a correction which varies sinusoidally with angular orientation. To take advantage of this, the instrument takes its six measurements and fits a sinusoid to the resulting points as best it can, as shown in Fig. 1-7c. The average value gives the "spherical equivalent" component of the prescription, while the peak-to-peak value and phase angle of the sinusoid determine the "cylinder" and "cylinder axis" components.

From this it is evident that the simplicity of use of this instrument camouflages an intricate and subtle measurement process involving rotation of an image source, linear movement of a lens, and a determination of focus. It also camouflages a calculation of the Fourier components of a waveform represented by six points.

Finally, the instrument carries out the entire measurement process on

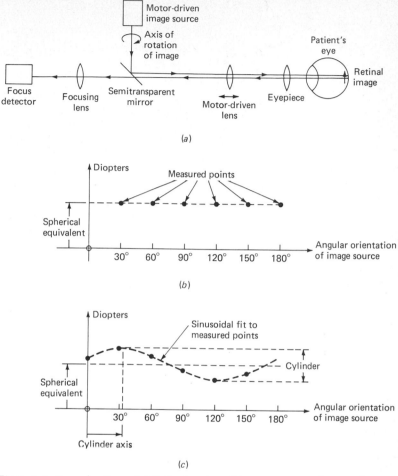

Figure 1-7. *Eye refraction.* (a) *Optical system;* (b) *measurement of an eye having no astigmatism;* (c) *measurement of an eye having astigmatism.*

each eye with an invisible, infrared image source while the patient views a visible, binocular target appearing to be located at infinity. More than anything else, it is this contrast between "what you see" and "what you get" which characterizes the "smart" instruments made possible by microcomputers.

Automatic calibration is a particularly valuable feature in a measuring instrument. It requires two capabilities:

1   The measuring circuit must be automatically switchable from the input transducer to either of two standard inputs, one which should give a "zero" measurement and one which should give a "full-scale" mea-

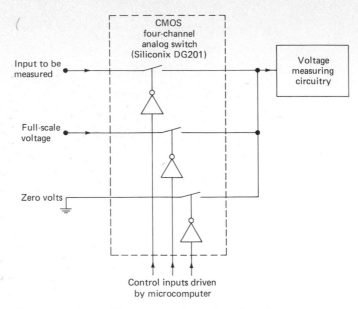

Figure 1-8. *Autocalibration switching of a voltage input.*

surement.   Measurements are made and results stored for these two
standard conditions.

2   Subsequent measurements must be normalized to these two stored results.   The control required for the first step and the calculating capability required for the second are already built into a microcomputer-
based instrument.   The input switching for a voltage input can use
complementary metal-oxide semiconductor (CMOS) analog switches
for fast, reliable, solid-state switching, as in Fig. 1-8.

The grocer's scale shown in Fig. 1-9 furnishes a closely related capability. The grocer first places a container on the scale and presses a "tare"
button.   The microcomputer will zero the display of weight.   Subsequent
measurements are then calculated and displayed using this *arbitrary zero
reference.*

Sophisticated handling of a device can be more easily achieved in a
microcomputer-based instrument than otherwise.   The microcomputer-
based PROM programmer shown in Fig. 1-10 enters data into a programmable read-only memory (PROM).   PROMs are extremely useful for storing
the instructions which make up the software of a microcomputer-based instrument.   They suffer from rather wide variations in the amount of current,
or voltage, required to change the state of a specific bit during programming.
As discussed in Sec. 4-1, the PROM programmer pulses the bits to be
changed and monitors the results.   Then it selects the number of pulses required for the programming of each bit on the basis of how many it actually

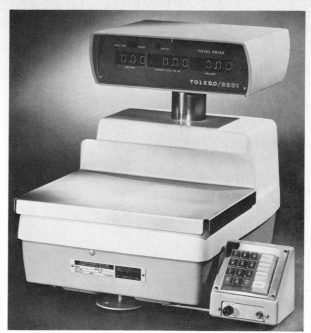

Figure 1-9. Grocer's scale. (Toledo Scale Division of Reliance Electric Co.)

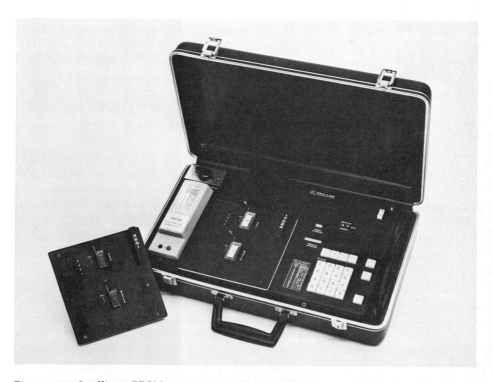

Figure 1-10. Intelligent PROM programmer. (Pro-Log Corp.)

*Figure 1-11. Automatic type-
writer. (Xerox Corp.)*

needs to change its state, plus an added percentage to provide the reliability
of "overprogramming." At the same time, it minimizes the time and the
heating of the PROM necessary to achieve this result.

Another example of sophisticated device handling is used in the automatic typewriter system shown in Fig. 1-11. As complete lines are read from
the cassette tape-storage unit, the microcomputer types these lines in alternate directions, typing one line from left to right and the next from right to
left, to achieve typing speeds of up to 350 words per minute.

A *"smart" output display* enables an instrument to show exactly what
is significant to a user. The "selective-level measurement set" shown in
Fig. 1-12 is used to test telephone frequency-multiplexing equipment, where
it gives a decimal display of the telephone-channel identity, the calculated
frequency, and the measured result. In addition, each voice-channel signal
level is represented by the height of a point above the X axis on a cathode-
ray-tube (CRT) display. The measurement currently being made is represented by a flashing marker. If the signal level on one channel is outside the
user-defined limits, the decimal display can be used to locate the channel
designation in the multiplex hierarchy (for example, mastergroup number,
supergroup number, group number, and channel number) as well as to obtain a more accurate decimal readout of this signal level.

Some instruments use *sophisticated data reduction* to provide the information which a user wants rather than the data which is generated
directly. Consider a gas or liquid chromatograph which performs the ana-
lytical separation of complex chemical mixtures in order to determine the
amount of each chemical present in a sample. The amplified output is in
the form of a voltage versus time, as shown in Fig. 1-13. The quantitative information in this waveform resides in the *area* under each peak. Extracting
this information is complicated by a drifting baseline, the riding of one peak

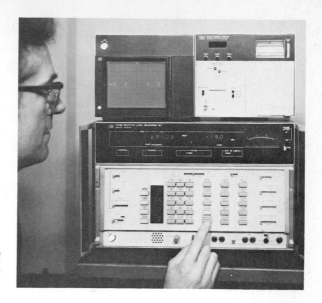

Figure 1-12. *Selective-level measurement set. (Hewlett-Packard, Ltd.)*

upon another (component 2 upon component 1), and peaks fusing together (components 3 and 4). The instrument shown in Fig. 1-14 computes the areas accurately and automatically, printing out time and area for each peak.

Some instruments take advantage of a microcomputer's ability to utilize *bulk data storage.* Thus the "smart" computer terminal shown in Fig. 1-15 employs dual floppy-disk storage which requires the interactive control discussed in Sec. 4-4. The terminal can store half a million words of data and program instructions, permitting flexible interaction with the user. In addition, the terminal can temporarily store large amounts of data so that

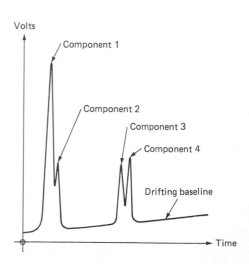

Figure 1-13. *Output of a gas chromato-graph.*

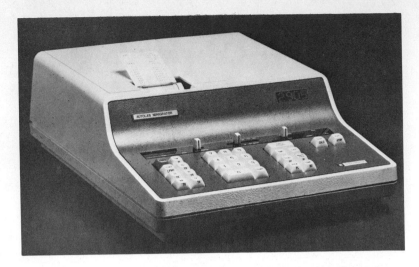

Figure 1-14. *Chromatographic computing integrator.* (Spectra-Physics.)

peak loads on the communication lines and at the central computer can be reduced.

A microcomputer-based instrument can incorporate extensive *error control*, both to detect when errors occur and to reduce these sources of

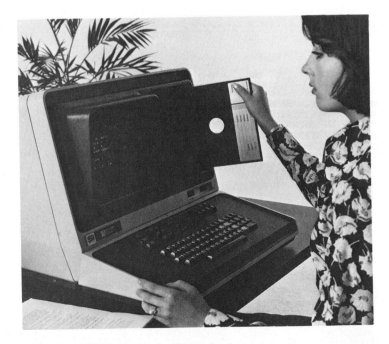

Figure 1-15. *Batch terminal.* (Sycor, Inc.)

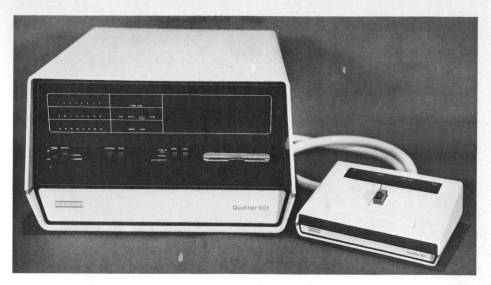

Figure 1-16. Self-testing IC tester. (*Fairchild Systems Technology Division.*)

error.   For example, when data is transferred from a microcomputer to a floppy disk, it is usual to add a "cyclic redundancy check character" (CRCC) as a means for achieving error detection.   Then the data is read back from the floppy disk in order to make a CRCC check.   If this is unsuccessful, the data can be written again and checked.   If this continues to be unsuccessful, then the data can be transferred to a different location on the disk and a note made not to use the first location any more.

Self-test capability fosters user confidence in the successful operation of an instrument.   Furthermore, if the instrument fails, the self-test capability may also help diagnose the source of the trouble.   Thus the integrated-circuit (IC) tester shown in Fig. 1-16 takes into account the three variables which occur in IC testing: the tester, the program (read in through an optical card reader), and the IC to be tested.   Each time a program is loaded, the tester checks both itself and the program data before going on to test the IC. Thus the user can maintain a high degree of confidence that if the tester *says* the IC is faulty, then indeed the IC *is* faulty, and not the tester or the program.

Flexible design is a valuable attribute of a microcomputer-based instrument.   For example, the CRT computer terminal shown in Fig. 1-17 is actually one of an evolving family of terminals.   The hardware is modular, permitting specific hardware functions to be modified by changing one of the internal printed-circuit boards.   Likewise, the function of any key can be modified by changing the microcomputer software.

Flexible remote control of several instruments can be achieved using a standard interface bus to interconnect the instruments with a controller.

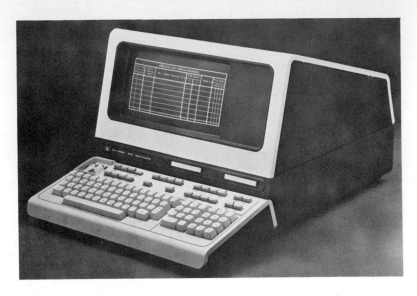

Figure 1-17. Flexibly designed CRT terminal.   (Hewlett-Packard Co.)

The system shown in Fig. 1-18 employs a programmable calculator to control all the instruments shown, achieving an automatic test capability for a specific test situation using standard instruments.   While the figure shows one manufacturer's equipment, any manufacturer's equipment can be used on this same interface bus.   It need only meet the requirements of the inter-

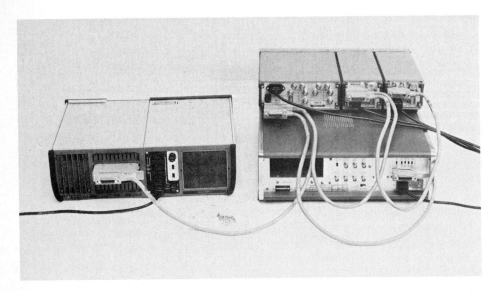

Figure 1-18. Standard instruments + programmable calculator + interface bus = automatic test equipment.   (Hewlett-Packard Co.)

nationally accepted interface-bus standard.* For example, the signal generator of Fig. 5-22 is designed for this standard interface bus as is the waveform generator of Fig. 5-23. An instrument which incorporates a microcomputer can accept setup information over this bus and, if it is a measuring
instrument, transmit measured results to the controller, a printer, or a plotter, as discussed in Sec. 5-10. Compatibility with the interface bus should
enhance the usefulness, and hence the market, of many instruments.

A more appropriate interface for many microcomputer-based instruments requires transmission of data over a single pair of wires, coding each
character of data in the same asynchronous format used by a teletype. Using
a universal asynchronous receiver transmitter (UART) integrated circuit,
this is easily accomplished, as discussed in Sec. 5-9.

* Originated by Hewlett-Packard Company, this standard has been adopted by the IEEE
  and is under consideration by the International Electrotechnical Commission.

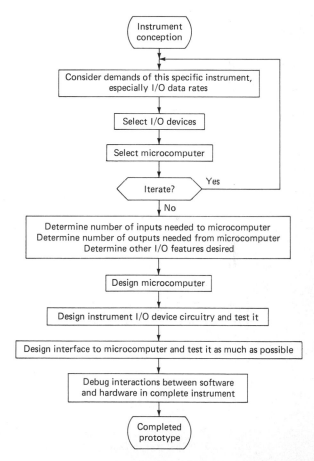

Figure 1-19. Overview of in-
strument-design steps.

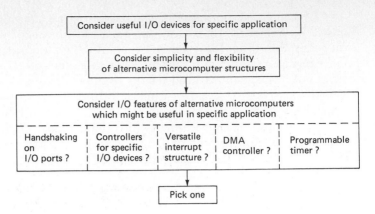

Figure 1-20. *Hardware considerations for microcomputer selection.*

1-2 DIMENSIONS OF THE DESIGN PROBLEM

The design of any instrument involves a sequence of interactive decisions. In the design of a microcomputer-based instrument, virtually all design decisions are affected by which microcomputer is chosen. Both the hardware needs and the software needs of the instrument bear upon this choice. Any of several microcomputers may be able to meet these needs. Nevertheless, since the choice of a microcomputer will have a far-reaching effect upon how these needs are met, this decision must be made initially.

In this section, we will take a somewhat simplistic overview of the design process. Thus, Fig. 1-19 illustrates a series of steps beginning with the

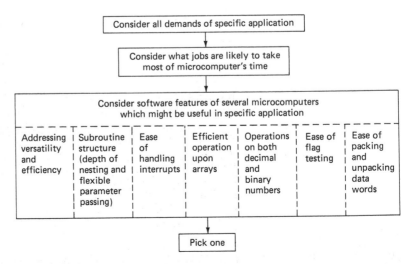

Figure 1-21. *Software considerations for microcomputer selection.*

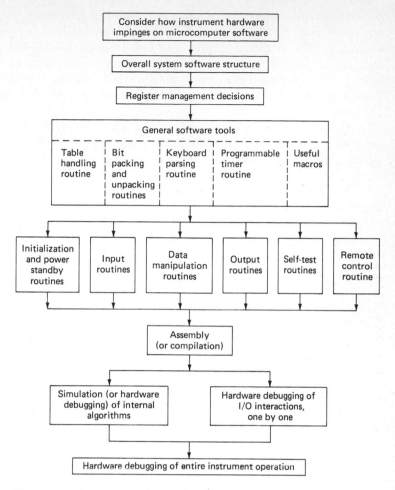

Figure 1-22. Instrument software development.

function of the envisioned instrument and the choice of a microcomputer. As shown, we may iterate in the decision of a microcomputer as we gain a better feeling for the needs of the instrument and the capabilities of a specific microcomputer.

There may be an overriding impetus to use a specific microcomputer which has nothing to do with the requirements of the instrument. For example, if we have designed a previous instrument with a certain microcomputer, all the software development aids and prototyping hardware which were useful then are available now. Furthermore, our familiarity with this microcomputer is a very real asset.

If we are faced with choosing the microcomputer, both hardware and software questions must be considered. A large number of the hardware

questions concern the interactions between the microcomputer and the instrument's input and output (I/O) devices. Many of these hardware considerations, shown in Fig. 1-20, involve terminology which will be described
later in this book. The intent at this time is to place these considerations within the context of the overall design process. In like manner, Fig.
1-21 raises some of the software considerations involved in microcomputer
selection.

Because software development is such an overriding factor in the design of a microcomputer-based instrument, this aspect of Fig. 1-19 is expanded into Fig. 1-22. Again, the terminology will become more meaningful later.

In a sense, then, Figs. 1-19 to 1-22 provide an overview of the remaining chapters of the book. It might be helpful, from time to time, to return to these four figures in order to place ideas, techniques, and devices
into the context of the design of a complete instrument.

REFERENCES

An intriguing article on the history of the development of microcomputers
plus a vivid view of their impact upon our world is provided by G. Bylinsky,
Here Comes the Second Computer Revolution, *Fortune*, November 1975,
pp. 134–184.

An extensive, technical overview of microcomputers and their impact
upon the design engineer is contained in Microprocessors: A Special Issue,
Electronics, Apr. 15, 1976, pp. 74–174.

MICROCOMPUTER REGISTERS AND DATA MANIPULATION

2-1 AN OVERVIEW OF A MICROCOMPUTER

We can think of a microcomputer as consisting of six parts, as shown in Fig. 2-1. Data within the microcomputer is operated upon *one word* at a time. Typical *word lengths* for different microcomputers are 4 bits and 8 bits. The six parts of a microcomputer behave as follows:

1   The *clock* gives rise to the timing of all operations, so that events which must take place in sequence will do so in an orderly and unambiguous fashion.

2   The *CPU,* or *central processing unit,* coordinates all activities within the microcomputer. It sequences the execution of instructions. In so doing, it coordinates the movement of data from inputs into the micro-computer. It manipulates that data so as to fit the operation of the mi-crocomputer to its application. Also, it coordinates the movement of data from the microcomputer to outputs.

3   Each *output port* is like four or eight windows (corresponding to the 4 or 8 bits making up the word length). Executing an output instruction in the CPU is like opening or closing each window so as to correspond

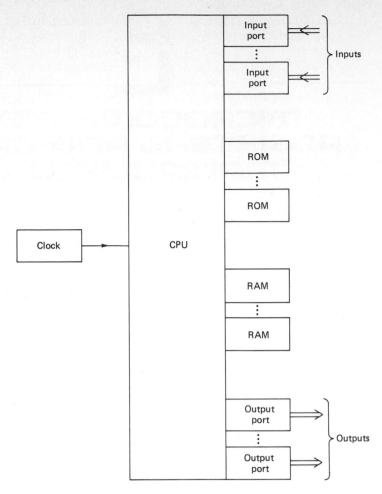

Figure 2-1. Simplified view of a microcomputer.

to each bit in a word. The windows remain open or closed in this pattern until modified by the execution of a subsequent output instruction.

4   Each *input port* is like another set of windows which are all opened
simultaneously to let in whatever may be outside. These windows are
opened momentarily at a time specified by the CPU and then closed
again.

5   The *ROMs*, or *read-only memories*, contain the instructions which implement the algorithms fitting the microcomputer to its application.
They also contain any fixed constants and fixed tables which are useful
in this process. The term "read-only" implies that the instrument
designer determines these algorithms, constants, and tables once and

for all as part of the design process. As a result, the generally useful microcomputer becomes *dedicated* to the needs of a specific instrument.

6 Finally, the *RAMs*, or *random-access memories*,* provide for the temporary storage of data which is either obtained from input ports or generated within the CPU as part of the algorithmic processes required of the application.

These six parts form the essence of all microcomputers. Later we will consider additional parts peculiar to some microcomputers (for example, control inputs which can *interrupt* the normal operation of the microcomputer or *hold* it in a state of suspended animation).

The term *microprocessor* is sometimes used in a general way to mean this microcomputer structure, in contrast to the transducers, actuators, displays, and other things which are needed to meet the requirements of the instrument. More typically, the term microprocessor is used to designate the large-scale integration (LSI) chip, or integrated circuit, which includes the CPU. Sometimes (particularly among the early microprocessors to appear on the market) some standard integrated circuits augment the microprocessor chip in order to construct a fully functioning CPU which can communicate with, and control, input ports, output ports, RAM, and ROM. On the other hand, some microprocessor chips include not only a self-contained CPU but also one or more of the other parts of the microcomputer such as the clock or input/output ports.

2-2 THREE STAGES IN THE DESIGN
OF A MICROCOMPUTER-BASED INSTRUMENT

The previous section provides an overview of the six basic parts of a microcomputer. As designers, we are interested in the various ways of interacting with these parts to design an instrument. These interactions can be categorized into three stages:

1 The *hardware* considerations needed to put together a microcomputer structure, such as that shown in Fig. 2-1.
2 The *hardware* considerations needed to bring the microcomputer structure together with the remaining instrument components (for example, transducers, displays).
3 The *software* considerations leading to the sequence of instructions which the microcomputer will execute so that the various functions of the microcomputer, and thereby the instrument, will take place. These

---

* A more appropriate designation for a RAM is a *read-write memory*, indicating the ability first to write data into it and then, later, to read data out.

software considerations will result in a *program* for the microcomputer which, at the time of manufacture of the instrument, will become the 1s and 0s manufactured into ROMs.

Postponing the hardware considerations until later, this chapter is devoted to the rudimentary building blocks for this third stage in the design process. We will consider how various microcomputers manipulate data among *registers*. Defined liberally, the term *register* will mean a storage location into which data can be written, or from which data can be read, or both. This might be one of the registers in the CPU, a word in RAM or ROM, an input port, or an output port.

2-3 MICROCOMPUTER INSTRUCTIONS AND THE ROLE OF THE PROGRAM COUNTER

Throughout the remainder of this chapter, the manner in which specific microcomputer instructions affect the contents of specific registers will be discussed. Commercially available microcomputers will be used to provide examples. A more thorough description of some of these microcomputers is provided in the appendixes.

A helpful way to undertake the study of this chapter is to make a parallel study of a specific microcomputer *at the register level*. Then each time a feature, approach, or problem is discussed here, see how it is handled for the specific microcomputer. Not only will this provide valuable insights into the functioning of the different registers and instructions for that microcomputer, but it will also provide a specific vehicle for examining how some of the more subtle things we will discuss might be carried out in a specific instance. The problems at the end of the chapter will, by and large, assume this kind of familiarity with a specific microcomputer.

Many microcomputers use an 8-bit word length for the ROMs in which instructions are stored. This is common not only for those microcomputers whose instructions manipulate 8-bit data words, but also for those microcomputers whose instructions manipulate 4-bit data words. In addition, the 8-bit word length of a ROM turns out to be a restrictively small number of bits for many of the instructions that it is desirable to have in a microcomputer instruction set. Consequently, most microcomputers use instructions of several word lengths. Some instructions will be 8 bits in length and some will be 16 bits in length. In several microcomputers, some instructions will even be 24 bits in length.

Since all these instructions will be stored as successive 8-bit words in ROM, it is common to refer to these ROM words as forming the successive *bytes* of an instruction word. Figure 2-2 illustrates the data word length and the two alternative instruction word lengths typical of *4-bit* microcomputers. The designation "4-bit microcomputer" or "8-bit microcomputer"

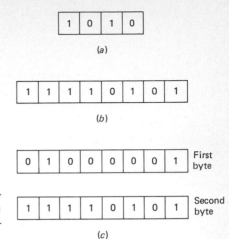

Figure 2-2. Data word and instruction words for a typical 4-bit microcomputer. (a) 4-bit data word; (b) 1-byte instruction; (c) 2-byte instruction.

indicates the number of bits in a data word. Intel Corporation's 4004 micro-computer (the first commercially available microcomputer, introduced in 1971) has exactly this structure, as does Intel's 4040 (the updated version of the 4004) and Rockwell International Corporation's PPS-4 microcomputer.

The potential problem of determining whether an instruction in ROM is a 1-byte instruction or a 2-byte instruction is solved in three steps:

1 When power is first turned on, the CPU automatically goes to a certain location in ROM where it knows it will see the first byte of the first instruction.
2 That first byte, by its coding, will tell the CPU whether this is a 1- or a 2-byte instruction. If it is a 2-byte instruction, the CPU will automatically get the second byte also.
3 When the CPU has completed the execution of the present instruction, it will automatically be looking to take the next instruction from a location in ROM which will contain the first byte of the next instruction.

The mechanism used to access successive instructions in ROM involves a *control register* in the CPU called the *program counter*. Each location in a ROM has a unique *address*. When the execution of an instruction is completed, the program counter will *point* to the location of the first byte of the next instruction in ROM; that is, it will contain the address of this first byte, as shown in Fig. 2-3. In this figure, the program-counter contents are shown both as a 12-bit binary number and as a three-digit *hexadecimal* number.

Hexadecimal code is a convenient, concise way to represent both addresses and register contents. It codes each successive group of 4 bits of a binary number as one character, using the coding shown in Fig. 2-4. To il-

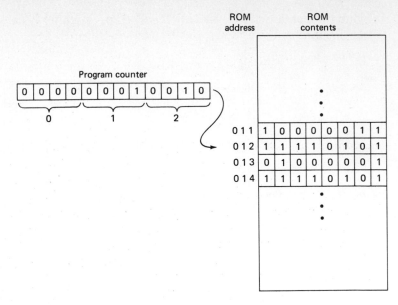

Figure 2-3. *The program counter is a pointer to ROM.*

Figure 2-4. Hexadecimal Code

Binary code	Hexadecimal code
0000	0
0001	1
0010	2
0011	3
0100	4
0101	5
0110	6
0111	7
1000	8
1001	9
1010	A
1011	B
1100	C
1101	D
1110	E
1111	F

lustrate this, note that an arbitrary 12-bit binary number N can be expressed in its decimal equivalent form using the relationship

$$N = 2048b_{12} + 1024b_{11} + 512b_{10} + 256b_9$$
$$+ 128b_8 + 64b_7 + 32b_6 + 16b_5$$
$$+ 8b_4 + 4b_3 + 2b_2 + b_1$$

where $b_{12}, \ldots, b_1$ are the bits of the binary number. But

$$N = 16^2 \times (8b_{12} + 4b_{11} + 2b_{10} + b_9)$$
$$+ 16 \times (8b_8 + 4b_7 + 2b_6 + b_5)$$
$$+ 1 \times (8b_4 + 4b_3 + 2b_2 + b_1)$$

or

$$N = 16^2 \times h_3 + 16 \times h_2 + 1 \times h_1$$

where h_3, h_2, and h_1 are the characters of the hexadecimal numbers. For illustration, consider the following examples:

$$(001101001010)_{\text{binary}} = (34A)_{\text{hexadecimal}}$$
$$(00000000)_{\text{binary}} = (00)_{\text{hexadecimal}}$$
$$(0000001111111111)_{\text{binary}} = (03FF)_{\text{hexadecimal}}$$

The diagram of Fig. 2-3 is repeated in Fig. 2-5 using hexadecimal code to represent the contents of the program counter, the ROM address, and the ROM contents. To begin the next *instruction cycle*, the CPU will take the address contained in the program counter (012), send it out to ROM, which will return the contents of this address (F5) to the CPU. Then the program counter will be automatically incremented to address 013. The CPU will look at the instruction it has *fetched* from ROM (F5) and decide whether it is a 1- or a 2-byte instruction. If it is a 1-byte instruction, it will *execute* the operation coded by the instruction, F5. If it is a 2-byte instruction, it will fetch the second byte of the instruction, automatically increment the program counter again, and then execute the resulting 2-byte instruction. Thus the *instruction cycle* for a 1-byte instruction consists of two phases:

Fetch cycle
Execute cycle

whereas the instruction cycle for a 2-byte instruction consists of three phases:

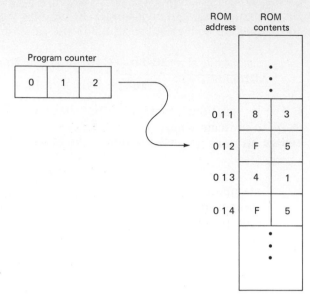

Figure 2-5. *The program counter points to ROM.*

Fetch cycle
Fetch cycle
Execute cycle

Because the program counter automatically increments after each fetch cycle, it is only necessary to store instructions in successive locations in ROM in order to have them executed successively.

On occasion, it is desirable to be able to deviate from this lock-step sequencing of instructions. For example, we may wish to "jump unconditionally" to an arbitrary address, say 1F5. The instruction to do this for Intel's 4004 and 4040 microcomputers is a 2-byte instruction:

41F5

After the CPU fetches the first byte, 41, it knows (by the presence of the 4 in the most significant hex digit position) that this is the 2-byte "unconditional jump" instruction. It reads in the second byte, F5, from ROM. Then, to execute this instruction, it loads the 1F5 part of this instruction into the program counter. As a result, the instruction to be next executed will be fetched from address 1F5.

Incidentally, notice that in Fig. 2-5 the program counter is set to fetch the instruction at address 012, namely, F5. For the Intel 4004 and 4040 microcomputers, this is a 1-byte instruction. At the end of its execution, the program counter will be pointing to address 013 and will next pick up the 2-byte instruction 41F5 which we have just discussed. Consequently, the

F5 byte in address 012 is treated very differently from the F5 byte in address 014.

2-4 ADDRESSING MODES

In the last section, we saw how the program counter served as a pointer to ROM to indicate where the next instruction to be executed could be found. In this section, we will consider various ways in which an instruction can designate:

1   Data operands—that is, which registers are to be operated upon by a data-manipulating instruction (using the term *register* to include an input port, an output port, a RAM address, a CPU register, or the address of fixed data or a table entry in ROM).

2   Jump address operands—that is, what address is to be used by a jump instruction as it modifies the program-counter contents.

In the first case, one possibility is to assign a unique address to each register and then to designate the registers involved in the execution of an instruction as part of the instruction word. The disadvantage of this approach is that if there are many registers to distinguish among, long instruction words will be required to handle these addresses. As a consequence, a variety of ways are used to address data operands.

Accumulator addressing specifies that the operand associated with this instruction is always contained in one specific register in the CPU. If the operation is to be carried out, the operand must first be moved to this specific register, commonly called the *accumulator* or A *register*. An example of this type of instruction is complement the accumulator, in which each bit of the accumulator is complemented (that is, $0 \rightarrow 1$ and $1 \rightarrow 0$). For the many instructions which involve two operands, one of the operands will typically be in the accumulator. Most microcomputers have just one accumulator.

Scratchpad register addressing identifies any one of several CPU registers as the source of an operand, often to be operated upon in conjunction with the contents of the accumulator. An example of such an instruction is add register R to the accumulator, where R designates one of several *scratchpad registers** in the CPU. Two advantages accrue with this mode of addressing. It is fast, since the operand is already in the CPU. Also, it permits 1-byte instructions which access any one of several operands since the *address field* of the instruction is small (for ex-

---

* General-purpose registers.

ample, only 3 bits of the instruction word are needed to designate
   which of eight scratchpad registers contain the operand).
Full direct addressing includes the full address of the operand in the instruction, perhaps necessitating a second and third byte in the instruction to
   achieve a full 16-bit address.
Page-zero direct addressing is a way to achieve direct addressing with a
   2-byte instruction. If the lower 8 bits of an address are considered to be
   the address within a specific *page*, while the upper bits specify the
   page number, then *page-zero* direct addressing assumes that the page
   number is zero. It thus permits direct access to any of the 256 memory
   locations identified by the 8-bit address on page zero.

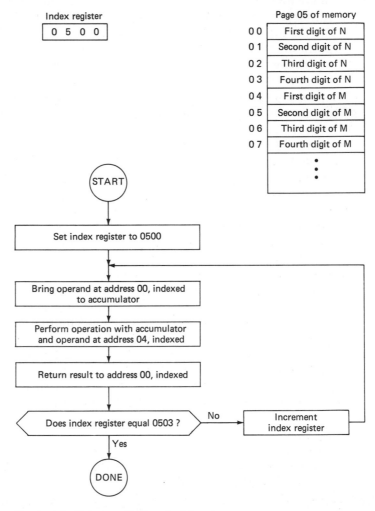

Figure 2-6. *One use of indexed addressing.*

Indexed addressing adds an offset (perhaps one 8-bit byte) contained in the instruction to the contents of an "index register" in the CPU. This permits the address of an operand to be modified during successive passes through a *loop* of instructions, as shown in Fig. 2-6. For the purposes of illustration, if we wished to add two four-digit decimal numbers together, where each memory location holds one digit, there would be two problems. The operands must be accessed and the decimal addition must be carried out appropriately. We are concerned here only with properly accessing the operands; we will discuss how decimal addition can be carried out later, complete with the carries between digits. Note that the first time through the loop the first digit of M is added to the first digit of N and the result is returned to the location which initially held the first digit of N, thereby replacing it. During the second pass through the loop the second digits are added. This continues four times, resulting in the addition of all four digits. Of the microcomputers we will discuss, only the Motorola 6800 has this convenient means of modifying the addresses of data operands.

Indirect addressing uses a CPU register, perhaps one of the scratchpad registers, as a pointer to RAM (or to ROM for accessing a table). This, again, permits a 1-byte instruction to access an operand anywhere in memory. It is also the commonly used means for incrementing the address of an operand during successive passes through a loop of instructions. But the pointer must first be set up to point to a memory location, requiring one or more additional instructions. This mode of addressing gains efficiency when the same address is used a second time, as when the result of an operation is returned to the memory location of one of the operands. It also gains efficiency when successive locations in memory are accessed one after another, as mentioned above, for successive passes through a loop of instructions.

Doubly indirect addressing uses another CPU register, a *register pointer* having 3 or 4 bits, to point to any one of perhaps 8 or 16 scratchpad registers as the location of a pointer to memory, as indicated in Fig. 2-7. This achieves the effect of having several alternative pointers to RAM. In so doing, it necessitates an additional instruction any time this register pointer is changed. Repeating the algorithm to add 2 four-digit numbers, we can again achieve the goal of accessing successive locations at two different places in memory during successive passes through a loop of instructions. The result is the same; only the mechanism for carrying it out is different. Some microcomputers have just one pointer to memory but have an additional register whose contents can be swapped with the pointer. The effect of this is identical to having two pointers to memory plus a 1-bit register pointer to indicate which pointer is in effect.

Immediate addressing uses the second byte of an instruction as a fixed, 8-bit operand which can be loaded into a register. Some microcomputers

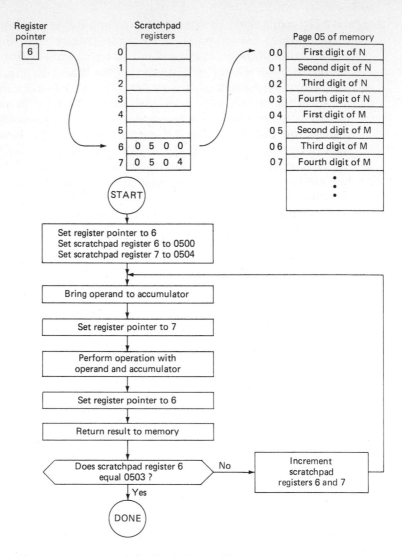

Figure 2-7. One use of doubly indirect addressing.

also have 3-byte immediate instructions in order to load a 16-bit register with a fixed 16-bit operand. This is useful for loading a scratchpad
register with a 16-bit pointer to memory.

The preceding addressing modes were concerned with data operands. As
stated previously, an instruction can also use an operand to change the contents of the program counter. These jump instructions likewise make use of
a variety of addressing modes:

Full addressing is immediate addressing with enough bytes in the instruc-

tion (typically 3 bytes for an 8-bit microcomputer) to hold the complete
new address to be loaded into the program counter. By changing the
entire program-counter contents, full addressing permits the next instruction to be taken from any ROM location.

Present-page addressing is immediate addressing which interprets the second byte of an instruction as the lower 8 bits of a full address. It is
used by some microcomputers to create a 2-byte jump instruction,
where the corresponding jump instruction to an arbitrary address
would require 3 bytes. Present-page addressing loads the second byte
of the instruction into the lower 8 bits of the program counter.

Relative addressing interprets the second byte of an instruction as a signed
number ranging between roughly −128 and +128. This form of
addressing provides a useful way to form jump instructions. The second byte is "added" to the program counter in order to jump to a
nearby location in ROM. The philosophy here is that only occasionally do we want to jump to an arbitrary location requiring a full ROM
address. More often we want to jump to an address which is somewhat
near the address of the present instruction's location in ROM, and it is
economical to do this with a 2-byte instruction rather than a 3-byte instruction. Present-page addressing does this reasonably well except
when we approach the end of a page and want to jump "nearby," if
nearby happens to be on the next page. Relative addressing will thus
tend to permit us to get by with 2-byte jump instructions somewhat
more often than present-page addressing. Actually what happens is
that relative addressing tends to make us insensitive to page boundaries, whereas with present-page addressing, we have some incentive to
locate programs carefully with respect to page boundaries.

Indirect addressing loads the contents of a scratchpad register into the program counter. It provides a means for setting up a variable address for
a jump instruction under program control. Some microcomputers can
do this with one instruction. Others require the more devious approach of transferring data first from a scratchpad register to a "stack"
memory (to be defined and discussed in Sec. 2-7) and from there to the
program counter.

A specific microcomputer will employ several of these modes of addressing,
as illustrated in Fig. 2-8. For more complete information on the addressing
modes for a specific microcomputer, refer to the data in the appendixes or to
the analogous manufacturer's information for a microcomputer not discussed there.

2-5 ASSEMBLY LANGUAGE

Up to this point, we have been skirting the issue of how to represent a program, or segments of a program, for a microcomputer. What we want to do

Figure 2-8. Addressing Modes of Some Microcomputers

	Data operands									Jump address operands				
	Number of accumulators	Number of scratchpad registers	Full direct addressing	Page-zero direct addressing	Indexed addressing	Number of indirect address pointers	Number of scratchpad registers used for doubly indirect addressing	Immediate addressing —1 byte operands	Immediate addressing —2 byte operands	Full addressing	Present-page addressing	Relative addressing	Indexed addressing	Indirect addressing
4-bit microcomputers														
Intel 4004	1	16	No	No	No	0	8	Yes	Yes	Yes	Yes	No	No	Yes
Intel 4040	1	24	No	No	No	0	12	Yes	Yes	Yes	Yes	No	No	Yes
Rockwell PPS-4	1	1	No	No	No	0	2	Yes	Yes	Yes	Yes	No	No	Yes
8-bit microcomputers														
Fairchild F8	1	64	No	No	No	1	2	Yes	Yes	Yes	No	Yes	No	Yes
Intel 8008	1	6	No	No	No	1	0	Yes	No	Yes	No	No	No	No
Intel 8080	1	6	Yes	No	No	3	0	Yes	Yes	Yes	No	No	No	Yes
Motorola 6800	2	0	Yes	Yes	Yes	0	0	Yes	Yes	Yes	No	Yes	Yes	Yes
RCA COSMAC	1	32	No	No	No	0	16	Yes	No	No	Yes	No	No	Yes
Rockwell PPS-8	1	1	No	Yes	No	0	2	Yes	No	Yes	Yes	No	No	Yes
SMS Microcontroller	1	7	No	No	No	1	0	Yes	No	Yes	Yes	No	Yes	No

is describe instructions, and their addresses in ROM, in an easily manageable fashion. This is the basic role which an *assembly language* fulfills.

A specific microcomputer will have an assembly language defined by
its manufacturer. Each instruction will be designated by a short nickname,
a *mnemonic,* such as CLR for an instruction which will "clear" the accumulator to all zeros. The manufacturer will have his own convention for desig-
nating what registers are involved in the operation. The manufacturer will
also indicate what *address labels* are permissible for associating with the
address of an instruction in ROM (or with the address of a directly addressed
variable in RAM). These address labels are used with a test for identifying
where to jump for the next instruction. Finally, the manufacturer will select
a convention for representing the constants used by immediate instructions.

In order to use examples to illustrate points, we will need an assembly
language. However, we will not want to restrict ourselves, in our examples,
to doing only those things permitted by the register structure and instruction
set of a specific microcomputer. Consequently, we will define some assembly language ground rules which will serve our general needs. Specific
instructions will be defined and used where they are needed. At the same
time, the appendixes will provide the mnemonics and instruction definitions given by the manufacturers of several specific microcomputers. In
working problems using a specific microcomputer (either one specified in
the appendixes or one specified with the manufacturer's information), two
alternatives are reasonable:

1   Use our assembly language ground rules together with the manufac-
    turer's mnemonics and instruction definitions.
2   Use the manufacturer's assembly language in its entirety.

Of course, if we develop software which is actually to be assembled into *object code* (that is, the 1s and 0s to be stored in ROM) using the manufacturer's
assembler, then we must necessarily use the second alternative above.

The chart of Fig. 2-9 provides our general ground rules. The format
shown at the top of the chart puts no specification on the number of character spaces reserved for each field, as this is not really necessary for "pencil
and paper" purposes.

2-6   TESTS

One of the powerful capabilities of computers, microcomputers included, is
the ability to test a Boolean (that is, two-valued) variable and, on the basis of
its value, continue with one set of instructions or another. In Figs. 2-6 and
2-7, we saw one of the most powerful ways to use such a test. A loop of instructions was carried out repeatedly until a test was satisfied, at which
point we broke out of the loop and were done.

Figure 2-9. Assembly Language Ground Rules

		Fixed-field format		
Address label	Mnemonic	Register	Operand	Comments
P1	ADD	M		Keep adding M into ac-
	JNC		P1	cumulator until it
	LOD	2,A		overflows.

Address labels

Address labels must be unique, alphanumeric, and begin with a letter.
None is needed except to identify destinations of jump instructions.

Mnemonics

Specify type of instruction. See the appendixes.

Registers

Used only when the instruction can have any of several operands.

Accumulator	A
CPU scratchpad register	1, 2, 3, . . .
Memory address pointed to	M
Immediate data	I

For a microcomputer with two-address instructions:
Destination register, source register

Operands

Address labels of jump instructions or directly addressed variables: FIX.
Identification of indexed instructions or variables: 3,X.
Specification of "immediate" data using one of the following forms, where 'nn'
represents any appropriate number of characters:

Hexadecimal number	H'nn'
Binary number	B'nn'
ASCII code character	C'nn'
Decimal number	nn (assumed, by default)

Comments

Used to clarify what the instructions are doing.
Irrelevant to the actual program—but not to a person reading it!
Any line beginning with an asterisk (*) is an entire line of comments.

To use tests effectively, we need to know:

1   What Boolean variables a microcomputer can test
2   How it uses such a test to branch, or jump, one way or another
3   How we can transform various kinds of two-valued decisions into one
    of these Boolean variables

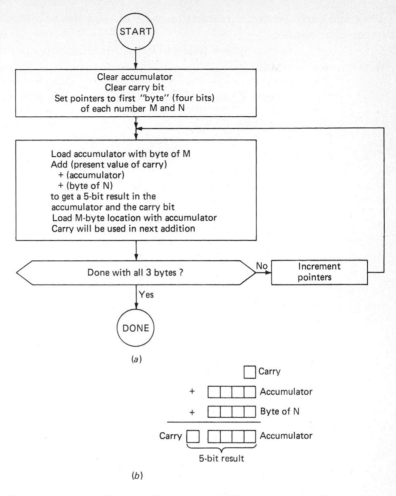

Figure 2-10. Algorithm for adding two 12-bit binary numbers with a 4-bit microcomputer. (a) Algorithm; (b) assumed function of add operation.

4 How we can transform multivalued decisions into an orderly sequence of two-valued decisions

For carrying out arithmetic and logical operations in a microcomputer, we find that often neither a 4-bit nor an 8-bit word size is large enough to handle some of the variables of a problem. The link which enables us to deal with any size numbers, 4 bits (or 8 bits) at a time, is the *carry*, or C, bit. Thus, when we want to add two 12-bit binary numbers together, we will use an algorithm like that shown in Fig. 2-10a. The carry bit is cleared initially. The addition of each set of two 4-bit numbers plus a 1-bit number can produce (at most) a 5-bit result, as shown in Fig. 2-10b, by adding

$$1111 + 1111 + 1 = 11111$$

Thus the carry bit can serve as the link between the addition of successive bytes of a number.

Some microcomputers will perform this addition operation directly; that is, they will add:

$$\underbrace{\text{(new C),(new A)}}_{\text{5-bit result}} \leftarrow \text{(A)} + \text{(operand)} + \text{(C)}$$

For other microprocessors, the only add instruction is

$$\underbrace{\text{(new C),(new A)}}_{\text{5-bit result}} \leftarrow \text{(A)} + \text{(operand)}$$

In this case, we must devise an algorithm for getting to the three-operand addition. Figure 2-11 shows one possibility. Figures 2-10 and 2-11 illustrate two tests, one in general terms ("Are we done with all three bytes?") and one in the very specific terms of testing the carry bit ("Does C = 1?"). Because it is a two-valued variable already, and because the desire to branch one way or another on the basis of the value of the carry bit arises naturally in many

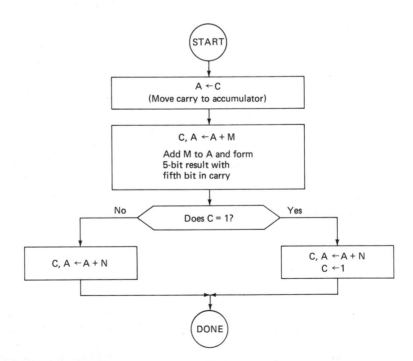

Figure 2-11. Addition algorithm.

algorithms (just as it did in our problem), the carry bit is one of the things which virtually all microcomputers can test.

There are two types of instructions which employ a test in order to branch either of two ways in a program. The first and more frequently used type is called a *conditional jump* or *conditional branch* instruction, and is of the form:

Jump to address ALPHA if carry = 1 †

Otherwise continue with the next instruction in sequence.

This is illustrated in Fig. 2-12a and b.

The second type is a *conditional skip* instruction. If the test is satisfied, the next instruction is skipped. By making this next instruction an unconditional jump, these two instructions form the equivalent of a single conditional jump instruction, as illustrated in Fig. 2-12c and d. However, it is important to realize that this approach changes the sense of the test; thus, in Fig. 2-12c and d, we continue on with the following instructions if C = 1 and jump to an arbitrary address if C = 0.

Of all the microcomputers listed in Fig. 2-8, only the two Rockwell microcomputers utilize skip instructions. Because of the need to combine a 1-byte skip instruction with an unconditional jump instruction to do the equivalent of a conditional jump, skip instructions would seem to result in more ROM words being used than do conditional jumps. However, both the Rockwell microcomputers perform a 1-byte unconditional jump to the present page and a 2-byte unconditional jump to anywhere; so they do not lose out here. In fact, it is interesting to note that the popular Intel 8080 microcomputer requires 3 bytes for *all* conditional and unconditional jumps, making no effort toward efficiency here. Instead, it gains efficiency in other ways, such as making powerful use of six CPU scratchpad registers.

The manner in which the jump address is formed varies between microcomputers, as indicated in the last five columns of Fig. 2-8. However, the information there is sketchy and needs the amplification gained by studying the instruction set of a specific microcomputer. For example, it appears from Fig. 2-8 that the Motorola 6800 microcomputer can jump to an arbitrary full address (a 3-byte instruction) or to an address relative to that presently in the program counter (a 2-byte instruction), or to an indexed address (a 2-byte instruction), or to an address formed indirectly. Actually, all conditional jump instructions use *only* relative addressing, while unconditional jumps use any of the four forms of addressing.

In an attempt to optimize between 2-byte and 3-byte instructions, several microcomputers use this approach of having an unconditional jump in-

---

† An alternative is to jump if carry = 0. Some microcomputers offer both alternatives as a programming convenience.

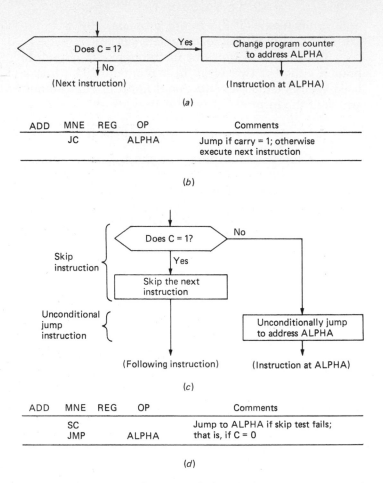

Figure 2-12. Conditional jump and skip instructions. (a) Jump if carry = 1; (b) assembly language representation of "jump if carry = 1"; (c) skip if C = 1 + unconditional jump ⇔ jump if C = 0; (d) assembly language representation of this skip instruction sequence.

struction which employs a full address, and conditional jump instructions which can jump only to a limited number of addresses (that is, which use relative addressing or present-page addressing).

At the expense of using two instructions in sequence, we can solve the problem of making conditional jumps *outside* the range of the available addressing mode using an approach identical to that employed with a skip instruction, as shown in Fig. 2-13, using a jump if carry = 1 instruction. Note that this structure again changes the sense of the test; that is, the combined effect of the two instructions is to jump if C = 0 and to continue in sequence if C = 1. In Chap. 6, we will discuss how the assembly language pro-

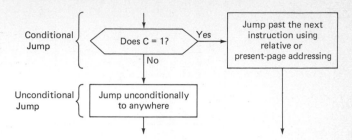

Figure 2-13. Forming a conditional jump to an arbitrary address.

gram is translated into the actual ROM contents for the program. We will see that symbols can be used for addresses, and the assembler automatically can select the addressing mode which is most concise. If the step represented in Fig. 2-13 is necessary, it will be done automatically. If not, the simpler representation will be used.

The carry bit of a microcomputer is only one of several things which can be tested. The chart of Fig. 2-14 illustrates the variety of variables which are tested in some representative microcomputers. Note the popularity of testing the carry bit and of testing whether the accumulator equals zero. As we will see, these two tests permit us to jump on the basis of individual bits of a word rather easily. Testing the most significant bit of the accumulator is useful in testing for the sign of a number when the sign is represented by the state of this bit. In addition, being able to test any one bit of the accumulator directly is a feature which can be bent to assorted useful ends. However, this last test, as well as the remaining tests, can be looked upon as convenience features of a specific microcomputer; they can be implemented, somewhat inefficiently, by other instructions plus one of the first two tests.

So far in this section, we have considered those Boolean variables which a microcomputer can test, and how it uses such a test to cause the program to branch either of two ways. Now we will consider how to transform any two-valued decision into one of these tests. To do this, certain instructions will be useful, and Fig. 2-15 indicates whether these are available with each of the microcomputers we have been discussing. For our ease of use as we go along, each of these instructions is given a mnemonic name and is described in Fig. 2-16. They will be described in more detail as we use them in examples.

We also will need a LOD instruction to load a *destination* register from a *source* register, as illustrated in Fig. 2-16. Every microcomputer has its own way to move data. An approach used by many microcomputers is to involve the accumulator as either the source register or the destination in all instructions which move data. But, in any case, all microcomputers not only move the data to the destination register but also leave it undis-

Figure 2-14. Variables Used for Conditional Jumps in Some Microcomputers

	Carry bit	Accumulator equals zero	Most significant bit of accumulator	Overflow	Combinations of the tests to the left	Parity of accumulator (i.e., even number of 1s)	External input(s)	Scratchpad register equals zero	Arbitrary bit in a RAM operand	Flag flipflops, set and cleared by program
4-bit microcomputers										
Intel 4004/4040	X	X					1			
Rockwell PPS-4	X	X					1	X		2
8-bit microcomputers										
Fairchild F8	X	X	X	X	X					
Intel 8008/8080	X	X	X			X				
Motorola 6800	X	X	X	X	X					
RCA COSMAC	X	X					4			
Rockwell PPS-8	X	X	X						X	
SMS Microcontroller	X	X	X				X	X	X	X

Figure 2-15. Useful Instructions for Forming Tests

	Subtract register from accumulator		Exclusive-OR register with accumulator		AND register with accumulator		"Compare" versions of one or more
Mnemonic →	SUB		EOR		AND		of the operations to the left
Register →	I	R or M	I	R or M	I	R or M	(see text)
4-bit microcomputers							
Intel 4004		X					
Intel 4040		X				X	
Rockwell PPS-4				X		X	
8-bit microcomputers							
Fairchild F8			X	X	X	X	X
Intel 8008/8080	X	X	X	X	X	X	X
Motorola 6800	X	X	X	X	X	X	X
RCA COSMAC	X	X	X	X	X	X	X
Rockwell PPS-8				X	X	X	
SMS Microcontroller				X		X	

Figure 2-16. Some Mnemonics and Their Descriptions

Mnemonic	Register	Operand	Description
SUB	I	H'F0'	A ← A − I, where I is the hexadecimal number F0
SUB	M		A ← A − M
SUB	3		A ← A − register 3
EOR	I	H'03'	A ← A ⊕ I. Exclusive-OR corresponding bits
AND	I	H'80'	A ← A AND I. AND together corresponding bits
LOD	A,M		A ← M and leave M unchanged
JMP		P1	Jump (unconditionally) to P1
JC		P2	Jump to P2 if carry (C = 1)
JNC		P3	Jump to P3 if no carry (C = 0)
JAZ		P4	Jump to P4 if accumulator is zero
JAN		P5	Jump to P5 if accumulator is not zero

Note: A is the accumulator; C is the carry bit; M is a designated memory location; 3 in the register field represents scratchpad register number 3; I is an operand located in the second byte of the instruction (an immediate instruction).

turbed in the source register. That is, all microcomputers use *nondestructive readout* from any source register.

Some microcomputers use *flag* flipflops to store the variables which can be tested. For example, when a subtraction is carried out, a "zero" flag flipflop is set if the result is zero; otherwise it is cleared. Then when a test for zero is made, it is this flipflop which is tested, not the accumulator contents. This approach makes possible the use of *compare* instructions which carry out a subtraction (or ANDing* or ORing* or exclusive-ORing*) in order to affect these flag flipflops without changing the contents of the accumulator. This is a powerful capability in that the operand being tested is left unchanged and ready for subsequent operations or tests. The last column of Fig. 2-15 indicates this capability.

We can classify the kinds of test we would like to make into two types:

1   Single, isolated tests
2   Sequences of tests to handle multivalued decisions

Single, isolated tests can be considered as one of three cases. In the first, we are directly interested in a Boolean variable, like the carry bit, which the microcomputer can test directly. We have already considered one example of this in Fig. 2-11, where we tested the carry bit in the process of implementing an addition algorithm.

A second case of an isolated test occurs when we want to match the contents of a register, or certain bits of a register (that is, the accumulator, a scratchpad register, a memory location, or an input port), bit for bit with some reference. An often recurring example arises when we desire to go through a loop of instructions a certain number of times, as happened in Figs. 2-6 and 2-10. In fact, this occurs so often that it is worth investigating what approach is especially efficient for a given microcomputer and then sticking with it. A common approach is to preset a scratchpad register to the number N of iterations desired, then go through the loop once, decrement N, test N for zero, and jump back to the beginning of the loop if N does not equal zero, as shown in Fig. 2-17. Because this need arises so often, Intel's 4004 and 4040 include a 2-byte ISZ instruction which will increment any one of 16 four-bit scratchpad registers and then jump if the result is not zero. By initially presetting the register to H'D' (D in hexadecimal code), the microcomputer will increment (to E and F) and jump back for two more iterations through the loop. The third increment will be to zero, and the microcomputer will go on. This ISZ instruction thus replaces the DEC, LOD, and JAN instructions of Fig. 2-17b.

Often we do not want to match the entire contents of a register but rather only one bit, or perhaps several bits. This can be done by using an AND instruction to mask off the bits in which we are not interested.

---

* To be defined shortly.

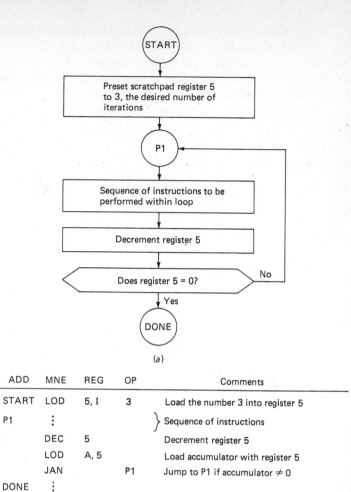

(a)

ADD	MNE	REG	OP	Comments
START	LOD	5, I	3	Load the number 3 into register 5
P1	⋮			} Sequence of instructions
	DEC	5		Decrement register 5
	LOD	A, 5		Load accumulator with register 5
	JAN		P1	Jump to P1 if accumulator ≠ 0
DONE	⋮			

(b)

Figure 2-17. Looping a fixed number of times. (a) Flowchart; (b) assembly language sequence.

Example 2-1. Jump to address ALPHA if the least significant bit of input port 5 equals 1.

ADD	MNE	REG	OP	Comments
	IN	5		Load accumulator from input port 5
	AND	I	B'00000001'	Mask off all but right most bit
	JAN		ALPHA	Jump to ALPHA if A ≠ 0

The AND instruction "ANDs" the accumulator with the binary number 00000001, bit by bit. The AND operation will produce a 1 in a specific bit position if and only if there are 1s in the corresponding bit position of the two operands. In this case the AND instruction forces zeros into all bit positions except for the rightmost bit. The rightmost bit of the result will be the same as the rightmost bit of the operand at input port 5.

Example 2-2. Jump to address BOB if the least significant digit of a two-digit number in register 4 equals H'D' (that is, the hexadecimal value D).

ADD	MNE	REG	OP	Comments
	LOD	A,4		A ← register 4
	AND	I	B'00001111'	Mask off leftmost 4 bits
	EOR	I	H'0D'	A ← A ⊕ "D"
	JAZ		BOB	Jump to BOB if A equals zero

The exclusive-OR operation EOR will complement those bits of the accumulator corresponding to the ones in H'0D' (= B'00001101'). It will leave the remaining bits of the accumulator unchanged. The EOR instruction is often used in this way to complement selected bits of the accumulator. Note that we could have used a subtract immediate instruction in this example as an alternative to the EOR instruction.

The third case of an isolated test occurs when we want to test whether the content of a register falls into one class of possibilities or not. Here we really only want to make one test which will draw this distinction. In general, we have difficulty doing this (using one test). However, it can be done for two common situations, illustrated by the following three examples.

Example 2-3. Jump to address P3 if either of the two most significant bits of input port 5 equals 1.

ADD	MNE	REG	OP	Comments
	IN	5		Load accumulator from input port 5
	AND	I	B'11000000'	Mask off six least significant bits of A
	JAN		P3	Jump to P3 if A ≠ 0

Example 2-4. Jump to address FIX if the least significant 4 bits of the accumulator equal any one of the six consecutive hexadecimal numbers A, B, C, D, E, or F.

ADD	MNE	REG	OP	Comments
	AND	I	H'0F'	Mask off the four most significant bits of the accumulator
	SUB	I	H'0A'	Subtract 0A
	JNC		FIX	Jump to FIX if no carry results

In this example, we make use of the SUBtract instruction in order to draw a distinction between 4-bit numbers which are equal to or greater than 0A, for which carry will equal zero, and numbers which are less than 0A. We assume that for the SUB instruction, the microcomputer takes the resulting borrow and puts it into the carry flipflop. (A few microcomputers put the complement of the resulting borrow into the carry.)

Example 2-5. Jump to address GO if the least significant 4 bits of the accumulator equal any one of the five consecutive hexadecimal numbers 7, 8, 9, A, B.

ADD	MNE	REG	OP	Comments
	SUB	I	H'07'	Subtract the lowest of the consecutive numbers to be tested for
	AND	I	H'0F'	Mask off most significant 4 bits
	SUB	I	H'05'	Subtract 05 in order to let the carry bit draw a distinction between 0 and 4 on the one hand and 5 to F on the other
	JC		GO	Jump to GO if carry = 1

Sometimes we wish to use a sequence of tests to make a multivalued decision. If the sequence is not long, the direct approach shown in Fig.

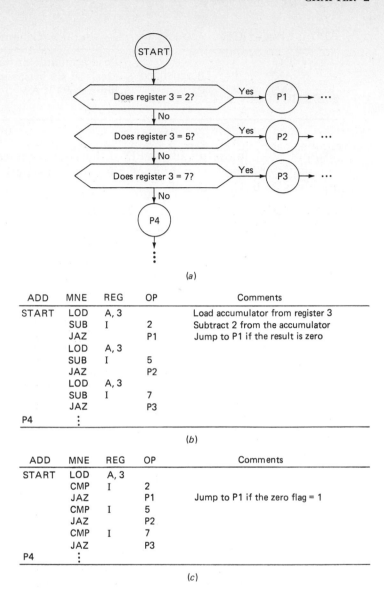

(a)

ADD	MNE	REG	OP	Comments
START	LOD	A, 3		Load accumulator from register 3
	SUB	I	2	Subtract 2 from the accumulator
	JAZ		P1	Jump to P1 if the result is zero
	LOD	A, 3		
	SUB	I	5	
	JAZ		P2	
	LOD	A, 3		
	SUB	I	7	
	JAZ		P3	
P4	:			

(b)

ADD	MNE	REG	OP	Comments
START	LOD	A, 3		
	CMP	I	2	
	JAZ		P1	Jump to P1 if the zero flag = 1
	CMP	I	5	
	JAZ		P2	
	CMP	I	7	
	JAZ		P3	
P4	:			

(c)

Figure 2-18. Direct approach for a multivalued decision. (a) Flowchart; (b) assembly language sequence; (c) use of compare instruction CMP.

2-18a and b makes sense. This direct approach can benefit from the compare instruction which some microcomputers have, as indicated in the last column of Fig. 2-15. Such an instruction will carry out a subtraction and set a "zero flag" if the result is zero but *will leave the accumulator unchanged.* Consequently, it is not necessary to load the accumulator repeatedly. The result is shown in Fig. 2-18c.

For multivalued decisions with more alternatives, a more systematic approach will be presented when we discuss the use of tables in Sec. 2-8.

2-7 SUBROUTINES AND STACKS

When we later consider the hardware aspects of the design of a microcomputer-based instrument, we will find that a "divide and conquer" approach helps to cut large unmanageable problems down into manageable pieces. Likewise, when we look at the software development for this same instrument, a "divide and conquer" philosophy provides a means for making headway without becoming overwhelmed. A useful structure here is the *subroutine*. In fact, it is so useful that many designers of microcomputer-based instruments organize the software so that the main program is nothing more than a sequence of subroutine calls, each of which is constructed around further subroutine calls, with some of these constructed around further subroutine calls, and so on. Two strong benefits result from this approach:

1   Each subroutine can be developed as a relatively short, well-understood, and relatively easily tested and debugged portion of the overall scheme.
2   The interactions between all the parts of the software (that is, between one subroutine and another one which calls it) are handled in a regular and well-identified way.

This second point is vital. Not only does it mean that we are provided with a manageable structure for *developing* a system. It also means we have a structure which is amenable to subsequent *modification* in order to improve performance or add new features *without* being set back because of subtle or forgotten interactions between parts of the software. Of course, for this to be a valid statement, we must document these interactions where they will be available to us when we, or someone else, are ready to modify our system software. Alternatively, we can use a higher-level compiler-type language like Algol to prepare the software and let it set up and handle these interactions automatically. We will discuss this alternative in Chap. 6.

The JMS instruction used to jump to a subroutine is similar to an unconditional jump in that it has an address associated with it which replaces the contents of the program counter. Thus it indeed causes an unconditional jump to an arbitrary location in ROM where the subroutine's instructions reside. The distinction between a jump to a subroutine and an unconditional jump lies in the ability to return to the calling program from a subroutine. This implies that just before the contents of the program counter are replaced by the address of the first instruction of the subroutine, these contents are set aside. Then to *return* from the subroutine,

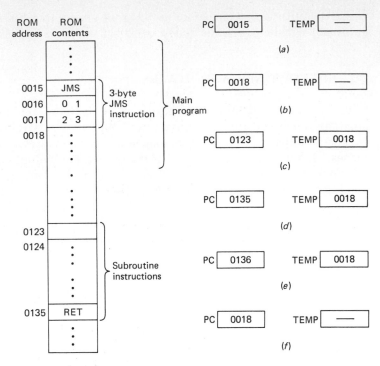

Figure 2-19. Subroutine call and return mechanisms. (a) Before fetch
cycle of JMS instruction; (b) at completion of fetch cycle of JMS instruction; (c) at completion of execution of JMS instruction; (d) sometime
later, before fetch cycle of RET instruction; (e) at completion of fetch cycle
of RET instruction; (f) at completion of execution RET instruction,
the CPU has returned to the next instruction after the JMS instruction in
the main program.

a RET instruction restores this set-aside address to the program counter.
This is illustrated in Fig. 2-19, which shows the ROM contents and also
the contents of the program counter (PC) and a temporary storage register
for the return address (TEMP) at various instants in time. Recall that
each instruction cycle consists of a fetch cycle, during which the CPU
"fetches" an instruction from ROM, and an execute cycle, during which
the CPU executes that instruction.

   This example made use of one temporary storage location, called
TEMP, as part of the mechanism for implementing a subroutine call and return. A more powerful approach makes use of a stack, or last-in first-out
memory structure, for storing return addresses. The stack consists of memory registers (located either in the CPU, in RAM, or split between the two)
which are addressed automatically during subroutine calls and returns.
The stack structure permits a main program to call a subroutine, which can
call another subroutine, which in turn can call another subroutine, and so

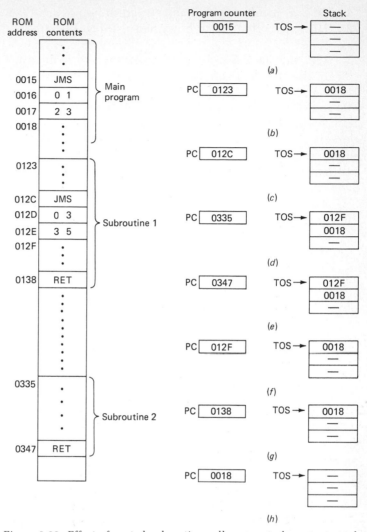

Figure 2-20. Effect of nested subroutine calls upon stack contents and program-counter contents. (a) Start main program JMS instruction cycle; (b) end of main program JMS instruction cycle; (c) start subroutine 1 JMS instruction cycle; (d) end of subroutine 1 JMS instruction cycle; (e) start subroutine 2 RET instruction cycle; (f) end of subroutine 2 RET instruction cycle; (g) start subroutine 1 RET instruction cycle; (h) end of subroutine 1 RET instruction cycle.

on. This nesting of subroutines is provided for by simply putting the successive return addresses onto the top of the stack (TOS) during successive calls and taking them off the top of the stack in reverse order during successive returns. This is illustrated in Fig. 2-20.

Three quick measures of the power of a microcomputer are:

1   Does it incorporate a stack structure?
2   How deep (that is, to how many storage locations) does the stack extend?
3   Can the stack also be used as temporary storage for register contents under program control or interrupt control?

The first two questions provide a significant point of comparison between microcomputers, since they indicate the ease and extent to which the software of a system can be developed in bite-size chunks. For example, Intel's 4004 has a stack, but it goes only three registers deep. This could be a real handicap if nesting subroutines five deep would be a natural way to organize the software for an instrument.

The third question will become more meaningful when we discuss interrupt structures in Chap. 3. Figure 2-21 compares our microcomputer list on the basis of these three questions.

In order to clarify the "interconnection" between a subroutine and any calling program, the documentation must specify:

1   In what registers the subroutine will look for parameters passed to it by the calling program
2   In what registers it will return results
3   What CPU scratchpad registers will be changed in the process of executing the subroutine
4   The names of other subroutines used by this subroutine

Perhaps the most useful place for this information is as comment lines at the beginning of the assembly language program for the subroutine. Then if the (assembly language) program is modified at some later time, this interconnection data will necessarily be available. Recall, from our assembly language ground rules of Fig. 2-9, that we can insert lines beginning with asterisks into a program and have them treated as comment lines and ignored by the assembler.

As an illustration, consider a subroutine for a 4-bit microcomputer to add two N-digit numbers X and Y and put the result back in the location from which X was taken. Assume that the digits of each number are stored in consecutive RAM memory locations. The parameters which must be passed to the subroutine are two pointers, each pointing to the first digit of one of the numbers. The parameter N must also be passed to the subroutine. The resulting comments might look like those shown in Fig. 2-22.

2-8   TABLES

One of the potent things we can do as we develop the software for algorithms is to take any aspects which are more random than they are regular and rep-

Figure 2-21. Stack Capabilities of Some Microcomputers

	Stack capability	Depth of stack	Location of stack	Used for register storage under program control	Used for automatic scratchpad register storage during interrupts
4-bit microcomputers					
Intel 4004	Yes	3	CPU	No	No
Intel 4040	Yes	7	CPU	No	No
Rockwell PPS-4	Yes[a]	Unlimited[a]	RAM	No	No
8-bit microcomputers					
Fairchild F8	Yes[a]	Unlimited[a]	RAM	No	No
Intel 8008	Yes	7	CPU	No	No
Intel 8080	Yes	Unlimited	RAM	Yes	No
Motorola 6800	Yes	Unlimited	RAM	Yes	Yes
RCA COSMAC	Yes[a]	Unlimited[a]	RAM	Yes	No
Rockwell PPS-8	Yes	33	CPU and RAM	Yes	No
SMS Microcontroller	No	—	—	—	—

[a] These stacks require subroutine call and return routines to be implemented in software. While calls and returns using these stacks are slow, an alternative, fast mechanism can be used for a few subroutines (in the case of the COSMAC) or for any subroutine which will not call further subroutines (in the case of the Rockwell PPS-4 or the Fairchild F8).

```
     *
     ****** N DIGIT BCD ADDITION SUBROUTINE ******
     *
     * UPON ENTRY:
     *    REG 1      = RAM PAGE OF OPERANDS
     *    REG 2,3    = POINTER TO FIRST DIGIT OF FIRST NO. & RESULT
     *    REG 4,5    = POINTER TO FIRST DIGIT OF SECOND NUMBER
     *    REG 6      = N, THE NUMBER OF DIGITS TO BE ADDED
     * UPON EXIT:
     *    CARRY WILL EQUAL 1 IF OVERFLOW OCCURS
     * REGISTERS CHANGED: ACCUMULATOR, REG 2,3,4,5,6
     * SUBROUTINES USED: NONE
     *
     DADD -------------
```

Assembly language instructions for this subroutine are called by the address label DADD

```
     RET
```

Figure 2-22. Comments for an N-digit addition subroutine called DADD.

resent the randomness by entries in a table. An appreciation of this process can be obtained from some examples.

Example 2-6. At the expense of dedicating a large portion of a page of ROM to a decimal multiplication table, we can drastically speed up, and simplify, the process of multiplying N-digit numbers. The appropriate table is shown in Fig. 2-23. It is entered by combining any two digits to be multiplied into an 8-bit address, entering the table at this address, and reading out the two-digit product. The rest of the algorithm to multiply N-digit numbers consists of decimal additions and shifting.

ROM address	ROM contents
00	0 0
01	0 0
02	0 0
03	0 0
	•
	•
	•
53	1 5
54	2 0
55	2 5
56	3 0
	•
	•
	•
97	6 3
98	7 2
99	8 1
	•
	•
	•

Figure 2-23. Decimal multiplication table.

Example 2-7. An instrument employing a cathode-ray tube as an output display offers the possibility to the designer of also displaying all the instrument setup information. A rationale for doing this is to get away from the appalling array of controls needed on some instruments and replace these with a single keyboard for entering all setup information. The CRT is then used both for output and for displaying what has been entered as setup information. The CRT can also be used to aid the setting-up process with messages prompting the user to enter certain data or to make specific initial tests. Each of these messages can be stored in a table as a string of alphanumeric characters coded with the commonly used ASCII code (American Standard Code for Information Interchange), as shown in Fig. 2-24. Use of the table requires a pointer to the start of each message. The display generator will pick up each successive character from the table and display it. A special NULL character (ASCII code = 0000000) can be used to mark the end of each message. When the display generator reaches a NULL character, it knows it has reached the end of the message and stops.

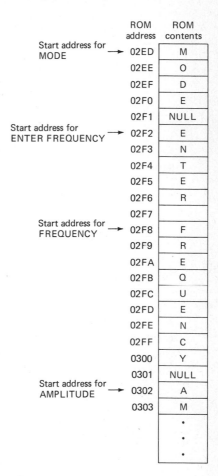

Figure 2-24. Table of display messages.

Example 2-8. Sometimes it is useful to code addresses, such as the "start addresses" of Fig. 2-24, and have a table which translates these

codes into addresses. Thus, if there are 32 or fewer of these start addresses, a 5-bit code number can be used to enter the table of Fig. 2-25
to carry out the translation. We will then use the resulting address to
set up the pointer to ROM, which accesses successive characters in the
table of Fig. 2-24.

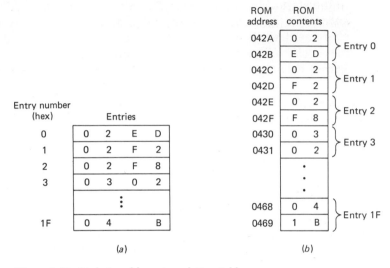

Figure 2-25. Code-to-address translation table.

Example 2-9. A convenient table technique involves coding the addresses of unconditional jump instructions. A table like that of Fig.
2-25 can be used to carry out the translation. In the previous example,
we used the address to set up a pointer. Here we use it to load the program counter in order to bring about the unconditional jump. Most
microcomputers have an indirect jump instruction, or sequence of instructions, which permits a scratchpad register to be loaded into the
program counter in order to do this. Refer to the rightmost column of
Fig. 2-8.

Example 2-10. In Fig. 2-18, we considered a direct approach to handling a multivalued decision. For a multivalued decision having
many alternatives, organizing the decision around a table has the advantage of regularizing the decision. Thus alternatives can be added,
changed, or deleted simply by changing the table. Also the com-

plexity of the decision process is confined to the table rather than being strung out in a long sequence of instructions of the form of Fig. 2-18b or c. Finally, using a table is a more efficient way to handle the decision (as measured by the number of ROM words needed) if there are many alternatives in the decision. Thus, if the multivalued decision can be cast into a comparison between a number K and any one of the binary numbers between 0 and N, then we need only use K as an entry into a table of addresses, just as was done in the last example.

Through these examples we have seen some of the opportunities for using tables. However, not only must information be sorted into a table, but also a suitable algorithm must be set up to *drive* the table, in order to get out the information desired.

We want to set our incentives toward putting "random" kinds of things into tables. We already have every incentive to do this when the alternative is exceptionally painful. However, we can help ourselves toward using tables as a general tool by developing a generally useful *table-driver* algorithm. This algorithm, written as a subroutine, should handle tables having an arbitrary (but small) number of bytes per entry (for example, 1, 2, 3, or 4). Its role is to translate a *base address* for a table, an *offset* into the table, and the *number of bytes per entry* of the table into an address for (the first byte of) the selected entry in the table. This is illustrated in Fig. 2-26.

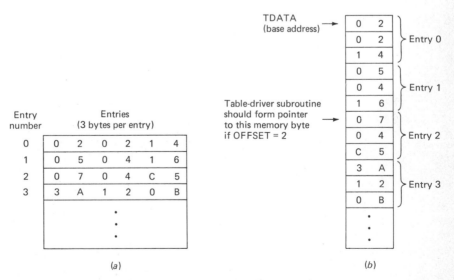

Figure 2-26. Table-entry example. (a) TDATA, a table containing data; (b) table constrained to ROM with 8-bit words.

The last section discussed subroutines and the passing of parameters to them. A parameter can be passed *directly,* as when an offset address is put in a scratchpad register. Parameters can also be passed *indirectly,* as when a memory pointer is set up to point to the first of several parameters needed by the subroutine. The subroutine can then access these parameters by incrementing the pointer to pick up each one as needed. This is particularly useful when the subroutine requires different sets of *fixed* parameters at different times. These sets can be stored in ROM and the appropriate set employed when calling the subroutine by loading the pointer appropriately.

In addition to passing a parameter to a subroutine directly or indirectly, we can pass a parameter *implicitly.* This is useful when a parameter can take on one of only a very few values. We can, in effect, have a separate subroutine for each value. In actual fact, we simply employ separate entry points to one subroutine. Thus, to simplify parameter passing to a table-driver subroutine, we will handle the "number of bytes per entry" as separate entry points, permitting this parameter to take on only a small number of values (that is, 1, 2, 3, or 4).

Figure 2-27 illustrates the scheme we will use for passing parameters to and from our table-driver subroutine. Thus the base address of the table and the offset into it are passed directly to the subroutine using the CPU's memory pointer P and another register which can hold a full address and which we will designate as the OFFSET register. Likewise, the resulting pointer to the selected entry in the table is returned to the calling program in P. The

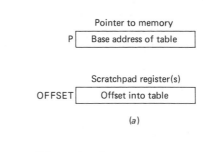

Pointer to memory

P | Base address of table

Scratchpad register(s)

OFFSET | Offset into table

(a)

If the number of bytes per entry is	Then call
1	TBL1
2	TBL2
3	TBL3
4	TBL4

(b)

Pointer to memory

P | Selected entry in table

(c)

Figure 2-27. Parameter passing to and from the table-driver subroutine. (a) Registers used to pass parameters to the subroutine directly; (b) implicitly passing the "number of bytes per entry" parameter to the subroutine; (c) location of the parameter returned by the subroutine.

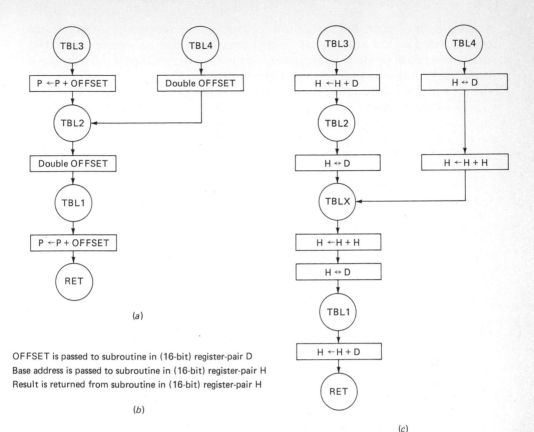

OFFSET is passed to subroutine in (16-bit) register-pair D
Base address is passed to subroutine in (16-bit) register-pair H
Result is returned from subroutine in (16-bit) register-pair H

(b)

ADD	MNE	REG	OP	Comments
TBL4	XCHG			H ← offset; D ←pointer
	DAD	H		Double offset (H ←H + H)
	JMP		TBLX	Jump to TBLX
TBL3	DAD	D		Add offset into pointer (H ←H + D)
TBL2	XCHG			H ← offset; D ←pointer
TBLX	DAD	H		Double offset
	XCHG			H ←pointer; D ←doubled offset
TBL1	DAD	D		Add offset into pointer
	RET			Return from subroutine

(d)

Figure 2-28. *Table-driver subroutine called by* TBL1, TBL2, TBL3, *or* TBL4. (a) *Flowchart;* (b) *parameter passing using the Intel 8080;* (c) *flowchart using Intel 8080 register-pair operations;* (d) *Intel 8080 assembly language subroutine.*

"number of bytes per entry" parameter is handled by calling the subroutine named TBL1 if a value of 1 is wanted, by calling the subroutine named TBL2 if a value of 2 is wanted, and so forth.

The table-driver subroutine is shown in generalized form in Fig. 2-28a. For illustrative purposes, it is also developed as it might be implemented using the Intel 8080 microcomputer. This microcomputer is particularly convenient for this purpose because it permits arithmetic operations to be carried out directly on full addresses. Another microcomputer would more typically handle the operations a byte at a time.

To illustrate the use of the table-driver subroutine, consider the following two examples.

Example 2-11. Consider the table DATA1 shown in Fig. 2-29. If the number of bytes per entry is three and if the offset is two, TBL3 is entered with

$$P = 0180 \qquad \text{and} \qquad OFFSET = 2$$

Upon returning from TBL3, we will have

$$P = 0186$$

	ROM address	ROM contents	
DATA1 →	0180	0	7
	0181	A	3
	0182	6	2
	0183	5	8
	0184	9	D
	0185	0	1
	0186	1	6
	0187	6	5
	0188	7	1
	0189	F	F
	018A	0	3
	018B	1	B
	·	·	
	·	·	
	·	·	

Figure 2-29. DATA1, a table.

Example 2-12. Consider the table DATA2 shown in Fig. 2-30. Again, if the number of bytes per entry is three and if the offset is two, TBL3 is entered with

$$P = 01FC \qquad \text{and} \qquad OFFSET = 2$$

Upon returning from TBL3, we should have

$$P = 0202$$

That is, our table-driver subroutine must carry out a proper addition into the full address of P, rolling over into the next page if this is appropriate. This is handled automatically with Intel 8080 register-pair operations. For another microcomputer which can add only single-byte operands, this aspect of the algorithm would require careful attention.

	ROM address	ROM contents	
DATA2 →	01FC	0	7
	01FD	A	3
	01FE	6	2
	01FF	5	8
	0200	9	D
	0201	0	1
	0202	1	6
	0203	6	5
	0204	7	1
	0205	F	F
	0206	0	3
	0207	1	B
		•	
		•	
		•	

Figure 2-30. DATA2 (same table in another location).

These last two examples have demonstrated the use of a table-driver subroutine which will permit us to get into tables easily. With this capability in hand, we are able to concentrate on the two important issues involving tables as we develop the software for an instrument:

1 What aspects of the software look more random than regular?
2 How can this randomness be translated into a table?

Our efforts with these two questions early in the development of the software for an instrument, and also as we run into raggedy randomness along the way, will return handsome dividends.

2-9 MEMORY ALLOCATION AND ASSEMBLER DIRECTIVES

As the development of the software for an instrument proceeds, several considerations arise concerning where we will locate the main program, subroutines, tables, and RAM variables. First, we must select the page numbers to be used for ROM and those to be used for RAM. A specific microcomputer will impose some constraints. For example, when power is first turned on, each microcomputer will go to a certain address on a certain page and expect to find its first instruction there. This page will necessarily want to be one of our pages of ROM.

As another example, the Motorola 6800 can directly address any operand on page zero as a 2-byte instruction, whereas it requires a 3-byte instruction to directly address an operand residing on any other page. As a result, users of the Motorola 6800 can aid the software development by making page zero a RAM page. Furthermore, if more than one RAM page is used, it helps to allocate page zero to the most frequently used variables. Any arrays of data which will be accessed indirectly with a variable pointer within a loop can just as well go onto another RAM page (if more than one RAM page is necessary). The full address needed by this pointer must be set up initially anyway, and the variables will not be accessed directly thereafter.

In the last section, we discussed the storage of addresses in tables. If all the addresses within one table contain the same page address, the table can be reduced to hold just the address within that page. Then the full address can be formed by joining the known page address to the 1-byte address within the page obtained from the table.

Another example occurs in the allocation of ROM to subroutines. For one thing, any microcomputer which makes use of 2-byte "present-page" conditional jump instructions can benefit by having each subroutine contained entirely on one page, since all its conditional jump instructions will then necessarily be to addresses on the same page. For another thing, the initial debugging of the software as it runs the instrument hardware is facilitated if each subroutine which is called from another page has its address set up in the peculiar fashion shown in Fig. 2-31. Then as the system is debugged, the subroutines can be changed and instructions can be added or deleted without affecting any of the calling addresses on the other pages. This is useful if each page of ROM is actually a separate ROM chip. A change in a subroutine will require a change in one chip, but it will not propagate changes onto other chips due to changed addresses. Ultimately these unconditional jumps at the top of each page can be removed, the SUBiP address labels of Fig. 2-31 changed to SUBi address labels, and the entire assembly language program reassembled.

Each of these situations provides a reason for being able to specify, as part of the assembly language program, where variables and different parts

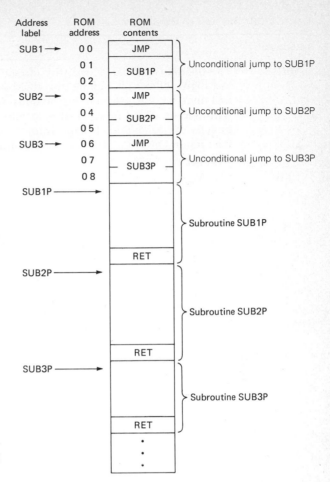

Figure 2-31. Subroutine addressing within a page during
system development.

of the program are going to be located in RAM and ROM. An assembly language will include *assembler directives* for the purpose of giving directions
such as these to the assembler as it goes about its job of translating an assembly language program into object code (that is, the 1s and 0s stored in
ROM). We will define the assembler directives of Fig. 2-32 to go along with
our assembly language ground rules of Fig. 2-9.

Example 2-13. As an example of the use of these directives, consider
Fig. 2-33. The EQU mnemonic tells the assembler that when it sees the
symbol TIMES in the operand field of an instruction of the main pro-

Figure 2-32. Assembler Directives

Mnemonic	Function
ORG	The operand associated with this directive is interpreted as a four hex-digit address. It defines the ROM address, or ORiGin, of the first byte of the program instructions which follow. Instructions will then be stored in successive locations until a subsequent ORG directive is encountered. If no initial ORG instruction is used, the instruction ORG 0000 is implied, meaning that the first instruction will be put in page 00 address 00
RMB	This Reserve Memory Bytes directive is used with the address label of data in RAM. The value of its decimal operand says how many bytes of RAM to reserve for this data
DB	This Define Byte directive is used to store constants and tables. It directs the assembler to interpret the operand as two hexadecimal digits and store them in the next word of memory (in ROM)
DC	This Define Character directive is similar to DB but is used to store characters in ASCII code form. It directs the assembler to interpret the operand as an ASCII code character
DW	This Define Word directive is used to store a four hex-digit address or number in ROM, most significant hex digits first
EQU	This EQUate directive is used to assign a value to a label
END	This directive defines the END of the assembly language program

gram or a subroutine, it should substitute the number 5. The program instructions will be assembled into consecutive addresses, beginning at address 00 00. When the assembler gets to the ORG 01 00 directive, it will skip over the remaining addresses on page 00 and put the first byte of Table 1 (namely, 1C) into address 01 00, the second byte (47) into address 01 01, and so forth. Again, when it gets to the ORG 02 00 directive, it will skip over the remaining addresses on page 1 and put the first byte of the first instruction of the SUB1 subroutine into address 02 00. The ORG 03 00 directive will cause the assembler to skip ahead and assign address 03 00 to the variable TEMP1. Address 03 01 will be assigned to TEMP2. Address 03 02 will be assigned to ARRAY1. The assembler then takes the decimal number 16, converts it to the hexadecimal number 10, and adds it to address 03 02 to come up with the next address assignment. Thus ARRAY2 identifies address 03 12. The net effect of these address allocations is shown in Fig. 2-34.

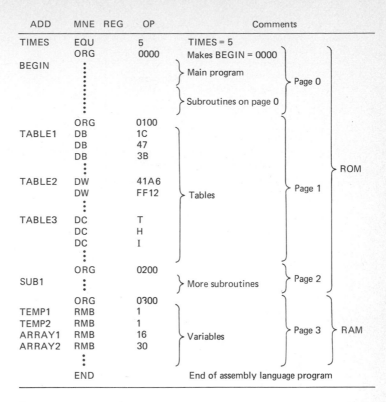

ADD	MNE	REG	OP	Comments
TIMES	EQU		5	TIMES = 5
	ORG		0000	Makes BEGIN = 0000
BEGIN	⋮			Main program
				Subroutines on page 0
	ORG		0100	
TABLE1	DB		1C	
	DB		47	
	DB		3B	
	⋮			
TABLE2	DW		41A6	
	DW		FF12	Tables
	⋮			
TABLE3	DC		T	
	DC		H	
	DC		I	
	⋮			
	ORG		0200	
SUB1	⋮			More subroutines
	ORG		0300	
TEMP1	RMB		1	
TEMP2	RMB		1	
ARRAY1	RMB		16	Variables
ARRAY2	RMB		30	
	⋮			
	END			End of assembly language program

Page 0

ROM

Page 1

Page 2

Page 3 RAM

Figure 2-33. Example program.

2-10 MACROS

Many assemblers provide the ability to define new instructions, called *macros*. We define each of these *macro instructions* with a *short* sequence of assembly language instructions. Then each time the assembler comes to one of our macros, it will substitute our defining sequence of assembly language instructions and assemble these into object code. This raises a major distinction between a macro and a subroutine. Each time a subroutine XCH is called, only the 3 bytes of the JMS XCH instruction are generated. If XCH were prepared as a macro, then *each* successive use of XCH would once again generate all the defining instructions.

For this reason, a macro is generally short. If it were more than a few instructions, we would write it as a subroutine so as to minimize the total ROM storage needed.

Macros serve us as an antifrustration tool as much as anything. Since the sequences of instructions which are replaced are short anyway, we could "just as well" write the sequences each time the need arises and forget

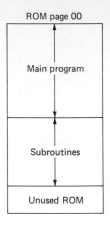

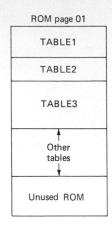

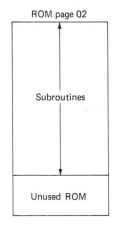

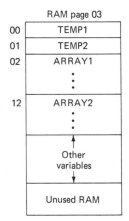

Figure 2-34. ROM and RAM allocation corresponding to Fig. 2-33.

macros. On the other hand, if the instruction set for the microcomputer we are using does not include a CLB instruction to CLear Both the accumulator and the carry bit and yet we find ourselves repeatedly wanting to do this, then it makes sense to figure out once and for all an efficient way to do this with the instruction set at hand and define CLB as a macro.

This is especially valuable after we have become intimately familiar with the instruction sets of several microcomputers and have made a decision to use a specific one in the design of an instrument. While enjoying the convenient instructions of the microcomputer we are using, nevertheless we may have a tendency to desire some of the instruction capability available in another microcomputer. Macros permit us to create them (but, of course, not with the efficiency available in the other microcomputer).

Several examples will illustrate our procedure for defining a macro. Of course, if we are actually writing assembly language programs for a specific manufacturer's assembler, the procedure must be modified as needed to suit that assembler.

Example 2-14. Using the Motorola 6800, which does not have an instruction to clear its two accumulators A and B, create a macro CAB to do this.

ADD	MNE	REG	OP	Comments
CAB	MACRO			Define CAB as a macro, not as an address label
	CLR	A		Accumulator A ← 00
	CLR	B		Accumulator B ← 00
	ENDM			End of macro definition

Notice that the mnemonic CAB to be defined does not appear in the mnemonic field. Instead, it appears in the address label field, simply as a place of convenience. When the assembler gets to this line of instructions, it will see the word MACRO in the mnemonic field and will know what is happening. Whenever it subsequently sees CAB in the mnemonic field, it will treat that line of assembly language code as if it actually consisted of the two lines

CLR A

CLR B

and assemble accordingly.

Example 2-15. The Intel 4004 and 4040 microcomputers do not directly address RAM. However, we might set aside scratchpad register-pair 14 to be used by macros for this purpose. That is, we will never put anything else into register-pair 14 and expect it to still be there after executing one of these macros. Below is shown the macro definition for a WRD instruction which will WRite the contents of the accumulator Directly into the RAM location whose address label is written into the operand field.

ADD	MNE	REG	OP	Comments
WRD	MACRO		LOC	Define WRD as a macro
	FIM	14	LOC	Register-pair 14 ← LOC
	SRC	14		Set pointer to RAM
	WRM			RAM ← accumulator
	ENDM			End of macro definition

To use this to write the accumulator contents into a RAM location TEMP1, we have, simply:

ADD	MNE	REG	OP	Comments
	WRD		TEMP1	TEMP1 ← accumulator

where TEMP1 is a location in RAM which has been defined using the RMB assembler directive of Fig. 2-32.

Notice that the address location LOC used in the macro definition is simply a dummy variable. It indicates how the operand associated with this macro is to be used.

2-11 BIT PACKING AND UNPACKING

In the process of using RAM memory, tables, input ports, and output ports, the fixed word length of a microcomputer is often large relative to the variables in which we are interested, particularly if it is an 8-bit word length. At the same time, many instrument designers decide all hardware-software tradeoffs in favor of minimum hardware at the expense of extra software (that is, extra ROM words). Almost every real-life incentive pushes toward minimizing hardware. Reduced parts count will reduce manufacturing cost and tend to simplify the debugging of a malfunctioning system. Power and cooling requirements will be reduced. Size will be decreased and reliability will tend to increase. Replacement-part inventories will be simplified.

How does the fixed word size of a microcomputer impinge upon this desire to minimize hardware?

1 The number of input ports required will be minimized if we arbitrarily *pack* unrelated inputs together. With 15 input lines, some of which are related to each other, the hardware will be minimized if we forget what is related to what and simply use two 8-bit input ports to handle

these 15 input lines. These inputs can subsequently be *unpacked* within the microcomputer into whatever groups are meaningful.

2   Likewise the number of output ports required will be minimized if output variables which are unrelated are nevertheless *packed* together to form 8-bit output words. Again, if we have 22 output lines, we have every hardware incentive to pack them into three 8-bit output ports.

3   If the software would seem to require the handling of an array of 48 one-bit variables, then the straightforward approach is to store these in 48 consecutive words of RAM. However, we have a strong incentive to *pack* and *unpack* these variables into six 8-bit words if it means that our total RAM requirements will all fit into one RAM chip instead of two (or two instead of three). It might be argued that we are only decreasing RAM at the expense of increasing ROM. On the other hand, ROM is cheaper and consumes less power than RAM; so the tradeoff makes sense. Also ROM is denser than RAM in terms of words per package; so this tradeoff tends to reduce size.

4   In Sec. 2-8, we discussed tables whose entries might extend over several ROM word lengths. For example, each entry of the table in Fig. 2-25 consisted of 2 bytes while each entry of that in Fig. 2-26 consisted of 3 bytes. We again have an incentive to *pack* the data into tables so that each entry requires one byte instead of two (or two instead of three).

The general problem of bit packing consists of taking some number of bits from a *source* word S, shifting them appropriately to some new position within the word, and then inserting them into this new position in a *destination* word D without disturbing the remaining bits of D.

Example 2-16. One approach to bit packing is illustrated in Fig. 2-35, using a subroutine called PACK. Before entering this subroutine, we need to move the "source" word, from which bits will be taken into one scratchpad register, labeled S for our convenience here. Likewise, the "destination" word, to be packed, needs to be moved to another scratchpad register D. Then two more "mask" registers SM and DM need to be loaded, perhaps using immediate instructions. The SM mask has 1s corresponding to the source bit positions of S. The DM mask has 0s corresponding to the destination bit positions of D.

    The subroutine begins by first seeing if the source and destination bit positions are already aligned. If they are, the ANDing of the two masks SM and DM will produce all zeros. If they are not, both the source word and the source mask are rotated right one position, assuming the availability of the rotate instruction shown in Fig. 2-35d.

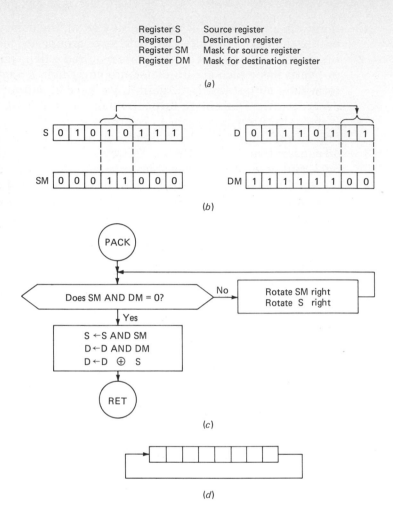

Figure 2-35. PACK subroutine. (a) Scratchpad registers upon entry; (b) example of operation; (c) PACK algorithm; (d) assumed rotate right instruction.

Again the check for alignment is made. This procedure is continued until alignment is attained. Then the rotated source word S is ANDed with the SM mask to force zeros into all bit positions of S not involved in the packing. Next the destination word D is ANDed with the DM mask to force zeros into the bit positions of D to be packed. Finally S is exclusive-ORed (or ORed or added) to D. This will produce 1s in the result wherever the selected bits of the source word equal 1 and the unselected bits of the destination word equal 1. To carry out this entire algorithm, a typical microcomputer will require many LOD instruc-

tions to load the accumulator with an operand from a scratchpad register, carry out an operation, and then load a scratchpad register with the
result.

Before going on, note a potential source of disaster with this
algorithm. What will happen if SM has three 1s while DM has two 0s?

The algorithm to pack data can be drastically simplified if:

1   The destination register is initially all zeros.
2   The source register is already aligned with the destination register and
    has zeros in all the extraneous bit positions.

In this case, simply move the destination word to the accumulator and
exclusive-OR the source word to it.

Example 2-17. Form a packed word from four sources S1, S2, S3, and
S4, which are already appropriately aligned and each having zeros in
its extraneous bit positions.

$$A \leftarrow S1$$

$$A \leftarrow A \oplus S2$$

$$A \leftarrow A \oplus S3$$

$$A \leftarrow A \oplus S4$$

At this point, the packing is complete. The result can be loaded into
any desired location from the accumulator.

These two alternative approaches to this problem of forming a packed
word illustrate two extremes. The first approach pays a severe penalty for
its generality. The second approach requires some planning in how and
where its component parts are formed, but then makes the packing almost
trivial.

Unpacking specific bits from a word consists of two steps:

1 Masking to make all extraneous bits equal to zero
2 Shifting right or left to align the bits as desired

Even if shifting is required, the procedure is quite simple.

Example 2-18. A selected table entry has been moved to the accumulator. The bits of interest are shown in Fig. 2-36a. Unpack these bits and align them in the rightmost position of the accumulator. The algorithm is shown in two forms in Fig. 2-36b and c. The rotate right instruction is assumed to be of the form shown in Fig. 2-35d.

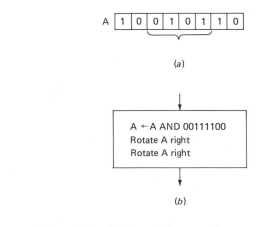

Figure 2-36. Example of unpacking data. (a) Bits of interest; (b) algorithm in flowchart form; (c) algorithm in assembly language form.

2-12 ARRAYS

Often the variables of a problem do not stand alone as single 4- or 8-bit words of data. Rather, a single variable may extend over several words (for example, a 10-digit decimal number). Or we may use 128 eight-bit words to store consecutive samples of data from an analog-to-digital converter.

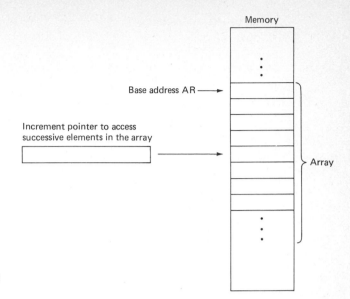

Memory

Base address AR ⟶

Increment pointer to access
successive elements in the array

Array

*Figure 2-37. Addressing
data in an array.*

Each of these is an example of an *array.* Our distinguishing characteristic of an array will be an operational one. We will access each element of
an array in succession by incrementing (or decrementing) through the array
from one end to the other. The tool for accessing data in an array is thus a
memory pointer which can be incremented or decremented, as in Fig. 2-37.
The alternative indirect-addressing modes, listed in Fig. 2-8, determine how
a specific microcomputer will access successive elements in an array. The
two examples of Figs. 2-6 and 2-7 have already provided a rudimentary view
of accessing successive elements in an array, or actually in two arrays.

To access every element in an array (in which the number of elements
is equal to NUM) from beginning to end involves three steps:

1   Initialize a pointer to the base address of the array. Initialize a
    scratchpad register N to NUM. We will use N as a counter.
2   Access one element of the array. Carry out the desired operation.
    Decrement the counter N. Increment the pointer P.
3   Test the counter for zero, and branch back to step 2 if it is not yet zero.
    Otherwise, the operation on the array has been completed.

This procedure is illustrated in Fig. 2-38.

Some microcomputer manufacturers have recognized that operations
upon arrays are of fundamental importance to many, if not most, users. In
recognition of this, they have tailored the instruction set of their microcomputer to combine several of the steps shown in Fig. 2-38 into one instruction.
The extent of this tailoring of an instruction set so as to be efficient in the
handling of arrays is indicated for several microcomputers in Fig. 2-39. The

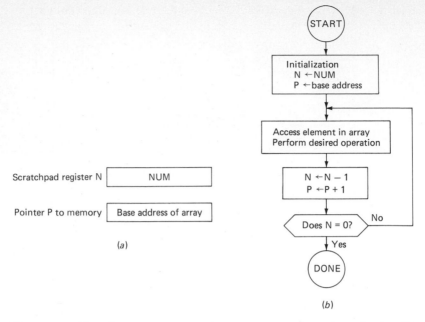

Scratchpad register N | NUM

Pointer P to memory | Base address of array

(a)

START → Initialization N ← NUM, P ← base address → Access element in array, Perform desired operation → N ← N − 1, P ← P + 1 → Does N = 0? — No (loops back) / Yes → DONE

(b)

Figure 2-38. *Algorithm to access every element in an array.* (a) *Initialization;* (b) *flowchart.*

Rockwell microcomputers go far in this direction. In fact, the last column is intended to indicate that Rockwell's PPS-8 microcomputer can form various combinations of the following operations into a single (one-byte!) instruction:

1 Move data from A to M or from M to A or exchange M and A (or do not move data at all).
2 Increment or decrement P, the pointer, to M.
3 Test for a boundary and skip if one is encountered.
4 Test for completion of a program loop (that is, compare P with an "end address" in another register) and skip if equal.
5 Exchange pointers.

To do this, the PPS-8 has a rich and varied instruction set so the user can do 1 alone (as A ← M or M ← A or M ↔ A), or 1 and 2 and 3 together, or 1 and 2 and 3 and 4 and 5 together.

Example 2-19. In Sec. 2-7, we discussed the use of a stack to store return addresses for subroutines. If a microcomputer stack can only

Figure 2-39. Array-oriented Instructions of Some Microcomputers

	M ← A, increment P	A ← M, increment P	A ← A (operation) M, increment or decrement P	Increment P, test P and jump	Increment R, test R and jump	Output port ← M, increment P	M ↔ A, decrement P, test P and skip	Increment P, test P and skip	Decrement P, test P and skip	Move data, increment P, test P or R and skip, and exchange pointers
4-bit microcomputers										
Intel 4004/4040					X					
Rockwell PPS-4							X	X	X	
8-bit microcomputers										
Fairchild F8	X	X	X	X						
Intel 8008/8080										
Motorola 6800										
RCA COSMAC		X				X				
Rockwell PPS-8	X						X	X	X	X
SMS Microcontroller										

handle return addresses, we might wish to create another stack, located in RAM, to handle data under program control. This is useful, for example, to set aside the contents of one or more scratchpad registers temporarily, knowing that we will restore them later. Registers can be *pushed* onto the stack to set them aside. Subsequently they can be *popped* back from the stack to the registers. One popular way to create such a stack will be discussed in the next section.

Another way to create this stack is to set aside a fixed number of consecutive addresses (perhaps eight) in RAM for the stack. The lowest address might then be designated the "top of the stack." Each "push" will move all the data in the stack up one word, throwing away the word in the highest address. This makes room so that the data to be pushed onto the stack can now go into the "top of the stack" location. At the same time, data previously pushed onto the stack is maintained in order within the stack. "Popping" the stack reverses this procedure, first moving the word at the "top of the stack" back to a scratchpad register and then moving each word to one lower address within the stack. This is illustrated in Fig. 2-40a and b.

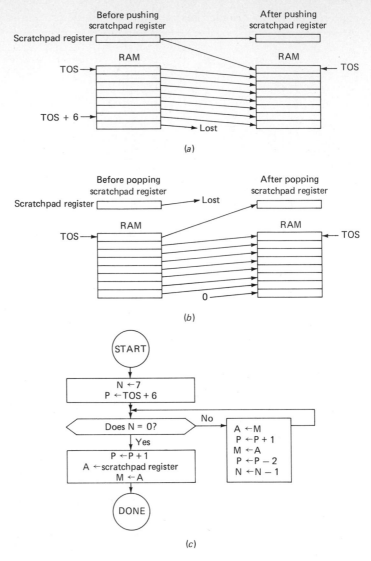

Figure 2-40. Pushing and popping data. (a) Pushing data onto the stack; (b) popping data from the stack; (c) algorithm for pushing.

An algorithm for "pushing" is shown in flowchart form in Fig. 2-40c. It uses a scratchpad register N as a counter and assumes that all moves of data must include the accumulator A as either the source register or the destination register.

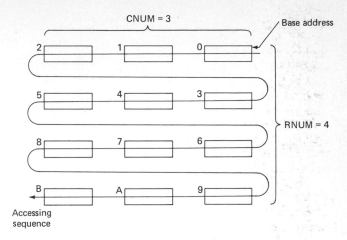

Figure 2-41. Two-dimensional array.

Sometimes data is most naturally handled as a *two-dimensional* array, as will occur in storing 128 samples of data from a 10-bit analog-to-digital converter. Each sample can be stored in two consecutive words in RAM (for an 8-bit microcomputer). The total data storage using this regime would then be 128 × 2, or 256 words.

To operate upon all samples in the array, one after another, it is convenient to think of the array as consisting of "rows" and "columns" of bytes of memory as shown in Fig. 2-41, where the number of rows in the array is designated RNUM and the number of columns is designated CNUM. If the base address for the array points to the byte of memory in the upper right-hand corner, we can think of the successive bytes in memory as running across each row, from least significant byte to most significant byte, and then on to the next row.

***

Example 2-20. Construct a flowchart for a general algorithm which will carry out an (unspecified) operation upon each row of the two-dimensional array of Fig. 2-41, starting at the base of the array and working across each row from right to left.

We will call two scratchpad registers RC and CC and use them as counters to keep track of rows and columns, respectively. Also P will once again designate a pointer to memory. The algorithm is shown in Fig. 2-42.

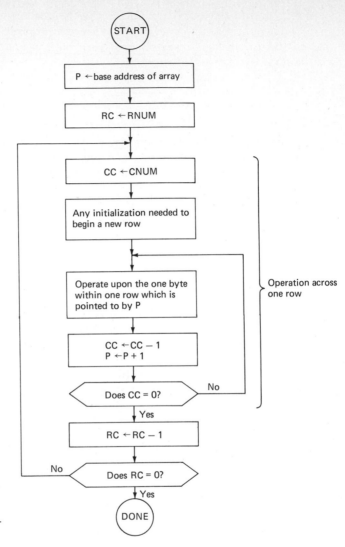

Figure 2-42. General two-
dimensional algorithm.

2-13 POINTERS

Pointers have served us well in previous sections as a means for forming an
indirect address. They have permitted us to increment from one address to
the next in order to access the data in an array using a loop structure.
     In this section we will consider how, on occasion, an operation can be
expedited by manipulating a pointer. An algorithm sometimes seems to involve a rather tedious rearrangement of an array of data. If we only realize
it, the same algorithm can, on occasion, be implemented much more directly

by manipulating the *pointer* to the array of data. Some designers always seem to manipulate an array while others seek to manipulate a pointer. This has led to the observation that some designers seem to be "array people" while others are "pointer people."

Example 2-21. Consider again the problem discussed in Example 2-19 of creating a stack out of eight words in RAM. There we relocated the entire array for either a "push" or a "pop" operation. A far better implementation of a stack (and the approach taken by all microcomputers which use a stack located in RAM) involves the manipulation of a pointer rather than an array. In Example 2-19, we identified a *fixed* location in RAM and called it the "top of the stack." The more expeditious approach uses "push" and "pop" operations to manipulate the contents of a pointer which, in turn, identifies a variable location in RAM as the top of the stack. This is illustrated in Fig. 2-43a, where P is a scratchpad register used as a pointer to memory. We use the notation

P.H = high-order 8 bits of the 16-bit register P

P.L = low-order 8 bits of the 16-bit register P

to identify the two halves of a 16-bit register. POINTER and POINTER + 1 are RAM addresses which hold the stack pointer when we are not doing a stack manipulation. The notation M(POINTER) means the contents of the memory location whose address is labeled POINTER. TOSIN is an address in RAM which will be set up as the TOp of Stack INitially, when power is first turned on, as indicated in Fig. 2-43b.

The PUSH algorithm, shown as a subroutine (note the "Return" at the end) assumes that the data to be pushed will be in a specific scratchpad register R. The stack pointer is first moved from RAM to the CPU register used as a pointer to RAM. Then the algorithm moves the contents of the register R to be "pushed" to the RAM address pointed to, increments P, restores the contents of the P register to RAM, and returns. The POP algorithm simply undoes what the PUSH algorithm did.

The proper use of a stack requires that every POP be preceded by a PUSH; that is, we cannot very well take data out of a stack which was not previously put there. Consequently, the stack contents can safely start at address TOSIN with no worry about the pointer ever backing up below TOSIN (unless the software is improperly prepared, so that POPs and PUSHes do not pair up). Likewise, if we reserve only eight

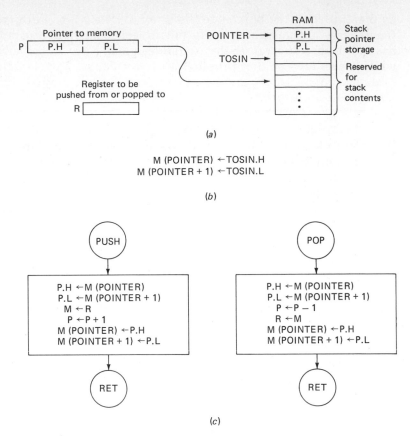

(a)

$$M (POINTER) \leftarrow TOSIN.H$$
$$M (POINTER + 1) \leftarrow TOSIN.L$$

(b)

PUSH

P.H ←M (POINTER)
P.L ←M (POINTER + 1)
M ←R
P ←P + 1
M (POINTER) ←P.H
M (POINTER + 1) ←P.L

RET

POP

P.H ←M (POINTER)
P.L ←M (POINTER + 1)
P ←P − 1
R ←M
M (POINTER) ←P.H
M (POINTER + 1) ←P.L

RET

(c)

Figure 2-43. Creation and use of a stack pointer. (a) RAM and pointer arrangement; (b) initialization of stack; (c) PUSH algorithm and POP algorithm.

addresses in RAM for the stack contents, we want to ensure that no more than eight words are ever pushed onto the stack at any one time, or we might overrun other variables stored in RAM. However, notice that the *only* consequence of reserving as large a stack as we desire is that there is less memory available for other variables.

As a final comment, the PUSH and POP algorithms consisted mostly of moving the stack pointer back and forth. By dedicating a specific CPU register to the stack function, a microcomputer manufacturer adds this capability almost painlessly.

Another use of pointers in instrument design concerns the tailoring of the function of the instrument to a few different classes of users. For example, the instrument of Fig. 1-12 which tests the equipment which frequency-multiplexes telephone calls is set up with various "plans" built into it. Each plan specifies how individual telephone channels are multiplexed into "groups," groups into "supergroups," and supergroups into "mastergroups." More than one plan is needed to handle the international market for the instrument, since different nations have standardized upon similar, but not identical, plans.

One solution is to develop the algorithm for each plan as a separate entity. This algorithm can be put into its own special ROM chip or set of ROM chips. Then, to tailor the instrument to each plan, the manufacturer inserts the appropriate ROMs into the instrument.

An alternative is to develop one general algorithm which will handle all plans. The distinctions among different plans are handled with

1 Pointers to constants
2 Pointers to Boolean values to be tested

Both of these are contained in a table. A separate table is what distinguishes a specific plan. Since the tables are concise, it is not unreasonable to include many plans in the instrument together with a switch which points to the table, and hence the plan, to use. Figure 2-44 illustrates the nature of these tables.

Before discussing how the constants in these tables are used, consider the alternatives for entering constants into an algorithm:

1 As immediate data
2 As the contents of a labeled address in ROM
3 As the contents of an address in ROM which is accessed by a pointer

The first choice is the most efficient way to access a constant since the addressing of the location of the constant is implicitly understood; the constant forms the second byte of the instruction. Storing constants as immediate data has the disadvantage that they then become buried throughout the software for the algorithm. Any changes in these constants requires a hunt for them, unless they are labeled using EQU assembler directives.

Storing constants in labeled addresses in ROM using the DB and DW assembler directives of Fig. 2-32 permits us to locate all the constants for the algorithm together in one place. In addition, the name we use for the address label of the constant helps us to locate it (for example, FREQ1 or INDEX3).

Storing constants in a table like that of Fig. 2-44 requires, and permits, us to set up a pointer to access a specific constant. Neither of the previous two addressing modes allows this variability. It can be achieved using indexed instructions (as with the Motorola 6800) or indirect addressing (as with most other microcomputers). In the case of indirect addressing, prior

ROM address	ROM contents		Meaning of contents	
00	3	2	Constant 1, digits 1, 2	Plan 0
01	5	6	Constant 1, digits 3, 4	
02	1	4	Constant 1, digits 5, 6	
03	3	1	Constant 2, digits 1, 2	
04	4	2	Constant 2, digits 3, 4	
05	0	5	Constant 3, digits 1, 2	
06	0	0	Value 1	
07	0	1	Value 2	
08	1	6	Constant 1, digits 1, 2	Plan 1
09	7	8	Constant 1, digits 3, 4	
0A	0	0	Constant 1, digits 5, 6	
0B	2	6	Constant 2, digits 1, 2	
0C	1	5	Constant 2, digits 3, 4	
0D	0	3	Constant 3, digits 1, 2	
0E	0	0	Value 1	
0F	0	0	Value 2	
10	0	0	Constant 1, digits 1, 2	Plan 2
11	0	0	Constant 1, digits 3, 4	
12	0	0	Constant 1, digits 5, 6	
13	2	3	Constant 2, digits 1, 2	
14	0	0	Constant 2, digits 3, 4	
15	0	0	Constant 3, digits 1, 2	
16	0	1	Value 1	
17	0	1	Value 2	

Figure 2-44. Tables for "plans."

to getting an operand, we can call a little subroutine which will form the address of the operand. It will read a switch which indicates the plan number. It will then go to a table holding the base address for that plan, move this to a pointer to memory, and add in a number which has been passed to the subroutine in a scratchpad register representing the offset of the table entry within the plan. These *offsets*, as compared with absolute addresses, will have been defined with the EQU assembler directive of Fig. 2-32. For example, for the offsets of Fig. 2-44:

ADD	MNE	REG	OP
CONSTANT1	EQU		0
CONSTANT2	EQU		3
CONSTANT3	EQU		5

The analogous procedure for indexed addressing is simpler. Again the offsets are defined using the EQU mnemonic. To address a specific constant, the index register is first loaded with the base address of the plan. Then an indexed instruction is executed:

ADD	MNE	REG	OP
	LOD	A	CONSTANT2, X

This loads the accumulator A from the memory address formed by adding the number represented by CONSTANT2 to the contents of the index register X.

This scheme provides a way to access a constant for a specific plan. Now consider how a general algorithm can be organized so that the *differences* between variations (for example, the differences between "plans") can be handled by pointers to tables. Consider the nature of these differences.

1 *Alternative operands.* We may need to add a constant (for example, a carrier frequency) at a certain point in the algorithm. If all variations include this addition but use different constants, the constant can be handled within the table.

2 *Alternative controlling constants.* Sometimes a variation can be handled by going through a loop a variable number of times (for example, add register 3 to the accumulator N times). Again if all variations go through this same loop, but the number of times varies between variations, this can be handled within the table.

3 *Alternative branches.* If all else fails for a portion of the algorithm, a Boolean value in a table can be tested and a branch made. A segment of the algorithm can apply for some variations and can be completely bypassed for other variations.

2-14 MICROCOMPUTER SPEED AND MEMORY EFFICIENCY

In comparing microcomputers, it is easy to come away with the frustrating feeling that there is no one "best" microcomputer for a specific instrument design. In reality, there are probably many microcomputers which will meet the requirements—or there may be none. Many applications can be met with a rather "slow" microcomputer as long as the requirements are even slower. Since many instruments must only look fast to a human operator, they can employ a "slow" microcomputer and still appear instantaneous. For example, a slow microcomputer like the Intel 4004 [with a 10- or 20-microsecond (μs) instruction cycle for 1- or 2-byte instructions] can still execute between 50,000 and 100,000 instructions per second. A fast microcomputer such as the Intel 8080 (with instruction cycles between 2 and 9 μs) or Motorola 6800 (with instruction cycles between 2 and 12 μs) might average about 250,000 instructions per second. Consequently, *either* "slow" *or* "fast" represents a high rate of executing instructions.

Comparing the duration of the instruction cycles of several microcomputers is not a very good indicator of which one is best for a particular application, even if speed is of primary interest. Of greater significance is a comparison of the times required by several microcomputers to execute a specific algorithm which is regarded as being "typical" or "important" in the application of interest. Alternatively, comparisons between microcomputers can be made for several standard or "benchmark" algorithms which are typical of many applications.

Once again it is important to emphasize that speed is likely not to be a deciding factor. For, even if one microcomputer can execute a benchmark algorithm (or, for that matter, the entire routine required by an instrument) four times faster than another microcomputer, that fact is irrelevant as long as the slower microcomputer is fast enough to satisfy the application.

Because of this weak dependence upon the speed of a microcomputer, another figure of merit is often used in comparing microcomputers. Again we are interested in benchmark algorithms, but now our interest focuses upon the number of words in ROM needed to store the algorithm. Some microcomputers have powerful instruction sets and thus need relatively few instructions to implement an algorithm. More typically, a microcomputer will be outstanding at doing one kind of thing and "middle of the road" at doing another.

To carry out a benchmark comparison of several microcomputers, it is necessary to become thoroughly immersed in the workings of each one so that a "best" implementation of the benchmark algorithm can be achieved for that microcomputer. However, the *value* of the benchmark comparison comes after this work is done. It comes when we are able to view the *result* of such an application-oriented comparison of the microcomputers without concerning ourselves any longer with how each one implemented the algorithm. In the final analysis, if one microcomputer can implement the entire software for an instrument in four pages of ROM while another requires six pages of ROM, this represents one reason for preferring the former microcomputer.

Example 2-22. Using the benchmark algorithm flowcharted in Fig. 2-45a, compare our list of microcomputers on the basis of ROM words needed as a primary criterion (and speed as a secondary criterion). This subroutine, DADD, is to add together two 8-digit decimal numbers X and Y, located in RAM, and put the result back into the location from which X was taken. It is assumed that the pointers to RAM have already been set up in the CPU before entering the subroutine. Like-

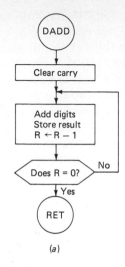

(a)

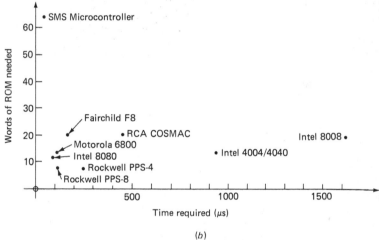

(b)

Figure 2-45. Benchmark algorithm. (a) The DADD subroutine; (b) comparison.

wise, it is assumed that scratchpad register R has been set up to count the digits.

The resulting comparison is shown in Fig. 2-45b. Several comments seem appropriate. The Intel 8008 and the RCA COSMAC do not have instructions for handling decimal digits directly. Consequently their routines have been prepared assuming that only one digit is stored in each byte of RAM, requiring eight iterations (just as for the 4-bit microcomputers) as well as a binary-to-decimal correction following the addition of each pair of digits. The SMS Microcontroller also

does not handle decimal digits directly. However, because it is particularly effective in operating upon selected bits within a byte of data, its
routine has been prepared assuming that corresponding digits of X and
Y are packed together into the same byte of RAM. The Fairchild and
Rockwell microcomputers are more efficient if the data is carefully located at a memory boundary. Any such helpful decisions have been
assumed for all of the microcomputers.

The SMS Microcontroller uses a 16-bit ROM word length to hold
its instructions. In order to provide a meaningful comparison, the
number of ROM words actually required by the SMS unit has been multiplied by 2 to obtain an equivalent number of 8-bit ROM words.

PROBLEMS

Many of these problems are intended to be worked in terms of a specific microcomputer. Refer either to one described in the appendixes or to
one for which you have a manufacturer's user's manual or equivalent information.

2-1 Minimum systems. Some microcomputers have been optimized to include at least some capability in each of the six areas shown in Fig. 2-1
with a minimum of parts. What is the least number of chips necessary
to do this for some specific microcomputer? How much capability
does this minimum chip count offer in each of the six areas?

2-2 Microcomputer word length. For a specific microcomputer, determine
the data word length; the length of one byte of an instruction (that is,
the ROM word length); the different instruction word lengths possible.

2-3 Hexadecimal numbers. Find the hexadecimal equivalents of the following binary numbers:
  (a) 00100111   (d) 1111111111111110
  (b) 01001110   (e) 0000000000000001
  (c) 10011100   (f) 0110101010111101

2-4 Hexadecimal numbers. Find the binary equivalents of the following
hexadecimal numbers:
  (a) 80   (c) E0   (e) 52
  (b) C0   (d) A3   (f) 01

2-5 Hexadecimal numbers. Find the decimal equivalent of the following
hexadecimal numbers:
  (a) 0F   (c) 35   (e) 0100
  (b) 10   (d) 00FF   (f) 0200

2-6 Data operands. For a specific microcomputer, list all "registers" which can be accessed for data operands.

2-7 Data operands. For a specific microcomputer, list the mnemonics of those instructions which address data operands using
    (a) Accumulator addressing
    (b) Scratchpad register addressing
    (c) Full direct addressing
    (d) Page-zero (or another specific, single page) direct addressing
    (e) Indexed addressing
    (f) Indirect addressing
    (g) Doubly indirect addressing
    (h) Immediate addressing

2-8 Jump address operands. For a specific microcomputer, list the mnemonics of those jump instructions (unconditional jump, conditional jump, and jump to subroutine) which form the jump address using:
    (a) Full addressing
    (b) Present-page addressing
    (c) Relative addressing
    (d) Indexed addressing
    (e) Indirect addressing

2-9 Indirect addressing. For a specific microcomputer, what are the ways, if any, for moving a variable address set up in a scratchpad register into the program counter?

2-10 Assembly language. Our assembly language ground rules make use of five separate fields—for the address, mnemonic, register(s), operand, and comments. Some microcomputer assembly languages use only four fields—for the address, mnemonic, operand, and comments. For a specific microcomputer, what are the different ways in which the register(s) involved in an operation is (are) identified?

2-11 Assembly language. Some microcomputer assembly languages use a "free-field format" in which the different fields are *not* identified by which character positions across a line they fall into. For a specific microcomputer, what constraints do you see taken to distinguish:
    (a) Address labels
    (b) Mnemonics (in addition to using standard names)
    (c) Registers
    (d) Labels for operands (data and jump addresses)
    (e) Immediate data

2-12 Branching. Considering a specific microcomputer,
    (a) Does it use flag flipflops for its tests? If so, what "compare-type" instructions are available which affect nothing but the flag flipflops?

(b) What can it test? For tests involving more than one bit, specify it in words or with a Boolean equation.

(c) Does it use conditional jump (that is, branch) instructions?

(d) Does it use conditional skip instructions?

(e) What addressing modes are possible with these conditional instructions?

2-13 Branching. If you have just completed the assembly language program for an instrument organized around a specific microcomputer and are now doing the assembling yourself, by hand, how do you decide what addressing mode to use for each jump instruction (assuming your microcomputer offers a choice)? Make a flowchart for your decision algorithm.

2-14 Looping. For a specific microcomputer, write the assembly language equivalent of Fig. 2-17b to iterate three times. How many bytes of ROM do these instructions require?

2-15 Testing. For a specific microcomputer, write an assembly language sequence (using as few ROM words as possible) to jump to an address P1 if the accumulator:

(a) Equals all 1s.

(b) Has its two most significant bits equal to 1.

(c) Has its two most significant bits equal to 0.

(d) Has either its least significant bit or its most significant bit equal to 1.

(e) Has either its least significant bit or its most significant bit equal to 0.

(f) Has its least significant four bits equal to one of the hexadecimal numbers 0, 1, or 2.

(g) Has its least significant four bits equal to one of the hexadecimal numbers 1, 2, or 3.

(h) Contains an odd number of 1s.

(i) Contains exactly one 1, located in any bit position.

2-16 Subroutines. The Rockwell PPS-8 microcomputer has a convenient way for a calling program to pass "immediate" data to a subroutine. A jump to subroutine instruction can be followed by any desired constants which the subroutine can then access (while at the same time incrementing the return address which is on the top of the stack so that upon return from the routine these constants will be skipped over). For some other specific microcomputer, can you find any way of passing immediate data to a subroutine other than the obvious one of loading it into a scratchpad register?

2-17 Subroutines. For a specific microcomputer:

(a) How are return addresses for subroutines handled?

(b) If the microcomputer incorporates a stack, where is it located?

Does it require any initialization when power is first turned on?

(c) Does the CPU handle return addresses automatically during calls and returns, or must extra instructions be included for this purpose? If so, what is used?

2-18 Subroutines. Consider that we are using a microcomputer which incorporates a stack for subroutine return addresses. Within a certain subroutine SUB1, we inadvertently use an *unconditional jump* to SUB2 (instead of a *jump to subroutine* SUB2) where SUB2 is another subroutine. What will be the effect of this programming error when the program is run on the microcomputer?

2-19 Tables. For a specific microcomputer, develop the assembly language sequence of instructions which will set up the pointer to memory as described in Example 2-8. Assume that the tables of Figs. 2-24 and 2-25 have been changed appropriately so that both are on the same page. Furthermore, assume that the pointer to memory initially points to the desired entry of Fig. 2-25. Could the resulting sequence be handled as a subroutine? Would it make sense to handle it in this way?

2-20 Tables. If your microcomputer can form either indirect or indexed jump addresses, develop the assembly language sequence of instructions to jump to an address which is stored in a table, as discussed in Example 2-9. Assume that the pointer to memory is already set up to the desired entry of Fig. 2-25 and that both this table and the addresses to be jumped to are on the same page. Could the resulting sequence be handled as a subroutine? Would it make sense to do so?

2-21 Tables. For a specific microcomputer, develop a flowchart and an assembly language subroutine for the table-driver algorithm of Fig. 2-28a. Specify where the subroutine expects to find the parameters P and OFFSET passed to it by the calling routine. Minimize the number of ROM words needed to store the subroutine.

2-22 Memory allocation. For a specific microcomputer, how is memory allocation constrained, or biased, by
(a) The start-up mechanism when power is turned on?
(b) Addressing modes for jump addresses?
(c) Addressing modes for data operands?
(d) Any other considerations?

2-23 Assembler directives. Under what circumstances might it be useful to give a fixed constant a label, using the EQU directive?

2-24 Assembler directives. Sometimes the term *pseudooperation* is given to an assembler directive which does not generate any object code (that is, 1s and 0s for the ROM program) during the assembling process. With this definition, which of the assembler directives of Fig. 2-32 are pseudo-ops?

2-25 Macros. For a specific microcomputer, define as efficiently as possible (that is, minimizing ROM words) a macro for any of the following instructions which are not already members of the microcomputer's instruction set:

(a) RAR, Rotate the Accumulator Right, moving the least significant bit into the most significant bit position.

(b) ADC, ADd Carry to accumulator.

(c) ACM, Add Carry, and M to accumulator, where M is the memory register pointed to.

(d) INC R, INCrement scratchpad register R.

(e) XCH R, EXCHange accumulator and scratchpad register R.

2-26 Macros. Define a macro for "your" microcomputer which you wish were actually one of the microcomputer's instructions, and which is short enough to warrant being treated as a macro.

2-27 Bit packing. For a specific microcomputer, define a macro PAK which will form a packed word in the (uncleared) accumulator from the word M already pointed to (by the pointer to memory) and the next word in memory. Assume the two words are already aligned and have zeros in the extraneous bit positions.

2-28 Bit packing. How would the table-driver subroutine of Sec. 2-8 have to be modified if all tables were constrained to reside in the pages having zeros in the two most significant bits of their binary address and if the "number of bytes per entry" were passed to the subroutine (now called TABLE) packed into these two bits? The two bits might code 1, 2, 3, or 4 bytes per entry as 00, 01, 10, 11. For the specific microcomputer considered in Prob. 2-21, rework the problem subject to the change (and with the one entry point called TABLE).

2-29 Bit unpacking. For a specific 8-bit microcomputer, define a macro SR4 (Shift Right 4 places) which will move the four most significant bits to the four least significant bit positions and then zero the four most significant bit positions. Alternatively, for a specific 4-bit microcomputer, define a macro SR2 which does the analogous operation.

2-30 Arrays. For a specific microcomputer, modify the algorithm of Fig. 2-38 into a *subroutine* which accesses each element in the array sequentially from the *highest* to the *lowest* address. Assume that upon entering the subroutine the memory pointer points to the base address of the array. Also assume that NUM is located in some convenient place, but specify where this is. Develop both a flowchart and an assembly language subroutine.

2-31 Arrays. To do an operation (using a specific microcomputer) upon an entire array of less than a page in length, does it help to locate the array either at the beginning of a page or at the end of a page? Explain.

2-32 Arrays. To do the operation of adding the two 4-digit numbers together shown in either Fig. 2-6 or Fig. 2-7 (whichever is appropriate for a specific microcomputer):

(a) Does it help to locate either, or both, arrays adjacent to a page boundary? Explain.

(b) Does it help to have both arrays on the same page? Explain.

(c) Does it help to have the arrays in corresponding positions on two separate pages? Explain.

2-33 Two-dimensional array. Repeat Example 2-20, except scan each row from left to right.

2-34 Pointers. Using a specific microcomputer, create a data stack using the algorithms of Fig. 2-43. Minimizing the ROM words required, write assembly language subroutines for:

(a) PUSH   (b) POP

2-35 Pointers. For a specific microcomputer which cannot form jump addresses using indexed addressing, but which can use indirect addressing, write the subroutine discussed in the text for reading out of the table of Fig. 2-44. Assume that the plan number is a binary number located in RAM at an address labeled PLAN. Show how you are assuming all tables are organized, labeled, and located within one page of ROM.

2-36 Benchmark algorithm. For a specific microcomputer, develop the algorithm of Fig. 2-45a subject to each of the following criteria (one at a time):

(a) Minimize ROM words

(b) Minimize time required

How do the results in each case compare with the data of Fig. 2-45b?

REFERENCES

An excellent capsule summary of the relationship between the register structure and instruction set of a specific microcomputer (Motorola 6800) and its assembly language is provided by S. Levine, Assembly Language for μPs, Electronic Design, Dec. 20, 1975, pp. 58–63.

For a more complete, detailed presentation of the register structure, instruction set, assembly language characteristics, and hardware considerations for a specific microcomputer, obtain the user's manual and the assembly language programming manual for the microcomputer from the manufacturer.

MICROCOMPUTER HARDWARE

3-1 ALTERNATIVE PHILOSOPHIES

Since the introduction of microcomputers in 1971 with Intel's 4004, the manufacturers of successive microcomputers have pursued a variety of alternative design objectives. The manufacturer of each new microcomputer has been able not only to capitalize upon an evolving technology but also to envision an evolving multifaceted market. Consequently, in looking at microcomputers, we find that a variety of directions have been taken. Some of these conflicting directions are:

1   Incorporation of all the components of Fig. 2-1 within a *self-contained chip set*.
2   Organization so as to achieve some minimal capability in each of the six areas defined in Fig. 2-1 with *minimum chip number* (for example, one or two chips). Optimizing for this also implies a self-contained chip set.
3   Development of a CPU chip which *interfaces easily* with standard, general-purpose chips for the memory, input, and output functions.

4   Organization to be efficient as a *large-capacity system* (for example, large memory, or large input-output capability).
5   Optimization as a *fast controller* rather than as a versatile, general-purpose processor.
6   Partitioning of chips so as to permit *arbitrary data word length*.
7   Microprogramming capability so as to achieve an *arbitrary instruction set*.

The Intel®4004/4040 and the Fairchild F8 microcomputers are good examples of self-contained chip sets. The 4004 chips* are each constructed as a 16-pin dual-in-line package (DIP) and include special timing circuitry on each chip so that data, instruction addresses, and instructions can be trans-

* Designated the MCS-4® chip set by Intel.

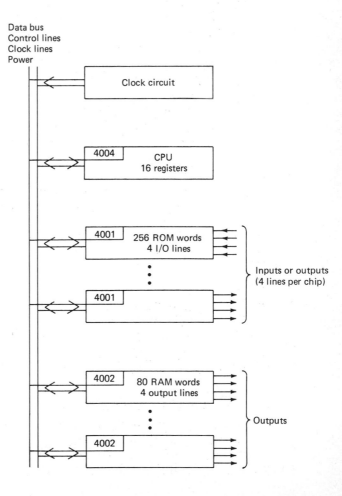

Figure 3-1. Intel 4004 (alias MCS-4) chip set.

ferred between chips over a four-line *data bus*. This general configuration
is illustrated in Fig. 3-1. Without this sharing of the data bus, it would be
impossible to obtain the general versatility of a microcomputer using chips
having only 16 pins. These small chips permit sophistication to be built
into an instrument with very little hardware.

The Intel MCS-40® uses the 24-pin, 4040 CPU chip. This is a more sophisticated CPU than the 4004 (as indicated in Chap. 2). It also has a few
more control lines to simplify expansion to many RAM and ROM chips.
Otherwise, it uses the same RAM and ROM chips to achieve the same advantage of a concise system structure.

The Fairchild F8 uses 40-pin packages, as do many other microcomputers. By using a self-contained chip set with an 8-bit data bus for transferring instruction addresses, instructions, and data between chips, 16 of the 40
pins on each chip have been made available for two 8-bit I/O ports, for either
input or output. This is an unusual tradeoff and an outstanding feature of
the F8. The minimum system is shown in Fig. 3-2. With its two chips and

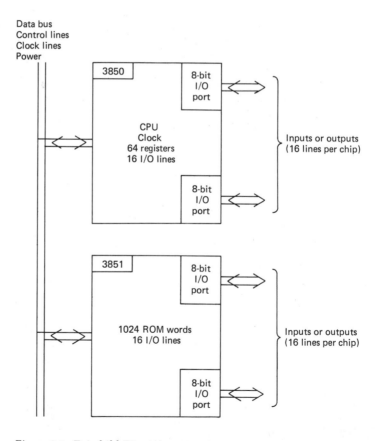

Figure 3-2. Fairchild F8 minimum system.

its 32 I/O lines, it is a strong contender for the many applications where small size is a desirable attribute. Another chip in the chip set, discussed in Appendix A2, permits expansion of the RAM capability for those applications where 64 words are not enough.

The Rockwell PPS-4 and PPS-8 are further examples of microcomputers built up from self-contained chip sets. These two are efficient in handling a large amount of memory and in handling sophisticated I/O devices directly. For example, they include specialized controller chips for printers, cathode-ray-tube (CRT) displays, and floppy disks.

The RCA COSMAC is a strict example of the other end of the specialization versus generalization spectrum. It is strictly a CPU but interfaces easily with standard logic components for RAM, ROM, and I/O.

The Intel 8080 and the Motorola 6800 fall into the category of potent general-purpose CPUs which use standard RAM and ROM. Each has a ver-

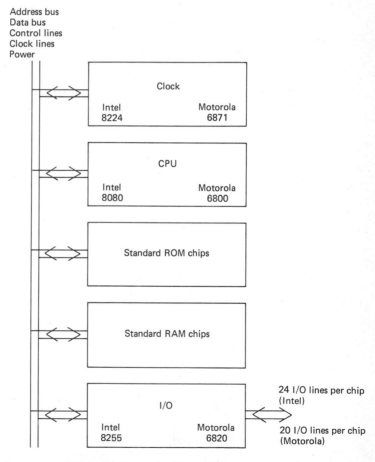

Figure 3-3. Intel 8080/Motorola 6800 systems.

satile I/O chip and a special clock chip, as shown in Fig. 3-3. They can be efficiently expanded to large-capacity systems. The Intel 8008 is the less powerful predecessor of the 8080 and requires the addition of quite a few standard logic chips before it is a fully functional CPU which can communicate with memory and I/O.

All the microcomputers discussed so far use MOS or CMOS* technology to achieve a high density of devices in a small package. For example, the Intel 8080 packs 5000 MOS transistors into a silicon chip which measures only 164 × 191 mils, or about 0.03 square inch! A price paid for the use of MOS technology is that the resulting microcomputer is slow compared with a microcomputer using bipolar-transistor technology. As a result, the very fast "controllers" and "microprogrammable" devices are bipolar—but end up requiring either larger chips or more chips.

The bipolar SMS Microcontroller makes drastic tradeoffs in order to be a fast controller. It includes only eight instructions (MOVE, ADD, AND, XOR, indexed jump, unconditional jump, conditional jump, and load immediate). On the other hand, these instructions identify not only a source and a destination register, but also *which bits* of the source and destination registers are to be operated upon. Some of the instructions can also "right rotate" the operand from the source register an arbitrary number of places before carrying out the operation. With 16-bit instruction words, this special-purpose microcomputer executes instructions on 8-bit data words at

* Metal-oxide semiconductor or complementary metal-oxide semiconductor.

Figure 3-4. SMS Microcontroller. (Scientific Micro Systems.)

the extremely fast rate of one every 300 nanoseconds (ns)—that is, 3.3 million instructions per second. As shown in Fig. 3-4, the complete microcomputer is packaged on a printed-circuit board, using large 64-pin DIP packages for CPU, RAM, ROM, and clock. While the Microcontroller comes in several sizes, the System 20 shown is partitioned with CPU, clock, and 2K (2048 words) of ROM in one chip, 256 words of RAM in another chip, and eight 8-bit I/O ports.

There is a specialized segment of the microcomputer market for which speed and flexibility (of architecture and data word length) go together. The manufacturers of minicomputers fall into this segment. The opportunity afforded here by LSI (large-scale integration) microcomputer technology is again reduced size and power consumption as well as simplified

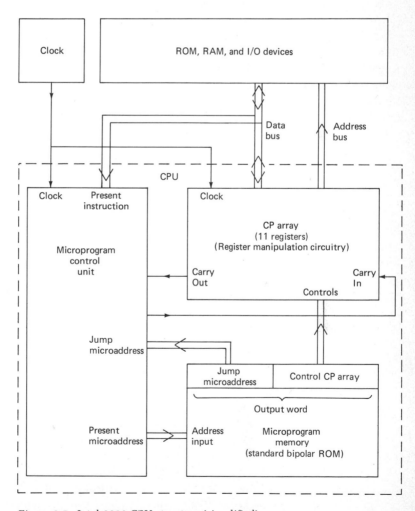

Figure 3-5. Intel 3000 CPU structure (simplified).

manufacturing, troubleshooting, and inventorying of parts. The drawback of this approach is that it adds an extra degree of freedom to the design process since the CPU itself must now be defined and designed.

Intel's 3000 bipolar microcomputer chip set is representative of this class of devices. The chips form a CPU having the structure of Fig. 3-5. The "CP array" is created using 2-bit-wide slices of circuitry on each chip (Intel 3002). That is, 2 bits of each register and 2-bits worth of circuitry to manipulate the contents of these registers are located in each chip. In addition, the CP array includes a *carry look ahead* chip (Intel 3003) to speed up the settling time across this array of 3002s. The "microprogram control unit" takes each instruction (from the memory outside the CPU) and breaks it down into a sequence of microinstructions which control the operation of the CP array. Each microinstruction includes an optional test so that the next microinstruction will either be taken in sequence or be taken from the "jump microaddress." These microinstructions are stored in the "microprogram memory," made up of standard bipolar ROM. If each microinstruction is executed in 125 ns, a microcomputer instruction consisting of four microinstructions will have an instruction cycle time of 0.5 μs. Not only does it execute each instruction fast, but these instructions can be tailored to the application so that it executes desirable algorithms especially fast. In addition, it can be especially efficient in its use of program storage (that is, memory outside the CPU) for these algorithms.

3-2   LOADING CONSIDERATIONS

As we proceed to construct a microcomputer from microprocessor chips together with, perhaps, standard ROMs and RAMs and standard I/O circuit devices, we must deal with the compatibility of devices which are to be interconnected. Likewise, when building up an instrument by connecting assorted devices to microcomputer input and output ports, we must again be concerned with the interconnections.

The specifications for the output of a device will indicate that unequivocal outputs are produced, provided that:

1   The voltage on each output line is properly identified as being within one voltage range to represent a logic 1 and another voltage range to represent a logic 0, as shown in Fig. 3-6. In this figure the logic levels have been defined *positive-true*; that is, the more positive of the two ranges has been identified as representing logic 1. While this is commonly done, it is not universally done (for example, the Intel 4004/4040 microcomputers use negative-true definitions of logic levels).

2   The output is not *loaded* beyond the capability of the device to maintain its output voltage in the appropriate voltage range. We cannot casually interconnect two arbitrary devices without first ascertaining that

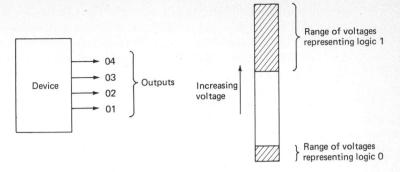

Figure 3-6. Output-voltage ranges.

the output device has sufficient *drive capability* to satisfy this loading requirement. The two circuits of Fig. 3-7 illustrate the two *worst-case* loading situations for one of the output lines of a Motorola output port (Motorola 6820, Peripheral Interface Adapter). Consider first the case of Fig. 3-7a in which the output is supposed to be at the higher of the two logic levels, representing a logic 1. In this case, the output line can be represented by a voltage source equal to the minimum permissible power-supply voltage for the chip [5 volts(V) − 5 percent = 4.75 V] in series with a resistance. The actual resistance will vary from one chip to the next owing to manufacturing tolerances. However, the worst-case specification covers this tolerance. Since Motorola wants the output voltage for a logic 1 to be anywhere between 2.4 and 4.75 V, the worst-case load is one which pulls the output voltage down by causing current to flow out of the output, as shown. Motorola

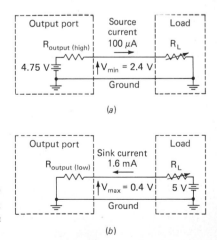

Figure 3-7. Worst-case loading of Motorola 6800 output port. (a) Worst-case equivalent circuit with output high; (b) worst-case equivalent circuit with output low.

says that in spite of their own manufacturing tolerances, they will guarantee that the logic 1 output voltage will never drop below 2.4 V provided the output line is never asked to source more than 100 microamperes (μA) of current. This provides a specification with which we can make decisions.

Example 3-1. What is the minimum resistance to ground R_L which can be hung on an output line which will still ensure that the logic 1 output voltage will be greater than 2.4 V?

$$R_L = \frac{V_{min}}{I_{max}} = \frac{2.4}{100 \times 10^{-6}} = 24{,}000 \text{ ohms } (\Omega) = 24 \text{ k}\Omega$$

In the case of a logic 0 output, the worst-case circuit is shown in Fig. 3-7b. The model for the output line is now a resistor to ground, or 0 V, since the other power-supply voltage for the chip is 0 V. The worst-case load in this instance is one which tends to pull the output voltage up. Motorola promises, in their specifications, that as long as the output line is not asked to *sink* more than 1.6 milliamperes (mA) of current, a logic 0 output will never rise above 0.4 V. Again, we can make design decisions with such information.

These specifications, and indeed the design of the MOS output circuitry, have been chosen for direct compatibility with various TTL* families. This is a useful, and important, compatibility since:

1   TTL has been, for many years, the leading series of logic families. It includes a wider variety of devices than any other logic family (although CMOS is gaining ground). It also includes families which meet various tradeoffs between speed and power. The three most popular TTL families are 74LSxx (low-power Schottky), 74xx (the original, "standard" TTL), and 74Sxx (high-speed Schottky). For example, a "hex inverter" (a 14-pin package containing six inverters) in these three families would be designated 74LS04, 7404, and 74S04, respectively.

2   TTL inverters and noninverting buffers provide a good interface between the relatively weak outputs of a microcomputer and higher-

---

* Transistor-transistor logic.

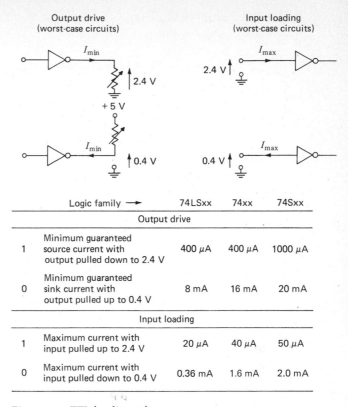

Figure 3-8. TTL loading rules.

Logic family →		74LSxx	74xx	74Sxx
Output drive				
1	Minimum guaranteed source current with output pulled down to 2.4 V	400 μA	400 μA	1000 μA
0	Minimum guaranteed sink current with output pulled up to 0.4 V	8 mA	16 mA	20 mA
Input loading				
1	Maximum current with input pulled up to 2.4 V	20 μA	40 μA	50 μA
0	Maximum current with input pulled down to 0.4 V	0.36 mA	1.6 mA	2.0 mA

power devices. They increase the current-driving capability by a factor of at least 10. Furthermore, "TTL compatibility" has become a widely used specification for the input-loading and output-drive capability for most digital devices. These loading specifications and drive capabilities are shown in Fig. 3-8 for each of the three families mentioned above.

Example 3-2. How many 74LSxx TTL inputs will a Motorola output line drive? Comparing Fig. 3-7 with Fig. 3-8, we have *two* criteria to satisfy. A logic 1 on the Motorola output line will drive as much as 100 μA before being dragged down to 2.4 V. Therefore, it can drive *five* 74LSxx inputs, since each of them will draw less than 20 μA for a total of 20 × 5 = 100 μA.

On the other hand, a logic 0 on the output line will sink as much as 1.6 mA before being dragged up to 0.4 V. Therefore, it can drive *four* 74LSxx inputs, but not five, since

$$4 \times 0.36 = 1.44 < 1.6$$

but

$$5 \times 0.36 = 1.80 > 1.6$$

Since the Motorola output line must be able to take the devices attached to it both high and low, it can drive a maximum of four 74LSxx devices.

Example 3-3. How many 74xx TTL inputs will a Motorola output line drive? For logic 1, *two* inputs gives

$$2 \times 40 \ \mu A = 80 \ \mu A < 100 \ \mu A$$

whereas *three* is too many. For logic 0, *one* input gives

$$1 \times 1.6 \ mA = 1.6 \ mA$$

which is just barely satisfactory. Consequently, a Motorola output line can drive one "standard" (that is, 74xx) TTL input, but no more than this.

Example 3-4. How many 74Sxx TTL inputs will a Motorola output line drive? Going through the same analysis, the output line can pull two inputs high but not even one low; so it cannot be used to drive 74Sxx logic devices.

CMOS is one other logic family which finds widespread use and therefore warrants our consideration here. It is a logic family with the very desirable characteristic of having inputs which look like open circuits. The typical current drawn by a CMOS input is 10 *picoamperes*, or

$$0.000000000010 \ ampere$$

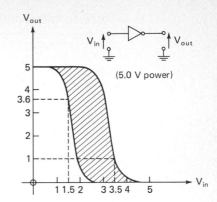

Figure 3-9. CMOS inverter input-output voltage relationships.

Consequently, almost any device can drive any number of CMOS devices.

In contrast with TTL and its fixed power-supply voltage requirement of 5.0 V ± 10 percent, CMOS logic can be operated with a power-supply voltage anywhere between 3 and 15 V (some devices can operate up to 18 V). To illustrate the specific relationship between input and output voltages, consider Fig. 3-9, which shows the input-output characteristic of a CMOS inverter operated with a 5-V power supply. As long as the input is below 1 V or above 4 V, we can be assured that the output has switched virtually all the way to 5 V or 0 V, respectively. The shaded region represents the uncertainty we can expect from one device to another. We avoid the uncertainty by keeping inputs above or below the uncertain region.

When connecting the output of a device to the input of a CMOS device, notice that if the output is specified as "TTL compatible," it will satisfy logic 0 requirements. On the other hand, a specification which says "the output can source 40 microamperes at 2.4 volts" (a typical specification which is useful for TTL) does not answer the question we want answered. Rather, for a CMOS load, we want to know what voltage to expect from an *unloaded* output, since a CMOS input looks like an open circuit. If the CMOS is operated at 5 V, we would like the input voltage to be close to 5 V for satisfactory operation.

Example 3-5. Can some lines of a Fairchild F8 output port drive TTL devices while others drive CMOS devices?

Consider the specifications of Fig. 3-10. The first and third lines, together with the TTL input data of Fig. 3-8, indicate that one 74xx device or one 74Sxx device or five 74LSxx devices can be driven from each output line. The second and third lines of Fig. 3-10 demonstrate satisfactory CMOS compatibility (provided any one output line is

Figure 3-10. Fairchild F8 Output-Port Specifications

Characteristic	Minimum	Maximum	Test conditions
High output voltage	2.9 V	5.0 V	$I_{source} = 100\ \mu A$
High output voltage	3.9 V	5.0 V	$I_{source} = 30\ \mu A$
Low output voltage	0 V	0.8 V	$I_{sink} = 2.0$ mA

trying to drive only CMOS devices, not a mixture of TTL *and* CMOS devices; any TTL inputs will lower the logic 1 level below that needed by the CMOS inputs).

3-3 CLOCKING AND START-UP

A microcomputer will have explicit specifications for its clock inputs which may include:

1   Minimum and maximum allowable frequency
2   Tolerances on the high and low voltage levels
3   Maximum rise and fall times of the waveform edges
4   Pulse-width tolerance, if the waveform is not a square wave
5   The timing relationships between clock phases, if two clock-phase signals are needed

For example, Fig. 3-11 illustrates the clock requirements of the Intel 8080, which requires two clock phases ϕ_1 and ϕ_2. These waveforms must be as specified. Otherwise operations which must occur in sequence, with sufficient time between them, will not occur properly.

Recognizing the sensitivity of an entire microcomputer to proper clock waveforms, the typical approach taken by microcomputer manufacturers is to provide the clock either as an integral part of the microprocessor chip itself (for example, F8, Microcontroller) or as a special chip (for example, 8080, 6800, 4040, PPS-4, PPS-8). Usually the clock will derive its stable frequency from a quartz crystal, which is sometimes included within the clock chip. Other clock chips require an external quartz crystal.

Start-up of the microcomputer's operation when power is turned on is typically accomplished with a "reset" input to the CPU. Activating the reset input will force a certain address into the program counter, from which point the microcomputer will begin executing instructions. As an example of a reset mechanism, the Motorola 6800 looks for a rising edge on its Reset input to initiate operation. The RC circuit of Fig. 3-12 keeps the Reset input

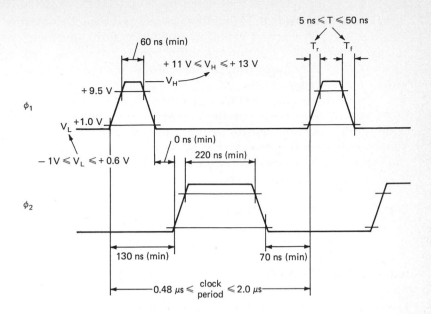

Power supply voltages = + 12 V, + 5 V, − 5 V (and 0 V)

Figure 3-11. Intel 8080 clock requirements.

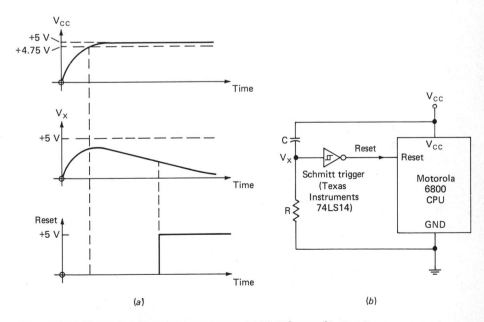

Figure 3-12. Motorola 6800 start-up circuit. (a) Waveforms; (b) circuit.

from rising until some time after the power for the microcomputer itself has reached 5 V. The actual values of resistance and capacitance needed depend upon how fast the power-supply output rises to 5 V when power is turned on. The Schmitt trigger causes Reset to snap when it changes, providing a sharp edge for the CPU.

Some microcomputers include automatic clearing of scratchpad registers upon reset. Others require the user to do any such operations, if desired, under program control as an *initialization routine*. If the CPU has a stack pointer pointing to a stack in RAM, then loading an initial address into the stack pointer would be one step in this initialization routine.

3-4 ADDRESS BUS/DATA BUS SYSTEM ORGANIZATION

A widely used approach to system organization is portrayed in Fig. 3-13. This approach is not only important for those microcomputers which are intrinsically organized in this way (for example, Intel 8008/8080, Motorola 6800, Rockwell PPS-4 and PPS-8, and RCA COSMAC), but it is also used in the instrument-development stage for every microcomputer which normally uses nonstandard ROMs (that is, microcomputers using a multiplexed bus). The manufacturers of such microcomputers also build special "prototyping" chips which allow standard ROMs to be used while developing an instrument in order to get it actually working.

As shown in Fig. 3-13, the CPU communicates with ROM, RAM, and I/O ports over a common *bus* consisting of:

1 Sixteen unidirectional address lines driven by the CPU. The upper eight lines, A15, . . . , A8, form the page number of a device. The lower eight lines, A7, . . . , A0, form an address within a page.

   The different devices on the bus are distinguished by different page addresses. Thus if input port 1 has page address 8, then the instruction to load the accumulator with the contents of "memory" page 8 (using any arbitrary address within the page, since it will be ignored) will "read" the data on the input port and load it into the accumulator.

2 Eight* bidirectional data bus lines. One word of data is transferred between the CPU and the addressed device. The direction of data flow is from the CPU to the device during a write (or load to memory) instruction. It is from the device to the CPU during a read (or load from memory) instruction.

3 Two unidirectional control lines, $\overline{\text{READ}}$ and $\overline{\text{WRITE}}$. These are high, or logic 1, when not being used. $\overline{\text{READ}}$ is driven low by the CPU to tell

---

* Four, for a 4-bit microcomputer.

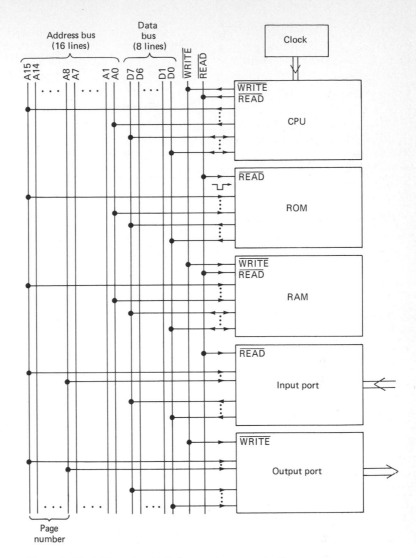

Figure 3-13. *Address bus/data bus system organization.*

the addressed device to put data onto the data bus for "reading" by the CPU. Similarly, $\overline{\text{WRITE}}$ is driven low by the CPU to tell the addressed device that the data on the data bus is to be "written" into it from the CPU.

A bidirectional data bus implies that any one line of the bus can be driven by any number of devices, but only by one device at a time. This is implemented by connecting only devices with *three-state* or *tristate* outputs

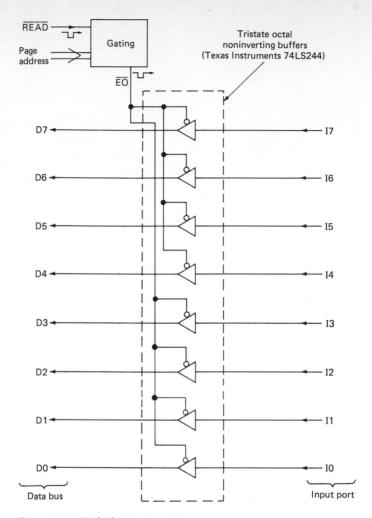

Figure 3-14. Eight-bit input port.

to the data bus. In fact, an input port is really nothing more than eight tri-state buffers, as shown in Fig. 3-14, plus gating to detect the page number and that READ has gone low. Each three-state buffer makes the output Di equal the input Ii when EO (enable output) is low. In this way the 8-bit input is put on the data bus. When EO goes high, the outputs Di go to a high-impedance state. They can no longer affect the data bus, being unable to pull the lines down to 0 V or up to 5 V.

 Incidentally, Fig. 3-14 portrays a convenient and widely used symbol-ism. Little circles are used to symbolize that the three-state buffers are ena-bled by a negative-true signal. In effect, a little circle represents an inver-

Figure 3-15. Dot symbolism. (a) Use of dot symbolism; (b) same device without
dot symbolism.

sion. Another way in which this symbolism is often used is illustrated in
Fig. 3-15a. It concerns the labeling of a device represented by a block. If
the output of the device is enabled by a negative-true signal, called $\overline{EO}$, then
we may write EO inside the block for the device together with a little circle
where the signal meets the block to symbolize that the output of the block is
enabled when this line goes low. Alternatively, we can leave off the circle
and label the signal $\overline{EO}$ inside the block as well as outside it, as in Fig. 3-15b.

The use of ROM chips in conjunction with the bus structure which we
have been discussing is identical to the use of an input port. ROM chips are
normally designed with three-state outputs. Consequently, as shown in Fig.

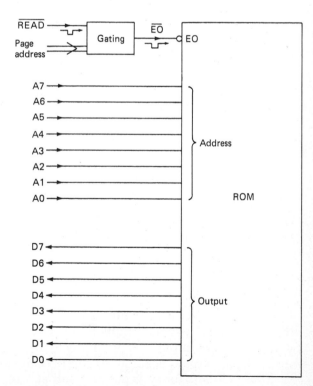

Figure 3-16. Connection of a
ROM chip to the bus.

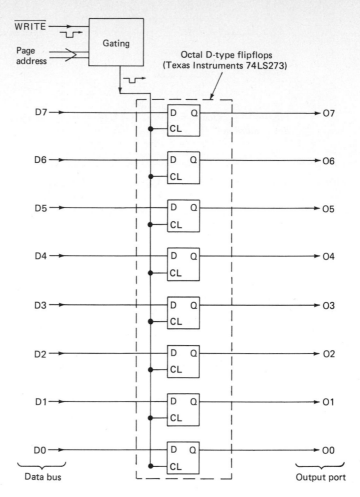

Figure 3-17. Eight-bit output port.

3-16, the page address must be decoded (assuming the ROM chip contains one page of address locations) together with the $\overline{\text{READ}}$ signal in order to put the contents of the addressed word onto the data bus when the CPU asks for it.

An output port does not ever drive the data bus, so it need not have three-state outputs. When it is addressed, and the $\overline{\text{WRITE}}$ line goes low, the data on the data bus must be *latched* and held until a subsequent $\overline{\text{WRITE}}$ to this output port occurs. Figure 3-17 shows an output port implemented with D-type flipflops. Each flipflop "remembers" what state it is in at the moment the clock input goes from low to high, and it remains in that state until the clock input goes from low to high again.

These circuits for an input port and an output port provide us with a

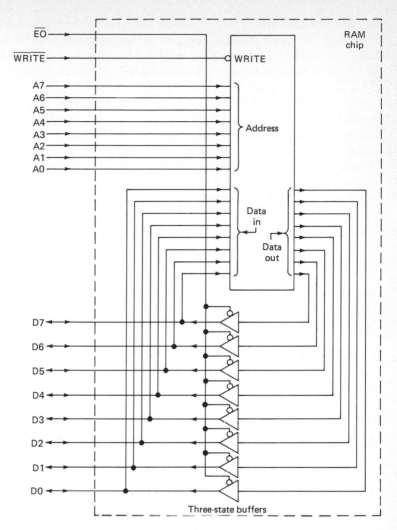

Figure 3-18. One approach to RAM design.

conceptual framework for the functioning of these devices. Some microcomputers use these actual circuits for I/O ports. More often, a manufacturer provides a special I/O chip which will typically be a larger chip (for example, a 40-pin package) and include at least two I/O ports, the ability to program each one to serve as either an input or an output port, and the gating
circuitry to detect a page address and either a READ or a WRITE signal. In
addition, it will typically have an extra input line and an extra output line
associated with each I/O port to "handshake" with the device connected to
the port, if desired. We will discuss handshaking in Chap. 5.

Connecting a RAM to the bus structure poses a complication which has not arisen with any of the previous devices. When addressing a page of RAM, the CPU is addressing the one device which will sometimes drive the data bus and at other times be driven from the data bus. As a result, the RAM must make provision for drawing this distinction from the $\overline{\text{READ}}$ and $\overline{\text{WRITE}}$ control lines.

One approach taken by RAM manufacturers is shown, in somewhat simplified form, in Fig. 3-18. To understand its operation, consider first the case in which we are not writing into it. The contents of the addressed location will appear on the data output of the inner block of circuitry. When the CPU wants to look at these contents, it need only make $\overline{\text{EO}}$ go low to enable the outputs of the three-state buffers and thus put the RAM output onto the data bus. On the other hand, to write into the RAM, first the output is disabled (by making $\overline{\text{EO}}$ go high) so that the data bus can be driven by the CPU alone. Once the address bus and the data bus have been set up by the CPU, it is only necessary to strobe the $\overline{\text{WRITE}}$ line with a negative pulse to transfer the data on the data bus into the addressed RAM location.

To use this RAM with an address bus/data bus microcomputer structure, the $\overline{\text{EO}}$ input is treated exactly like the $\overline{\text{EO}}$ input on a ROM or an input port. That is, it is enabled with the proper page address and with the $\overline{\text{READ}}$ pulse just as in Fig. 3-14 or Fig. 3-16. Likewise, the $\overline{\text{WRITE}}$ input is treated exactly like the strobe input to an output port. Just as in Fig. 3-17, the $\overline{\text{WRITE}}$ signal from the CPU is gated by the page address to produce a $\overline{\text{WRITE}}$ pulse for the RAM chip which is analogous to the strobe pulse for the output port.

Looking back, we have seen how each device can be hung on the bus. Each device has required some gating circuitry to gate a page address together with either a $\overline{\text{READ}}$ or a $\overline{\text{WRITE}}$ signal. A more systematic approach is to use 2 *one-out-of-eight binary decoders*, as shown in Fig. 3-19. A decoder is the first device we have discussed which has an $\overline{\text{EO}}$ (enable output) control, but which does not have three-state outputs. A three-state output does not make sense for a decoder. The function of the decoder is to make the addressed output go low (note the little circles on the outputs) while the other outputs remain high. If the decoder is disabled ($\overline{\text{EO}}$ high), all outputs remain high. For example, during an instruction to read input port 1, the CPU will generate an address

00000001   00000000

Page 1   Arbitrary address within the page

When the $\overline{\text{READ}}$ pulse occurs, the $\overline{1}$ output of the right decoder will go low, enabling input port 1. Meanwhile, all the other outputs of the right decoder remain high because they are not being addressed. The outputs of the left decoder *all* remain high because that decoder is not enabled at all (that is, $\overline{\text{WRITE}}$ remains high).

If more than eight devices are to be hung on the bus (for example, five pages of ROM, two input ports, three output ports, and a page of RAM), we

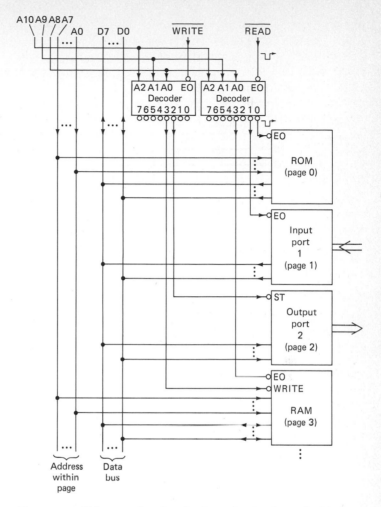

Figure 3-19. *Using two decoders in place of gating for each chip.*

need a decoder with more than eight outputs. Figure 3-20 shows an interconnection of eight-output decoders to resolve this difficulty.

The circuit of Fig. 3-19 for controlling devices on the bus is a good,
general solution to the problem. However, it does have some disadvantages:

1 It requires (at least) two decoders.
2 If CMOS decoders are used in order to minimize the loading of the bus
   (that is, the $\overline{\text{READ}}$, $\overline{\text{WRITE}}$, and page address lines), we must be concerned about the *propagation delay** of the decoders, since it is likely

   * The delay between a changing input and the resulting output change.

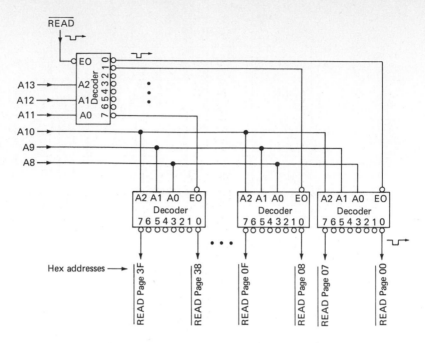

Figure 3-20. *Implementing the equivalent of a large decoder.*

to be relatively long (for example, as long as 300 ns for National Semiconductor's 74C42 decoder operated at 5 V).

3   If bipolar decoders are used in order to reduce propagation delay, we
must be concerned with the loading of the bus (for example, Intel's
3205 decoder has a propagation delay of only 18 ns but an input
loading of just a little less than a 74LSxx TTL input—0.25 mA to pull it
low and 10 μA to pull it high).

Whether or not loading is a problem in a specific case can be determined as
in Sec. 3-2. We will discuss potential problems arising because of propagation delays later in this section.

An alternative approach is available if each of the devices to be hung on
the bus has several enable inputs. In the case of having eight or fewer devices (that is, pages), the approach shown in Fig. 3-21 will provide the
needed control of the bus and yet avoid any decoders. This approach assumes that the enables are ANDed together, as is typical with multiple
enable devices. Thus the two $\overline{EO}$s on ROM page FE must both go low to
read from the ROM. The chip enable ($\overline{CE}$) input to the RAM chip must be
ANDed with both the output enable and the write signal, as in Fig. 3-22.

The use of multiple enables to control the bus can lead to weird page
numbers, as shown in Fig. 3-21. Those page numbers assume that all

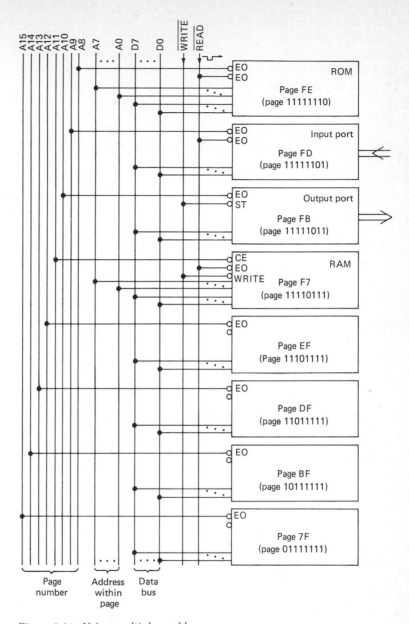

Figure 3-21. Using multiple enables.

enables are provided in *negated* form (that is, $\overline{EO}$, not EO), which is typical
of devices having just one or two enables.

How pages are numbered becomes important when the microcomputer
requires certain pages to be assigned to certain devices. For example, many
microcomputers look to page 00, address 00 for the first instruction when

power is first turned on. Notice that every page in Fig. 3-21 would be enabled under such circumstances, leading to a chaotic fight for control of the data bus. Needless to say, the first instruction executed would be rather different from anything planned. Successive instructions might, or might not, eventually get to the ROMs holding actual instructions.

If page 00 must be one of our pages, three alternatives are available:

1 Use decoders, as in Fig. 3-19.
2 Use inverters on the address lines to obtain $\overline{A15}$, $\overline{A14}$, . . . , $\overline{A8}$.

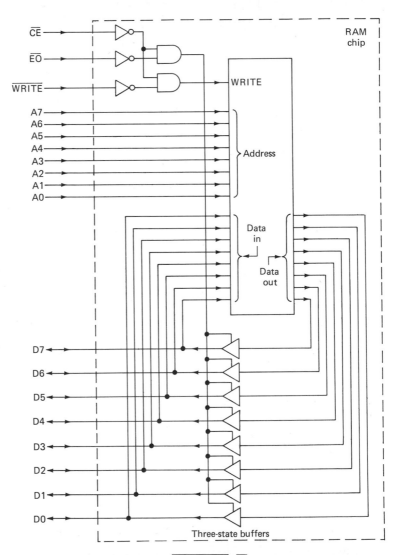

Figure 3-22. RAM design with chip enable ($\overline{CE}$).

Address lines →	A15	A14	A13	A12	A11	A10	A9	A8	Hex address		Address lines to detect	
	0	0	0	0	0	0	1	1	0	3	9	8
	0	0	0	0	0	1	0	1	0	5	10	8
	0	0	0	0	0	1	1	0	0	6	10	9
	0	0	0	0	1	0	0	1	0	9	11	8
	0	0	0	0	1	0	1	0	0	A	11	9
	0	0	0	0	1	1	0	0	0	C	11	10
	0	0	0	1	0	0	0	1	1	1	12	8
	0	0	0	1	0	0	1	0	1	2	12	9
	0	0	0	1	0	1	0	0	1	4	12	10
	0	0	0	1	1	0	0	0	1	8	12	11
	0	0	1	0	0	0	0	1	2	1	13	8
	0	0	1	0	0	0	1	0	2	2	13	9
	0	0	1	0	0	1	0	0	2	4	13	10
	0	0	1	0	1	0	0	0	2	8	13	11
	0	0	1	1	0	0	0	0	3	0	13	12
	0	1	0	0	0	0	0	1	4	1	14	8
	0	1	0	0	0	0	1	0	4	2	14	9
	0	1	0	0	0	1	0	0	4	4	14	10
	0	1	0	0	1	0	0	0	4	8	14	11
	0	1	0	1	0	0	0	0	5	0	14	12
	0	1	1	0	0	0	0	0	6	0	14	13
	1	0	0	0	0	0	0	1	8	1	15	8
	1	0	0	0	0	0	1	0	8	2	15	9
	1	0	0	0	0	1	0	0	8	4	15	10
	1	0	0	0	1	0	0	0	8	8	15	11
	1	0	0	1	0	0	0	0	9	0	15	12
	1	0	1	0	0	0	0	0	A	0	15	13
	1	1	0	0	0	0	0	0	C	0	15	14

Figure 3-23. Page selection using two enables (both in asserted form).

3   Use devices on the bus which have at least one of their enables in asserted form (that is, EO rather than all of the form $\overline{EO}$).

Manufacturers are increasingly recognizing the tremendous value of multiple enables, with some enables in asserted form and some in negated form.   Consequently, this problem of controlling a variety of devices on a bus should become progressively easier with time.

Given three enables on each device so that two are available for page selection, what are the ways of assigning page numbers, and selecting these pages, so as to differentiate among as many pages as possible?   If the two enables are both in asserted form, we can differentiate among 28 pages [a combination of eight things, two at a time = $(8 \times 7)/2$], as in Fig. 3-23.

For the many microcomputers which need page 00 to be one of the selected pages, the above scheme is inadequate.   However, by complementing

				Binary	address				Hex address		Address lines to detect	
Address lines →	A15	A14	A13	A12	A11	A10	A9	A8				
	0	0	0	0	0	0	0	0	0	0	$\bar{9}$	$\bar{8}$
	0	0	0	0	0	1	1	0	0	6	10	$\bar{8}$
	0	0	0	0	0	1	0	1	0	5	10	$\bar{9}$
	0	0	0	0	1	0	1	0	0	A	11	$\bar{8}$
	0	0	0	0	1	0	0	1	0	9	11	$\bar{9}$
	0	0	0	0	1	1	1	1	0	F	11	10
	0	0	0	1	0	0	1	0	1	2	12	$\bar{8}$
	0	0	0	1	0	0	0	1	1	1	12	$\bar{9}$
	0	0	0	1	0	1	1	1	1	7	12	10
	0	0	0	1	1	0	1	1	1	B	12	11
	0	0	1	0	0	0	1	0	2	2	13	$\bar{8}$
	0	0	1	0	0	0	0	1	2	1	13	$\bar{9}$
	0	0	1	0	0	1	1	1	2	7	13	10
	0	0	1	0	1	0	1	1	2	B	13	11
	0	0	1	1	0	0	1	1	3	3	13	12
	0	1	0	0	0	0	1	0	4	2	14	$\bar{8}$
	0	1	0	0	0	0	0	1	4	1	14	$\bar{9}$
	0	1	0	0	0	1	1	1	4	7	14	10
	0	1	0	0	1	0	1	1	4	B	14	11
	0	1	0	1	0	0	1	1	5	3	14	12
	0	1	1	0	0	0	1	1	6	3	14	13
	1	0	0	0	0	0	1	0	8	2	15	$\bar{8}$
	1	0	0	0	0	0	0	1	8	1	15	$\bar{9}$
	1	0	0	0	0	1	1	1	8	7	15	10
	1	0	0	0	1	0	1	1	8	B	15	11
	1	0	0	1	0	0	1	1	9	3	15	12
	1	0	1	0	0	0	1	1	A	3	15	13
	1	1	0	0	0	0	1	1	C	3	15	14

Figure 3-24. Page selection to include page 00.

two entire columns (that is, address lines) and being willing to detect these in negated form, we arrive at the scheme of Fig. 3-24. If some of our devices have one enable in negated form, we can assign them a page number such that an address variable must be detected in negated form (that is, page 81, 82, 41, 42, 21, etc.). Alternatively, we can put inverters on address lines A8 and A9 and detect when $\overline{A8} = 1$ and $\overline{A9} = 1$ instead of when $A8 = 0$ and $A9 = 0$. Consequently, the one table of Fig. 3-24 offers many possibilities.

Example 3-6. Reassign page numbers to the devices of Fig. 3-21 assuming each device has three enables, two in negated form and one in asserted form. Assign page 00 to the ROM at the top of Fig. 3-21.

All the devices except for the page 00 ROM can be implemented

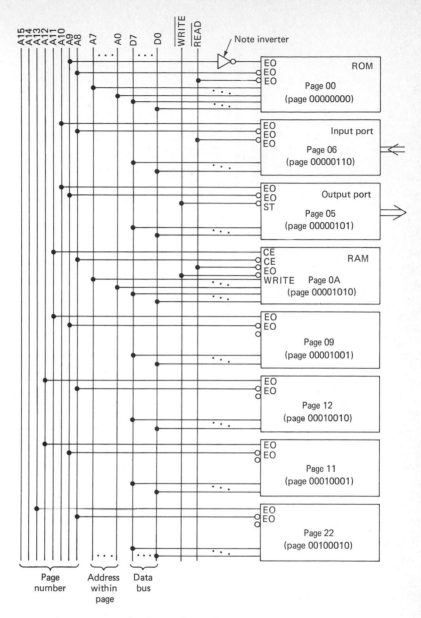

Figure 3-25. Using multiple enables and page 00.

directly, using page numbers in which one of the address variables to be detected must be in negated form while the other must be in asserted form. For page 00 we will need an inverter to complement the input to the asserted enable on the ROM. The result is shown in Fig. 3-25.

118

CHAPTER 3

	Binary address							Hex address		Address lines to detect	
Address lines →	A15	A14	A13	A12	A11	A10	A9	A8			

A15	A14	A13	A12	A11	A10	A9	A8	Hex		Detect	
[0]	0	0	0	0	0	0	[0]	0	0	$\overline{15}$	$\overline{8}$
[0]	0	0	0	0	0	[1]	1	0	3	$\overline{15}$	9
[0]	0	0	0	0	[1]	0	1	0	5	$\overline{15}$	10
[0]	0	0	0	[1]	0	0	1	0	9	$\overline{15}$	11
[0]	0	0	[1]	0	0	0	1	1	1	$\overline{15}$	12
[0]	0	[1]	0	0	0	0	1	2	1	$\overline{15}$	13
[0]	[1]	0	0	0	0	0	1	4	1	$\overline{15}$	14
[1]	[0]	1	1	1	1	1	0	B	E	15	$\overline{14}$
[1]	1	[0]	1	1	1	1	0	D	E	15	$\overline{13}$
[1]	1	1	[0]	1	1	1	0	E	E	15	$\overline{12}$
[1]	1	1	1	[0]	1	1	0	F	6	15	$\overline{11}$
[1]	1	1	1	1	[0]	1	0	F	A	15	$\overline{10}$
[1]	1	1	1	1	1	[0]	0	F	C	15	9
[1]	1	1	1	1	1	1	[1]	F	F	15	8

Figure 3-26. Page selection, including pages 00 and FF.

Before moving away from page-selection schemes, we will consider one which includes the detection of both pages 00 and FF. The Motorola 6800 microcomputer treats these two pages in a special way. The table of Fig. 3-26 shows an appropriate page-selection scheme for up to 14 pages.

Example 3-7. Repeat Example 3-6, but this time assign page 00 to RAM and page FF to ROM as might be done for the Motorola 6800 microcomputer.

A solution, based upon the table of Fig. 3-26, is shown in Fig. 3-27.

Thus far we have assumed that when the CPU tries to read data from a device on the bus, or write data to a device on the bus, the device is fast enough to respond in a manner which is satisfactory to the CPU. Actually, unless we take care in the design, this may easily be untrue. It is for the sole reason of solving such *timing problems* that RAM and ROM manufacturers produce variations of the same basic device which differ only in the specification for the maximum propagation delay. Of course, the faster device costs more. We would like to be able to ensure the proper operation of any

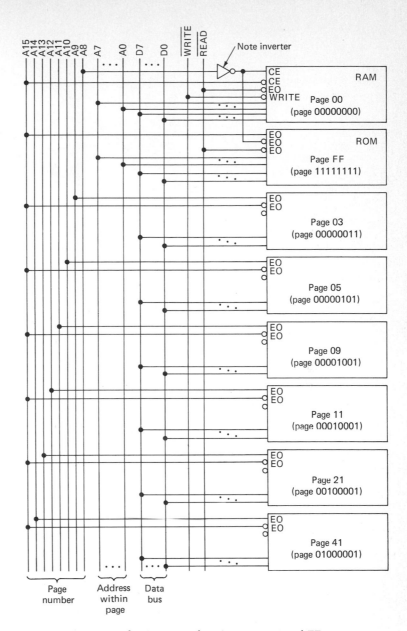

Figure 3-27. Page-selection example using pages 00 and FF.

instrument we are designing without paying a premium for faster devices than we actually need.

When a CPU attempts to execute a read instruction, it will put out an address and a READ control signal. The data must be returned to the CPU on the data bus within a certain time. As long as the device responds at

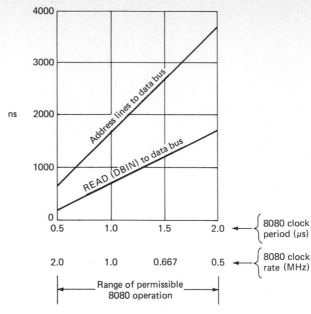

Figure 3-28. Intel 8080 requirements for devices to be
read from.

least this fast, it will be read correctly. As an example, Fig. 3-28 shows these
maximum permissible propagation delays for the Intel 8080 plotted versus
the clock rate, over the entire range of permissible clock rates. The plots are
only approximately correct, since they depend upon the actual clock waveforms used. They are derived from the "AC characteristics" section of the
8080 data sheet. Satisfactory reading from a device by the 8080 requires
that its address line to output *access time* t_A as well as its *chip enable to
output time* t_{CO} lie below the upper curve in Fig. 3-28, and also that its *output enable to output time* t_{OO} lie below the lower curve (since it will have
as its input the $\overline{READ}$ signal). If a decoder is interposed between the CPU
and the device in order to help with page selection, its propagation delay
must be included in the calculation.

In order to provide an idea of the propagation delays to be expected
from selected MOS and CMOS RAMs and ROMs, Fig. 3-29 gives data for
some popular devices (all of which are "TTL compatible").

Example 3-8. Assuming RAM page selection is done directly with
multiple-chip enables, what is the maximum Intel 8080 clock rate

Figure 3-29. Maximum Propagation Delays for Reading from Some Typical RAMs and ROMs

Type	Size	Characteristics	Enables	Max output enable to output time t_{OO} (ns)	Max chip enable to output time t_{CO} (ns)	Max access time (address to output) t_A (ns)
			(static) RAMs			
Intel 5101	256 × 4	CMOS (very low standby power)	1 CE 1 $\overline{CE}$	350	700	650
Intel 2111	256 × 4	MOS	2 $\overline{CE}$	700	800	1000
Intel 2111-2	256 × 4	Same as 2111 but faster	2 $\overline{CE}$	350	400	650
Intel 2111-1	256 × 4	Same as 2111-2 but faster	2 $\overline{CE}$	300	350	500
Motorola 6810A	128 × 8	MOS	2 CE 4 $\overline{CE}$	–	230	450
Motorola 6810A1	128 × 8	Same as 6810A but faster	2 CE 4 $\overline{CE}$	–	180	350
			ROMs			
Intel 2708	1024 × 8	Programmable and ultraviolet erasable	1 $\overline{EO}$		120	450
Intel 2316A	2048 × 8	MOS	3 (prog. polarity)		300	850
Motorola 6830A	1024 × 8	MOS	4 (prog. polarity)		300	500

All these RAMs and ROMs require only $+5$ V power except the 2708 ROM (which requires $+12$ V, $+5$ V, -5 V).

which will provide satisfactory reading of data from the least expensive version (that is, the slowest) of Intel's 2111, 2111-1, 2111-2 series of RAMs?

For satisfactory operation of the 2111, the maximum output enable to output time ($t_{OO} = 700$ ns) must lie below the lower curve of Fig. 3-28, giving a maximum clock rate on this account of about 1.0 MHz. In addition, both $t_A = 1000$ ns and $t_{CO} = 800$ ns must lie below the upper curve of Fig. 3-28, giving a minimum clock period of 0.6 μs, or a maximum clock rate of 1.7 MHz, on this second account. To satisfy both demands, the 8080 clock rate must not exceed 1.0 MHz.

The timing requirements for reliably writing data into a RAM are rather more difficult to handle.   A RAM will require:

1   A delay which exceeds some minimum *write delay* t_{AW} between the settling of the address inputs to the RAM and the start of the $\overline{\text{WRITE}}$ pulse.
2   A pulse width which exceeds some minimum *write pulse width* t_{WP}.
3   A delay which exceeds some minimum *chip enable to write delay* t_{CW}, between chip enables and the end of the $\overline{\text{WRITE}}$ pulse.
4   A time which exceeds some minimum *write recovery time* t_{WR} between the end of the $\overline{\text{WRITE}}$ pulse and the changing of the address lines.
5. A time which exceeds some minimum *data setup time* t_{DS} after the data is on the data bus and before the end of the $\overline{\text{WRITE}}$ pulse.
6   A time which exceeds some minimum *data hold time* t_{DH} after the end of the $\overline{\text{WRITE}}$ pulse during which the data must not change.

Minimum values for these six parameters are given in Fig. 3-30 for the same RAMs listed in Fig. 3-29.   The corresponding minimum values for Intel's 8080 CPU are plotted in Fig. 3-31 versus the 8080's clock frequency.   Again, these plots are only approximate inasmuch as they depend upon the specific clock waveforms used.

Example 3-9. Repeat Example 3-8; this time *write* to the Intel 2111 RAM from the 8080 CPU.

In this case, each of the six parameter values for the 2111 in Fig. 3-30 must lie below the corresponding curve of Fig. 3-31.   Note that every parameter, except t_{WP} and t_{DS}, is satisfied over the entire range. To satisfy $t_{WP} = 750$ ns, any clock period down to 0.78 μs will work, corresponding to any clock rate up to 1.3 MHz.   Likewise, any clock rate up to 1.0 MHz will satisfy $t_{DS} = 700$ ns.   So, the 8080 is constrained to a maximum clock rate of 1.0 MHz for reliable writing to the 2111 RAM.

Example 3-10. Subject to the conditions of Example 3-8, what is the maximum clock rate for the 8080 microcomputer which will permit reliable reading from, and writing to, the 2111 RAM?

Reliable writing can be carried out up to 1.0 MHz, the same maximum clock rate as for reliable reading.   Consequently, the maximum clock rate is 1.0 MHz.

Figure 3-30. Minimum Parameter Values for Writing into Some Typical RAMs

Type	Size	Characteristics	Write delay t_{AW} (ns)	Write pulse width t_{WP} (ns)	Chip enable to write delay t_{CW} (ns)	Write recovery time t_{WR} (ns)	Data setup time t_{DS} (ns)	Data hold time t_{DH} (ns)
Intel 5101	256 × 4	CMOS (very low standby power)	150	400	550	50	400	100
Intel 2111	256 × 4	MOS	150	750	900	50	700	100
Intel 2111-2	256 × 4	Same as 2111 but faster	150	400	550	50	400	100
Intel 2111-1	256 × 4	Same as 2111-2 but faster	100	300	400	50	280	100
Motorola 6810A	128 × 8	MOS	20	300	0	0	190	10
Motorola 6810A1	128 × 8	Same as 6810A but faster	20	250	0	0	150	10

In the structure we have been discussing, all input ports and output ports are "memory-mapped" so that, to the CPU, they simply appear to be the contents of specific memory locations. Alternatively, some microcomputers (for example, Intel 8080, RCA COSMAC, Rockwell PPS-4 and PPS-8) have special I/O instructions which require little more than the addition of

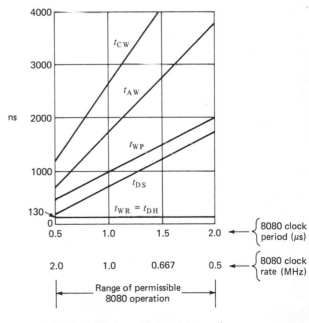

Figure 3-31. Intel 8080 minimum values for "write" parameters.

(Optimum clock waveforms are assumed)

two control lines, $\overline{\text{IN}}$ and $\overline{\text{OUT}}$, to the already discussed $\overline{\text{READ}}$ and $\overline{\text{WRITE}}$ lines. When an IN 5 instruction is executed, the 5 will be put on the address bus and can be used to distinguish input port 5 from the other input ports. The $\overline{\text{IN}}$ control signal is used exactly like $\overline{\text{READ}}$ to put the contents of input port 5 on the data bus.

Likewise, an OUT 2 instruction will put the number 2 on the address bus and pulse the $\overline{\text{OUT}}$ control line for strobing the data bus into output port 2 (just as $\overline{\text{WRITE}}$ strobes the data bus into RAM during an instruction writing to memory). Having the port number associated with the instruction provides an address without having to set up a memory pointer first, in contrast with "memory-mapped" I/O. On the other hand, sometimes it is useful to be able to set up a loop to read in from successive input ports. If the input ports are memory-mapped, the page number of a memory pointer can be incremented to point to successive pages during successive passes through the loop. Consequently, just the fact that a microcomputer has I/O instruction capability does not necessarily mean that we want to use it for all I/O ports.

3-5 MULTIPLEXED BUS SYSTEM ORGANIZATION

Some microcomputers completely avoid having an address bus between CPU and other devices. The Intel 4004/4040 divides each instruction cycle up into eight clock periods, as shown in Fig. 3-32. Successive 4-bit bytes of a 12-bit address are multiplexed over the 4-bit data bus to ROM during the first three clock periods, using the structure of Fig. 3-33. Then the two bytes making up the instruction are multiplexed back to the CPU during the next two clock periods. The instruction is executed during the final three clock periods. All chips in the microcomputer are clocked with a two-phase

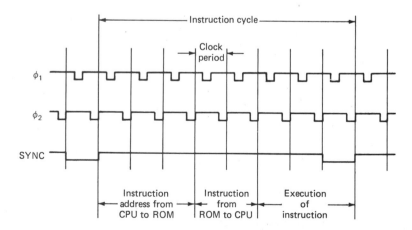

Figure 3-32. Intel 4004/4040 instruction cycle.

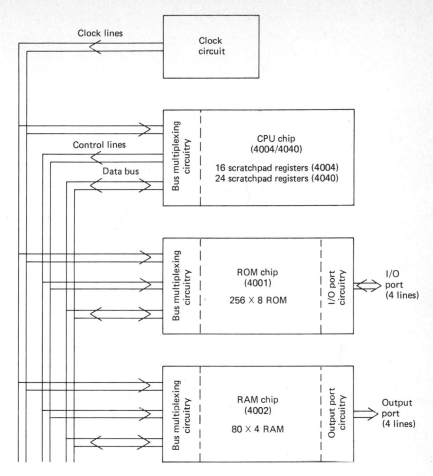

Figure 3-33. Intel 4004/4040 chip set.

clock. The CPU generates a SYNC signal which goes low for one clock period just before the beginning of each instruction cycle. This keeps all chips synchronized with the CPU as it goes through each instruction cycle.

The Intel 4004 uses the freedom which results from a missing address bus to construct a microcomputer with small, 16-pin chips. It pays the standard price that goes with multiplexing; namely, speed is sacrificed. With a maximum clock rate of 750,000 Hz, the rate of executing 1-byte and 2-byte instructions is 94,000 instructions per second and 47,000 instructions per second, respectively.

Notice that the "ROM" chip for this microcomputer does considerably more than a conventional ROM. It must also include the circuitry to latch the multiplexed address from the data bus and then, in return, to multiplex the ROM contents onto the data bus.

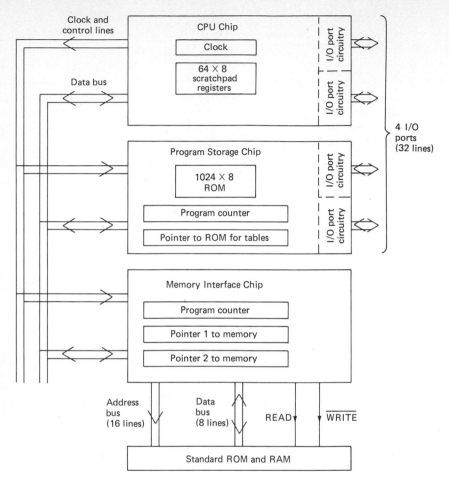

Figure 3-34. F8 chip set.

In their F8 microcomputer chip set, Fairchild has deleted the address bus in order to put two I/O ports in its place, as in Fig. 3-34. But rather than pay the "speed price" of multiplexing addresses on the data bus for every instruction, they have taken the program counter out of the CPU chip altogether and instead have put it into each chip containing ROM or interfacing to ROM. These duplicate program counters maintain identical contents by counting together. It is only when a jump instruction is executed that an address moves over the data bus between ROM chips.

The F8 chip set includes a "memory interface" chip which permits conventional RAM and ROM to be interfaced into the system with a standard address bus/data bus structure. Again, rather than transfer addresses over the data bus for every instruction, the memory interface chip includes a program counter and two pointers to memory. For operating upon arrays, the memory pointer involved in a specific instruction is automatically incremented. This results in fast instruction execution time. For example, the instruction for adding an operand in RAM to the accumulator takes 5.0 μs to execute. (The comparable instruction, but without automatic incrementing of the pointer, takes 3.0–5.0 μs for the Motorola 6800 depending on where in RAM the operand is located and whether the instruction is an indexed instruction. The comparable Intel 8080 instruction takes 3.5 μs but also does not include incrementing the pointer.)

3-6 FLAGS

When an instrument is organized around a microcomputer, the microcomputer can, under program control, tell various components in the instrument when to initiate an operation (for example, display an output result; start a motor running). In fact, with an accurate crystal clock, the timing *interrelationships* between assorted activities can be controlled precisely. When it is some component other than the microcomputer which must initiate an operation, four courses of action are possible:

1   The hardware for the instrument may be organized so that the operation can be initiated and carried out without making the microcomputer aware of the event. This goes against the philosophy of minimizing hardware by putting everything possible into the microcomputer. However, an operation which requires a faster response than that offered by any of the following three possibilities cannot be resolved without special, fast-responding hardware. In this case, the traditional techniques of logic design with SSI and MSI devices* become important.

2   The component wanting to initiate an operation can use a "flag" to tell the microcomputer. Then the microcomputer can, under program control, test this flag bit and initiate the operation only when the flag bit becomes set (that is, goes to logic 1).

3   The component wanting to initiate an operation can *interrupt* the microcomputer by means of a special input to the CPU. The microcomputer will stop what it is presently doing, carry out the desired operation under program control, and then go back to what it was doing. We will discuss the ramifications of this procedure in the next section.

4   If the operation to be initiated is a transfer of data into or out of the microcomputer's memory, or if the desired operation can be translated into such a transfer of data, then such an operation can be handled

---

* Small-scale integration devices (for example, gates, flipflops) and medium-scale integration devices (for example, counters, decoders, comparators).

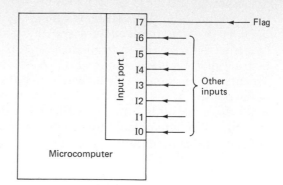

Figure 3-35. Reading in a flag through
an input port.

under *DMA*, or direct memory access, control. This is typically used to
move a block of data into or out of sequential memory locations under
conditions requiring extremely fast response. It will be discussed in
Sec. 3-8.

The process of testing a flag is extremely simple with those few microcomputers which include external flag inputs. Thus the Intel 4004/4040
have a TEST input pin on the CPU chip and have JT and JNT conditional
jump instructions which will cause a jump if TEST = 1 or if TEST = 0,
respectively. RCA's COSMAC microcomputer incorporates *four* such external flag input pins on the CPU chip. Having eight of its conditional jump
instructions used to test each of these for either 0 or 1, the COSMAC provides the user with a convenient, intrinsic flag-handling capability.
    The more generally available method for testing a flag is to bring it into
the microcomputer on one of the lines of an input port, as illustrated in Fig.
3-35. If the microcomputer instruction set includes a test of the most significant bit of the accumulator, the test of a flag can be facilitated by using the
most significant bit position of the input port for the flag input. Otherwise,
after loading the accumulator from the input port, the extraneous bits can be
masked off and the accumulator tested for zero.

Example 3-11. Test a flag brought in on bit 3 of input port 2. Jump to
address P1 if flag = 1.

ADD	MNE	REG	OP	Comments
	IN	2		A ← input port 2
	AND	I	B′00001000′	Keep only bit 3
	JAN		P1	Jump to P1 if flag = 1

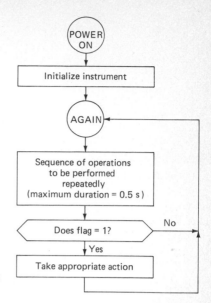

Figure 3-36. System software organization to check a
flag at least once every 0.5 s.

If the flag bit is in the least significant bit position (or the most significant bit position) and if the microcomputer can shift (or rotate) this bit of the
accumulator into the carry bit, then doing this and testing the carry bit provides an alternative to masking, as in Example 3-11.

Flags provide a flexible, minimum-hardware means for detecting slow
inputs to the microcomputer. The infrequent entry of data or setup information on the keyboard of an instrument by a user represents a typical example
which can be flagged to the microcomputer. As long as the microcomputer
scans any such slowly changing flags approximately once per 0.1–0.5 s, it
will not miss an entry when it occurs. In between scans, it can do its other
jobs.

Often an instrument's software can be organized so that a varied sequence of operations is executed over and over again, as in Fig. 3-36. The
sequence may be rather short or rather lengthy, depending upon what the instrument is supposed to be doing at the time of each pass through the sequence. However, as long as no combination of events makes any one pass
through the sequence last longer than 0.5 s or so, the scan of a keyboard flag
between passes will never miss an entry. When the instrument is not very
busy, this strategy may result in the keyboard flag's being scanned every millisecond or so. While this is extremely fast scanning for checking a keyboard, it does no harm. The result is a simple, flexible way to sense inputs
which occur infrequently.

The same strategy can be used for inputs which can occur at more fre-
quent intervals (for example, every millisecond). This is easy if each pass
through the sequence can be arranged so as to require less than a millisecond. If one pass may take considerably longer, the test of the flag input,

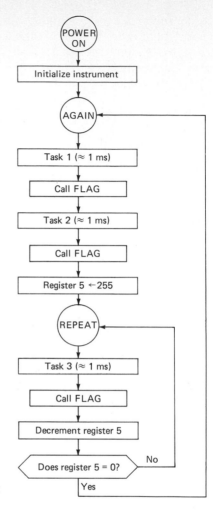

Figure 3-37. *System software organization to check a flag at least once every millisecond.*

and the action to be taken if the flag is set, can be written as a subroutine FLAG. Calls to this subroutine can then be interspersed throughout the sequence. This sounds more tedious than it actually is, because anything taking a long time to do in a microcomputer will include many loops; calling FLAG while inside the appropriate loops will provide the many calls needed while not requiring the *writing* of many JMS FLAG instructions, as illustrated in Fig. 3-37.

Sometimes the microcomputer may initiate the operation of a device in an instrument and know that shortly thereafter the device will set a flag which will require a fast response. For example, a microcomputer may start a printer motor running which moves a print head to the right across a page.

A sensor sets a flag as the print head crosses the left-hand margin, indicating both the position at which printing is to start and also that the motor is up to its constant running speed. If the flag is detected as soon as it is set and if successive characters are printed at equal time intervals, corresponding character positions in successive rows will be precisely aligned.

In the above example, the microcomputer can go into the *wait loop* of Fig. 3-38 after starting the printer, knowing that the sensor will shortly set the flag. The microcomputer gives its undivided attention to the flag as it waits. Incidentally, notice that if either the sensor or the motor operation malfunctions, the instrument will "hang up" in the wait loop. The user has no indication of what happened except that his instrument all of a sudden stopped working. Figure 3-39 illustrates how this situation affords an effective, and yet almost free, self-test indication. By putting a counter in the wait loop (which, under normal circumstances, should never have enough time to reach zero), we can test the counter for zero. If excess time is detected, the instrument can flash a "malfunction" light and display a diagnostic number to the user indicating the nature of the malfunction.

3-7 INTERRUPT CAPABILITY

Most microcomputers provide *interrupt capability,* permitting a device in an instrument to interrupt what the microcomputer is doing so that it can perform a service for the device. When finished, the microcomputer returns to its previous task. Generally, however, a microcomputer does not let a device do this without prior permission.

Within the CPU there is an *Enable Interrupt* flipflop which can be set or cleared under program control. It is also *automatically cleared* when power

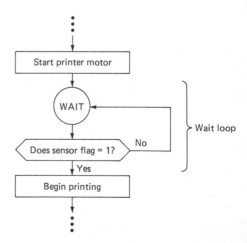

Figure 3-38. Use of a wait loop.

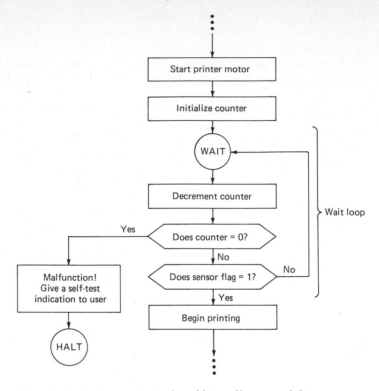

Figure 3-39. *Easy opportunity for adding self-test capability.*

is first turned on and after an interrupt occurs. Whenever the Enable Interrupt flipflop is cleared, the microcomputer locks out interrupts. A device trying to interrupt the microcomputer will be ignored.

The ability of the microcomputer to lock out interrupts automatically when power is first turned on gives it a chance to execute an initialize routine without interruption. Then, when everything is set up, the microcomputer will begin the operation of the instrument. In the course of the operation, the microcomputer may expect an event to occur, sooner or later, which needs immediate attention. It will execute an instruction setting the Enable Interrupt flipflop. Then it will continue doing whatever tasks need doing. To detect exactly when an event occurs, the CPU typically has an $\overline{\text{INT}}$ (that is, INTerrupt) control line which must be driven low by the occurrence of the event. At the completion of each instruction cycle, the CPU looks to see if the Enable Interrupt flipflop is set and if $\overline{\text{INT}}$ is low. If both of these are true, it clears the Enable Interrupt flipflop and goes into an "interrupt mode."

What happens next varies considerably from one microcomputer to another. However, in general terms, the following occur:

1   The contents of the program counter must be temporarily set aside so as to be available when the CPU is ready to return to where it left off when interrupted.

2   The program counter must be loaded with an address of an *interrupt service routine*. This routine does exactly those things needed by the device causing the interrupt. In this sense, the response to an interrupt is identical to the response after breaking out of the wait loop of Fig. 3-38.

3   Any of the CPU registers (for example, accumulator, carry, specific scratchpad registers) which are needed by the service routine must have their contents temporarily set aside at the beginning of the service routine and restored at the end of it. Otherwise, the service routine may change some of these contents as it uses the registers for its own purposes. For example, the interrupted program may have just finished setting up a memory pointer. If the service routine changes this memory pointer for its own purposes and leaves the new pointer for the unsuspecting interrupted program, chaotic results will occur when the CPU returns to the interrupted program.

4   The device which caused the interrupt, by making $\overline{INT}$ go low, must be appropriately manipulated by the microcomputer so that $\overline{INT}$ will be high again.

5   If subsequent interrupts are to be permitted, the Enable Interrupt flip-flop must be set again.

6   Finally, control is returned to the interrupted program by restoring the contents of the program counter previously set aside.

Two of these steps, 1 and 3, require the temporary storing, and subsequent restoring, of at least some registers in the CPU. Some microcomputers make this easy and quick by permitting "pushes" of scratchpad registers onto a stack and subsequent "pops" to restore them (see Fig. 2-21). Other microcomputers have enough scratchpad registers to permit reserving a few for this purpose. If RAM locations can be directly addressed, accumulator and registers can be moved to specific RAM locations.

One of the serious limitations of Intel's 8008 (which is resolved well in the 8080) is its inability to provide a good solution to this problem. Moving registers to RAM requires setting up a pointer to RAM. This would seem to necessitate destroying the previous contents of this pointer to RAM, which we certainly must not do. A solution for this problem requires the addition of two registers, configured as I/O ports, to the microcomputer. This permits the accumulator to be moved out to one port followed by one of the registers making up the pointer. The other register making up the pointer can then be moved to the accumulator. Now the new pointer can be formed and the accumulator and other registers moved to RAM.

The simplest use of an interrupt in an instrument occurs when we only permit one device to interrupt the CPU. In this case we can measure the rel-

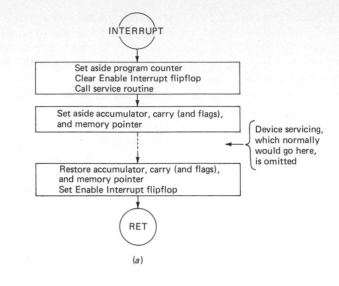

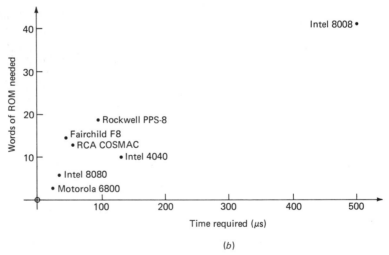

Figure 3-40. Benchmark comparison of interrupt servicing.   (a) Flowchart;
(b) comparison of microcomputers.

ative effectiveness of microcomputers with the "benchmark program"
shown in flowchart form in Fig. 3-40a.   While the number of scratchpad registers to be set aside is somewhat arbitrary, setting aside a memory pointer is
a reasonable minimum.   The graph of Fig. 3-40b compares our set of microcomputers on this basis for both ROM storage needed and speed.   The Intel
4004, the Rockwell PPS-4, and the SMS Microcontroller are not included be-

cause they do not permit interrupts. The Intel 8008 is included with the assumption that its hardware includes two 8-bit registers set up as I/O ports. It is assumed that the RCA COSMAC, with 16 possible memory pointers, and the Intel 4040, with 12, have enough to dedicate one to the interrupt service routine for this purpose only.

The Motorola 6800 is dramatically efficient at this benchmark program because it does everything automatically. Two specially located words of ROM hold the full address of the interrupt service routine. One word of ROM holds the RTI (ReTurn from Interrupt) instruction which restores all CPU registers and flags, sets the Interrupt Enable flipflop, and restores the program counter to return to the interrupted program.

Looking at the entry to and exit from the interrupt service routine of Fig. 3-40a, we note the similarity to a subroutine structure. The one thing missing is the address of the entry point. Some alternatives which are provided by different microcomputers are:

A fixed, absolute address in ROM (for example, page 0, address 3 for the Intel 4040)

An arbitrary address taken from a fixed location in ROM (for example, from page FF, addresses F8 and F9 for the Motorola 6800)

An arbitrary address taken from a specific scratchpad register (for example, register 1 for the RCA COSMAC)

One of several possible addresses which the CPU requests from the interrupting device at the time of the interrupt (for example, page 0, address 00, or 08, or 10, or 18, or 20, or 28, or 30, or 38 for the Intel 8008/8080)

Previously we considered the case of an instrument in which only one device would ever interrupt the microcomputer. Actually, regardless of which interruptible microcomputer we are using, we can almost as easily handle an interrupt from any number of devices provided we constrain all but one of the devices from interrupting at any one time. In this case, we know which interrupt service routine will be appropriate when the interrupt occurs. Therefore, before setting the Enable Interrupt flipflop, we can move the entry address for this service routine to the specific location in memory in which the CPU expects to find this entry address when an interrupt occurs. Alternatively, the interrupt service routine can execute a jump indirect instruction, using the contents of a scratchpad register to provide the address needed for a routine to service the device. As a third alternative, the interrupt service routine can execute an unconditional jump to a *RAM* location which has previously been loaded with the three bytes of an unconditional jump to the routine which services the device.

A few microcomputers make it almost trivial to accept an interrupt from any one of several devices and get to that device's service routine. For example, Intel's 8259 Programmable Interrupt Controller permits the 8080 to be interrupted from any one of eight sources (expandable up to 64 sources), using eight separate "interrupt" input lines. The CPU is *vectored* to one of eight addresses for the entry point to the appropriate service routine, as discussed in Appendix A3. In addition, devices are assigned priorities so that a higher-priority device can interrupt the service routine of a lower-priority device. Consequently, one device can interrupt the service routine of another device, which previously interrupted the service routine of another device, and so on up to eight levels deep. With an "unlimited" stack in RAM, the 8080 simply sets aside successive program-counter contents and scratchpad registers onto the stack. Then, as the highest-priority service routine is completed, the stack is unfolded to pick up where the next lower service routine left off when it was interrupted, and so on.

The whole idea of having interrupt capability is to provide a quick response to a device. If only one device can interrupt, it is a straightforward process to determine how long the response will take (that is, the duration of the service routine). If several devices can interrupt each other, the response time for a lower-priority device can only be specified in terms of a minimum response time (which occurs if its service routine is not interrupted) and a maximum response time (which occurs if each higher-priority device interrupts the service routine of the one just below it). It is our job, as designers, to make sure that any response time within this range will be satisfactory, or else to find an alternative solution to the problem.

Example 3-12. An Intel 8080 microcomputer provides for interrupts from three devices, D1, D2, and D3. D1 has the lowest priority and D3 the highest. The service routines for each take the following times (if they are not interrupted):

$$\text{Time for D1} = 120 \ \mu s$$

$$\text{Time for D2} = 90 \ \mu s$$

$$\text{Time for D3} = 65 \ \mu s$$

Taking all possible combinations of interrupts into account, determine the actual range in the response time for each of the devices.

$$\text{Time for D3} = 65 \ \mu s$$

$$90 \ \mu s \leqslant \text{Time for D2} \leqslant 155 \ \mu s$$

$$120 \ \mu s \leqslant \text{Time for D1} \leqslant 275 \ \mu s$$

3-8 DIRECT MEMORY ACCESS

Direct memory access (DMA), when it is an available resource of a micro-computer, permits the accessing of memory without having the CPU in-volved. It is typically used to transfer an array of data into, or out of, RAM from a device outside the microcomputer.

A typical minicomputer application occurs in the transfer of records between the minicomputer and a magnetic-disk storage unit. Some microcomputer-based instruments use relatively low-cost "floppy-disk" storage units in much the same way.

Another application arises from the need to refresh a character display repeatedly on a cathode-ray tube or a "multiplexed" display on seven-segment LED* numeric indicators. If each successive character to be dis-played is stored in a successive RAM location, the display can obtain each character automatically using DMA. To change the display, the CPU need only change the data stored in the appropriate locations in RAM.

Successive samples of a voltage waveform can be collected using an 8-bit analog-to-digital (A/D) converter. They can then be stored in RAM by using each successive "conversion done" output of the A/D converter to ini-tiate a DMA cycle. After all the desired samples have been collected, the data can be processed under program control.

An outstanding example of efficient DMA operation is provided by the Rockwell PPS-8 microcomputer and its DMA controller, depicted in Fig. 3-41a in simplified form. The controller serves up to eight different input or output ports. Any time the device associated with a specific I/O port is ready for a data transfer, it signals the DMA controller (shown as "Initiate DMA n"). The controller then initiates a "DMA Request" signal to the CPU. At the completion of the present instruction cycle, the CPU stops what it is doing and puts its three-state output to the address bus, data bus, $\overline{\text{READ}}$, and $\overline{\text{WRITE}}$ lines into the high-impedance state and returns a "DMA Acknowl-edge" signal to the DMA controller. The CPU then remains in a state of sus-pended animation until the controller terminates its DMA Request. This is necessary to preclude the kind of fight for control of RAM by CPU and DMA controller depicted in Fig. 3-42.

Having received the DMA Acknowledge signal, the controller looks at the Initiate DMA inputs to decide which is the highest-priority device re-questing service. Upon deciding this, it accesses the corresponding regis-ters for that channel, shown in Fig. 3-41b. These registers have been pre-viously set up under program control by the CPU. The controller puts the Address register contents on the address bus to RAM. Then the controller looks at the I/O Mode bit to decide on the appropriate control pulses to gen-erate for the $\overline{\text{READ}}$ or $\overline{\text{WRITE}}$ lines to RAM and for the control line to the I/O port (to strobe an output port, or to enable an input port).

---

* Light-emitting diode.

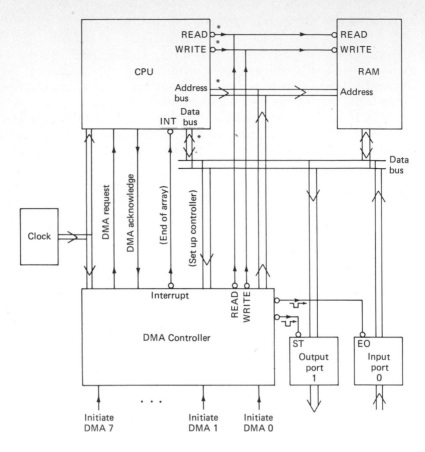

* CPU floats these three-state outputs during DMA operations

(a)

Figure 3-41. Rockwell PPS-8 DMA control. (a) Circuit (simplified); (b) DMA controller registers.

Once the data transfer has taken place, the controller increments the Address and Record Length registers. If the Record Length register rolls over from FF to 00, the controller looks at the Record Cycle Mode bit. Depending upon the state of this bit, the controller will either send an interrupt signal to the CPU or load the Address, Record Length, I/O Mode, and Record Cycle Mode registers from the contents of the channel 7 registers. The interrupt informs the CPU that the desired block of data has been transferred. Loading from the channel 7 registers is a capability permitted to any one of the seven channels, channel 0 through channel 6. It permits the channel using this "record cycle mode" to run continuously, resetting itself automatically from the channel 7 registers. Of course, the use of this mode precludes the use of channel 7 as a DMA channel.

DMA channel number	I/O mode (1 bit)	Record cycle mode (1 bit)	Address (14 bits)	Record length (8 bits)
0	⬚	⬚		
1	⬚	⬚		
2	⬚	⬚		
3	⬚	⬚		
4	⬚	⬚		
5	⬚	⬚		
6	⬚	⬚		
7	⬚	⬚		

(b)

Figure 3-41. (Continued)

After completing this DMA cycle, the controller checks to see if another DMA operation is being requested. If so, it services it. If not, it terminates the DMA Request signal to the CPU, which then comes out of its suspended-animation state and continues where it left off.

The RCA COSMAC microcomputer takes an interesting approach to

Figure 3-42. Improper control of RAM. (Rand Renfroe.)

providing DMA capability. It uses a specific 16-bit scratchpad register in the CPU as a DMA address register. It also has a $\overline{\text{DMA-IN}}$ and a $\overline{\text{DMA-OUT}}$ control line to the CPU. To use the DMA channel for data input to RAM, the address register must be initialized to the first RAM address into which the data will be put. Then each time $\overline{\text{DMA-IN}}$ is driven low by a device, the CPU will stop what it is doing at the completion of the present instruction cycle, put a word of data from the device onto the data bus, put the DMA address out to RAM, and generate a $\overline{\text{WRITE}}$ pulse to RAM. Then it picks up normal operation again with the next instruction cycle. With the DMA mechanism built into the CPU chip, its implementation is almost a casual extension of the normal CPU operation. It would have been useful if another scratchpad register had been dedicated to the function of record-length counter. It could simply shut down further DMA transfers when it reached zero and either be tested for zero or cause an interrupt.

3-9 PROGRAMMABLE TIMERS

We have seen a variety of hardware features of different microcomputers in previous sections. In this section, we will look at a feature which is not typical but which gives a specific microcomputer an interesting capability.

Fairchild's F8 microcomputer includes a *programmable timer* on each of its Program Storage Unit chips.* For example, the F8 microcomputer system shown in Fig. 3-43 incorporates two of these chips plus a CPU chip to provide a system with 64 scratchpad registers, 2048 words of ROM, 48 I/O lines (that is, 6 I/O ports), 2 vectored interrupt inputs, and 2 programmable timers. Each timer can be used to generate a program-initiated delay. For example, if a microcomputer-based instrument includes an electromechanical device, such as a printer or a stepper motor which must be driven by the microcomputer, it will need to generate pulses having a specified pulse width. Or it will need to wait a specific time between one action and the next. If these intervals were measured in microseconds, a "wait loop" in the program sequence would serve well. However, with an electromechanical device, the interval is likely to be measured in milliseconds and may be repeated over and over again (for example, to make a stepper motor take successive steps).

If we cannot afford to tie up the CPU with these long wait loops, the usual means for generating an output pulse of specified duration is to drive a *one-shot,* as shown in Fig. 3-44a. Each pulse requires a positive transition on the input to the one-shot. The pulse width is set by the external RC timing circuit. A *time interval* can be achieved by using appropriate circuitry to interrupt the microcomputer at the end of the pulse.

---

* Also on its "Static Memory Interface" chip, discussed in Appendix A2.

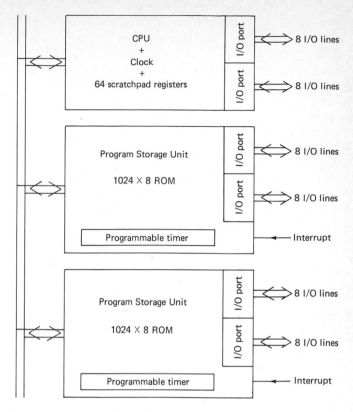

Figure 3-43. Three-chip Fairchild F8 microcomputer.

The programmable timers in the F8 microcomputer permit the elimination of all one-shots used to generate output pulses and time intervals. As shown in Fig. 3-44b, the programmable timer generates an interrupt at the end of a specified time interval. If an output pulse is being generated, this bit of the word in the output port can be complemented (with an EOR immediate instruction) to turn off the pulse.

As long as the instrument never needs more than one pulse or time duration at a time, a single programmable timer will solve all pulse and time-duration requirements. When the pulse or time duration is begun, a pointer can also be set up in a RAM location. Then, when the interrupt occurs, the pointer can be used by the interrupt service routine to determine what action to take, as in the examples which follow shortly.

The Fairchild F8 programmable timer is an 8-bit counter which is preset by the CPU with an output instruction. It is counted every 15.5 μs*

* When using a 2-MHz clock.

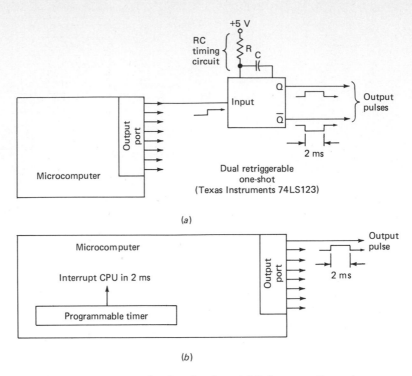

Figure 3-44. Generation of a "long" pulse. (a) Pulse generation using a one-shot; (b) pulse generation using the F8 programmable timer.

and has a maximum range of 255 counts (that is, 3.953 ms) before an interrupt occurs. The counting continues after the interrupt, generating a new interrupt every 3.953 ms. To stop the F8 timer, it is loaded with FF (hexadecimal).

Example 3-13. Using the ground rules of Sec. 2-8 for tables, form a table in which each entry contains any data and pointers associated with each specific use of a programmable timer. Call this table TIMETABLE (that is, label the base address of the table TIMETABLE). The offset address used for entering TIMETABLE is to be loaded into the register called OFFSET which is used by the table-driver subroutine.

The ith entry of TIMETABLE will contain three items, as shown in Fig. 3-45: (1)An 8-bit number, TIMEi, which will be preset into the timer to determine the duration of time before an interrupt occurs. (2) An 8-bit number, NOFFi, which gives the offset address of the next use

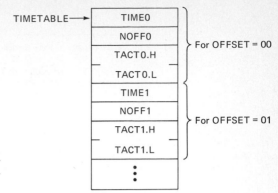

Figure 3-45. Format of TIMETA-
BLE, a table used with a programmable timer.

to be made of the programmable timer when the present use is completed. One common "next use" will be to turn the timer off. The in-
clusion of an arbitrary "next use" will permit a variety of interesting
capabilities, to be explored in subsequent examples. (3) A 16-bit full
address, TACTi, of the "action routine" to be used when the interrupt
occurs. Each action routine will do a specific job, such as "clear the
second bit of output port 3" (to terminate a pulse on that output line).

Example 3-14. Develop a subroutine, called TIMER, which will initiate the use of a programmable timer using the table of the last example.
    To initiate this use, we need to pass to TIMER a parameter desig-
nating the desired entry. This is loaded into the register called
OFFSET. Calling TIMER will start the programmable timer. Upon return from the TIMER subroutine, we can initiate the operation which
will be terminated by the programmable timer. For example, we might
"set the second bit of output port 3" to initiate a pulse on that output
line.
    This use of the TIMER subroutine when initiating an event which
is to last for a specified time is illustrated in Fig. 3-46a. The TIMER
subroutine itself is shown in Fig. 3-46b. Calling TBL4 causes the
memory pointer of the CPU to point to the first byte of the entry in
TIMETABLE pointed to by OFFSET. This first byte, TIMEi, is then
loaded into the programmable timer, starting its operation.

Example 3-15. Develop the interrupt service routine which will service the programmable timer.

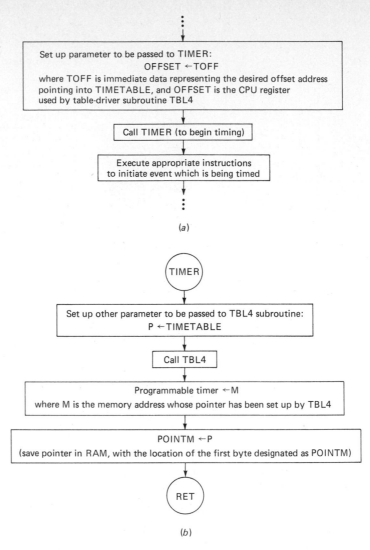

Figure 3-46. TIMER subroutine and its use when initiating a timed event. (a) Initiating a timed event; (b) TIMER subroutine.

This service routine is shown in Fig. 3-47. It stores, and eventually restores, the contents of any CPU registers which would be changed by the service routine. Then it pulls two items out of TIME-TABLE. NOFFi is one of these. It is set aside in the CPU register called OFFSET and not disturbed, or used, until the end of the service routine. At that time, it will be used to initiate another cycle of the timer (or to turn off the timer by loading FF into it) with a call to TIMER.

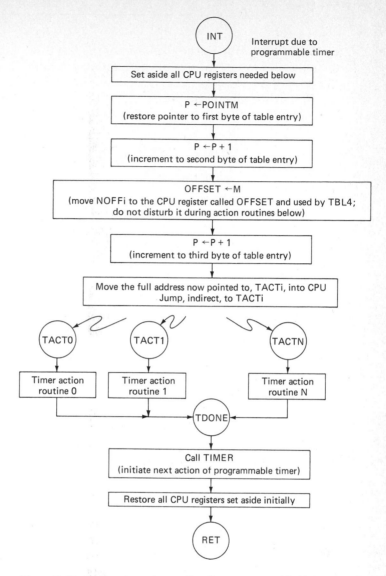

Figure 3-47. *Interrupt service routine for programmable timer.*

The other item pulled out of TIMETABLE is the full address of the action routine, TACTi, which carries out the actions needed at the end of this programmed time interval. Note that each of these action routines ends with an unconditional jump to the address labeled TDONE.

Example 3-16. How is the structure of the last three examples used for a "one-shot" event, such as the generation of a single positive pulse on the second bit of output port 3 having a duration of 1 ms?

First, we might use the zeroth entry in TIMETABLE (that is, the entry for OFFSET = 00) to do nothing but turn the programmable timer off:

$$\text{TIME0} = \text{FF (turn off timer)}$$

$$\text{NOFF0} = 00^\dagger$$

$$\text{TACT0} = 00^\dagger$$

† Actually, this value is irrelevant, since the timer is going to be turned off. We will never get the interrupt which leads to the use of this value.

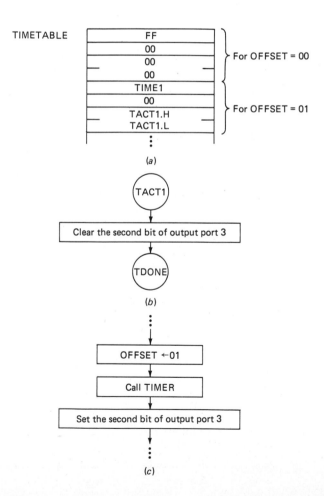

Figure 3-48. Generation of a single, 1-ms pulse. (a) TIMETABLE contents for a "one-shot" event; (b) action routine 1; (c) program segment to generate the desired 1-ms pulse.

If the next entry in TIMETABLE (that is, for OFFSET = 01) is the entry used for the generation of this pulse, then TIMETABLE will be as shown in Fig. 3-48a, where TIME1 stands for the number to be loaded in the programmable timer to give 1 ms.

The action routine for the case when OFFSET = 01 (with address TACT1) is shown in Fig. 3-48b. The only thing left to do is to initiate the pulse when desired, as in Fig. 3-48c.

Example 3-17. Generate a continuous 1.0-kHz square wave on the first bit of output port 3. Show how to initiate and how to terminate the square wave under program control.

Figure 3-49a shows the required contents of TIMETABLE, where

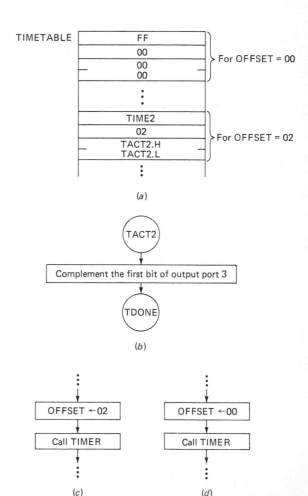

Figure 3-49. Initiation and termination of a 1.0-kHz square wave. (a) TIME-TABLE contents; (b) action routine 2; (c) program segment to initiate a continuous square wave; (d) program segment to terminate the square wave.

TIME2 stands for the number to be loaded in the programmable timer to give 0.5 ms. Each successive interrupt finds OFFSET = 02 and complements the desired output line.

Termination of the square wave requires only "initiating" a new time delay with OFFSET = 00, which loads FF (hexadecimal) into the programmable timer, turning it off. This is shown in Fig. 3-49d.

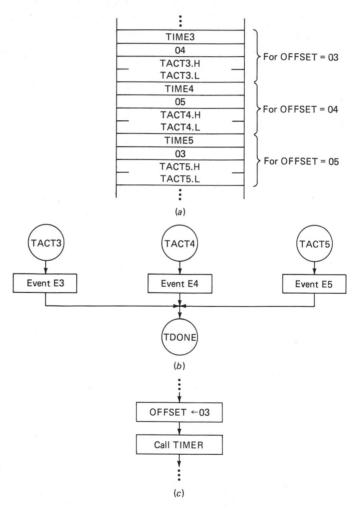

Figure 3-50. *Continuously repeating sequence of three events.* (a) *TIMETABLE contents;* (b) *action routines;* (c) *program segment to initiate sequence.*

Example 3-18. Generate a continuously repeating sequence of three events, . . . , E3, E4, E5, E3, E4, E5, ...

See Fig. 3-50 for the solution. The numbers TIME3, TIME4, and TIME5 determine the time intervals between these events.

Example 3-19. Generate a pulse lasting a second.

Using the F8 programmable timer, the maximum time interval before an interrupt occurs is 3.953 ms. If we count 255 interrupts, each time interval can be somewhat less than this in order to get to 1 s. See

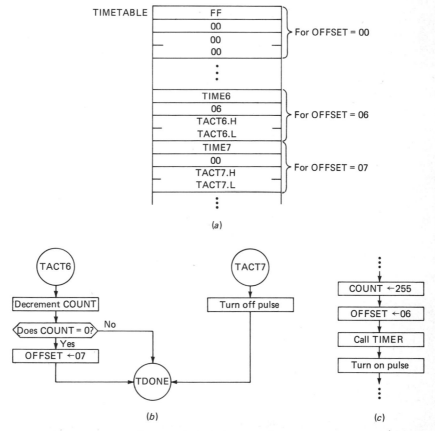

Figure 3-51. Generation of a 1-s pulse. (a) TIMETABLE contents; (b) action routines; (c) initiation of pulse.

Fig. 3-51. Between the two numbers we store in TIMETABLE for TIME6 and TIME7, we can obtain a very accurate pulse width, if we desire it. We need only determine the extra time introduced between one interrupt and the starting of the next time interval of the programmable timer and choose TIME6 and TIME7 to compensate for this extra time.

This programmable timer is such a generally useful device that with the iteration of ideas which takes place as new microcomputers are developed, a programmable timer will undoubtedly become an included feature of many future microcomputers. It is also likely to appear in new peripheral chips for present microcomputers.

PROBLEMS

3-1 Microcomputer design philosophy. Discuss how a specified microcomputer design has been optimized relative to the seven criteria of Sec. 3-1.

(a) What special chips does the manufacturer provide for the components of Fig. 2-1? Is there a special I/O chip? If so, how can it be used?

(b) What is the smallest number of chips needed to provide at least some capability in each area defined in Fig. 2-1? What is the extent of this minimum capability in each area?

(c) Does the microcomputer use standard RAM and ROM? If not, is there a "prototyping" chip which permits use of standard RAM and ROM in order to develop a system?

(d) How does the instruction set handle memory addressing? Does the number of instructions needed to set up an address vary with memory size?

(e) Would you characterize the microcomputer as a fast controller or versatile, general-purpose processor? Give at least one specific point supporting your position.

(f) Is the data word length arbitrary? If so, what are the largest and smallest possible data word sizes?

(g) Is the instruction set microprogrammable by a user? If so, what operations can be performed upon registers under microprogram control?

3-2 Loading. For a specific "TTL compatible" microcomputer:

(a) List the "TTL compatible loading rules" for the connections to input and output devices through the I/O ports, analogous to Fig. 3-8.

Driver	Driven			
	74LSxx	74xx	74Sxx	Input port
74LSxx	20	5	4	
74xx	20	10	8	
74Sxx	50	12	10	
Output port				—

Figure P3-1.

(b) Are these connections also "CMOS compatible" to CMOS logic operating with 5-V power? While CMOS drive capability varies among manufacturers, assume a logic 0 drive capability of 0.2 mA at 0.4 V and a logic 1 drive capability of 0.2 mA at 2.4 V.

3-3 TTL compatibility. For a specific microcomputer, and using the data of Prob. 3-2 and Fig. 3-8, complete the loading-rule chart shown in Fig. P3-1. In each case, show the maximum number of devices which can be driven by each driver.

3-4 CMOS compatibility. Consider the connection between the output of a microcomputer and the input to a CMOS device operating with 5-V power. If the microcomputer output can actually rise above +5 V or drop below 0 V, connection to a CMOS device may actually destroy it unless (as is usual) the microcomputer's output is incapable of driving more than 10 mA under these conditions. As shown in Fig. P3-2, a CMOS device includes a diode-protection circuit on each input (normally used to protect against destruction by static charges incurred

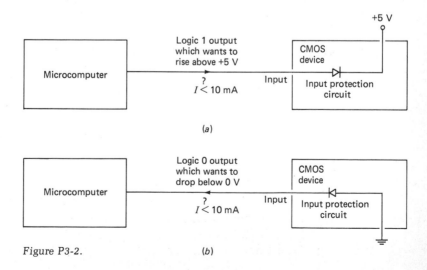

Figure P3-2.

during assembly into circuits). The figure illustrates that voltage inputs tending to rise above 5 V will be pulled down to 5 V with a diode clamp. Similarly, voltage inputs tending to drop below 0 V will be pulled up to 0 V.

For a specific microcomputer, can outputs exceed the 0- to 5-V range desired by CMOS devices? If so, can the input currents which result exceed the safe value of 10 mA? As an example of the manner in which this might be specified, consider Intel's 4289 Standard Memory Interface chip which permits standard RAM and ROM to be used by the Intel 4004/4040 microcomputers. Its specification lists a maximum output "clamp current" of 10 mA with an output clamped at -1 V. (The specification is made at -1 V in order to take advantage of the diode voltage drop in the clamp circuit.) There is no corresponding problem when an output goes high, since the 4289 power-supply voltages are $+5$ V and -10 V.

3-5   Clock waveforms. High reliability in a microcomputer clock waveform is sometimes obtained by using a crystal oscillator whose frequency is an integral multiple of the desired microcomputer frequency. This is then counted down and the counter outputs gated appropriately to obtain the needed waveforms. Determine integer values for K, L, and M in Fig. P3-3 and the value of T so as to satisfy the Intel 8080 clock-waveform requirements of Fig. 3-11 with as high a microcomputer clock frequency as possible. Constrain

$$K + L + M = 10 \text{ or } 16$$

so that either a decade or a binary counter can be used directly to obtain the waveforms. Assume that the required nonoverlap of the trailing edge of ϕ_1 and the leading edge of ϕ_2 will be resolved without any special considerations. Also assume all rise and fall times will be 10 ns. What is the resulting maximum microcomputer clock rate?

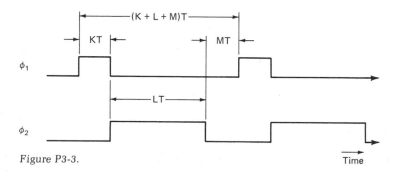

Figure P3-3.   Time

3-6   Clock waveforms.

(a) Use the approach of Prob. 3-5 on another specific microcomputer. What is the maximum microcomputer clock rate obtained in this way?

(b) What is the minimum clock rate obtained using this same circuit and changing only the frequency of the crystal oscillator? (This assumes that the microcomputer clock is not permitted to operate below a specified frequency.)

3-7   Reset mechanism.

(a) For a specific microcomputer, is the reset input sensitive to a voltage level or to a voltage transition? What is this input requirement for resetting?

(b) How does the microcomputer determine the address from which the first instruction will be taken?

(c) Does the reset mechanism clear any CPU registers? If so, which ones?

(d) Does the CPU undertake any other actions in response to a reset input?

(e) Is there a stack pointer in the CPU which must be initialized under program control?

3-8   Loading of address bus/data bus structure. Consider the loading requirements of a specific RAM, ROM, and general I/O port for a specific microcomputer.

(a) Make a loading chart, in the form shown in Fig. P3-4, for the maximum number of each device (when considered alone) which can be driven by each bus line specified.

(b) If the manufacturer of the microcomputer offers a "bus driver" chip to help the microcomputer handle this load, make a loading chart for it also.

3-9   Special I/O chip. Consider a microcomputer chip set which includes a special I/O chip having at least two I/O ports on it.

			Driven		
	Driver	I/O port	RAM	ROM
CPU {	Address bus			
	Data bus			
	READ, WRITE			
Bus driver {	Address bus			
	Data bus			
	READ, WRITE			

Figure P3-4.

(*a*) Can each port be set up as either an input port or an output port? Is this "hard-wired," or is it done under program control as part of the microcomputer's initialization routine? What setup variations are possible?

(*b*) Does the chip include multiple-chip enable inputs (to help with page selection)?

(*c*) Does it include special control inputs for "handshaking" between the CPU and the device connected to each I/O port? For data input, this would be an "input ready" input and an "input acknowledge" output. For data output, this would be an "output ready" output and an "output received" input (or some such names). If so, what alternatives exist for their use?

3-10 Page selection. If a microcomputer uses 1024 × 8 ROMs, the two most significant bits of the address on each ROM select a page (that is, 256 words) of ROM. How would you modify the scheme of Fig. 3-19 to use these ROMs together with 256 × 8 RAMs, input ports, and output ports? Show the circuit and label the page address(es) of each device.

3-11 Page selection.

(*a*) For a specific microcomputer, will the page-selection scheme of Fig. 3-24 satisfy the requirements for specific pages? Or does the microcomputer use any specifically designated page numbers *not* included among those of Fig. 3-24 (for start-up, etc.)? If Fig. 3-24 is satisfactory, how many pages can be selected with two enables, both in negated form? With two enables, both in asserted form? With two enables, one asserted and one negated?

(*b*) If the scheme of Fig. 3-24 is *not* satisfactory, derive one which is. Use a format analogous to that of Fig. 3-24, which has as many pages as possible (subject to the constraints on specifically designated pages imposed by the CPU), and which uses two enables for page selection (in various combinations of asserted and negated form).

3-12 Page selection. Modify the page-selection scheme of Fig. 3-24, again using two enable inputs (in various combinations of asserted form and negated form) for page selection, but including page FF (and not page 00) among the pages selected. Make a chart analogous to that of Fig. 3-24 having as many rows as possible. Assume that when power is turned on, the CPU will look for its first instruction on page FF.

3-13 Page selection. The page-selection scheme of Fig. 3-24 assumes that the RAM and ROM chips to be hung on the bus each have 256 words (or less). Modify the page-selection scheme of Fig. 3-24 so as to handle 1024 × 8 ROM chips, 256 × 8 RAM chips, and I/O ports. Assume each device has two enable inputs in various combinations of asserted form and negated form available for page selection. Also assume that page 00 must be included. Make a chart analogous to that of Fig. 3-24 having as many rows as possible.

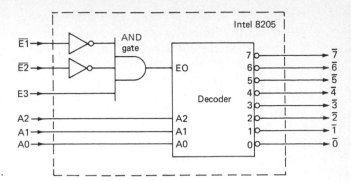

Figure P3-5.

3-14 Page addressing. Intel's 8205 low-power Schottky decoder shown in Fig. P3-5 operates exactly like each of the decoders shown in Fig. 3-19 except that it has gating on the EO input. Using a page-selection scheme which combines the ideas of Fig. 3-24 with those of Fig. 3-19, how many pages can be selected if the address inputs on all decoders are tied to A8,A9, and A10 and if $\bar{E}_1$ on each decoder is tied to either $\overline{READ}$ or $\overline{WRITE}$?

3-15 CPU timing constraints. For a specific microcomputer:

(a) Define how you want (or expect) the microcomputer clock waveforms to change versus frequency over the frequency range of the microcomputer. This will permit you to pin down exact timing relationships for the remainder of this problem.

(b) Construct a "read timing" chart analogous to that of Fig. 3-28 giving the CPU's timing expectations for devices to be hung on the bus and from which data will be read.

(c) Do the same thing for a "write timing" chart analogous to that of Fig. 3-31.

3-16 Timing constraints. Using a specific microcomputer, and having the charts of Prob. 3-15 in hand, determine the maximum reliable microcomputer clock rate for each case below.

(a) For a specific ROM and assuming page selection can be carried out directly with the enables, as in Fig. 3-21.

(b) For the same ROM but with a CMOS inverter (worst-case propagation delay = 90 ns) to help with page selection, as in Fig. 3-27.

(c) For the same ROM but with a CMOS decoder (worst-case propagation delay = 300 ns) to carry out page selection, as in Fig. 3-19.

(d) For reading and writing from a specific RAM subject to the page-selection approach of part (a).

(e) For the same RAM as in part (d) but subject to the page-selection approach of part (b).

(f) For the same RAM as in part (d) but subject to the page-selection approach of part (c).

3-17 Capacitive loading. When manufacturers make specifications relating either to speed or to propagation delay, these specifications are made subject to two assumed *test conditions*. One of these is a resistive load, and specifies a worst-case loading in the sense discussed in Sec. 3-2. The other is a worst-case capacitive load. For example, the Intel 8080 specifies propagation delays assuming a worst-case capacitive load on the address lines of 100 picofarads (pF).

All the RAMs and ROMs of Fig. 3-29 list a maximum input capacitance of 8 pF or less. A CMOS gate will have a typical input capacitance of 5 pF. Printed-circuit-board wiring might be estimated as adding a capacitance of roughly 30 pF/ft (for 0.025-in.-width conductor on standard G10 glass epoxy board).

(a) What are the specifications on capacitive loading for address, data, READ, and WRITE lines for a specific microcomputer organized around an address bus/data bus structure?

(b) What is the capacitive loading of the inputs to each of the components which can be hung on the bus?

(c) For a minimum system to operate at the microcomputer's maximum clock rate, how much capacitance can be taken up by the wiring for each line of the address bus/data bus structure?

(d) If the manufacturer provides a "bus driver" chip, how does its capacitive drive capability compare with that of the CPU?

3-18 Capacitive loading. The maximum propagation delay versus capacitive loading for a CMOS decoder, National Semiconductor's 74C42, is shown in Fig. P3-6. An MSI device such as this has enough internal complexity so that the variation in propagation delay versus capacitive loading is a second-order effect. In contrast, a CMOS inverter, the 74C04, has a shorter propagation delay, and therefore one which is much more dependent upon capacitive loading.

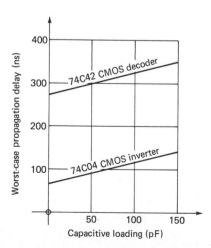

Figure P3-6.

(a) Determine the maximum clock rate which will permit reliable reading of an Intel 2708 ROM by the Intel 8080 if the page selection is done with the 74C42 decoder. Assume the capacitive loading of the ROM and its wiring upon the decoder is 15 pF.

(b) Rework the problem of part (a) assuming the availability of an identical ROM in all respects except that it has any number of EO (enable output) inputs in either asserted or negated form so that page decoding can be carried out without any extra decoders or inverters.

(c) Rework the problem of part (b), but assume all EO inputs on *all* devices are available in negated form only and that the page-selection scheme of Fig. 3-24 is used with 74C04 inverters on some of the address lines. Assume nothing else loads the output of the inverter used to drive this ROM and that the total (wiring + input) capacitive load is 15 pF.

(d) Rework the problem of part (c), but assume six devices are driven by this inverter, for a total capacitive load of 90 pF.

3-19 Page formation. Using two Intel 2111 (256 × 4) RAMs, interconnect them appropriately to obtain a 256 × 8 RAM. Show the interconnections of the control inputs ($\overline{CE}$, $\overline{CE}$, $\overline{EO}$, $\overline{WRITE}$), the address bus (A7, . . . , A0), and the I/O lines (I/O4, . . . , I/O1) and how the I/O lines are to be connected to the data bus of the microcomputer (D7, . . . , D0).

3-20 RAM structures. Motorola's 6810 128 × 8-bit RAM, shown in Fig. P3-7, has a rather different organizational structure from that of Fig. 3-22.

(a) What control inputs (that is, chip enables and read-write input) are needed to enable the output in order to read data out of the RAM onto the data bus?

(b) What control inputs are needed to write data into the RAM?

(c) During a write operation, the read-write input cannot be used in the same way as the $\overline{WRITE}$ input of Fig. 3-22, because this would lead to a fight on the data bus between the CPU's data output to the RAM and the RAM's (inadvertent) data output after being enabled and before $\overline{WRITE}$ goes low. Our job is to avoid causing such fights among three-state devices. To use the 6810, we need to find a read-write signal which is logic 1 at the time needed to read and logic 0 at the time needed to write—but the read-write line can stay at these levels well beyond the permissible times for actually reading and writing. The actual timing for reading and writing must be determined by one chip enable input (or an ANDing of several chip enable inputs) which enables the chip at a time which is satisfactory for *both* reading and writing.

Deriving these signals from the CPU of a specific microcomputer can be difficult and may lead to a less-than-maximum clock rate unless special circuitry is added. The Motorola 6800 CPU generates an appropriate read-write signal directly, which goes low only when a

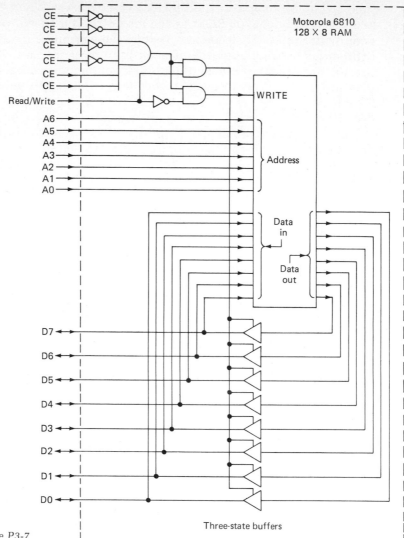

Figure P3-7.

"write" operation is to be executed. Since it stays low during most of
the execute cycle, the clock phase ϕ_2 is used as a chip enable. It de-
fines a proper time for writing (as well as for reading).

For another specific microcomputer, and with the control signals
available from its CPU, can you derive appropriate inputs for this RAM?
If so, what is the maximum rate at which the microcomputer can be
clocked with this RAM, assuming page selection is done solely with
chip enables? Use the RAM data of Figs. 3-29 and 3-30.

3-21 Page formation. Using two of the Motorola 6810 (128 × 8) RAMs of

Prob. 3-20, interconnect chip enables appropriately so as to form a 256 × 8 RAM. Label the connections to the data bus and to the address bus lines A7, . . . , A0. Show whatever interconnections are appropriate between the extra chip enables to get as many of these as possible for the "256 × 8 RAM."

3-22 Use of $\overline{\text{IN}}$ and $\overline{\text{OUT}}$ control lines. Consider a microcomputer which has not only $\overline{\text{READ}}$ and $\overline{\text{WRITE}}$ control lines (by whatever name they are actually called) but also $\overline{\text{IN}}$ and $\overline{\text{OUT}}$ control lines which are used in conjunction with special IN and OUT instructions.

(a) How is the address of a device, associated with the IN or OUT instruction, translated into an address coming out of the CPU?

(b) For this microcomputer, what advantage is there to using the IN and OUT instructions rather than "memory-mapping" all I/O ports?

(c) What disadvantage is there?

(d) Is it possible to select between input port 2 and a separate and distinct output port 2? What is involved?

(e) If all input ports except one are memory-mapped, what will the connections to this one input port look like?

(f) Repeat part (e) for one output port.

(g) Repeat parts (e) and (f) for one input port and one output port.

3-23 Multiplexed bus system organization. For a microcomputer which uses a multiplexed bus system organization:

(a) Show a timing diagram (or timing diagrams) analogous to Fig. 3-32 to indicate how the bus is used at different times in the instruction cycle.

(b) How are the operations on the different microcomputer chips synchronized?

(c) What unusual design approaches does the microcomputer feature because of its use of a multiplexed bus (analogous to the duplicated program counters in the Fairchild F8 microcomputer)?

(d) How has the manufacturer taken advantage of the absence of pins for an address bus?

3-24 Flags. For a specific microcomputer:

(a) Are there any "flag inputs" which can be tested directly?

(b) Is there a "best" bit position on an input port to facilitate testing of a flag? Explain.

(c) Show the minimum sequence of instructions (that is, minimum ROM words) for reading in a flag on a "best" line of an input port and jumping on the basis of its state. Assume that the other lines of the input port are being used and are therefore not all zero.

3-25 Flags. For a specific microcomputer, make a flowchart and write an assembly language FLAG subroutine (minimizing ROM words used) which:

(a) Reads input port 1, which has eight distinct flags as inputs (or four, for a 4-bit microcomputer).

(b) Tests each bit, in sequence.

(c) Executes, or bypasses, an "action routine" ACTi corresponding to the state of each flag bit.

(d) Returns.

Assume that at the time FLAG is called, the accumulator, the carry bit, and at least one scratchpad register are available for use by this subroutine.

3-26 Flags. For a specific microcomputer operating at its maximum clock rate, what is the maximum time which can occur between the setting of a flag and the beginning of the instruction cycle for the first instruction servicing the device which set the flag?

(a) Assume that a wait loop of the form of Fig. 3-38 is used.

(b) Assume that a wait loop of the form of Fig. 3-39 is used.

3-27 Interrupt capability. Does a specific microcomputer include interrupt capability? If so:

(a) Where are the contents of the program counter put when an interrupt occurs?

(b) How does the CPU get to the first instruction of the interrupt service routine?

(c) How is the "state of the CPU" most easily set aside? That is, how are the accumulator, carry bit (and other flags), and any needed scratchpad registers moved aside to provide use of these registers to the service routine? Consider minimizing ROM words needed to do this.

(d) Is there an Enable Interrupt flipflop in the CPU? If so, how is it handled automatically, and under program control?

(e) Is the interrupt input sensitive to a level or to a transition?

(f) Is there an Interrupt Acknowledge output that will "handshake" with the device which caused the interrupt (and perhaps get it to turn off the interrupt)?

(g) Can the interrupt (and interrupt acknowledge, if it exists) be set up, under program control, to operate in any one of several ways? If so, then what are the alternatives?

(h) Is there more than one interrupt input? If so, can a higher-priority event or device interrupt the service routine of a lower-priority one? How are return addresses and register contents handled in this case? How does the CPU decide which device caused an interrupt?

3-28 Interrupt benchmark program.

(a) For a specific microcomputer, write an interrupt service routine in assembly language having the flowchart of Fig. 3-40a. Minimize ROM words needed.

(b) Assuming the maximum permissible microcomputer clock

Address	RAM page 01	
00	1	0
01	3	2
02	5	4
03	7	6
04	9	8
05	B	A
06	D	C
07	F	E

Figure P3-8.   Address number

rate, determine the speed of this routine as well as the number of ROM words needed.

(c) What is the maximum duration which can occur between the generation of an interrupt signal by a device and the execution of the first instruction which deals with that device? This time should include the maximum delay which can occur between the change on the interrupt line and when the CPU actually looks at that line. In the benchmark program, it includes all instructions down to, but not including, the instructions restoring the accumulator, carry, and memory pointer. Assume that the Enable Interrupt flipflop is set and that no other interrupts occur.

3-29 Interrupt-driven numeric display. Assume that an interrupt is made to occur every millisecond into a specific 8-bit microcomputer. Make a flowchart and write a subroutine (which minimizes time of execution) which will take the contents of page 01, addresses 00 to 07, and put out a packed word to an output port based upon these contents once every millisecond. The least significant four bits are to be one of the "address numbers" shown in Fig. P3-8, which identifies a specific digit location. The most significant four bits are to be the digit located in the RAM location specified by the address number.

During each successive interrupt, the next digit is to be put out. After "address number" F, the next interrupt must pick up "address number" 0. If you wish to rearrange the addressing, or the sequence in which digits occur on the output, just specify what you want. Also, state what initialization, if any, must take place when power is first turned on.

To change any of the (up to) 16 digits being displayed by the instrument using this display approach, it is only necessary to update the corresponding contents in RAM. In Chap. 5, we will discuss the display circuitry which uses this output port.

3-30 DMA. Does "your" microcomputer include DMA capability? If so:

(a) How is a DMA channel set up (under program control before a DMA input is permitted to occur)?

(b) How does an external device tell the microcomputer that it has data ready (or is ready to accept a word of data)?

(c) How does the microcomputer "handshake" with this device to tell it that it has accepted the data (or that the data is ready)?

(d) How is the DMA channel operation terminated after the desired array of data has been transferred?

(e) Are special hardware considerations involved in the use of the DMA channel?

(f) Can more than one DMA channel be set up simultaneously to handle overlapping requests from several devices? If not, what must be done in order to switch the use of the one channel from one device to another?

3-31 DMA-driven numeric display. Repeat Prob. 3-29 but actuate a DMA channel instead of an interrupt with the signal which occurs every millisecond. Also use only the contents of the least significant four bits of the addresses in RAM on page 01, address 00 to 0F, for data. Assume that the most significant four bits in each of these addresses has been loaded with the address number, 0 to F, during the initialization routine, when power was first turned on to the instrument. Each successive DMA output should read out one of these composite 8-bit words to an output port. What needs to be done after the output from address 0F in order to begin again at address 00?

3-32 Programmable timer. Using the table-driving approach of Sec. 3-9, develop TIMETABLE contents and flowcharts analogous to Fig. 3-49 for each of the following:

(a) Read input port 5 into successive locations in RAM, starting at an address labeled DATA and stopping after collecting 128 words. Let "TIMED" represent the number to be preset into the programmable timer to set the sampling interval. Initially clear a RAM location labeled DDONE. When the last sample is collected, put a nonzero number into DDONE and stop collecting any more samples. Then DDONE can be tested to see when the data collection is finished.

(b) Put out the contents of RAM location DTOAC to output port 6, which is connected to a digital-to-analog converter. Let "TIMEC" represent the number to be preset into the programmable timer to set the output rate. As each sample is put out, clear the contents of CFLAG (in RAM). CFLAG is a flag to the program which indicates that it can serve up another output sample into DTOAC.

3-33 Programmable timer. For a specific microcomputer, assume the availability of a programmable timer which is preset with an output to output port 2. Use page 01 of ROM to store all tables.

Output port 3

Line 1	Line 0	
0	0	
		Step
0	1	
		Step
1	1	
		Step
1	0	
....		Step
0	0	

Figure P3-9.

(a) Assuming the availability of the TBL4 subroutine described in Sec. 2-8, write an assembly language subroutine TIMER, flowcharted in Fig. 3-46.

(b) Write the interrupt routine of Fig. 3-47.

(c) Generate an output to a stepper motor causing output lines 0 and 1 output port 3 to step through the continuous sequence shown in Fig. P3-9. Use a RAM location MOTOR to hold the present state of the output to the motor. Each step should last 4 ms (for a stepping rate of 250 steps per second). Use "TIME4" as the table entry to achieve this. Show all the items involved in doing this, analogous to Fig. 3-49. Show each program segment in both flowchart form and assembly language form, minimizing ROM words.

(d) Modify part (c) so as to generate a number of steps equal to the contents of SNUM, where SNUM is a RAM location. Do not initialize the stepper-motor position, but rather simply increment from the initial contents of MOTOR.

(e) Modify part (d) using the contents of SNUM as a signed number. If its most significant bit is a zero, step as in (d), counting SNUM down to zero. If its most significant bit is a one, step in the opposite direction (. . . , 00, 10, 01, 00, . . .), counting SNUM up (through all ones) to zero.

3-34 Programmable timer. Consider a specific microcomputer in which the location used for a subroutine return address can be loaded with an arbitrary address, handled as data and under program control.

(a) Show how to modify the interrupt routine of Fig. 3-47 by putting the address TDONE into this subroutine return address location before executing the indirect jump to TACTi. Then each action routine can be terminated with a 1-byte RETurn from subroutine instruction instead of an unconditional jump to TDONE (which probably requires 2 or 3 bytes).

(b) What are the advantages and the disadvantages of this alternative?

3-35 Multiple programmable timers. Develop flowcharts corresponding to Figs. 3-46 and 3-47 for handling three independent timers. Use a RAM location labeled TNUM to indicate which timer is being updated at any one time. Assume that the interrupt routine is entered from three separate entry points and that, after the appropriate CPU registers are set aside, each of these three entries sets its own number (0, 1, or 2) into TNUM. Then each of these three routines jumps to a common address for one common routine from then on. Minimize the number of ROM words used.

3-36 Programmable timer.

(a) If TIMETABLE is stored in page 01 of ROM and page 02 is a page of RAM, can an entry in TIMETABLE be set up, under program control, with a variable entry? Explain.

(b) If so, show how to generate any one of ten specific square-wave frequencies between 1 Hz and 1kHz. Use a number from 0 to 9 to indicate which frequency is desired. Assume the appropriate "TIMEi" values for the programmable timer are stored in a table called FREQ.

REFERENCES

Some of the considerations involved in using CMOS logic, including the kind of variability occurring between manufacturers, are discussed by R. Walker, C-MOS Specifications: Don't Take Them for Granted, *Electronics,* Jan. 9, 1975, pp. 103–107.

Some microcomputers have a CPU chip which includes a "Ready" or "Halt" input which can be used to stop its operation. This input, together with some extra circuitry, can be used to produce the fastest possible programmed control of a device, faster than either flag or interrupt control. The applicability of this approach to the control of a floppy disk by an Intel 8080 microcomputer is discussed by E. Fisher, Speed Microprocessor Responses, *Electronic Design,* Nov. 8, 1975, pp. 78–83.

MEMORY

4-1 ROMs, PROMs, AND EPROMs

For storage of programs, tables, and constants, read-only memories are available in several alternate forms:

1. ROMs—contents are *mask-programmed* by the manufacturer at the time the chips are made.
2. PROMs, or (field) programmable ROMs—contents are programmed by the user with a special PROM programmer as part of the process of fabricating an instrument.
3. EPROMs, or erasable PROMs—contents are again programmed by the user but can be subsequently erased. This permits a unit to be reprogrammed, should changes be desired in the original programming. In contrast, ROMs do not permit changes at all, and PROMs only permit previously unprogrammed bits to be programmed at a later date.

Any one of these three forms of read-only memory will provide reliable system operation. The choice among the three forms is usually clear-cut. EPROMs are the overwhelming choice during the development of an instrument, since this is a time when changes will invariably need to be made. In contrast, ROMs, with their significantly lower cost in large quantities, provide a natural choice to the manufacturer of large quantities of an instrument.

PROMs provide an extremely useful middle ground. Priced with EPROMs, but higher than ROMs, as shown in Fig. 4-1, PROMs present the instrument designer with the following valuable features once the software for the instrument has been developed and is providing satisfactory operation of the instrument:

1 PROMs provide a more reliable instrument than do EPROMs in the sense that the user cannot inadvertently erase any of the instrument's software.
2 PROMs are standard devices, available off the shelf from distributors. In contrast, ROMs must be obtained from a manufacturer, entailing a 6- to 10-week delivery time.
3 PROMs can be purchased, and used, in any quantity. ROMs entail an initial mask charge of $600–$1200 (which is averaged into the cost of each unit in Fig. 4-1).
4 PROMs permit a user to stock only one type of device and to maintain that stock at relatively low levels. ROMs entail the purchasing of at least 100 units at a time and the inventorying of parts for each programming variation used (for example, for each different page of ROM in an instrument).
5 PROMs encourage small modifications of an instrument to meet the needs of relatively small groups of customers. ROMs encourage the development of one instrument for everybody.

Because of these features, the sales of PROMs have overtaken the sales of ROMs.

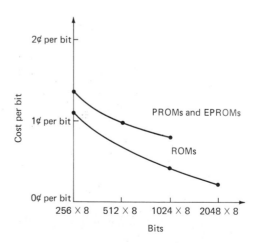

Figure 4-1. *Cost per bit for some typical ROMs, PROMs, and EPROMs (for a lot of 100).*

Address	Contents	
00	3	1
01	4	6
02	F	3
03	B	2
04	5	C
05	1	B
06	0	2

Figure 4-2. ROM contents.

Programming a ROM, PROM, or EPROM begins with a listing of the desired contents, as in Fig. 4-2. If a computer has been involved in the assembly process, this listing may be on paper tape or some such medium. In the case of a ROM, this listing is sent to the manufacturer. For a PROM or EPROM, this listing is used to program the device.

A *PROM programmer** like that shown in Fig. 1-10 permits entry from either the keyboard shown, a paper-tape reader, a computer, or copied from another PROM. This PROM programmer puts successive pulses onto each bit at the recommended rate and recommended voltage† of the PROM manufacturer, as in Fig. 4-3. Between pulses, it measures the output to determine when it crosses a threshold, indicating that it is 50 percent programmed. Then the PROM programmer can easily "overprogram" each bit by a constant percentage. For example, it might count pulses until the threshold is

---

* Used to program both PROMs and EPROMs.
† A voltage specification is usual for EPROMs, whereas a current specification is typical for "fusable-link" bipolar PROMs.

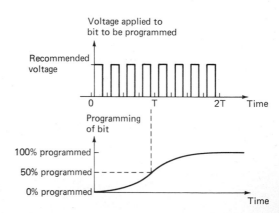

Figure 4-3. Overprogramming of an EPROM bit.

reached and then count back down to zero to double the number of pulses. Every bit is thus thoroughly programmed in a minimum amount of time. This "smart" PROM programmer uses an Intel 4004 microcomputer to provide this and a variety of other features. It even includes a timed ultraviolet source for erasing EPROMs.

For an understanding of the characteristics of a specific EPROM, consider the Intel 2708 EPROM pictured in Fig. 4-4a. In its use as a read-only memory, it has the close-to-ideal characteristics of Fig. 4-4b. Programming this EPROM is a multistep procedure. The device is powered normally, as shown in Fig. 4-4c. Then the device is written into almost exactly as if it were a RAM. When the Write Enable pin is raised to +12 V, the outputs (O1, . . . , O8) become data inputs. Both data and addresses are applied using the normal logic levels of Fig. 4-4b. Then successive addresses are written into, one after another, using the abnormal PROGRAM pulse of Fig. 4-4c as a write pulse. With minimum address and data setup times of only 10 μs, little time is wasted between successive PROGRAM pulses.

The heating of the chip which results during programming is evenly distributed, so as to be nondestructive, by an interesting approach. The programming for each address requires the application of 26 V on the PROGRAM input for a total time in excess of 100 ms. This is broken up by writing into each of the 1024 addresses, one after another, for no longer than 1 ms at a time. The complete programming takes a total of at least 100

(a)

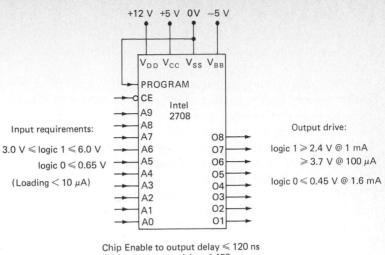

Input requirements:

3.0 V $\leqslant$ logic 1 $\leqslant$ 6.0 V

logic 0 $\leqslant$ 0.65 V

(Loading $<$ 10 μA)

Output drive:

logic 1 $\geqslant$ 2.4 V @ 1 mA

$\geqslant$ 3.7 V @ 100 μA

logic 0 $\leqslant$ 0.45 V @ 1.6 mA

Chip Enable to output delay $\leqslant$ 120 ns
Address to output delay $\leqslant$ 450 ns

(b)

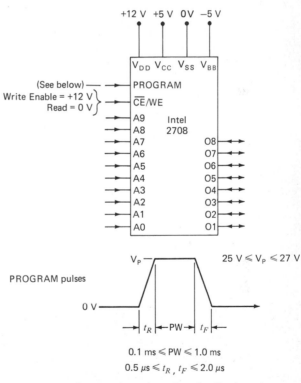

PROGRAM pulses

$25 V \leqslant V_P \leqslant 27 V$

0.1 ms $\leqslant$ PW $\leqslant 1.0$ ms

0.5μs $\leqslant t_R$, $t_F \leqslant 2.0 \mu$s

Programming each word requires N pulses, where

$N \cdot PW \geqslant 100$ ms

PROGRAM input current $\approx$ 10 mA

(c)

Figure 4-4. Intel 2708 EPROM with 1024 × 8 bits. (Intel Corp.) (a) Device, with quartz window removed; (b) read-mode characteristics; (c) programming characteristics.

scans, with each scan involving a "little bit" of writing into each of the 1024 addresses.

This programming procedure might be handled by a microcomputer-based, "smart" PROM programmer or as an auxiliary function of a general-purpose minicomputer system. After every ten scans or so, the Write Enable line can be dropped to 0 V and the contents of each address in the EPROM compared with the desired contents. This comparison can then be used as a basis for providing a certain percentage of overprogramming for each bit (or for determining that certain bits cannot be programmed). Erasing this EPROM requires placing the quartz window which forms the top of the integrated-circuit package within an inch or two of a high-intensity short-wave ultraviolet light for 20–30 min (depending upon the specific lamp used).

4-2 RAMs

The typical structure for the RAMs used with microcomputers is that shown in Fig. 3-22, with $\overline{\text{WRITE}}$, Enable Output, and one or more Chip Enable control inputs. It may have more than eight address lines, meaning that it contains several pages of RAM within one chip. It may have a word length of only 1 bit or of 4 bits, requiring the interconnection of several chips to obtain the desired word size, as in Fig. 4-5. Also it may have data output lines which are distinct from the data input lines. For use with a data bus, corresponding input and output lines need only be tied together.

All the RAMs listed in Fig. 3-29 are *static* RAMs, meaning that they will retain their data reliably (as long as power is maintained) regardless of whether any of the inputs change. In contrast, a *dynamic* RAM places specific requirements upon how often data must be accessed if it is to be retained. For example, Intel's 2107 (4096 × 1) dynamic RAM requires a "read" cycle to be performed on each of the 64 possible combinations of six address lines once every 2 ms. However, these 64 read cycles can be performed with the output actually disabled. Consequently, the refreshing of all dynamic RAM chips can be undertaken with a data selector which switches these six address lines from the address bus to the output of a 6-bit binary counter whenever there is an operation not involving RAM. Then a special refresh input is strobed. The 6-bit counter can be counted with the trailing edge of the strobe pulse.

The reasons that an instrument designer might choose to put up with dynamic RAMs and their refresh requirements are the same reasons which make them valuable to the computer industry:

1 The densest RAMs (that is, most bits per chip) are dynamic RAMs. A large dynamic RAM memory might require one-fourth the volume of a static RAM memory having the same total number of bits.

2 The least expensive RAMs are dynamic RAMs. Of course, because of

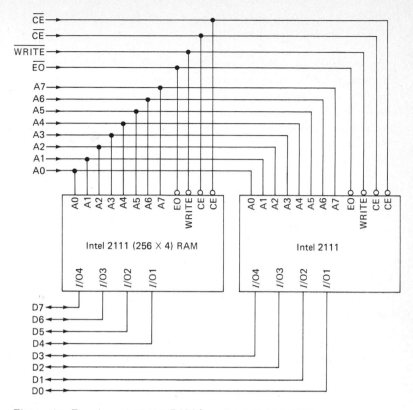

Figure 4-5. Forming a 256 × 8 RAM from two 256 × 4 RAMs.

the refresh circuitry, this economy is insignificant for the small amount of RAM required by many microcomputer-based instruments.

3 The standby-power dissipation when a dynamic RAM is being neither read from nor written into (but only refreshed at the minimum refresh rate) is significantly lower than that of a static RAM having the same number of bits (except in the case of a static CMOS RAM). Again, this will be significant only in large arrays of RAM chips.

The disadvantages of using dynamic RAMs instead of static RAMs are:

1 Refresh circuitry must be provided.
2 A minimum-size RAM memory for an 8-bit microcomputer will require eight RAM chips, since semiconductor-memory manufacturers produce dynamic RAMs with nothing but 1-bit word lengths, to optimize the chip design for a large number of bits.
3 In the event of power failure, the data in a dynamic RAM will be lost unless standby power and memory refresh are both provided. In contrast, a CMOS static RAM can maintain its data with almost negligible

power drain on a standby battery once the CPU has been shut down, as will be discussed in the next section.

To make it easier to use dynamic RAM in systems requiring a large amount of RAM, some microcomputer manufacturers provide a special interface circuit between their CPU and dynamic RAM. For example, the Fairchild F8 microcomputer has two chips for interfacing to standard memory chips, one of which is used with dynamic RAM. The refresh circuitry is included within this chip.

4-3 POWER-STANDBY CAPABILITY

A discouraging moment in the life of a user of an instrument which is set up by keyboard entry occurs when the room lights flicker. All the setup information stored in semiconductor RAM is lost when power is lost to the RAM, even momentarily.

This *volatility* of semiconductor RAM also means that the setup for this keyboard-driven instrument must be repeated each time power is turned on. Whether or not the setup procedure is slow and tedious is irrelevant to the instrument—but not to the user!

In this section, we will deal with a loss of power by shutting down the instrument in an orderly manner. Any data which warrants being saved will be saved. When power is restored, we would like to have the option of restarting the instrument automatically. Alternatively, we would like to restart the instrument in a "reset" state, retaining only setup data. In addition, we want to prevent any wild flailing by the microcomputer (for example, making a printer print garbage) both as it loses power and as it regains power.

A first building block for providing power-standby capability detects when power is failing while there are still some milliseconds of within-tolerance operation left. The same circuit which detects that power is failing can also be used to detect when power is restored. We will want this power-sensing circuit to have the characteristic shown in Fig. 4-6. The detection of power failure and restoration is shown for a microcomputer requiring the same 5.0 V ± 10 percent power-supply voltage as TTL logic. Its output is a logic level which is a logic 1 when power is up and logic 0 while power is down. The *hysteresis* in the characteristic is vital for handling a "brown-out" in which power just barely dips down to the point where power loss is detected and then rises again. The hysteresis provides time for the power-standby circuitry to go through a complete shutdown sequence of events without the premature interruption of being told to restart operations.

The power-sensing circuit of Fig. 4-7 provides the operation shown in Fig. 4-6. The voltage comparator shown is unusual in that it will provide

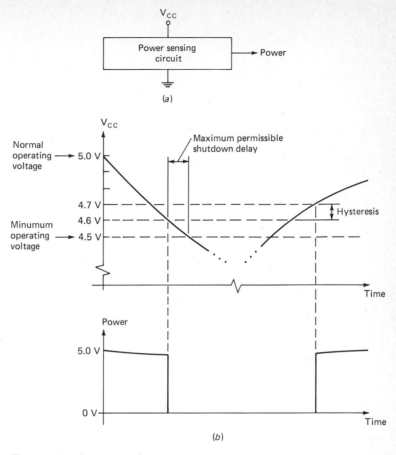

Figure 4-6. *Operation of a power-sensing circuit.* (a) *Symbol;* (b) *circuit operation.*

rated operation over the broad power-supply voltage shown and adequate operation for our purposes as V_{cc}, the power-supply voltage, shuts all the way down to 0 V. The zener diode looks like a 2.4-V battery as long as V_{cc} is greater than 2.4 V, making

$$V_x = 2.4 \text{ V} \qquad \text{for } V_{cc} \geqslant 2.4 \text{ V}$$

The zener diode looks like an open circuit for V_{cc} less than 2.4 V, giving

$$V_x = V_{cc} \qquad \text{for } V_{cc} \leqslant 2.4 \text{ V}$$

In contrast, V_y is proportional to V_{cc}. The proportionality constant is dependent upon Power, the comparator output, because of the feedback resistor R_h. Thus

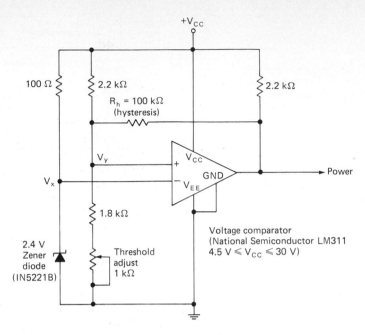

Figure 4-7. *Power-sensing circuit.*

$$V_y = K_{ph} \cdot V_{cc} \qquad \text{when Power is high}$$

and $\qquad V_y = K_{pl} \cdot V_{cc} \qquad$ when Power is low

where $\qquad K_{ph} > K_{pl}$

It is this resistor R_h which gives rise to the hysteresis in the characteristic.

In the power-up condition, V_y is greater than V_x and Power = logic 1 (actually V_{cc}). As V_{cc} decreases, V_y decreases toward V_x. When it comes within approximately 1 mV of V_x, the comparator output begins to drop. The feedback resistor R_h then accentuates the dropping of V_y and causes the comparator output to snap to logic 0. This snap action helps ensure the unambiguous interpretation of Power, the circuit output.

A second building block for providing power-standby capability is the shutdown circuit shown in Fig. 4-8. This circuit will use a signal from the microcomputer, $\overline{\text{Enable Shutdown}}$, to specify *when* shutdown can occur *after* a power loss has been detected by Power, the output of the comparator circuit. When power is restored, operation will resume immediately as $\overline{\text{Shutdown}}$ goes high. The state of the $\overline{\text{Enable Shutdown}}$ signal from the microcomputer is ignored.

A third building block is a CMOS RAM with battery backup, as shown in Fig. 4-9. When $\overline{\text{Shutdown}}$ goes low, the RAM will be disabled for further writing, as one of its chip enables (CE) is driven low. As the power-supply

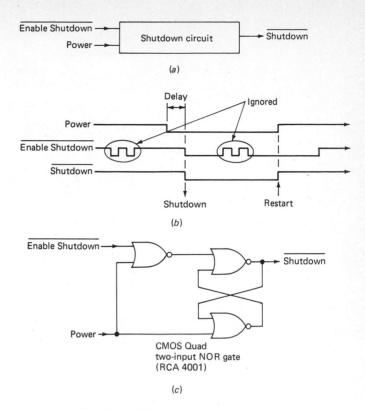

Figure 4-8. Shutdown circuit. (a) Symbol; (b) circuit operation; (c) circuit.

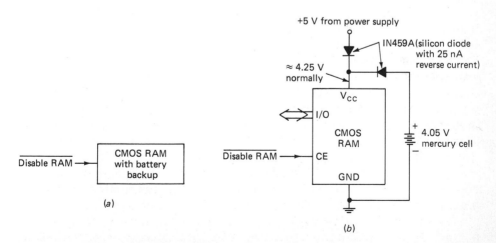

Figure 4-9. Battery backup for CMOS RAM. (a) Symbol; (b) circuit.

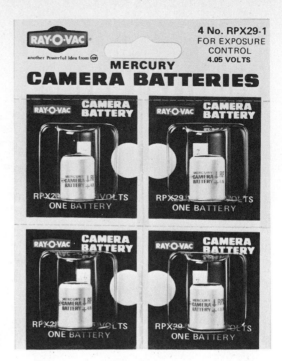

Figure 4-10. 4.05-V mercury cells. (Ray-O-Vac Division of ESB Incorporated.)

voltage on the CMOS RAM drops further, the diode in series with the mercury cell begins to conduct. The RAM supply voltage stabilizes at about 3.5 V. This circuit assumes that the CMOS RAM will retain its data with a supply voltage below 3.5 V (for example, the Intel 5101L will retain data down to 2.0 V).

As an example of the backup capability provided, a 256 × 8 CMOS RAM consisting of two Intel 5101L (256 × 4) RAM chips will draw less than a maximum of 30 µA, and "typically" 0.4 µA, in standby. To meet this demand, the small* 4.05-V mercury cell shown in Fig. 4-10 with its 190-milliampere-hour rating can supply a steady 11 µA at an almost constant voltage for a period of 2 years, the shelf life of the cell.

A fourth building block in providing power-standby capability is the microcomputer's "reset" or "restart" mechanism. Some microcomputers look at the logic level on a reset input to the CPU and reset continuously as long as this input is enabled. Other microcomputers look for a voltage transition (for example, a rising edge) on a reset input to initiate a specific start-up sequence. In either case, this automatic initialization terminates as the CPU goes to a specific location in ROM to fetch the first instruction of our program. We will use the Power signal from the power-sensing circuit of Fig.

* 0.5-in. diameter × 0.625-in. length.

4-7 to do the resetting in either case above. This is done in lieu of an independent start-up circuit, like that of Fig. 3-12.

If the microcomputer resets on a voltage transition, it is likely to flail about wildly as the power-supply voltage drops below specification. It will do so again as power is restored, before the supply voltage has risen within specification. Disabling the CMOS RAM protects its contents. If there is a concern over these wild flailings creating "irrational" behavior of devices tied to the output ports, the output ports can be disabled as well. Alternatively, some microcomputers have a "stop" input on their clock chip. In this case, Shutdown can be used to stop the clock.

Our fifth and final building block is the power-on switch detect circuit of Fig. 4-11. The double-pole, double-throw switch shown is the power switch for the instrument. During the microcomputer's initialization routine, the Switched On output of this circuit can be used as a flag to the microcomputer. If it is equal to logic 0, then power is coming on because the power switch has just been turned on. If it is equal to logic 1, then the power switch has been on for some time, but no ac power has been present at the power plug. This circuit is useful if we want to draw a distinction between these two cases. In the first case we may want to present a "reset" instrument to the user. In the second case we may want to continue with the same operations which were going on when power failed. Incidentally, the 22-MΩ resistors in this circuit not only provide the time constant which makes the circuit work; they also protect the mercury cell (and the

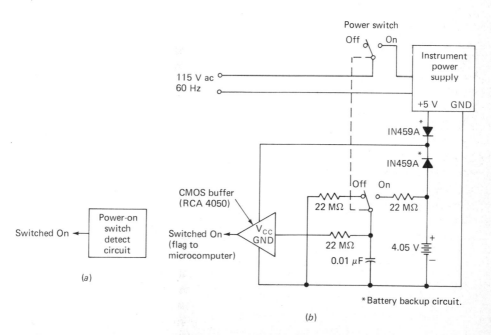

Figure 4-11. Power-on switch detect circuit. (a) Symbol; (b) circuit.

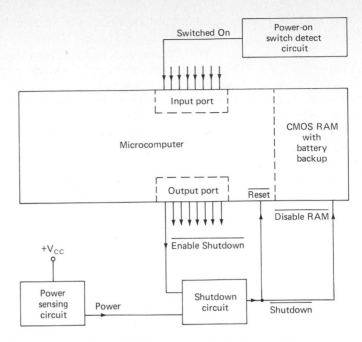

Figure 4-12. "Save RAM" power-standby interconnections.

CMOS RAM it backs up) and the CMOS buffer against an accidental short between the terminals of the power switch with its 115 V ac.

With these building blocks, we are ready to implement a "Save RAM" form of power-standby capability, the interconnection for which is pictured in Fig. 4-12. This capability will save the contents of the CMOS RAM, but nothing else. When power is restored, the microcomputer can use the Switched On flag of Fig. 4-11 to decide whether to start from scratch or to begin a new cycle of its operation. This approach assumes that the instrument's operation is cyclic and that it can afford the loss of that part of the cycle in progress when power died (to say nothing of all the cycles which did not take place while power was down).

The $\overline{\text{Enable Shutdown}}$ signal from the microcomputer is used to prevent shutdown at inopportune times lasting as long as the "maximum permissible shutdown delay" of Fig. 4-6. This line will normally be low, permitting Power to cause shutdown the moment a power failure is detected. If the microcomputer is about to initiate a routine which will result in the change of several words in the CMOS RAM, it can prevent Power from causing a shutdown in the middle of this routine by driving $\overline{\text{Enable Shut-down}}$ high at the beginning of the routine and low again at the end of it.

When an instrument is stopped in the middle of its operation because of a power failure, it may be difficult to decide what action to take when power is restored. While the "Save RAM" approach may be best, it is not the only possibility. A "Save state" approach saves not only the RAM contents but also all the CPU register contents. Then when power is restored, all register contents will be identical to their previous values. The CPU can pick up with the very next instruction which would have been executed when power failed.

In order to do this, we must have a microcomputer in which all the CPU registers can be moved out to the CMOS RAM. This includes accumulator, carry bit (or flag bits), scratchpad registers, and the contents of the stack or of the stack pointer (if there is one). Of course, for a CMOS CPU like the RCA COSMAC this step is unnecessary, provided the CPU retains its register contents when the clock is stopped (as is true of the COSMAC). Rather, the CPU must only be put on battery backup also and Power used to stop the clock.

An additional desirable (but not absolutely necessary) capability for picking up exactly where we left off is provided by *nonmaskable interrupt* capability. This type of interrupt permits the microcomputer to be interrupted *regardless* of the state of the Enable Interrupt flipflop. Some microcomputers provide this capability directly with a separate input (for example, Motorola 6800, Rockwell PPS-8, Fairchild F8). Others provide the equivalent capability of enabling at least one interrupt while others are disabled (for example, Intel 8080 when used with its 8259 Programmable Interrupt Controller). Finally, *any* interruptible microcomputer can enable interrupts internally and then use one line of an output port to control the disabling of all but one interrupt signal.

Given these two capabilities, we can use the interconnection of Fig. 4-13 to provide "Save state" power-standby capability. In contrast with the "Save RAM" approach, this time the Enable Shutdown line is kept high all the time. When a power failure occurs, Power will initiate a nonmaskable interrupt. Its service routine moves all CPU registers out to the CMOS RAM and *then* drives the Enable Shutdown line low. From this point on, operation is the same as for Fig. 4-12 until after power is restored and Switched On has been checked. If Switched On is high, then Enable Shutdown is driven high, the CPU registers are restored, and a return from interrupt instruction is executed to load the program counter with the instruction address which was set aside when the nonmaskable interrupt occurred (when power failure was first detected).

For an instrument which executes a variety of tasks, we may want to execute any one of several different kinds of restarting tasks when power is restored, depending on where in the program the operation was stopped by power failure. For example, consider an instrument whose normal operation involves the cyclic repetition of many tasks, as in Fig. 4-14. The use of PFAIL (a word in RAM), as shown, will provide the restarting routine with a pointer which says where among all the tasks it stopped. Each Increment PFAIL instruction is inserted in the program to tell the restarting routine to do something different. Such a pointer might be used with either the "Save RAM" or the "Save state" approach for providing power-standby capability.

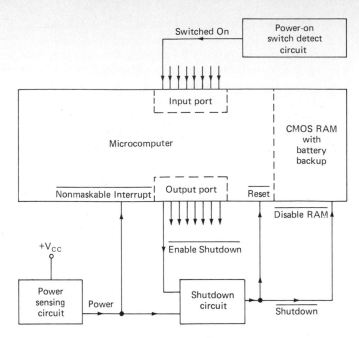

Figure 4-13. "Save state" power-standby interconnections.

4-4 FLOPPY DISKS

A storage medium which combines bulk storage, fast access (as measured by human response times), nonvolatility (that is, data retention when power is lost), and reasonably low cost is the floppy disk. In addition, since the disks (or "diskettes") themselves are both removable and low in cost, this medium facilitates insertion of extensive setup information and data files into an instrument.

To understand how the use of a floppy disk can augment the capability of an instrument, we will look first at the characteristics of a floppy-disk drive itself. Then we will look at the characteristics of a floppy-disk controller and its interaction with a microcomputer.

Floppy-disk data storage was created by IBM and is used in their 3740 data entry system. As a consequence, IBM has established a de facto standard, both for the floppy disks themselves and for the formatting of data upon the disk. Many manufacturers of floppy-disk drives, like that in Fig. 4-15, have designed their drive for compatibility with the IBM diskette. Then it is up to the designer of the floppy-disk controller to decide whether or not to use IBM's data format.

Compatibility brings with it the opportunity to transfer data directly from an instrument into a large computer. It means compatibility not only

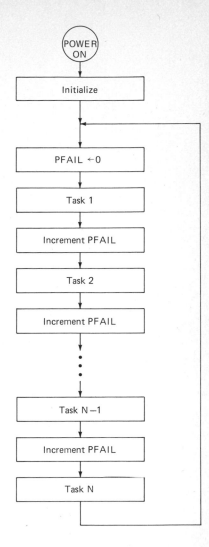

Figure 4-14. Formation of a PFAIL pointer.

with IBM equipment but also with all other equipment which utilizes the IBM standard.

Incompatibility with the IBM format permits more data to be stored on a disk. A little less than 2 million data bits can be stored on an IBM-compatible disk in the form of almost a quarter of a million 8-bit bytes. In contrast, a special format permits about 3 million data bits to be stored. The reason for this discrepancy will become evident shortly, when we discuss formatting of data on the disk.

The floppy disk itself is an oxide-coated Mylar disk, 7.8 in. in diameter and permanently packaged in an 8 × 8-in. plastic jacket. The drive clamps the center of the disk and rotates it inside the stationary jacket. A slot in the

Figure 4-15. Floppy-disk drive. (California Computer Products, Inc.—Cal-Comp.)

jacket allows a read-write head to have access to the 77 circular tracks used by an IBM-compatible drive. With 48 tracks per inch, adjacent tracks are spaced approximately 0.02 in. apart and are 0.012 in. wide. Another hole in the jacket permits optical sensing of an index hole on the disk which marks the starting point for each track. A reflective tab is mounted on the jacket of a disk which can be written into. The "write" electronics of the drive are automatically disabled if this reflective tab is not present.

The floppy disk in the drive of Fig. 4-15 rotates at a speed of 360 rpm. Data is transferred to or from the disk 1 bit at a time at a nominal rate of 250,000 bits per second, or 1 bit every 4 μs. This occurs after the read-write head is positioned at the desired location on a specific track, with the head lowered into contact with the disk for data transfer. It indicates how fast a record will be transferred to or from the microcomputer once it has been accessed. That is, successive 8-bit words are transferred every 32 μs.

With each revolution of the disk taking 167 ms, it takes an average of 83 ms to access a new record on the same track. However, if a record is on a randomly located track, the access time can be dominated by the time required to move to the required track, at 6 ms per track, plus the 16 ms required to lower the head onto the disk. Even in the worst case, this total access time is only 0.6 s.

During writing, a 16-bit "cyclic redundancy check character" (CRCC) is appended to each record. This consists of the remainder left over after dividing the 1s and 0s making up the record by a specific 17-bit binary number. The division is carried out bit by bit using "modulo-2" division, which can be implemented solely with a shift register and exclusive-OR gates and which provides good error-detection characteristics. Subsequent reading of the record will include dividing both the record and the extra CRCC bits by the same 17-bit binary number. If no errors have occurred, the remainder from this operation will be zero. On the other hand, if any errors have occurred, it is extremely likely that a nonzero remainder will result from this division.*

The maximum error-rate specification of 1 error per 10^9 bits read is reduced to a maximum specification of 1 error per 10^{12} bits read, if error detection is followed by 10 more attempts at reading. By reading and checking each record after it is written, the user can thus extend the reliability by a factor of 1000 or so.

Because the read-write head actually contacts the floppy disk, both head wear and disk wear take place. The interface minimizes this wear by retracting the head except when a data transfer takes place. The head life is specified for 10,000 hours of head-to-disk contact. If the disk drive spent one-fifth of a day every day transferring data, this would yield a head life of 5 calendar years. After this time, the error rate could be expected to rise above the specified values. The disk wear resulting from head-to-disk contact yields a disk-life specification of 1 million passes per track. This is extrapolated by the manufacturer to a disk life of 2 years in a "heavy-duty" application.

This reliability information is provided to give some feel for the quality of a memory medium which is significantly less reliable than the *floating-head* disk drives used in more expensive minicomputer-based systems. There, the disk turns sufficiently fast to permit the read-write head to float slightly above the surface of the disk on a thin layer of air, thus eliminating the wear resulting from head-to-disk contact. On the other hand, a floppy-disk unit is significantly more reliable than a paper-tape, cassette-tape, or cartridge-tape unit.

To the controller which interfaces it to a microcomputer, the floppy-disk drive of Fig. 4-15 consists of the inputs and outputs shown in Fig. 4-16. The design of an instrument employing several floppy-disk drives is facilitated by the Select input, which enables all inputs and outputs. Thus all the other input and output lines on all drives are tied together and to the controller. The controller enables one drive at a time using the $\overline{\text{Select}}$ lines. All outputs are *open-collector*,† and only the selected drive can pull an output line low. Otherwise the line is pulled high by a pull-up resistor.

The $\overline{\text{Ready}}$ line is the only line which is not disabled when $\overline{\text{Select}}$ goes high. It indicates that the floppy disk is inserted correctly, that the door is closed, and that the dc voltages and the disk speed are correct. It goes high anytime any of these conditions are *not* met.

Since track positioning is achieved with a stepper motor,‡ the inputs are incremental in nature. Each $\overline{\text{Step}}$ pulse moves the read-write head in-

---

* Both the generation of the CRCC bits during writing and the division and testing of the remainder during reading can be implemented with Motorola's MC8503 universal polynominal generator, a single 14-pin IC. See Prob. 4-15.

† See Prob. 4-3.

‡ Discussed in Sec. 5-7.

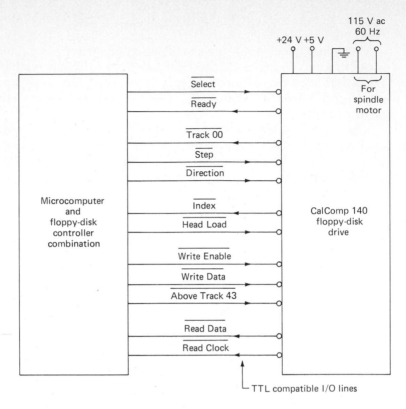

Figure 4-16. Floppy-disk drive I/O.

ward to the next higher track number, if the $\overline{\text{Direction}}$ input is high. If $\overline{\text{Direction}}$ is low, a $\overline{\text{Step}}$ pulse will move the head outward to the next lower track number. When track 00 is reached, the $\overline{\text{Track 00}}$ output goes low and further outward stepping is inhibited. When power is first turned on, the head can be stepped out until the position reference provided by the $\overline{\text{Track}}$ $\overline{00}$ output is reached. Thereafter, desired track positions can be attained by counting from one position to the next.

The leading edge of the 4-μs pulse on the $\overline{\text{Index}}$ output represents the beginning of a track. It is derived from the index hole in the floppy disk and therefore occurs once per revolution. $\overline{\text{Head Load}}$ moves the read-write head into contact with the disk.

To write data onto the floppy disk, $\overline{\text{Write Enable}}$ must be taken low. Then the write current reverses direction on the trailing (rising) edge of each $\overline{\text{Write Data}}$ pulse, causing a magnetic-flux change to be written onto the disk. Because the speed of the disk can vary somewhat (360 rpm ± 2.4 percent), it is necessary to write both data and clock information onto the disk. The commonly used "double-frequency recording" technique shown in Fig. 4-17 produces one flux change at the start of each clock period. It produces

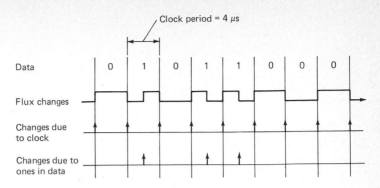

Figure 4-17. Double-frequency recording.

another flux change in the middle of the clock period *if* the data equals logic 1 during that clock period.

The Write Data input to the drive which will produce the flux changes of Fig. 4-17 can be generated using the circuit of Fig. 4-18*a*. A 1-MHz (megahertz) clock (four times the data frequency) counts the "2-bit Gray code counter" shown in Fig. 4-18*a* to create a 4-μs interval having four equal parts. The controller for the drive takes successive 8-bit words of data from the microcomputer (using DMA control) and converts them to serial form using the Gray code counter output A as a "Write Clock" input to shift successive bits out on a "Data" output. One AND gate then generates a "clock pulse" at the beginning of every 4-μs interval. A second AND gate generates a "data pulse" in the middle of every 4-μs interval *if* Data = 1 during that interval. These are ORed together and inverted to generate Write Data.

The controller makes the floppy-disk drive input labeled Above Track 43 in Fig. 4-16 go low whenever the read-write head is positioned at one of the inner tracks, numbered 44 to 76. It is used by the drive as a signal to decrease the write current for these tracks, to assure IBM compatibility.

To read data from a selected drive (for which the read-write head has been moved to the desired track and lowered onto the disk), the Write Enable input must be taken high. Then a *data-separator* circuit in the drive will look at the flux changes on the disk representing both clock and data, as in Fig. 4-17, and separate this into a Read Data output and a Read Clock output. Data separation simplifies the controller circuitry.

These two outputs can have any one of several optional formats. For applications using IBM 3740-type address marks (in which some of the "clock" flux changes are omitted to provide a unique address), a "phase-lock loop" (PLL) data-separator circuit is used and the outputs have the format shown in Fig. 4-19*a*. The controller accumulates the bits read from *both* the Read Clock and Read Data outputs into 8-bit bytes. Thus the 8-bit output shown in Fig. 4-19*a* would form a data byte of 58 (hexadecimal) and a clock byte of FF. Clock bytes are always equal to FF except when an address mark is created on the disk, as will be discussed shortly.

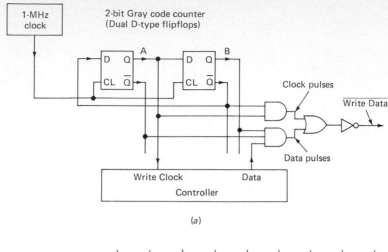

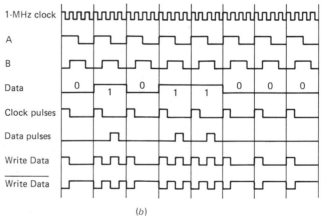

Figure 4-18.   *Generation of* Write Data.   (a) *Circuit;* (b) *timing diagram.*

For applications not requiring IBM compatibility, a simpler "one-shot" data separator* takes advantage of a flux-change format on the disk in which the "clock" flux changes are never omitted.   The resultant output format is shown in Fig. 4-19b.   With this format, the rising Read Clock transitions can be used by the controller to clock the data into a shift register, as in Fig. 4-19c, so as to reconstruct 8-bit words in a particularly simple way.

Before discussing how a controller for a floppy-disk drive operates, it is appropriate to consider the IBM 3740 formatting of a disk.† As mentioned earlier, the disk is divided into 77 circular tracks.   A track is further divided

* Refer to Prob. 4-17.
† Refer to IBM Publication GA21-9182-0 for more specific details.

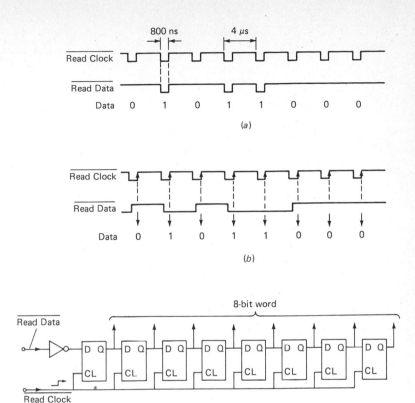

Figure 4-19. $\overline{\text{Read Data}}$ and $\overline{\text{Read Clock}}$ formats. (a) Format using PLL data separator for IBM compatibility; (b) format using simpler one-shot data separator; (c) serial to parallel conversion using the format in (b).

into 26 *sectors*, each of which contains 128 bytes of data (8 bits per byte). In addition, each sector contains 60 other bytes, as shown in Fig. 4-20a, divided into an identification portion and a data portion, with gaps after each to permit some reaction time for the microcomputer to make a decision on what to do next. For example, a gap of 17 bytes will last $17 \times 8 \times 4 = 544$ μs. The gaps also provide the slack needed when writing onto the disk so that newly written data in one sector does not run over into the beginning of the next sector if the disk rotates slightly faster than its nominal speed (but within the speed tolerance of 360 rpm $\pm$ 2.4 percent).

Designing an instrument for IBM compatibility presupposes that the commonly available *initialized* disks will be used. Such a disk is purchased with the address marks and track/sector identification shown in Fig. 4-20 already properly recorded for each sector. In addition, only tracks 00 to

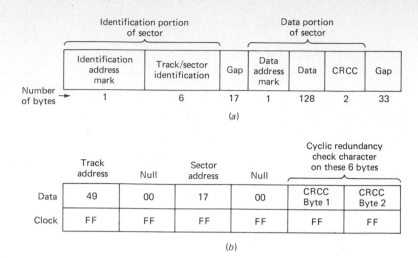

Figure 4-20. IBM 3740 disk format for sectors. (a) Overall sector format—188 bytes (8 bits per byte); (b) the 6 bytes making up the identification portion of the sector, shown for track 49, sector 17.

73 are used. The controller looks for the beginning of a sector by looking for the Identification Address Mark (an 8-bit byte for which Data = FE, Clock = C7). Then it verifies the track address and sector address, including a cyclic redundancy check to help ensure reliable reading.

Verifying the track address in this way enhances the reliability of operation. If the mechanism for stepping from track to track malfunctions, the track address read from the disk will remain unchanged, providing malfunction indication as we build self-test capability into the instrument.

After verifying track and sector addresses, the controller waits for the Data Address Mark (an 8-bit byte for which Data = FB, Clock = C7). Then it either reads or writes 128 bytes of data. When writing, it appends two cyclic redundancy check character (CRCC) bytes to these 128 data bytes, to provide for subsequent error-detection capability on this data. During a read operation, all 130 bytes are used to form a 16-bit remainder (which should be zero) for the cyclic redundancy check.

The IBM format for a complete track is shown in Fig. 4-21. As men-

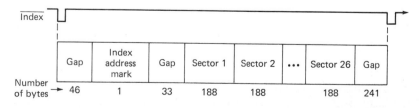

Figure 4-21. IBM 3740 disk format for tracks.

tioned earlier, the $\overline{\text{Index}}$ output of the drive consists of a pulse occurring once per revolution of the disk when the index hole in the disk is optically sensed. The leading edge of this pulse marks the beginning of the track. The beginning of the track is also marked, 46 byte-times later, by an Index Address Mark (an 8-bit byte for which Data = FC, Clock = D7). Following another gap, the 26 sectors occur. These are followed by another gap at the end of the track.

    Data can be stored in any of the sectors on any of tracks 01 to 73. Using IBM's terminology, each sector contains one *record*, consisting of up to 128 bytes of data. A *data set* consists of any number of consecutive records, extending over any number of tracks. Track 00 is used as a table of contents for the disk. As shown in Fig. 4-22, sector 07 of track 00 is used to provide an alphanumeric label for the disk as a whole so that an instrument or computer can search through several floppy-disk drives to see if any of them contains a disk with a certain label. This permits an instrument employing several drives to be independent of which drive is used for reading which information. Sectors 08 to 26 are used to label data sets and to specify their *extent* (that is, the addresses of the first and last sectors of each data set). The format information shown in Fig. 4-22 represents the minimum information needed, with all options left unused (for example, write protect;

Figure 4-22. IBM 3740 Disk Format for Track 00

Sector number	Use
01–06	Reserved
07	Labeling information for the entire floppy disk
08	Labeling information for one data set
09–26	Labeling information for up to 18 more data sets

(a) Sector usage

Byte number	Contents	
1	V	Used to identify that this sector is used as a "volume
2	O	label"
3	L	(as it should be, for IBM compatibility)
4	1	
5		
6		
7		User-defined disk label
8		(one to six alphanumeric characters, starting in byte 5)
9		
10		
11–79	blank	
80	W	(indicates that IBM standard labels are used)
81–128	blank	

(b) Labeling of disk in sector 07

Figure 4-22. (*Continued*)

1	H	Identifies that this sector is being used for a data-set
2	D	label (unused sectors are initialized to DDR1 to iden-
3	R	tify that they are unused)
4	1	
5	blank	
6		
7		
8		
9		User-defined name of data set
10		
11		
12		
13		
14–24	blank	
25	1	Tells the system that all 128 data bytes in each sector
26	2	contain actual data
27	8	
28	blank	
29		Track number
30		
31	0	First sector of data set
32		Sector number
33		
34	blank	
35		Track number
36		
37	0	Last sector of data set
38		Sector number
39		
39		
40–128	blank	

(*c*) *Labeling of data sets in sectors 08–26*

creation date). From this format information, it is evident that an IBM-compatible instrument not only must create data sets on tracks 01 to 73 but also must identify them on track 00.

As a specific example of the interactions between a floppy-disk drive and a microcomputer, we will consider Rockwell's 42-pin LSI chip floppy-disk controller, shown in Fig. 4-23. This is just one of the peripheral controllers which make the PPS-8 family of chips unusually powerful. The PPS-8 microcomputer handles floppy-disk selection, control of track position, and head loading under program control, through its I/O ports, as in Fig. 4-24. The $\overline{\text{Ready}}$ line is used to generate an interrupt.

The transfer of data is handled one *record* (that is, the 128 bytes within one sector) at a time under DMA control. When the transfer is complete, the

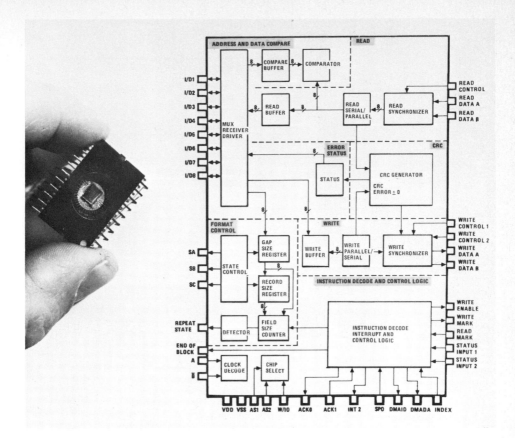

Figure 4-23.   Floppy-disk controller.   (Rockwell International Corp.)

controller interrupts the CPU.   After a "read," the CPU checks the status of the controller to determine whether an error was detected (that is, whether a nonzero remainder resulted from the CRC calculation).   If so, the read operation might be repeated until no error is detected, aborting with a malfunction indication after 10 unsuccessful tries.   After a "write," the CPU performs a "read " in order to carry out a CRC check on the newly written data. Again, suitable error routines are handled under program control.

The actual transfer of a record involves the use of not one, but two, DMA channels.   One channel handles the RAM location to be used for the source, or the destination, of the 128 bytes of data.   The other channel picks up 15 RAM words which are parameters used to describe the format of the identification information within a sector.   In this manner, either the IBM format of Fig. 4-20 or an alternative format can be used.   This DMA channel must be reinitialized as it enters each new sector.   Using the "record cycle mode" discussed at the end of Sec. 3-8, this can be done automatically.

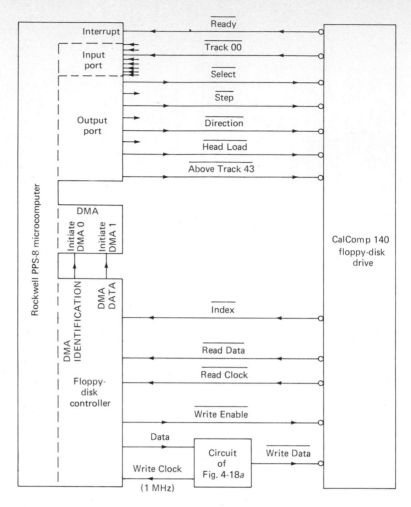

Figure 4-24. Structure of floppy-disk interface.

Then, as each new sector passes under the read-write head, the controller picks up the parameters it needs to make a comparison. For example, before getting to the Identification Address Mark, the controller will have read a word from RAM having the same data pattern. After a match with the address mark occurs, another DMA cycle reads in the desired track number from RAM for the next comparison. This continues through the entire iden-tification portion of the sector. If the wrong sector has been identified, the controller tries again on the next sector. When the correct sector has been identified during a read operation, the controller waits for a match with the Data Address Mark and then initiates a data transfer between RAM and each successive byte on the disk, using the other DMA channel. For a write operation, the controller generates a gap, Data Address Mark, data record, CRCC bytes, and the final gap. That is, it fills out the complete sector following the identification portion of the sector, as illustrated in Fig. 4-20a.

Because the CPU is idled during each DMA transfer for 4 μs (in the PPS-8 microcomputer operating at its maximum clock rate), we can determine the percentage of time during which the CPU is idled by these DMA operations (after the DMA channels have been set up). The identification check for each sector requires the DMA transfer of 15 words from RAM, taking 60 μs. The duration of an IBM sector is

$$188 \text{ bytes} \times 8 \text{ bits per byte} \times 4 \text{ } \mu\text{s per bit} = 6016 \text{ } \mu\text{s} \approx 6 \text{ ms}$$

Therefore, an unsuccessful identification of a sector idles the CPU for only 1 percent of this 6-ms interval. A successful identification is followed by the DMA transfer of 128 words to or from RAM, idling the CPU for an additional 512 μs, for a total of 572 μs. Consequently, a successful identification of a sector idles the CPU for just under 10 percent of this 6-ms interval, leaving 90 percent of its time available for other activities.

PROBLEMS

4-1 EPROM compatibility. Consider the use of the EPROM, whose specifications are given in Fig. 4-4, with a specific microcomputer. Alternatively, use another EPROM for which you have data. Are the input and output voltages and current characteristics compatible with those for the microcomputer's address bus, data bus, and READ lines? Explain.

4-2 Bipolar PROM use. The smallest (that is, fewest bits) PROM available is a 32 × 8 bipolar, fusable-link PROM packaged in a 16-pin DIP. An example is the Signetics 82S123 PROM shown in Fig. P4-1. This

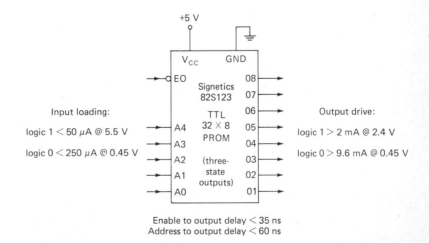

Figure P4-1.

PROM might be used to "personalize" an instrument for different groups of users with the storage of up to 32 constants.

(a) For a specific microcomputer, how many of these PROMs can be hung on the address bus/data bus structure, assuming no other load on the bus?

(b) What is the implication of having only five address lines when using this PROM in the configuration of Fig. 3-19?

4-3 Bipolar PROMs with open-collector outputs. Some bipolar PROMs have open-collector outputs. They can pull an output line low, but look like an open circuit when the output is supposed to go high. Consequently, the bus lines driven by the outputs must have pull-up resistors attached, as shown in Fig. P4-2.

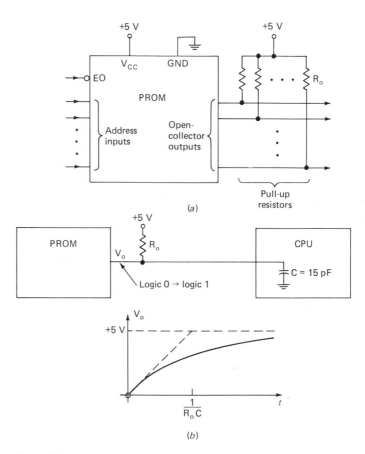

Figure P4-2.

(a) For a specific microcomputer, what is the minimum resistance which these pull-up resistors can have such that the CPU can still drive the bus? Assume that the CPU has no other load (and that the open-collector PROM is disabled).

(b) What is the maximum resistance which these pull-up resistors can have such that they can still drive the (resistive) load presented by the CPU? Assume that the CPU is the only load for the PROM.

(c) What is the maximum resistance which these pull-up resistors can have such that they can drive the capacitive load of wiring and CPU input (represented as a total of 15 pF in the figure) and have the voltage rise to a logic 1, as seen by the CPU, within 200 ns after a PROM output changes from logic 0 to logic 1?

4-4 RAMs with separate I/O lines. Figure P4-3 illustrates the Intel 5101 (256 × 4) CMOS RAM with its data inputs DIi and its data outputs DOi. Show the interconnections between two 5101s to achieve a 256 × 8 RAM for connecting to an address bus/data bus structure.

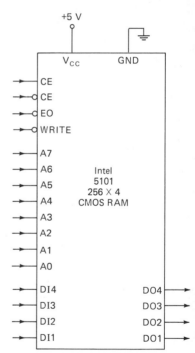

Figure P4-3.

4-5 Dynamic RAM. For a specific microcomputer, what CPU signal or signals could be used for determining when memory is not being accessed so that a refresh cycle can take place? Assuming the refreshing takes 500 ns, does this slow down the microcomputer?

4-6 Dynamic RAM. Consider a specific microcomputer which has a special chip for interfacing to dynamic RAM.

(a) What characteristics must a specific RAM meet in order to be usable with this chip?

(b) Are any other circuit elements needed (for example, transistors for switching heavy currents)? If so, show a typical circuit configuration.

4-7 Power-sensing circuit. In the power-sensing circuit illustrated in Fig. 4-7, the input impedance to the voltage comparator is hundreds of megohms.

(a) For the circuit values shown and Power $= V_{cc}$, what value of the threshold adjust potentiometer will make $V_y = V_x$, when $V_{cc} = +4.6$ V? This is the condition leading to the lower threshold of Fig. 4-6.

(b) With the values shown in Fig. 4-7 and with the value determined in part (a), what will the upper threshold voltage be?

4-8 Shutdown circuit. The circuit of Fig. 4-8 employs two NOR gates in a "latch" circuit whose output $\overline{\text{Shutdown}}$ will remain in either of two states if both its inputs are low. Which state it is in depends upon which input went low last. The truth table for a NOR gate is shown in Fig. P4-4. "H" stands for a high, or logic 1, signal and "L" stands for a low, or logic 0, signal. Denoting the output of the NOR gate on the left as the variable N, sketch N in the timing diagram of Fig. 4-8b and verify that the circuit performs as indicated.

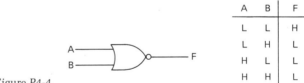

A	B	F
L	L	H
L	H	L
H	L	L
H	H	L

Figure P4-4.

4-9 Battery backup circuit. The circuit of Fig. 4-9b includes two silicon diodes having very low reverse current. How does the low reverse current of each diode serve a useful purpose in the circuit?

4-10 CMOS RAM. Consider a specific CMOS RAM for which you have data at hand.

(a) At how low a power-supply voltage will it retain data? Is this satisfactory, given the circuit of Fig. 4-9, or must modifications be made to that circuit? If modifications are necessary, how would you change it?

(b) What is its maximum standby current?

(c) Does this standby current depend upon whether or not the RAM is disabled?

4-11 Power-on switch detect circuit. As discussed in Prob. 3-4, if the input to a CMOS device rises above the power-supply voltage for the device, input current will flow through the diode-protection circuit.

(a) Does this factor affect the load on the mercury cell of Fig. 4-11 when power is lost?

(b) A typical input current to a (powered) CMOS buffer is 10 pA. What is the implication of this upon the circuit of Fig. 4-11 during normal operation of an instrument?

4-12 "Save RAM" power-standby capability. The circuit of Fig. 4-12 provides a variety of possibilities for power-standby operation. Describe possible ways in which an instrument might be designed to behave, in response to a power failure and power restoration, if the following occurred:

(a) The power-on switch detect circuit is removed.

(b) Both the power-on switch detect circuit and the shutdown circuit are removed.

4-13 "Save state" power-standby capability. With its ability to pick up where it left off in executing the program of an instrument, the "Save state" approach to power standby would seem to have less need of a shutdown circuit than the "Save RAM" approach. It is in its interactions with devices external to the microcomputer that the shutdown circuit becomes especially useful. Give an example of some aspect of the operation of an instrument which might benefit from the use of the shutdown circuit in conjunction with use of the "Save state" approach.

4-14 PFAIL pointer. The use of a pointer such as this provides another approach to the problem alluded to in Prob. 4-13. Give an example of some aspect of the operation of an instrument which might benefit from this approach, and which cannot use the shutdown circuit as an alternative.

4-15 Cyclic redundancy check (CRC) circuit. Motorola's MC8503 universal polynomial generator can both generate a remainder for writing on a disk and check for a zero remainder while reading from a disk. While this circuit can utilize any one of six "polynomials," Fig. P4-5 shows the control inputs, Data Input, Data Output, and All Zeros output for one of these.

(a) Explain the sequence of control inputs which would be used in a floppy-disk controller during a write operation.

(b) Do the same for a read operation.

(c) If no error occurs during a read operation, the shift register outputs (Q1, . . . , Q16) just before the last 16 shifts are equal to the next 16 bits on Data Input. Explain why the last 16 shifts then clear the shift register outputs to all zeros.

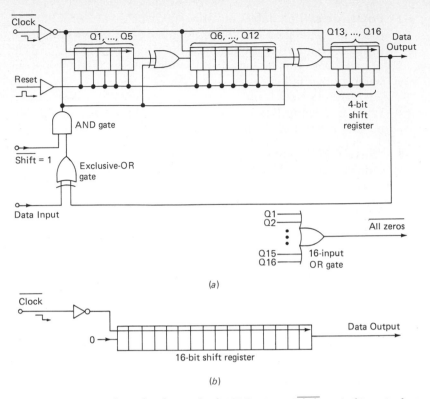

(a)

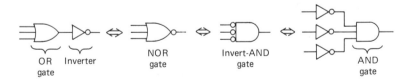

(b)

Figure P4-5. (a) Cyclic redundancy check (CRC) circuit ($\overline{\text{Shift}}$ = 1); (b) equivalent circuit with $\overline{\text{Shift}}$ = 0.

4-16 Generator for $\overline{\text{Write Data}}$. Using the equivalence shown in Fig. P4-6, implement the gating part of Fig. 4-18 using one "Triple 3-input NOR gate" IC package.

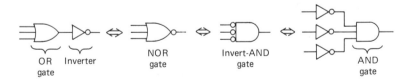

Figure P4-6.

4-17 One-shot data separator. For the circuit shown in Fig. P4-7:
    (a) Take the "Flux changes" waveform of Fig. 4-17 and make a timing diagram for A, B, $\overline{\text{B}}$, C, D, $\overline{\text{Read Clock}}$, and $\overline{\text{Read Data}}$.
    (b) Are your outputs identical with the waveforms of Fig. 4-19b?

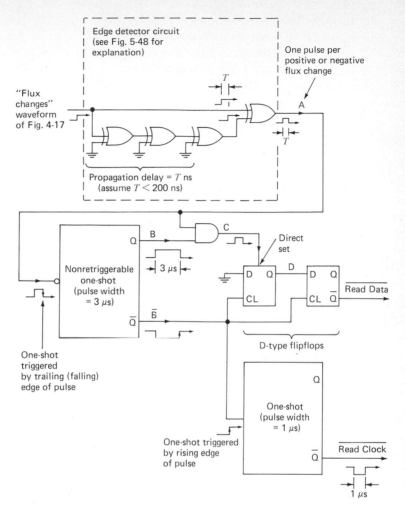

Figure P4-7.

(c) Why must the B one-shot be nonretriggerable; that is, why must it ignore any negative-going input transitions occurring while its output is generating a pulse?

(d) Under what circumstances will a positive pulse occur on C and thereby direct set flipflop D?

(e) What is the function of flipflop D?

4-18 Floppy-disk data format. (a) Consider the definition of a non-IBM-compatible disk format to transfer as many bytes of data as possible between one complete track on the disk and N consecutive RAM addresses. The format is to consist of a gap of 10 bytes following the leading edge of the Index output, N data bytes, two CRCC bytes, and a gap of at least 10 bytes before the next $\overline{\text{Index}}$ pulse occurs. Accounting for the worst-case spindle speed of the disk (360 rpm $\pm$ 2.4 percent) in your calculation, determine the value of N.

(b) If the probability that any one bit is transferred erroneously (on the first try) is 1 in 10^9, what is the probability of transferring these N + 2 bytes without error? Assume errors occur independently of each other.

(c) What is the probability of transferring the 130 bytes of data and check characters of an IBM-compatible floppy-disk record without error, assuming the same error probability for each bit?

4-19 Floppy-disk timing. For an IBM-compatible disk, how long does the microcomputer have between the interrupt at the end of reading the record from one sector (to check the CRC remainder and to set up to read the record from the next sector) before the read-write head gets to the next sector?

4-20 Floppy-disk timing. For an IBM-compatible disk:

(a) What are the minimum and the maximum possible times which it will take to write the contents of 1024 consecutive addresses in RAM onto a floppy disk, in consecutive sectors on one track? Assume that all sectors are first written and then all of them are checked (and that they all check OK, so that no rewriting is necessary). Neglect the time required by the CPU, counting only the time dictated by the disk itself.

(b) Describe the conditions leading to the minimum time.

(c) Describe the conditions leading to the maximum time.

(d) In each of these cases, determine the percentage of time during which the CPU is idled by DMA transfers.

REFERENCES

The selection of a suitable PROM for a specific application, as well as a listing of available PROMs and some of their characteristics, is provided by J. Metzger, PROM's Proms, Promises, *Electronic Products*, June 16, 1975, pp. 45–48.

A concise discussion of PROMs and their programming is presented in the 32-page booklet, "PROM User's Guide," available from Pro-Log Corp. (2411A Garden Road, Monterey, CA 93940).

A survey of the characteristics of available static and dynamic semiconductor RAMs is given by E. Hnatek, Chipping Away at Core: Another Round, *Digital Design*, July 1976, pp. 31–42.

INPUT-OUTPUT

5-1 I/O CONTROL

The most fundamental function of a microcomputer in an instrument is to
accept and interpret the inputs to the instrument and to generate its outputs.
Some interactions between the microcomputer and an I/O device can be controlled by the CPU alone, as in Fig. 5-1a. For example, the CPU acts on its
own to update certain numeric displays to be discussed in Sec. 5-6. The display is treated like a write-only memory (WOM). Each numeric indicator is
addressed and written into with a new digit whenever the CPU is ready to do
this. The display does not talk back. It is always ready for a new digit
whenever the CPU gives it one.

In contrast, some interactions between a microcomputer and an I/O device are controlled almost entirely by the device alone, as in Fig. 5-1b.
These data transfers take place under DMA control, as discussed in Sec. 3-8.
Whenever the device is ready for the next data transfer, it initiates this
transfer and executes it without the "knowing" participation of the CPU. It
is true that the device waits until completion of the present instruction
cycle, that the CPU suspends its operation during the DMA transfer, and that
the address in memory which is accessed comes from a DMA controller.

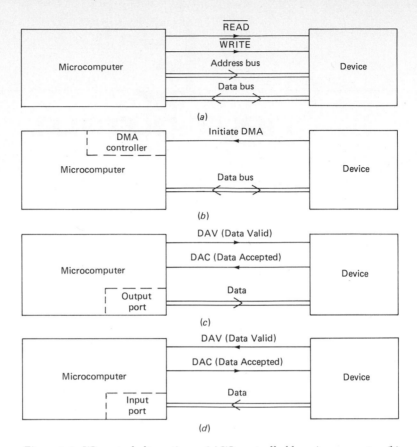

Figure 5-1. *I/O control alternatives.* (a) *I/O controlled by microcomputer;* (b) *I/O controlled by device;* (c) *data output controlled by handshaking;* (d) *data input controlled by handshaking.*

Nevertheless, from the point of view of the CPU, the transfer is automatic. From the point of view of the device, the transfer takes place at its command.

Handshaking control of data transfer between a microcomputer and a device, as in Fig. 5-1c and d, permits reliable data transfer in many situations where neither of the previous two approaches is satisfactory. Handshaking uses the successive steps shown in Fig. 5-2 for the transfer of each word between microcomputer and device. The "talker" (either microcomputer or device) is the source of the data. The "listener" is the recipient of the data. As shown in Fig. 5-2, the following steps transfer the data words W0, W1, W2, . . . :

1 With DAV (DAta Valid) = 0, the data word Wi is put out by the talker.
2 As soon as it sees that DAC (Data ACcepted) = 0, the talker makes DAV = 1 to tell the listener that the data is valid. The talker must maintain this data until DAC = 1.

Figure 5-2. Handshaking for Successive Data Transfers

	Talker	Listener
Data	DAV (data valid)	DAC (data accepted)
W0	0	0
W0	1	0
W0	1	1
W1	0	1
W1	0	0
W1	1	0
W1	1	1
W2	0	1
W2	0	0
W2	1	0
W2	1	1
W3	0	1
W3	0	0
.	.	.
.	.	.
.	.	.

3   The listener makes DAC = 1, signifying it has accepted the data (and is no longer looking at the data lines). The listener must keep DAC = 1 until it sees DAV = 0.

4   The talker makes DAV = 0 as an acknowledgment of the DAC = 1 signal. At the same time, it puts the next word to be transmitted on the data lines. It must now wait for DAC = 0 before making DAV = 1 to initiate the next data transfer.

5   The listener, knowing that its DAC = 1 signal has been seen by the talker, now makes DAC = 0 to permit initiation of the next data transfer.

The data lines required for transferring data between a microcomputer and a device may consist of a portion of an I/O port, an entire I/O port, or several I/O ports. If several I/O ports are used, it is irrelevant that they cannot be loaded, or read from, simultaneously. In this case the microcomputer simply does not handshake until it has loaded, or read from, all the I/O ports involved in the data transfer.

Some microcomputers leave it to the user to create the DAV and DAC handshake lines, as illustrated in Fig. 5-3. This provides a completely versatile approach. However, it also entails packing data to generate the output handshake signal and unpacking data to read the input handshake signal.

Other microcomputers provide handshake lines in conjunction with each I/O port. Thus Motorola's Peripheral Interface Adapter for use with

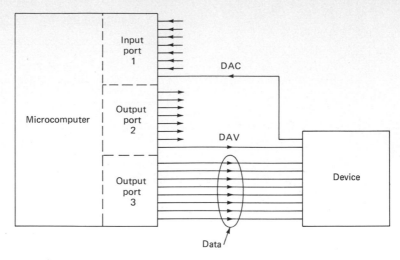

Figure 5-3. Creation of handshake lines.

their 6800 microcomputer includes two I/O ports plus handshake lines for each, as shown in Fig. 5-4. Each port and the operation of its handshake lines are set up under program control as part of the initialization routine for an instrument. The handshake input line can be tested as a flag. Alternatively, it can be set up so that a transition on this line generates an interrupt. In fact, the handshaking can be set up to be done automatically (using handshake lines in negated form, $\overline{\text{DAV}}$ and $\overline{\text{DAC}}$). Thus, if I/O port A is set up as an input port as in Fig. 5-5a, then when the device driving input port A is ready, it handshakes with a negative-going transition on $\overline{\text{DAV}}$

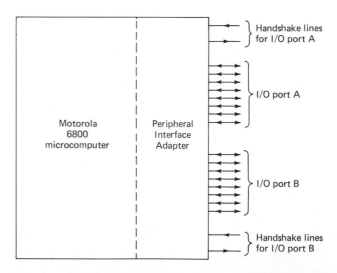

Figure 5-4. Motorola 6800 automatic handshaking capability.

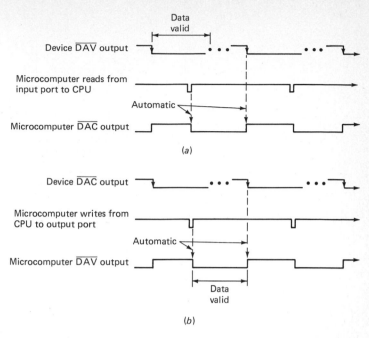

Figure 5-5. *Automatic handshaking by microcomputer.* (a) *Automatic handshaking during input to microcomputer;* (b) *automatic handshaking during output from microcomputer.*

which generates an interrupt. As the microcomputer interrupt service routine reads this data from input port A, the $\overline{DAC}$ line goes low (that is, DAC = 1) automatically. $\overline{DAC}$ goes high again automatically when the next $\overline{DAV}$ negative-going transition occurs.

In a similar manner, I/O port B can be set up as an output port as in Fig. 5-5b. Then writing to output port B will also drive the $\overline{DAV}$ output line low automatically. The device driven by output port B acknowledges that it has accepted this data with a negative-going transition on $\overline{DAC}$ which makes the $\overline{DAV}$ output line go high automatically and also generates an interrupt.

Using an interrupt input for handshaking permits the microcomputer to be particularly effective in transferring arrays of data to or from relatively slow devices without getting tied up and unable to do much else simultaneously. Also, the automatic handling of the output handshake line both simplifies the software and speeds up the hardware. It is a common feature among microcomputers which have handshake lines included on a general I/O chip (for example, Intel 8080, Motorola 6800, and Rockwell PPS-8).

The implication up to this point has been that each device to be connected to the microcomputer communicates through its own I/O port(s), leading to the "star" I/O structure of Fig. 5-6. This approach minimizes the hardware needed by a device to handle data transfers, since its data lines and

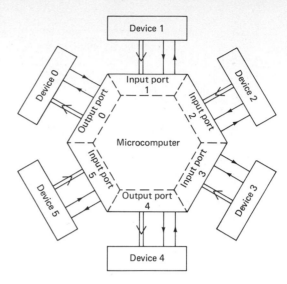

Figure 5-6. Star I/O structure.

handshake lines are not shared with other devices. It also permits the hand-shaking of data transfers with slow devices in which the input or output lines can be tied up for long intervals while the microcomputer waits for the slow device to accept data or generate new output data. Also, an output port can be used to hold data for a device, thus simplifying its hardware.

A star I/O structure has the disadvantage of requiring a large number of I/O lines connected to the microcomputer. If the microcomputer is located on one printed-circuit board while the I/O devices reside elsewhere, a multitude of connectors and cables fan out like tentacles from this microcomputer board. Having this multitude of I/O lines gives rise to a multitude of opportunities for the instrument to fail. It also provides an irregular structure if we want to provide the instrument with the capability to test itself for various types of failure.

The hardware between a microcomputer and its I/O devices can be regularized with a bus structure. One possibility is shown in Fig. 5-7, in which all devices are memory-mapped, as discussed in Sec. 3-4 in conjunction with the interconnection of I/O ports with the CPU. In effect, this locates each I/O port in the corresponding device circuitry. The "bus drivers" shown provide a higher drive capability than the CPU itself can provide. They also prevent damage to the CPU due to the inadvertent mishandling of these bus lines, which now reach throughout an instrument. An example of a low-power-Schottky TTL bidirectional bus driver is shown in Fig. 5-8.

The circuit of Fig. 5-7 also includes a "vectored" interrupt capability. When any device interrupts the CPU, the CPU is automatically "vectored" to the interrupt service routine for that one device (rather than to a general interrupt service routine which must determine which device interrupted).

This bus structure can provide a handshaking capability identical to

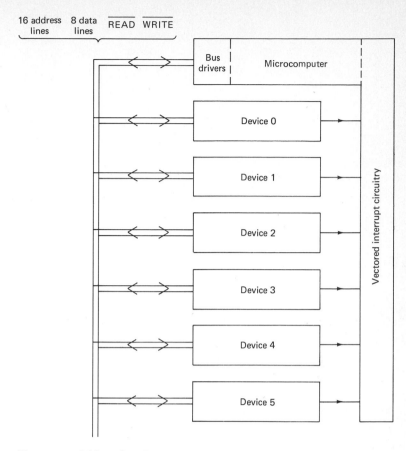

Figure 5-7. *Address bus/data bus I/O structure.*

that discussed in conjunction with Fig. 5-4. In fact, an easy and effective way to achieve this for a microcomputer having a general I/O port chip which includes handshaking capability is to embed one of these chips into the circuitry for each device. This provides an alternative to the use of the vectored interrupt circuitry of Fig. 5-7.

For a microcomputer which includes IN and OUT instructions together with $\overline{\text{IN}}$ and $\overline{\text{OUT}}$ control lines, only a small number of address lines need be brought out on the bus to I/O devices. It is only necessary to use the address to distinguish between the different devices (and different registers within one device), since none of the RAM and ROM memory accesses will affect the $\overline{\text{IN}}$ or $\overline{\text{OUT}}$ control lines. A microcomputer which memory-maps all I/O ports can also be set up to provide the same convenience to the device circuitry, using the approach of Fig. 5-9. In this case, page 07 is shown as dedicated to all I/O devices, whereas pages 00–06 are dedicated to RAM and ROM.

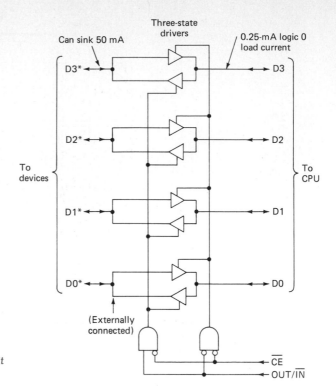

Three-state drivers

Can sink 50 mA

0.25-mA logic 0 load current

D3*   D3

D2*   D2

To
devices

To
CPU

D1*   D1

D0*   D0

(Externally
connected)

Figure 5-8. Intel 8216 4-bit
bidirectional bus driver.

CE
OUT/IN

5-2 I/O TIMING

A device which infrequently interacts with a microcomputer does not cause any potential timing problems. There is plenty of time to do the other things required of the microcomputer while still checking a flag for this slow device periodically to see if it needs servicing.

Potential problems with I/O timing arise in the transfer of an array of data between a microcomputer and a device at a relatively high rate. These problems are complicated if the data transfer continues for so long that the microcomputer is needed elsewhere.

Successful transfer of data from the microcomputer to a device depends upon the proper interrelationship among the three time intervals shown in Fig. 5-10:

1   T_{DEVICE}, the time interval between successive readings of data by the device, that is, between successive negative-going $\overline{DAC}$ transitions.
2   T_{MICRO1}, the time taken by the microcomputer from this $\overline{DAC}$ notification until the next word of data is ready (and $\overline{DAV}$ is lowered).
3   T_{MICRO}, the total time taken by the microcomputer to service the device. This includes T_{MICRO1} plus the time needed to increment a pointer to memory (if the data is coming from an array in memory) plus the time

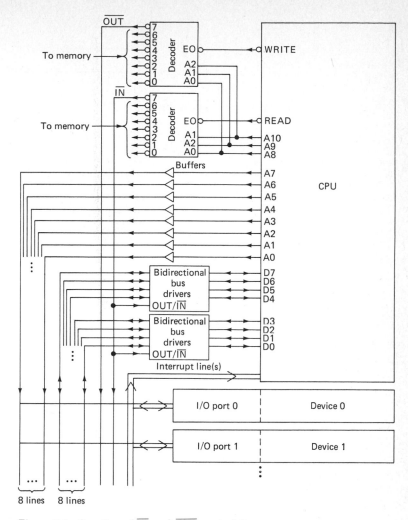

Figure 5-9. Creation of $\overline{\text{IN}}$ and $\overline{\text{OUT}}$ control lines.

needed to decrement and test a record-length variable for terminating data transfers at the proper time.

How these last two time intervals arise can be seen from the service routine of Fig. 5-11, which assumes that the device interrupts the microcomputer as it lowers the $\overline{\text{DAC}}$ line. This example assumes that the microcomputer need not expend any effort determining which device caused the interrupt— either because it has vectored interrupt capability or because there is only one device which can interrupt at this time. In Fig. 5-11, Pointer is the CPU register which points to the RAM address designated as M. PARRAY (stored in RAM) represents the pointer to the data to be transferred. LENGTH, also

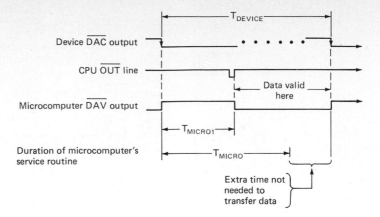

Figure 5-10. *Definitions of time intervals involved in transferring data to a device.*

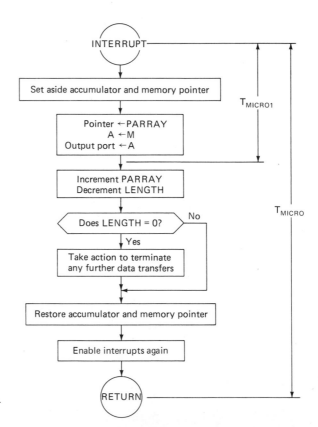

Figure 5-11. *Service routine defining* T_{MICRO1} *and* T_{MICRO}.

stored in RAM, indicates how many words in the array remain to be transferred.

To avoid any *underflow* errors, we must satisfy the *necessary* (but not
sufficient) condition:

$$T_{MICRO1(max)} < T_{DEVICE(min)} \tag{5-1}$$

In contrast, the following condition is *sufficient* to ensure no underflow
errors:

$$T_{MICRO(max)} < T_{DEVICE(min)} \tag{5-2}$$

However, on occasion this inequality can be violated, as shown in Fig. 5-12.
As long as the interval between the end of T_{MICRO1} and the end of T_{DEVICE} (labeled OK) never goes negative, an underflow error will never occur. This
leads to another *necessary* (but not sufficient) condition involving the
average time required to service the device $T_{MICRO(avg)}$, which must be satisfied in order to avoid underflow errors:

$$T_{MICRO(avg)} < T_{DEVICE(min)} \tag{5-3}$$

Inequality (5-3), which relaxes the sufficient condition expressed by
inequality (5-2), is useful if T_{MICRO} is not constant. Such a circumstance can
arise if the service routine is initiated by an interrupt but is, itself, interrupted by a higher-priority device. Alternatively, it can happen if the service routine is entered under flag control (rather than interrupt control) and

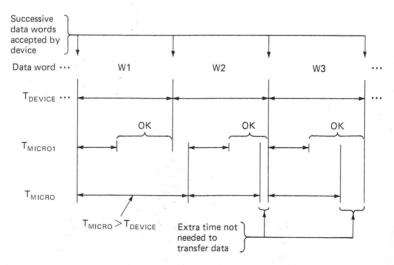

Figure 5-12. *Timing constraint for reliable data transfer from microcomputer
to device.*

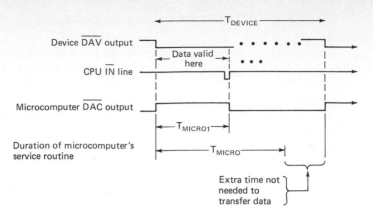

Figure 5-13. *Definitions of time intervals involved in transferring data from a device.*

if the CPU has been doing more than waiting for the flag in a wait loop.

As designers, our job is to avoid designing occasional erratic operation into an instrument. Consequently, we are usually compelled to satisfy inequality (5-2). However, we may know enough about the instrument to permit occasional, slight violations of inequality (5-2). If the device interface is equipped to flag the microcomputer when an underflow error occurs, we can use this to go back and try the data transfer again, if this provides acceptable performance. Alternatively, we can use it as a "self-test" mechanism to indicate an instrument malfunction, if we are convinced this should *never* happen under normal circumstances.

Successful transfer of data from a device to the microcomputer means that the microcomputer must accept each word of data before the device replaces it with the next word. If it does not meet this deadline, an *overrun* error occurs (for which the device should be set up to flag the microcomputer). The timing constraint in this case is shown in Fig. 5-13. T_{DEVICE} is the time interval between the generation of successive words by the device. T_{MICRO1} is the time interval starting when a new word is first available to the microcomputer and ending as that word is read in through an input port. T_{MICRO} is again the total time required by the microcomputer to service this device.

With these definitions, the same conditions given by inequalities (5-1), (5-2), and (5-3) apply to the successful transfer of data into the microcomputer from a device. As an example of the times involved, if the device is a cartridge-tape unit, a new word of data may be put out by the cartridge-tape unit every 160 μs. If the device lowers its $\overline{DAV}$ line and the microcomputer does not respond by reading in this data within 160 μs, the tape unit either drops the present word and puts out the next word or misses the next word while holding onto the present word. In either case, the cartridge-tape interface detects that no handshake occurred in time, so it sets an overrun error flag for the microcomputer.

Example 5-1. For a microcomputer in which DAV and DAC are implemented as flags, and which does nothing else while reading in 128
words from a device, show the service routine for this device in flowchart form.

    The handshaking scheme of Fig. 5-2 must be implemented in
software. This is illustrated in Fig. 5-14. Since nothing else is
competing for the CPU, the pointer in the CPU can be set up initially and left until the process is done. Likewise, a CPU scratchpad register can be used as a record-length counter for the duration of the
transfer of this array of data into RAM.

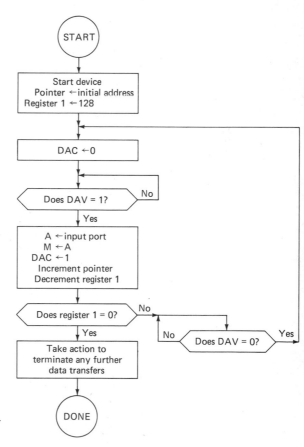

Figure   5-14. Handshak-
ing with flags.

5-3   DATA BUFFERING WITH FIFOs

The last two sections have dealt with the problem of transferring an array of data between a microcomputer and a device.   In Sec. 5-1, we considered how handshaking can provide reliable data transfer, subject to a timing constraint.   Section 5-2 treated this timing constraint in detail.   It also discussed how a device can raise an error flag to the microcomputer if this timing constraint is ever violated; that is, if the microcomputer does not execute a proper handshake before the device must deal with the next word of data.

In the interests of minimizing the hardware of an instrument, we can do no better than the approach provided in the last two sections for coupling a device to a microcomputer.   If the timing is "close," we do well to consider how a service routine can be rewritten or how the testing of a handshaking output flag from a device can be expedited.   However, when all else fails, the use of a *FIFO* provides an easy-to-apply, relatively inexpensive alleviation of this timing constraint.

A FIFO, or first in, first out memory, is also sometimes called an "elastic store" for its ability to accept data at one data rate and emit it at another rate.   In effect, if we put several words of data into a FIFO, they will be available to a device connected to the FIFO output whenever the device is ready for them.   If the device asks for more than these several words, the FIFO will refuse to handshake.   This becomes useful, as will be discussed shortly, when the FIFO can hold many words (up to some maximum, such as 32 or 64).

As an example of FIFO characteristics, consider the 32×9 FIFO of Fig. 5-15.   In its typical use with an 8-bit microcomputer, only an 8-bit word length would be used, the ninth input being grounded.   On the input side, successive words can be loaded into the FIFO by handshaking for each one, using the DAV_{IN} and DAC_{IN} lines shown.   This can be continued for up to 32 words, if none are removed from the output during the process of loading these 32 words.   More generally, the FIFO can continue to be loaded until it no longer raises its DAC_{IN} (Data ACcepted) line.   At this point, the FIFO has accepted the last word but is indicating that it is full and cannot accept further data.   At some later time the DAC_{IN} line can be checked again, and if high, the handshaking of subsequent words of data can be continued.

Once loaded into the FIFO, the successive data words "ripple through" the FIFO structure and line up in order at the output.   An important characteristic time of a FIFO, for our purposes, is the ripple-through time $T_{RIPPLE\ THROUGH}$.   This is the time it takes for an input-data word to appear at the output of an initially empty FIFO.

The FIFO of Fig. 5-15 uses an "array-type" organization analogous to that of Example 2-19 for organizing a stack.   This organizational approach moves data automatically from register to register to carry out the FIFO function.   As a consequence, it is relatively slow (for a FIFO), but fast enough for microcomputer applications.   The alternative "pointer-type" organization

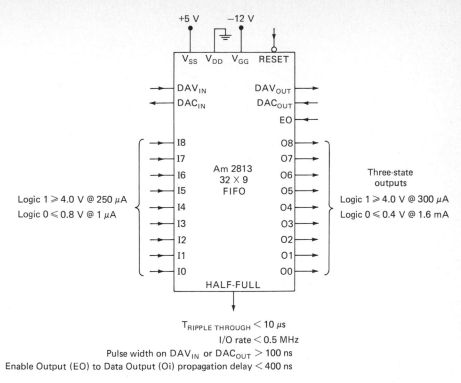

+5 V   −12 V

Vss VDD VGG RESET

DAVIN   DAVOUT
DACIN   DACOUT
                          EO

I8   Am 2813   O8
I7   32 X 9   O7
I6   FIFO   O6
I5   O5
I4   O4
I3   O3
I2   O2
I1   O1
I0   O0

Logic 1 ⩾ 4.0 V @ 250 µA
Logic 0 ⩽ 0.8 V @ 1 µA

Three-state
outputs
Logic 1 ⩾ 4.0 V @ 300 µA
Logic 0 ⩽ 0.4 V @ 1.6 mA

HALF-FULL

$T_{\text{RIPPLE THROUGH}} < 10\ \mu s$
I/O rate < 0.5 MHz
Pulse width on DAV_{IN} or $DAC_{OUT} > 100$ ns
Enable Output (EO) to Data Output (Oi) propagation delay < 400 ns

Figure 5-15. 32 × 9 FIFO. (Advanced Micro Devices, Inc.)

used by some FIFOs is analogous to that of Example 2-21 for organizing a stack. It permits an input-data word to an otherwise empty FIFO to appear at the output virtually instantaneously.

The timing required for the output from the FIFO is completely independent of that on the input. Assume that the Enable Output line is tied high in Fig. 5-15 so that the three-state output lines are never in the high-impedance state. Then if DAV_{OUT} is high, a data word is available on the output and will remain there until a handshaking operation transfers it to a device. This can be continued with successive words in the FIFO until DAV_{OUT} no longer rises, indicating that the FIFO is empty (except for a possible data word rippling from the input toward the output).

If instead of tying EO high all the time, EO is tied to DAC_{OUT}, then successive words from the FIFO can be put directly onto the data bus of a microcomputer's address bus/data bus structure. Since the output data does not actually change until DAC_{OUT} goes low, it will be stable during the reading from FIFO to CPU. Used in this mode, DAV_{OUT} can be used as a flag to indicate whether a word is ready. If so, it is simply read into the CPU. This satisfies the FIFO's handshaking requirement at the same time that the data is read.

As long as the handshaking logic between the output of one FIFO and

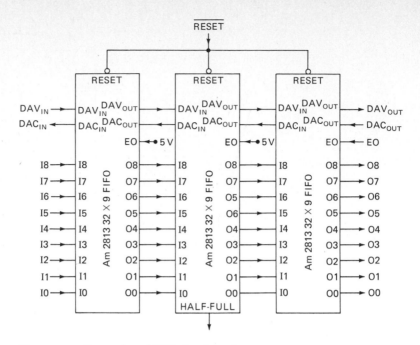

Figure 5-16. Expansion of FIFO depth to obtain a 96 × 9 FIFO.

the input to another is compatible (perhaps with the addition of one or two inverters) and as long as the loading requirements between outputs and inputs are compatible, an arbitrarily deep FIFO can be made. These conditions are satisfied in Fig. 5-16 to produce a 96 × 9 FIFO.

Expansion of FIFO word length by combining several FIFOs is not as easy because of the need to combine handshaking lines properly. In general, careful consideration must be given to when data is accepted on inputs and when data changes on outputs. Otherwise, occasionally erratic operation is likely to result. The best solution is to use a 4-bit-wide FIFO (such as Fairchild's 3341, a 64 × 4 FIFO) for handling 4-bit word lengths, and an 8-bit-wide FIFO for handling 8-bit word lengths.

The FIFO of Fig. 5-15 has a useful HALF-FULL output. If HALF-FULL = 1, the FIFO is more than half full; otherwise the FIFO is less than half full. When looking at the FIFO input, this provides an indication of whether the FIFO has been emptied out halfway from a previously full condition. In contrast, DAC_{IN} only indicates whether the FIFO is completely full or not. When looking at the FIFO output, HALF-FULL indicates whether the FIFO has been filled up halfway from a previously empty condition. Again, we will find circumstances when this is more helpful than looking at DAV_{OUT}, which only indicates whether the FIFO is empty or not.

Since we know that the input to a FIFO will handshake if it is not full, we can tie a FIFO directly to an address bus/data bus structure as the

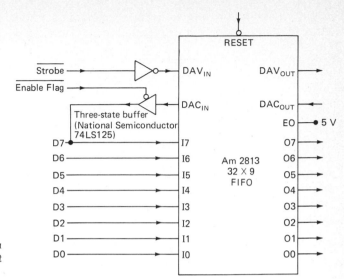

Figure 5-17. Treating a FIFO as an elastic output port.

"elastic" output port shown in Fig. 5-17. The DAC_{IN} line can be read back into the CPU through a three-state buffer (or three-state inverter) as shown. This bit is tested as a flag to indicate whether or not the FIFO is full. If not, successive words can be strobed out to the FIFO until it is finally filled (or until the transfer of the entire array has been completed).

To determine the timing requirements necessary for successful data transfer in the above mode, consider that the FIFO, and hence the device, is being operated under flag control, not interrupt control. Furthermore, consider that while the device being driven by the FIFO is in operation, the instrument carries out the cyclic sequence of events shown in Fig. 5-18. Both blocks shown may take a variable amount of time. We are interested in the maximum amount of time taken $T_{CYCLE(max)}$ to pass through both blocks once. We are actually interested in the time taken from the step in the upper block just after the last word of data is written out until the CPU has processed all instructions around the loop and writes out the first word of data for the next

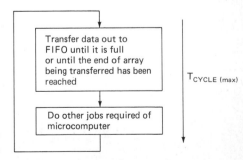

Figure 5-18. Timing definition for the cyclic testing of a FIFO flag for output from the CPU.

cycle. This time is almost exactly the same as the time T_{CYCLE}. Successful data transfer only requires that the following *sufficient* condition be satisfied:

$$T_{CYCLE(max)} < \text{FIFO DEPTH} \times T_{DEVICE(min)} - T_{RIPPLE\ THROUGH} \qquad (5\text{-}4)$$

This inequality is closely related to inequality (5-2) since

$$T_{CYCLE(max)} = T_{MICRO(max)}$$

when operating under flag control. The FIFO alleviates the timing constraint of inequality (5-2) by a factor almost equal to the depth of FIFO (since $T_{RIPPLE\ THROUGH}$ is relatively small). This is a factor of 32 for the FIFO of Fig. 5-15.

For a FIFO having three-state outputs, an "elastic" input port can be created, as in Fig. 5-19. This circuit has two "enable" inputs. One permits DAV_{OUT} to be tested as a flag. The other transfers the data word on the FIFO output into the CPU while simultaneously handshaking the next word in the FIFO up to the output. These two enable inputs can be decoded with an address to distinguish each of them from the other and from other input ports. As discussed earlier, DAV_{OUT} is first tested, and then, if it is equal to one, a word is transferred to the CPU. If it is equal to zero, the FIFO has been emptied and the CPU can go back to its other tasks for another cycle, as in Fig. 5-20. With the definition of $T_{CYCLE(max)}$ shown, inequality (5-4) again expresses the timing constraint required for successful data transfer.

For interrupt control, the HALF-FULL output can be used to generate the interrupt. When a FIFO is used as an elastic output port, a negative-

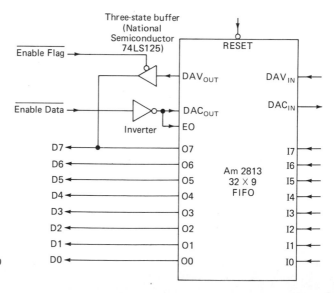

Figure 5-19. Treating a FIFO as an elastic input port.

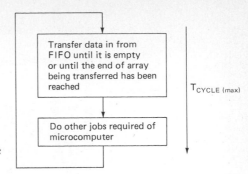

Figure 5-20. Timing definition for the cyclic
testing of a FIFO flag for input to the CPU.

going transition on the HALF-FULL output indicates that the FIFO has been
half emptied since it was last filled. If this negative-going transition is used
to generate the interrupt, the *necessary* condition for successful data transfer
analogous to inequality (5-1) is

$$T_{\text{MICRO1(max)}} < \frac{\text{FIFO DEPTH} \times T_{\text{DEVICE(max)}}}{2} - T_{\text{RIPPLE THROUGH}} \qquad (5\text{-}5)$$

Actually, if this *necessary* condition is met, the *sufficient* condition analogous to inequality (5-2) will almost assuredly be met automatically. This
only requires that after filling up the FIFO, the service routine must terminate before the FIFO empties out halfway again.

Using a FIFO as an elastic input port and operating it under interrupt
control requires the generation of an interrupt when a positive-going transition on the HALF-FULL output occurs. Again, inequality (5-5) provides the
timing constraint which must be met for successful data transfer.

5-4 KEYBOARDS AND SWITCHES

The manual control of an instrument as well as the manual entry of setup information can be handled with a keyboard, using modular keyswitch components like those of Fig. 5-21. A manufacturer of keyswitch components
typically will provide keys having whatever legends we desire. Different
colors can provide color coding for groups of keys. Keyswitches are
printed-circuit-board mounted, providing simplicity of wiring, possibly encoding logic, and a connector to the microcomputer.

The alternative to a keyboard for manual entry of setup information
into an instrument tends to be an assortment of toggle switches, slide
switches, rotary switches, or "push-push" ganged switches to choose among
alternative modes of operation or parameter values. Thumbwheel switches
provide an alternative to a keyboard for entering numerical information.
We will discuss the use of such *fixed-position* switches later in this section.

Figure 5-21. Modular key-switch components. (Texas Instruments Inc.)

Before the days of microcomputer-based instruments, fixed-position switches were the common way of entering setup information into an instrument. At that time, a keyboard provided a relatively cumbersome alternative. Now, just the opposite is true. In fact, there are a variety of reasons why keyboards seem to be displacing fixed-position switches on the front panels of instruments:

1 A keyboard provides a *clean-cut look* to an instrument. All the manual setup and control functions of the instrument can be gathered together in an orderly array.

2. A keyboard eliminates *front-panel clutter*. For an instrument which can operate in any of several modes, each of these modes requires its own kind of setup information. A "top of the line" oscilloscope provides an outstanding example. A jumble of alternatives is required to set it up for different triggering modes, vertical input modes, and display modes. With the normal front panel of the past, most of the fixed-position switches provide setup alternatives for modes of operation

other than the mode being used at any one time. As a consequence, these unused switches provide confusion, distraction, and clutter to the user. In contrast, a keyboard together with an appropriate display of the setup information chosen provides the user with a minimum of extraneous front-panel clutter.

3 A keyboard provides *one overall approach to manual setup and control.* Its use can be accounted for even in the earliest stages of the development of an instrument. As the development progresses, changes and additions to the setup and control of the instrument can be handled as straightforward changes in the tables and action routines which "parse" the keyboard (as discussed in Sec. 7-1), perhaps with the addition of one or more keys to the keyboard array. Such changes and additions produce a minimum of trauma in the designer of the front panel.

4 A keyboard provides a *systematic input* to a microcomputer. The hardware needed to enter inputs from the keyboard can be handled once and for all, as we shall see, using one standard LSI circuit which can accommodate more keys than we will ever be interested in building into a front panel.

5 A keyboard permits *remote setup and control.* Since all keyswitches are momentary-action switches, these switches in themselves do not represent the setup information. They only provide the ability to enter or to change this information. The setup information itself must be represented as a separate and distinct front-panel function. As a consequence, the remote control of an instrument simply involves disabling the front-panel keyboard and entering analogous data in the same format from a remote instrument communicating through a connector on the back of the instrument. This remotely obtained setup information can still be displayed on the front panel. We will discuss this remote control of an instrument in Sec. 5-10.

6 A keyboard enhances front-panel-switch *reliability.* Keyswitch manufacturers tend to concentrate upon reliability as a major design criterion. Perhaps even more important, all the front-panel switches are mounted and used in the same way, with the help of a printed-circuit board. Consequently, there are no awkward front-panel-switch interconnections and no assemblage of cables reaching from the heart of the instrument out to each separate front-panel switch.

The use of a keyboard does raise the need for displaying the setup information as a separate front-panel function. The "smart" signal generator of Fig. 5-22 shows an approach which uses "annunciator" lights (that is, on-off lights) aligned with specific keyswitches to serve this function. A seven-segment decimal display indicates the synthesized frequency output of the instrument. This use of annunciator lights permits an easy-to-implement keyboard approach in which setup information is represented in a manner not too different from that inherent in the use of fixed-position

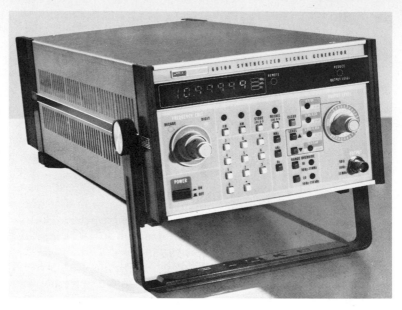

Figure 5-22. Keyswitch-annunciator light approach to the display of setup information. (John Fluke Mfg. Co.)

switches.   A more complex instrument having its setup information displayed in this manner might tend to have a cluttered look.

In contrast, the "smart" waveform generator of Fig. 5-23 separates the keyboard function from the setup-display function.   For a more complex in-

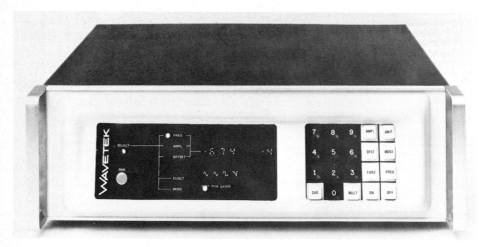

Figure 5-23. Separation of keyboard-input function from setup-information-display function. (Wavetek.)

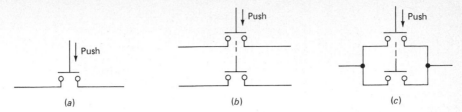

Figure 5-24. *Conventional mechanical keyswitches.* (a) *Representation of a mechanical keyswitch;* (b) *representation of a double-pole keyswitch;* (c) *interconnecting for improved reliability.*

strument, this approach permits the display of only that information which pertains to the mode of operation of interest. Everything else is blanked out.

Either of these approaches permits the user to be notified of any deficiencies in the setup information (for example, "You have not yet entered the signal amplitude you desire") by blinking an appropriate annunciator light.

Conventional mechanical keyswitches depend upon a switch closure between two contacts, as shown schematically in Fig. 5-24a. With a life expectancy typically in excess of 1 million operations, these switches are acceptable for most operations. Many manufacturers offer "double-pole" versions of their keyswitches, as in Fig. 5-24b. Since "switch failure" often means lack of contact closure, the reliability of the switch can be increased by tying the two poles together in parallel, as in Fig. 5-24c, and using it as a single-pole switch.

An alternative way to achieve a higher reliability from a keyswitch is to use a completely different mechanism such as a capacitive effect, an inductive effect, or a Hall effect. However, none of these permit the simple encoding permitted by keyswitches employing a contact closure. Consequently, we will discuss only the encoding of conventional mechanical keyswitches.

National Semiconductor's MM5740AAF keyboard encoder is a specialized 40-pin LSI chip designed specifically to provide an ASCII-coded output from a teletype keyboard. As such it includes some features which we will ignore.* One of these is a three-state output which is too slow (2.5-μs propagation delay) to provide data bus communication at normal microcomputer clock rates.

The keyboard encoder chip requires an external, relatively slow clock input which can be met with the simple Schmitt trigger RC oscillator shown in Fig. 5-25. Also shown is a "keybounce mask" capacitor which masks out the contact bounce characteristic of a mechanical switch when it is first depressed. If this problem is not solved in one way or another, it can appear to

* See National's data sheet and also their Application Note AN-80.

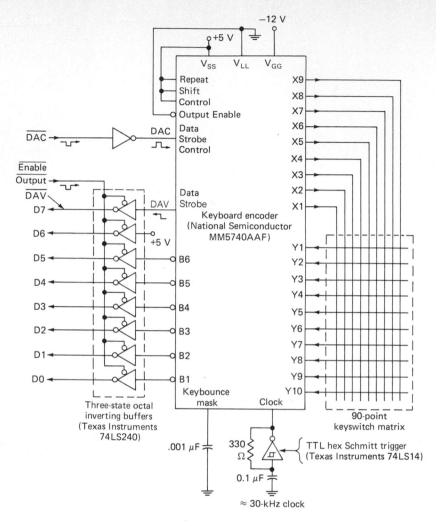

Figure 5-25. *Keyboard encoder setup for flag control.*

the microcomputer that the same key has been depressed several times (within a few milliseconds) instead of just once. The 0.001-microfarad (μF) value shown for this capacitor ensures proper operation even if the key-switches take as long as 8 ms to settle.

Each keyswitch, when depressed, closes a circuit between one Xi line and one Yi line. The keyboard encoder scans this array by driving one of the nine Xi output lines high and then checking each of ten Yi input lines, in turn, to see if one of them is high. The encoder continually scans this 90-point matrix, looking at each key once every 3 ms, if a 30-kHz clock is employed.

Assume that no key is presently depressed and that the output register

(B1, . . . , B6) has been cleared with the $\overline{\text{DAC}}$ handshake line. When a key is depressed, it will be detected within 3 ms. The encoder detects that the key is newly depressed on this scan and ignores the key on subsequent scans until it is released again. In detecting the newly depressed key, it loads the output register with a *key code* determined by which junction in the 90-point keyswitch matrix was closed. It also sets the DAV (DAta Valid) handshake flag. These outputs remain hung up indefinitely until the *leading edge* of the $\overline{\text{DAC}}$ handshake signal occurs (because it is the leading edge, $\overline{\text{DAC}}$ cannot be tied to $\overline{\text{Enable Output}}$ but must occur after $\overline{\text{Enable Output}}$).

This keyboard encoder employs a "two-key rollover" technique to handle the case of a second key being depressed before the first is released. All other keys are ignored until the presently depressed key is released. This feature helps avoid errors in which the user's finger depresses one key firmly and an adjacent key slightly. It also resolves a fast succession of

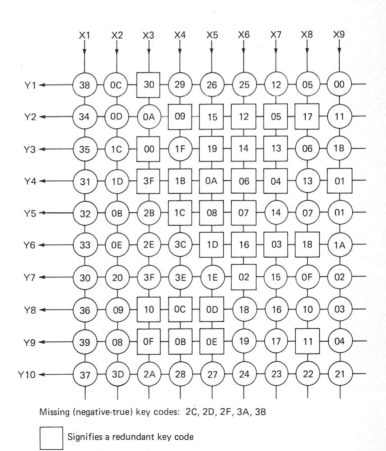

Missing (negative-true) key codes: 2C, 2D, 2F, 3A, 3B

☐ Signifies a redundant key code

Figure 5-26. Hexadecimal key codes corresponding to each possible position of a keyswitch.

keyswitch inputs when a second key is depressed before a first is completely released.

As was indicated earlier, this keyboard encoder chip was designed specifically for teletype-keyboard application. Consequently, we will take the key codes which result and use them for our own purposes. A more expensive alternative is to use the more general chip MM5740xxx and pay a ROM mask charge to specify any coding we desire for up to *nine* outputs. Using the MM5740AAF teletype chip, we can pick Xi-Yi intersections to use so as to obtain the 45 key codes for *every* number from 0 to 44 (in negative-true form). Actually we can obtain all but five of the 64 possible combinations of the six output lines (B1, . . . , B6). Figure 5-26 shows these negative-true hexadecimal encodings for each position of the 90-point matrix.

Example 5-2. Select a key code for a small 16-key instrument such that "digit" keys (0, . . . , 9) are coded

Key name	Hex key code
0	00
.	.
.	.
.	.
9	09

and the remaining six "function" keys (F0, . . . , F5) are coded

Key name	Hex key code
F0	10
.	.
.	.
.	.
F5	15

Using this coding, the B5 output line distinguishes between a digit key and a function key.

The chart of Fig. 5-27 shows the location for each of the 16 keys.

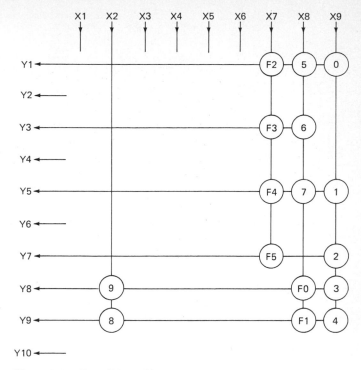

Figure 5-27. Encoding 16 keys.

The circuit of Fig. 5-25 is set up for flag control of a keyboard. The key code and the $\overline{\text{DAV}}$ handshake signal are read into the CPU periodically. The most significant bit of this 8-bit word, $\overline{\text{DAV}}$, is tested, and if zero, the entire word represents a valid key code. The CPU must then drive $\overline{\text{DAC}}$ low to handshake with the keyboard encoder. In this case $\overline{\text{DAC}}$ might be the CPU's $\overline{\text{OUT}}$ line, suitably decoded for this device.

If it were desired to use this circuit under interrupt control, DAV could drive an interrupt line directly. In this case only a three-state hex inverter package would suffice to drive data bus lines D0, . . . , D5 as in Fig. 5-28. The effect of the other two data bus lines D6 and D7 could be masked out after reading into the CPU's accumulator. This avoids the ambiguity which results from their floating during an IN instruction.

An alternative scheme for reading up to 64 keyswitches into an 8-bit microcomputer is shown in Fig. 5-29. It assumes the availability of a standard I/O chip which can be configured into one input port and one output port. The diodes shown prevent multiple keyswitch closures from shorting output lines together. The 10-kΩ pull-up resistors provide unambiguous inputs to the input port when switches are depressed. If the output port

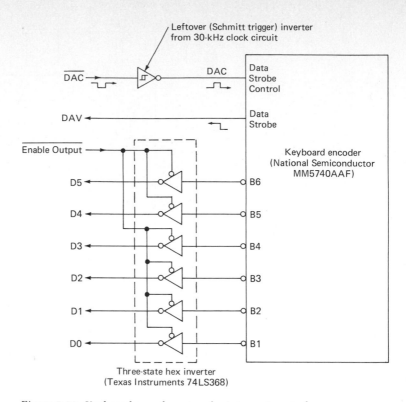

Figure 5-28. Keyboard encoder setup for interrupt control.

normally is loaded with all zeros, the input port can be tested periodically as a flag to determine whether any key is depressed (no keys depressed is read in as all ones). While it would be more convenient to use pull-down resistors and test for all zeros, the loading characteristics of the "TTL compatible" I/O port inputs and outputs (probably) preclude this.

To eliminate the effects of contact bounce in the keyswitches, the keyboard should be serviced less often than every 10 ms or so (that is, a time interval exceeding the "maximum contact bounce time" specification for the keyswitches being used). Then the keyboard service routine carries out the procedure of Fig. 5-30, using a word in RAM labeled KEY to provide status information. The algorithm is initialized with KEY = 00. KEY is set to FF when a depressed key is first sensed. During the next time through the service routine, the key is read, its key code is stored in KCODE, and KEY is set to 01. Until this key is released, KEY remains at 01, inhibiting further reading of any keys.

The keyswitches are scanned by driving one output low at a time, reading the input port, and checking it for all ones. If it is not all ones, the location of the zero is determined. This scanning procedure must be carried out so as to associate a unique key code with each point in the keyswitch ma-

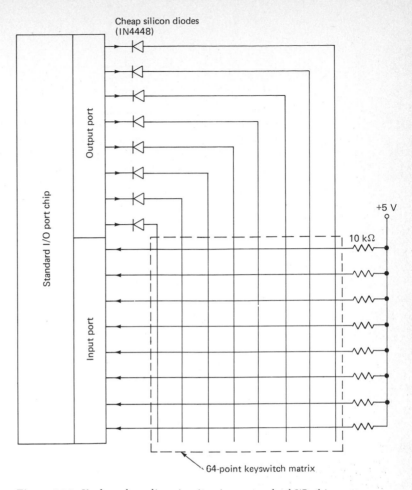

Figure 5-29. Keyboard reading circuit using a standard I/O chip.

trix. By including the test, "Is the key identified by KCODE still depressed?" this service routine provides the same "two-key rollover" capability discussed earlier.

Fixed-position switches come in many forms to serve a variety of purposes in microcomputer-based instruments. One common use is to select among any one of several options available to the user of an instrument. In such a case, the switch may well be mounted on a printed-circuit board within the instrument, where it will normally not be bothered. The DIP switches shown in Fig. 5-31 provide one low-cost means for achieving this function. Each rocker operates a single-pole, single-throw switch. The transparent cover shown protects against the inadvertent changing of the switch programming during the servicing of the instrument.

Thumbwheel switches serve the similar function of programming

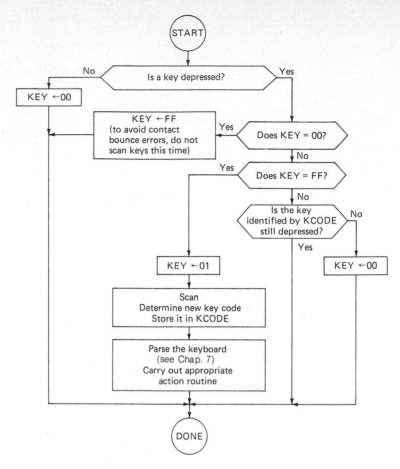

Figure 5-30. Keyboard service routine for the circuit of Fig. 5-29.

binary-coded-decimal information into an instrument. The unit of Fig. 5-32 provides printed-circuit-board mounting in an instrument, and either thumbwheel or screwdriver setting. These thumbwheel switches come in a variety of colors, permitting the color coding of different internal programming functions. Each digit switch has a circuit which looks like four single-pole, single-throw switches connected between the four outputs (8, 4, 2, 1) and the common (C) terminal. Which outputs are connected to the common terminal and which are left floating is determined by the digit position at which the switch is set, as shown in Fig. 5-32c. From one to six digits are available in an integral unit.

If several of these fixed-position switches are used in an instrument, they can be made to look like a "switch-programmed ROM," using the circuit configuration of Fig. 5-33. The decoder drives one of its output lines low, depending upon the address put out by the CPU. The contents of the

Figure 5-31. DIP switches for printed-circuit-board mounting. (AMP Inc.)

selected pair of thumbwheel switches (or the selected DIP switch) appear at
the inputs to the three-state inverters in negated form. When Enable Output
goes low, this data is complemented and put on the data bus. The diodes
serve to isolate between the closed switches corresponding to different addresses. Of course, if only two thumbwheel switches are needed (or one DIP
switch), the circuit is simpler, as in Fig. 5-34.

5-5 TRANSDUCTION

The evolution in instrument design which has taken place because of the
development of microcomputer technology is nowhere more evident than in
the sophisticated use of simple transducers or sensors. On-off sensors of a
variety of physical quantities can provide a sophisticated measurement
capability when used in *arrays* and when used to *time the occurrence of an
event*. A microcomputer combines the on-off data from several sensors with
ease and flexibility. It can give perceptive shadings of meaning to a complex input which has been transduced into a series of timed events.

The reading of Universal Product Code (UPC) symbols, as shown in
Fig. 5-35a, is used by grocery-product manufacturers to identify both the
manufacturer (with a five-digit number) and each of that manufacturer's
products (with another five-digit number). Each digit is coded with two
dark and two light bands, using the coding shown in Fig. 5-35b for the five
left-hand characters. The five right-hand characters employ the complement of this coding, where the complement is obtained by replacing
dark bands with light bands and vice versa. The entire symbol includes
coding for these 10 characters plus specific bar patterns for starting, stop-

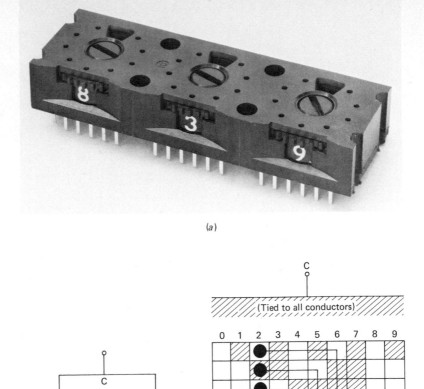

(a)

(b)

(c)

Figure 5-32. *Thumbwheel switch unit for printed-circuit-board mounting.* (Electronic Engineering Company of California—EECO.) (a) Unit; (b) symbolism; (c) circuit.

ping, separating halves of the symbol, and adding a check character. A wand used to scan UPC symbols need only distinguish between the low reflectivity of dark bands and the high reflectivity of light bands. A microcomputer can then derive the UPC data from the time intervals between the logic-level changes received from the wand.*

Phototransistors, shown in Fig. 5-36, can be used to provide on-off

---

* See the "M6800 Microprocessor Applications Manual" referenced at the end of this chapter.

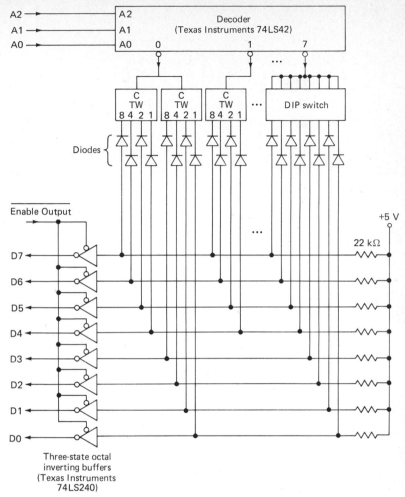

Figure 5-33. Switch-programmed ROM.

sensing in a variety of situations. The circuit characteristics of different devices extend from fast switching (for example, 4 μs) to high sensitivity [for
example, 20 mA/mW-cm² (milliamperes per milliwatt per square centimeter)
in a Darlington phototransistor].

An "optoelectronic reflective sensor" is used in the wand to read UPC
symbols and is used in a variety of other devices employing a marked-sense
card reader. It is constructed by housing a light-emitting diode (LED) and a
phototransistor together, as shown in Fig. 5-37. By controlling both the distance and the angular orientation of the sensor relative to the reflective surface being scanned, the on-off response characteristic is optimized.

The "optoelectronic switch" shown in Fig. 5-38 is a similar device in
which the LED is aimed directly at the phototransistor across a slot. It is

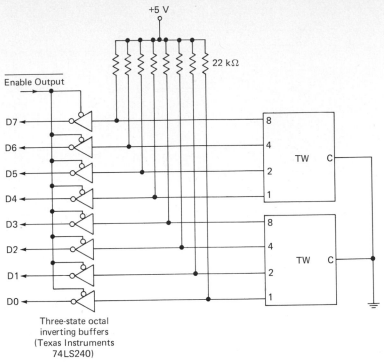

Figure 5-34. Single-word, switch-programmed ROM.

Figure 5-35. Universal Product Code. (a) Complete symbol; (b) coding of left-hand characters.

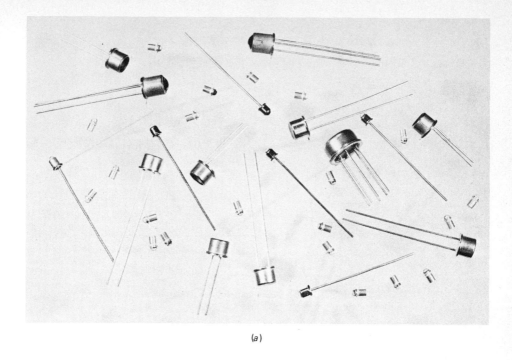

(a)

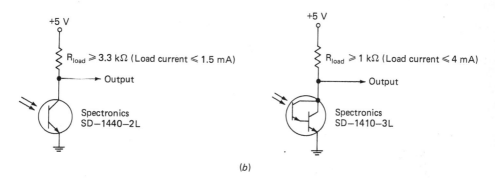

(b)

Figure 5-36. Phototransistors. (Spectronics, Inc.) (a) Devices; (b) circuit characteristics.

useful for sensing when a moving object crosses a fixed position. This, in turn, provides the makings of a limit switch or a simple position encoder, as in Fig. 5-39.

For situations where optical sensing is unsatisfactory, the $1\frac{1}{4}$-in.-long "Hall-effect switch" shown in Fig. 5-40 may be more suitable. In place of the LED, it has a magnet. In place of the phototransistor, it has a Hall-effect sensor. Instead of being actuated by an opaque mask, it is actuated by a ferrous-metal mask which diverts the magnetic flux away from the Hall

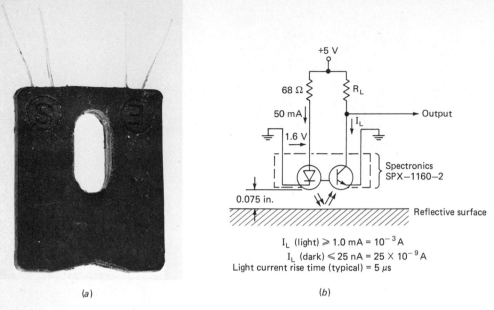

I_L (light) $\geqslant 1.0$ mA $= 10^{-3}$ A

I_L (dark) $\leqslant 25$ nA $= 25 \times 10^{-9}$ A

Light current rise time (typical) $= 5$ μs

(a)   (b)

Figure 5-37. *Optoelectronic reflective sensor.* (*Spectronics, Inc.*) (*a*) Device; (*b*) circuit characteristics.

sensor. Unlike magnetic pickups, the device does not depend upon movement of the mask. Consequently, its dynamic characteristics approximate those of the optoelectronic switch, detecting an on-off condition down to dc and up to 100 kHz.

An on-off position sensor which has evolved over many years is the miniature mechanical switch shown in Fig. 5-41. This switch is available in a variety of forms to permit on-off position sensing under a variety of circumstances. A single-pole, single-throw switch can be used as in Fig. 5-42*a* to provide a flag input to a microcomputer. However, the contact bounce inherent in the switch must not be permitted to cause faulty operation. When used as a limit switch, this circuit causes no problem, since we only wish to detect when the switch first closes. If it opens again momentarily because of contact bounce, this will be ignored, since we will have already initiated an action in response to the contact closure.

If we must sense when a mechanical switch opens again, following the detection of a closure, the switch must be "debounced." We can use the simple circuit of Fig. 5-42*a* again and debounce the switch in the software. Whenever a change is detected in the state of the switch flag, the CPU must ignore reading the flag again for the 5 ms or so needed to exceed the "maximum contact bounce time" specification of the switch. This can be achieved by going into a 5-ms wait loop or by using a programmable timer or by never sampling the flag more often than once every 5 ms. Alternatively,

(a)

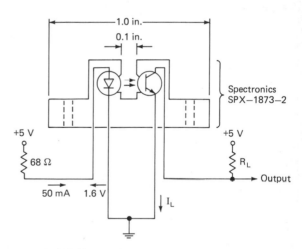

I_L (light) $\geqslant$ 1.5 mA
I_L (dark) $\leqslant$ 250 nA
Light current rise time (typical) = 8 μs
Light current fall time (typical) = 16 μs

(b)

Figure 5-38. Optoelectronic switch. (Spectronics, Inc.) (a) Device; (b) circuit characteristics.

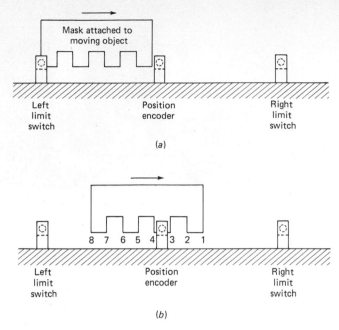

Figure 5-39. Optoelectronic limit switches and position encoder.
(a) Object at extreme left position of travel; (b) object, after
moving through three of the eight quanta boundaries, as measured by the position encoder.

if none of these "minimum hardware" solutions is desirable, then a single-
pole, double-throw switch can be used and debounced with either of the
latch circuits shown in Fig. 5-42b or c. A latch circuit will remain in the
last state to which it was forced, if inputs ever "float." Thus the floating
condition which occurs during contact bounce is ignored.

Some applications of mechanical switches warrant the development of
special-purpose integrated circuits to overcome their deficiencies. For example, the dual tones which are to be interpreted as digits from a telephone
receiver are generated with the help of the switches in a Touch-Tone* pad.
The dual-tone multifrequency detector shown in Fig. 5-43 includes logic to
ignore the first few cycles of each input frequency in order to prevent error
in detection due to switch contact bounce. Within 20 ms after receiving a
pair of high and low Touch-Tone frequencies, it generates a binary number
corresponding to the Touch-Tone digit together with a strobe pulse indicating the presence of valid data. When either tone disappears for more
than 10 ms, the circuitry resets and begins looking for the next digit.

* Bell Telephone patented.

(a)

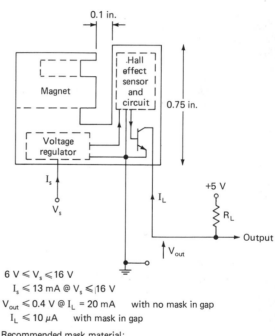

6 V $\leq$ V$_s$ $\leq$ 16 V

  I$_s$ $\leq$ 13 mA @ V$_s$ $\leq$ 16 V

V$_{out}$ $\leq$ 0.4 V @ I$_L$ = 20 mA   with no mask in gap

    I$_L$ $\leq$ 10 μA   with mask in gap

Recommended mask material:
1.0 mm (0.04-in.) thick Armco Electromagnetic Iron

Figure 5-40. Hall-effect switch. (MICRO SWITCH Division of Honeywell.) (a) Device; (b) circuit characteristics.

(b)

Figure 5-41. Miniature mechanical switch. (MICRO SWITCH
Division of Honeywell.)

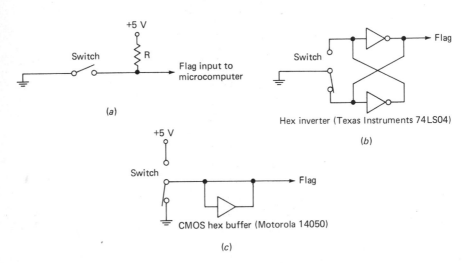

Figure 5-42. Mechanical switch circuits. (a) Use of a switch to create a flag; (b) switch-
debounce circuit; (c) alternative CMOS switch-debounce circuit.

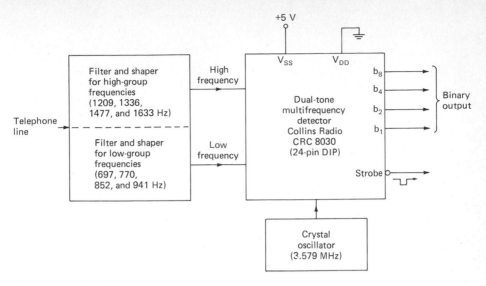

Figure 5-43. Touch-Tone detection circuit.

A pulse-generating transducer produces an input to a microcomputer which again has the simplicity of an on-off device. A microcomputer-based and highly sensitive meter for gauging gold-plating thickness bombards a sample with beta rays and picks up the resulting backscatter with a geiger tube. The count from the tube during a prescribed time interval is converted into micrometers of thickness using a calibration curve formed from a table in ROM. The gauge can determine thickness for different base metals and plating materials simply by using different look-up tables. It can be automatically calibrated by testing a known sample, perhaps located in the base of the instrument, before testing an unknown sample.

For a microcomputer having interrupt capability, each pulse can be used to provide a transition which will interrupt the microcomputer. The service routine simply counts the contents of a RAM address (or several addresses, for finer resolution). After the desired time interval, as specified by a programmable timer, the counting is terminated and the results used as desired. If the input rate is too high to be handled directly in this way, it can be scaled down using a TTL counter, as in Fig. 5-44.

For a microcomputer not having interrupt capability, each transition from the transducer (or from a scaler) can be used to set a flipflop by clocking it, as shown in Fig. 5-45. This flipflop is edge-triggered, looking only at the rising edge of the waveform from the transducer. This is useful when the transducer (or scaler's) output is a square wave. When the flipflop is cleared by the microcomputer after reading the flag, the transducer (or scaler) will not interfere with the clearing function.

The service routine to handle a pulse-generating transducer under flag

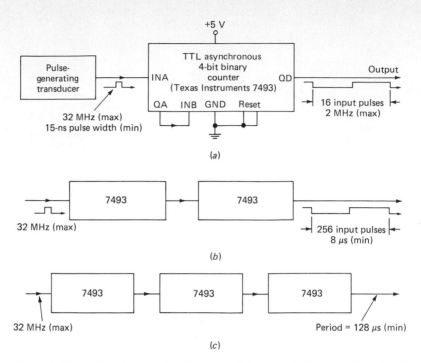

Figure 5-44. Scaling down fast pulse rates. (a) Scale of 16 scaler; (b) scale of 256 scaler; (c) scale of 4096 scaler.

control can derive a time interval, over which pulses will be counted, from the microcomputer's crystal clock. Thus, in Fig. 5-46, the flag input is looked at N times (where N can be an arbitrarily large number) extending over an interval of K2 cycles of the microcomputer clock. The wait loop is included so that the time K1 taken from TEST to TESTD is independent of the value of Flag.

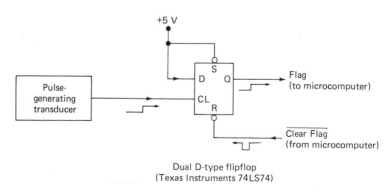

Figure 5-45. Flag circuit.

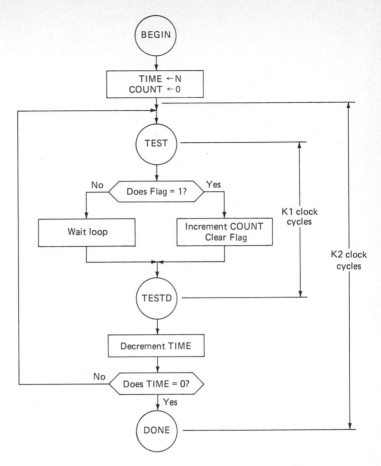

Figure 5-46. *Service routine for a pulse-generating transducer operating under flag control.*

The *quantization* of linear position can be achieved optoelectronically as in Fig. 5-39 if motion proceeds in only one direction, from one limit switch to the other. As the boundaries between successive quanta are crossed, a word in RAM can be incremented to *encode* this incremental data into an absolute position.

The more general problem of encoding absolute position from incremental data for bidirectional motion requires three optoelectronic reflective sensors or optoelectronic switches as in Fig. 5-47. One of these provides a "zero-reference" output Z. When Z = 1, the motion of the incremental encoding mask has moved to its left limit stop. As it changes from one to zero, this marks a "zero reference point" and is used to zero two words in RAM. POS represents the encoded position, which equals zero at this left limit stop. LASTAB is used to store the values of the other two sensors A and B

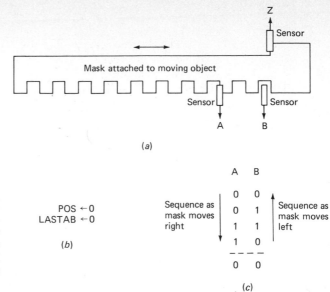

Figure 5-47. Bidirectional incremental encoder with zero reference. (a) Encoder shown located at zero reference point; (b) initial values of encoder variables; (c) output sequences.

POS ← 0
LASTAB ← 0

(b)

A	B	
0	0	
0	1	Sequence as mask moves right / left
1	1	
1	0	
0	0	

(c)

when they were last read. Initializing LASTAB to zero is done to correspond to A = 0 and B = 0 in the first quantum to the right of the zero reference point. As the encoding mask moves to the right, the outputs A and B pass through the sequence shown in Fig. 5-47c.

To use this encoder under flag control, the CPU must scan the sensors often enough so that no quanta changes are missed. For example, if the encoding mask, moving at maximum speed from left to right, causes A and B to change from 00 to 01 at one moment and from 01 to 11 a millisecond later, this corresponds to a speed of 1000 quanta per second. The sensors must be checked more often than this. Each check compares the new values read in for A and B with LASTAB. If they are the same, nothing is done. If they have changed, POS must be incremented or decremented, depending upon the sense of the change, as indicated in Fig. 5-47c. Also LASTAB must be updated to the new value.

Using an incremental encoder under interrupt control requires generating a pulse whenever A or B changes. The circuit of Fig. 5-48 uses exclusive-OR gates and Schmitt triggers to generate a positive pulse on the output OUT whenever either a positive or a negative transition occurs on either the A or the B input. Its operation is illustrated by the timing diagram of Fig. 5-48b. Note that each exclusive-OR gate makes its output equal to logic 1 if and only if its inputs are unequal. If OUT is used to interrupt the microcomputer, the service routine for this interrupt can go through the same procedure as discussed earlier for flag control.

The emphasis of this section has been upon simple transducers which permit sophisticated transduction because of the way they are used in conjunction with a microcomputer. Another application occurs in conjunction

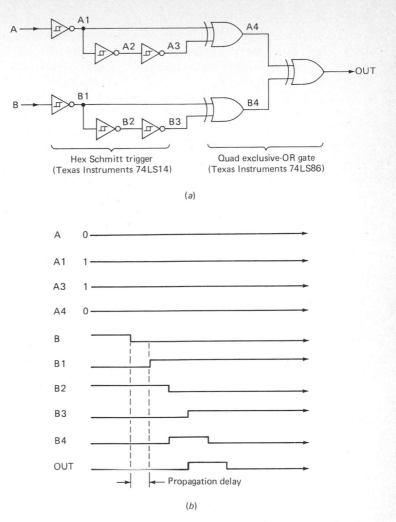

(a)

(b)

Figure 5-48. Dual-edge detector circuit. (a) Circuit; (b) timing diagram.

with automatic test equipment which involves user interaction. If the function of the test is to locate a faulty component on a printed-circuit board of digital logic, it often happens that the test equipment cannot make this determination solely on the basis of generating inputs and measuring outputs on the board's edge connector.

By having a user probe a succession of carefully selected points on the board, the test equipment can exercise edge connector inputs and check responses anywhere on the board. This provides a much stronger diagnostic capability than operating from the edge connector alone. The tester can direct the user through a sequence of probings with displayed instructions like PROBE IC 13, PIN 6. With the probe in place, the tester can run a test sequence over and over again. If the test fails immediately, the user is quickly ready to go on to the next test, to isolate the problem further. On the other hand, if the fault is an intermittent one, the user may want to linger. Raising the test probe is a convenient way for the user to signal the test equipment to go on to the next test. The probe only needs to be able to distinguish a floating input from a high or a low logic level.

The probe circuit of Fig. 5-49 uses the two lower voltage comparators to generate a PROBE RAISED flag. With the open-collector outputs of these two comparators connected as shown, the only way for PROBE RAISED to go high is for the output transistors on the outputs of both comparators to be turned off. This requires both differential inputs e_1 and e_2 to be positive. This, in turn, requires the probe input voltage to be between 1.1 and 1.9 V. The resistors to the probe input cause this to happen when the probe is raised, with a 1.5-V level.

Since the probe input must have a high impedance to avoid appreciably loading the circuit under test, the use of a comparator or its equivalent is required whether or not the PROBE RAISED feature is used. Hence this feature is available at virtually no increased cost.

Because of the needs of process-control engineers, many transducers are available which will transduce a physical quantity, like temperature or

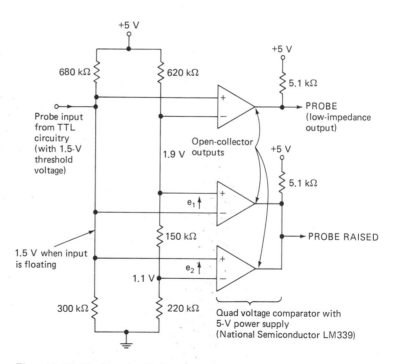

Figure 5-49. "Probe raised" detect circuit.

(a)

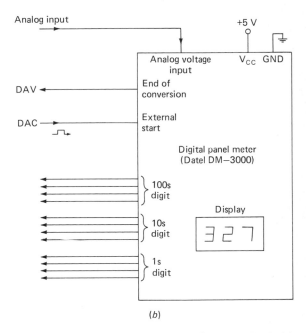

(b)

Figure 5-50. Digital panel meter. (Datel Systems, Inc.) (a)
Device; (b) circuit.

pressure, into a linearly proportional voltage. If a display of this quantity is
required on the front panel of the instrument, perhaps suitably scaled, a
digital panel meter like that of Fig. 5-50 will perform both the analog-to-
digital (A/D) conversion function and the display function. This meter displays a voltage between 0 and 999 mV. The decimal point can be sup-
pressed, if desired. As an A/D converter, it has the characteristics shown in
Fig. 5-50b and can be set up to carry out a new conversion at any rate from 0

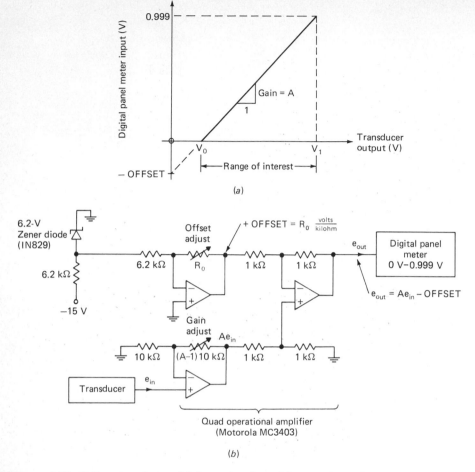

Figure 5-51. *Voltage translator.* (a) *Operational-amplifier translator characteristic;* (b) *circuit.*

to 250 samples per second, which is adequate for many transduction purposes.

Scaling the transducer output so that the numbers on a digital panel meter yield some desired meaning (for example, tenths of degrees Fahrenheit between 00.0° and 99.9°) can be carried out with an operational-amplifier voltage-translation circuit. Consider that the transducer generates a positive output voltage and that V_0 represents the transducer output voltage to be translated to a display of 0. Likewise V_1 represents the transducer output voltage to be translated to an output of 999 mV. Then the desired translation characteristic is shown in Fig. 5-51a. The circuit of Fig. 5-51b uses a single integrated circuit and some resistors to achieve this characteristic. The gain and offset potentiometers not only serve their expected functions of adjusting gain and offset voltages but also serve to compensate for operational-amplifier nonideal characteristics (for example, offset voltage), as long as these remain sufficiently constant in the instrument application. If this is not the case, higher-performance operational amplifiers can be used. The operational-amplifier performance is helped if the transducer output is not likely to change blazingly fast.

When a direct display is not desirable, an A/D converter is the needed device, available in modular form or in a DIP package. The A/D converter shown in Fig. 5-52a requires only the addition of a voltage comparator and an external 10-V reference to produce a 10-bit binary number proportional to an analog voltage input between 0 and 10 V.

As shown in Fig. 5-52b, the A/D converter is designed to operate conveniently in a bus-organized system. The conversion is begun when the CPU pulses the "Start" input, perhaps using an OUT instruction and decoding the $\overline{\text{OUT}}$ line with an address for this function. Then the CPU can go into a wait loop of roughly 20 μs, which tests DAV (DAta Valid) by executing an IN instruction (and decoding the $\overline{\text{IN}}$ line with an address which will pulse the

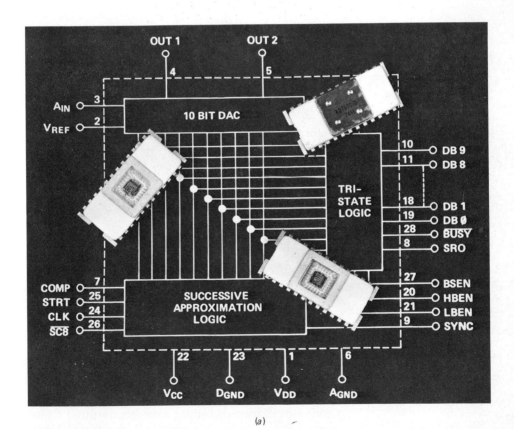

(a)

Figure 5-52. CMOS 10-bit A/D converter. (Analog Devices.) (a) Device; (b) circuit.

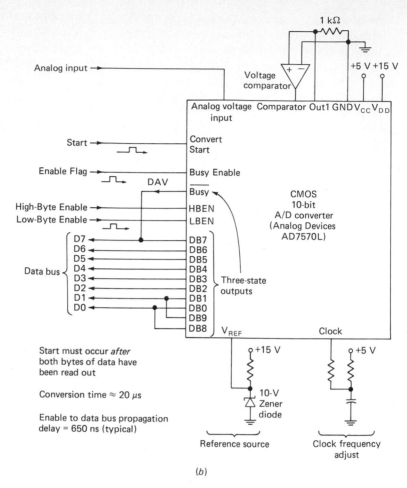

Figure 5-52. (*Continued*)

"Enable Flag" line). When DAV is read in as a logic 1, the conversion is complete. The lower 8 bits can be read with an IN instruction which decodes a second address to strobe the "Low-Byte Enable" line, putting this data onto the data bus. The upper 2 bits are enabled onto the bus with an IN instruction to a third address which strobes the "High-Byte Enable" line. The data remains latched in the A/D converter until the CPU generates another "Start" pulse.

An 8-bit version of this A/D converter differs only slightly. When DAV goes high, the 8 data bits can be put on the data bus with a "Byte Enable" input.

As an example of a convenient transducer for a microcomputer-based instrument which involves a pressure measurement, consider National Semiconductor's integrated-circuit pressure transducer shown in Fig. 5-53a.

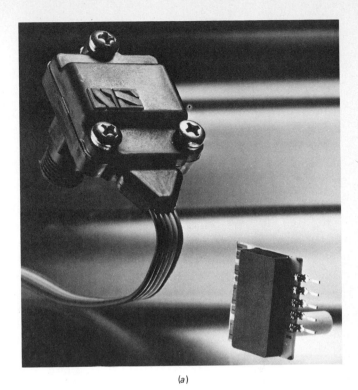

(a)

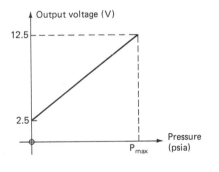

P_{max} (psia)	National Semiconductor device model number
15	LX1702A
30	LX1703A
60	LX1710A
100	LX1720A
300	LX1730A
1000	LX1740A
2000	LX1750A
3000	LX1760A
5000	LX1770A

±3 percent of span overall accuracy
±0.5 percent of span repeatability

(b)

Figure 5-53. Integrated-circuit pressure transducer. (National Semiconductor Corp.)
(a) Device; (b) characteristics.

The device provides the linear output shown in Fig. 5-53b, which can easily be translated down to a 0- to 10-V output range for conversion by a 10-V A/D converter. As shown in that figure, the device is available in many models to provide for the measurement of absolute pressure with a full-scale output ranging from atmospheric pressure up to 5000 psia (pounds per square inch

absolute).   National also configures this device into a *relative* pressure
gauge, for measuring pressure differences.

5-6   DISPLAY

In this section we will look at the means for generating front-panel displays
of the following types:

   1   Annunciators (that is, on-off lights)
   2   Numerics
   3   Alphanumerics

A popular and easy-to-use annunciator is a light-emitting diode (LED), such
as that of Fig. 5-54, which can be mounted directly in a front panel using the
mounting clip shown.   Alternatively, it can be printed-circuit (PC)-board-
mounted behind a translucent panel.   While most LEDs emit a ruby-red
light, green and yellow LEDs are also available.   When a LED is forward-
biased, its current must be limited externally because the LED itself causes a
constant voltage drop (of 1.6 or 2.4 V, typically).   A typical drive circuit is
shown in Fig. 5-55.

    The display of numeric information can be handled in any of several
ways.   Arrays of seven-segment LED displays, such as the one shown in Fig.
5-56*a*, can be PC-board-mounted in standard integrated-circuit sockets.
They are available in both the common-cathode configuration of Fig. 5-56*b*
and the common-anode configuration of Fig. 5-56*c* to permit alternatives in
the drive circuitry.

    Figure 5-57 illustrates one way in which seven-segment LED displays
can be driven from output ports using standard BCD*-to-seven-segment
decoder-drivers.   The 150-Ω resistors limit the current in each LED segment

---

    * Binary-coded decimal; see Sec. 7-4.

*Figure 5-54. Light-emitting diode and mounting clip.   (Hewlett-
Packard Co.)*

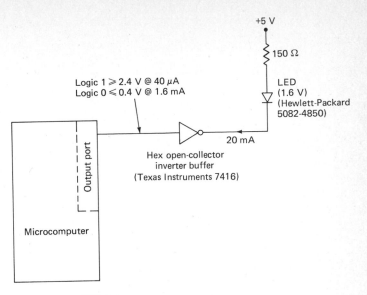

Logic 1 ⩾ 2.4 V @ 40 μA
Logic 0 ⩽ 0.4 V @ 1.6 mA

+5 V

150 Ω

LED
(1.6 V)
(Hewlett-Packard
5082-4850)

20 mA

Hex open-collector
inverter buffer
(Texas Instruments 7416)

Output port

Microcomputer

Figure 5-55. LED driver.

(a)

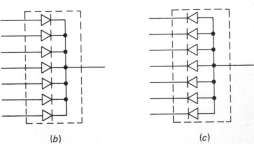

(b)

(c)

Figure 5-56. Seven-segment LED display. (Litronix, Inc.) (a) Typical unit; (b) common cathode; (c) common anode.

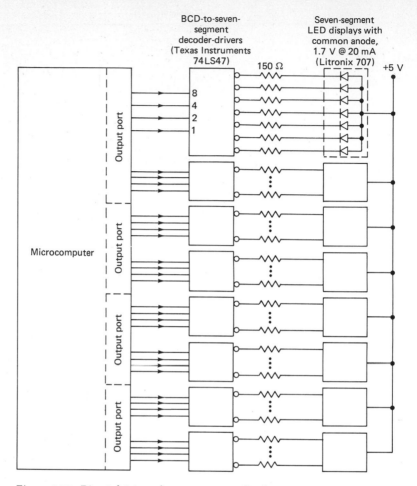

Figure 5-57. *Direct driving of seven-segment displays.*

to 20 mA.   A 74LSxx TTL decoder-driver is used on the assumption that the microcomputer output port can satisfy its 0.36-mA sink current input requirement, but perhaps not the 1.6-mA requirement of a standard 74xx TTL input.

If we use any decimal displays at all, we may want to use more than just one or two digits. In this case, the approach of Fig. 5-57 expends microcomputer output ports at a prodigious rate. In contrast, the approach of Fig. 5-58 uses decoder-drivers, each of which includes latches to hold the one BCD digit being displayed, to reduce the number of output ports required. The Signetics unit shown imposes very low input loading and has current-source outputs. It holds the 20-mA output current desired without the use of the current-limiting resistors of Fig. 5-57.   The one-of-eight decoder shown in Fig. 5-58 has "asserted" outputs so that the selected output is driven high, as required by the "strobe" input of the Signetics unit.   To

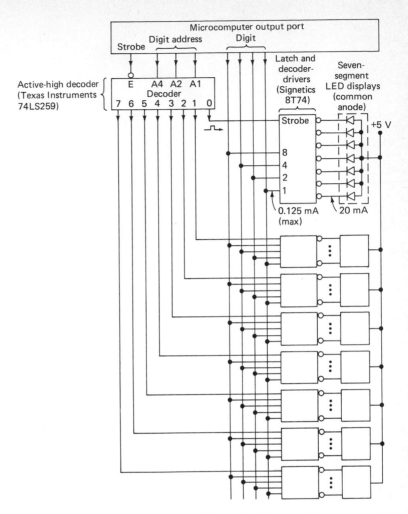

Figure 5-58. *Use of decoder-drivers having latches to reduce output-port requirements.*

understand how a digit is updated, consider that a 5 is to be displayed in the top display, having Digit address = 0. The output port must be put through the sequence:

Strobe	Digit address	Digit	Function
1	xxx	xxxx	Arbitrary output, but strobe disabled
1	000	0101	Set up digit address and digit
0	000	0101	Strobe
1	000	0101	Disable strobe

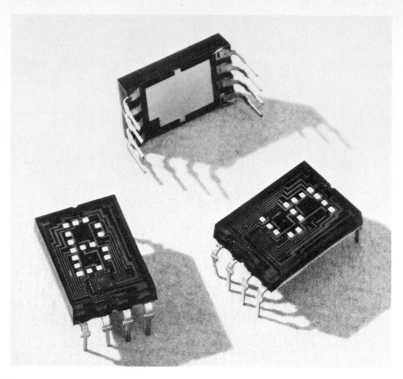

Figure 5-59. *Latch-decoder-driver-display combination.* (*Hewlett-Packard Co.*)

A device which carries the amalgamation of parts one step further than that of Fig. 5-58 is the combination latch-decoder-driver-display shown in Fig. 5-59. It is available in a form which provides a hexadecimal digit output. Alternatively, another model can be used if it is useful to blank the display by writing the hexadecimal character F into it or to obtain a minus sign by writing the hexadecimal character D into it. Each input looks like a 74xx standard TTL input, requiring the sinking of 1.6 mA to ground. Except for the buffers required to handle this load current, the circuit of Fig. 5-58 can substitute eight of these units for the eight latch-decoder-drivers and the eight seven-segment displays shown.

Rather than using an output port to drive a display, the display can be configured to look like "write-only memory." Not only does this save the use of an output port, but also it simplifies the updating of the display. For example, the circuit of Fig. 5-60 looks like a 74LSxx circuit to the address bus/data bus structure of a microcomputer. It includes two page-selection inputs for use as discussed in conjunction with Fig. 3-25. Within the selected page, writing to any of addresses 00–07 will update two digits (assuming an 8-bit microcomputer).

Another way to reduce the parts count is to *multiplex* the display, as in

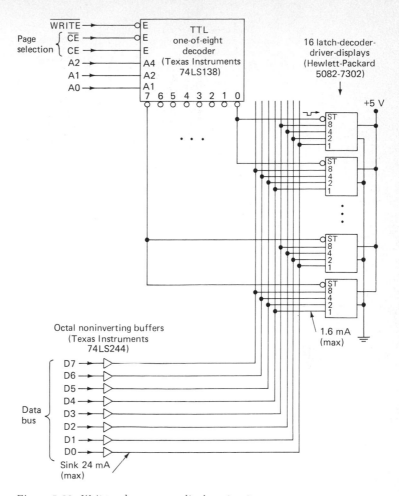

Figure 5-60. *Write-only memory display circuit.*

Fig. 5-61.   This approach drives an array of seven-segment displays from a single-BCD-to-seven-segment decoder.   Each of the eight displays shown is driven for 1 ms out of every 8 ms.   To obtain an average current of I_{avg} in each turned-on display segment, this requires an actual current per segment of

$$I_{seg} = 8\ I_{avg}$$

The circuit shown employs Darlington circuits for both "segment drivers" and "digit drivers," as shown in more detail in Fig. 5-62.   The specific segment driver used has a maximum drive capability of 50 mA.   This means that the average segment current is limited to $\frac{50}{8} = 6.25$ mA, which means that the display will be considerably less bright than if it were driven with

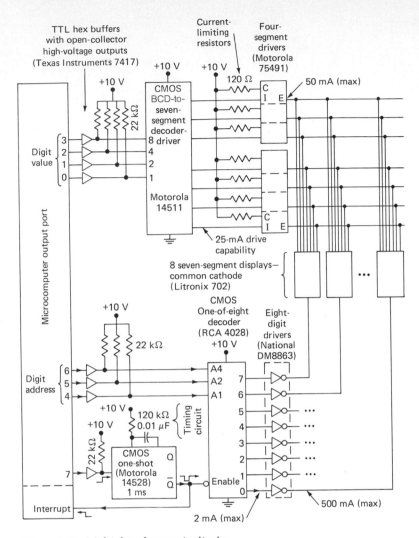

Figure 5-61. Multiplexed numeric display.

the constant 20 mA used in previous drive circuits. On the other hand, LED segments operated with a constant current are less bright than LED segments operated in a multiplexed mode and having the same value of average current. It might take a constant current of 8 or 9 mA to obtain the same brightness as is obtained with the average current of 6.25 mA of Fig. 5-61.

Each digit driver in Fig. 5-61 must turn on the current for as many as seven segments at one time (when an 8 is being displayed), for a total of $50 \times 7 = 350$ mA. These segment drivers and digit drivers need the 10-V swings provided by the CMOS outputs. Also, as shown in Fig. 5-62, the total voltage drop across drivers and LED segment is approximately 4 V. If a

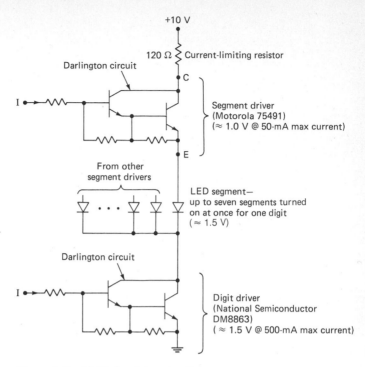

Figure 5-62. Multiplex drive circuit.

5-V supply were used, any variation in the 4 V would cause a large percentage change in the voltage across the current-limiting resistor and would significantly affect the current through the LED, and its brightness. For these two reasons, the multiplexed display is operated from a 10-V supply voltage. Assuming TTL-compatible output ports, this necessitates the buffering shown, to translate 0- to 5-V swings on the microcomputer outputs into the 0- to 10-V swings needed by the CMOS devices (when they are operated with a 10-V power-supply voltage).

The one-shot in this circuit serves two functions. First, it generates an interrupt every millisecond which is used to update the output port with the next digit address and its digit value. Also, it disables the display after 1 ms, which is about as long as a LED segment can operate with a 50-mA current without having its operating life adversely affected. A major risk inherent in a multiplexed display is that a malfunction in the multiplexing mechanism will leave one seven-segment display turned on constantly with an excessively high current. The one-shot shuts down the display in the case of a multiplexing malfunction, thereby protecting it.

If the eight displayed digits are stored in RAM in the packed form shown in Fig. 5-63a, the job of the interrupt service routine for the display is greatly simplified. Notice that each of the eight digits is packed with its

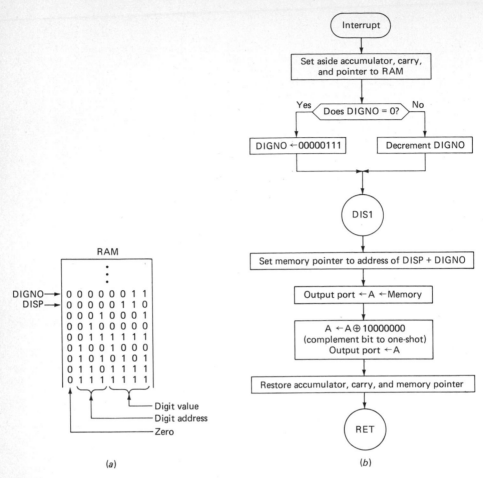

Figure 5-63. *Software for multiplexed numeric display.* (a) *RAM contents shown for a display of Blank, Blank, 5, 8, Blank, 0, 1, 6 (where blanking is achieved with digit value = 1111); (b) interrupt service routine for display.*

digit address in the most significant bits of the word. These bits might be inserted as part of the initialization routine when power is turned on. The service routine decrements DIGNO to obtain the number of the next digit address to be refreshed. When DIGNO reaches zero, it is preset to the highest address, which is seven in our case. DIGNO is used to pick one word out of the eight-word array DISP, which in turn is loaded into the output port. The most significant bit is then complemented to trigger the one-shot of Fig. 5-61, turning on the display for 1 ms.

A versatile alphanumeric display is shown in Fig. 5-64a. It is easy to use because the device includes memory and refresh circuitry so that it will, on its own, maintain the display of up to 32 characters on a panel 8.5 in. long

(a)

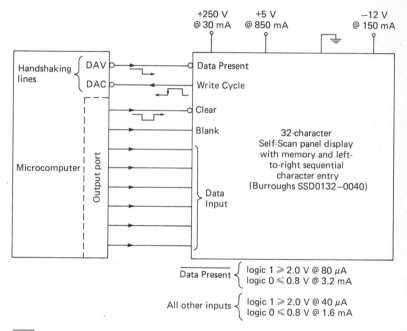

$$\overline{\text{Data Present}} \begin{cases} \text{logic } 1 \geqslant 2.0 \text{ V @ 80 } \mu\text{A} \\ \text{logic } 0 \leqslant 0.8 \text{ V @ 3.2 mA} \end{cases}$$

$$\text{All other inputs} \begin{cases} \text{logic } 1 \geqslant 2.0 \text{ V @ 40 } \mu\text{A} \\ \text{logic } 0 \leqslant 0.8 \text{ V @ 1.6 mA} \end{cases}$$

$\overline{\text{Clear}}$ pulse $\geqslant 33$ μs clears the display's memory.
When Blank = 1, the entire display is blanked. The display's
memory is not affected. This is useful for presenting
a blinking message.

A negative transition on the $\overline{\text{Data Present}}$ input initiates
the acceptance of one character into the display's memory and
causes Write Cycle to go high immediately.
When Write Cycle returns low again (1.0 to 33 μs later), the
data input can be changed and the next character
transferred to the display.

(b)

Figure 5-64. *Self-Scan® panel display.* (Burroughs Corp.) (a) Device; (b) circuit; (c) data-input
coding.

Code	Display	Code	Display	Code	Display	Code	Display
00	@	10	P	20	(blank)	30	0
01	A	11	Q	21	!	31	1
02	B	12	R	22	"	32	2
03	C	13	S	23	#	33	3
04	D	14	T	24	$	34	4
05	E	15	U	25	%	35	5
06	F	16	V	26	&	36	6
07	G	17	W	27	/	37	7
08	H	18	X	28	(	38	8
09	I	19	Y	29	)	39	9
0A	J	1A	Z	2A	*	3A	:
0B	K	1B	[	2B	+	3B	;
0C	L	1C	~	2C	,	3C	<
0D	M	1D	]	2D	–	3D	=
0E	N	1E	{	2E	.	3E	>
0F	O	1F	}	2F	╱	3F	?

(c)

Figure 5-64. (Continued)

by 2.25 in. high. As shown in Fig. 5-64b, the display is updated by first applying a logic 0 on the $\overline{\text{Clear}}$ input for at least 33 μs, clearing the display's memory, and initializing the display so that the next character to be entered will be displayed in the leftmost-character position. Successive characters to be displayed from left to right are now loaded into the display using the handshaking lines shown in Fig. 5-64b and the character codes shown in Fig. 5-64c. This code is a 6-bit subset of the 7-bit ASCII code, slightly modified for some nonalphanumeric characters.

Since each character requires no longer than 33 μs to enter, use of the "Write Cycle" handshaking input to the microcomputer under flag control seems appropriate. The display might be updated by loading the ASCII code for the 32-character message into a 32-word RAM array and then calling a display subroutine which outputs each character in turn. Alternatively, a scheme like that discussed in Prob. 5-20 permits fixed characters to be taken directly from a ROM array and appropriately mixed with variable characters taken from a RAM array.

This display is particularly versatile because the output, or outputs, to be displayed can be labeled on the display itself. This permits the display to be used in a variety of ways without confusion to the user. Several examples are shown in Fig. 5-65.

Other Self-Scan models include a 1 row × 16 character display (Model SSD1000-0041) having the same overall dimensions, costing roughly the same amount but having characters which are twice as large.

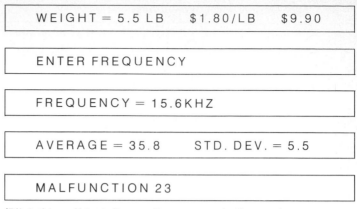

WEIGHT = 5.5 LB $1.80/LB $9.90

ENTER FREQUENCY

FREQUENCY = 15.6KHZ

AVERAGE = 35.8   STD. DEV. = 5.5

MALFUNCTION 23

(Blink this self-test diagnostic message to the user)

Figure 5-65. Examples of the use of an alphanumeric display panel.

5-7   ACTUATION

A recurring consideration in the design of microcomputer-based instruments is the buffering needed between the lines of an output port, with their limited drive capability, and the devices needing driving, with their variations in current and voltage requirements. Many microcomputers have output ports with just enough drive capability to drive one standard TTL (74xx) input. As shown in Fig. 3-8 and repeated in Fig. 5-66, this means that the output can pull a load of at least 1.6 mA down below 0.4 V. It also means that it can pull a load of at least 40 μA up above 2.4 V.

For microcomputers whose output ports cannot drive even one standard TTL input (for example, RCA's COSMAC using standard CMOS devices to construct output ports), possibly they will drive the low-power Schottky TTL (that is, 74LSxx) inputs described in Fig. 3-8. Then the buffering and drive circuitry can be built up out of 74LSxx devices. Alternatively, the outputs can be buffered up to TTL drive capability using the CMOS buffers described in Fig. 5-66.

For loads of up to 30 V and 40 mA, the standard TTL inverting buffer shown in Fig. 5-67*a* will energize the load with a logic 1 on the output port. If the load is inductive (for example, a solenoid, relay, or motor), the buffer needs to be protected against the inductive-voltage surge which occurs when the circuitry tries to turn off the current in the load suddenly. The low-cost rectifier shown in Fig. 5-67*b* provides this protection in a package which is smaller than a $\frac{1}{4}$-W resistor. The circuits of Fig. 5-67*c* and *d* provide higher current drive capability. In addition, the "protect circuit" of Fig. 5-67*d* includes a resistor to speed up *turn-off* of the current in an inductive load. While this can be omitted for a slow, nonrepetitively operating device like a solenoid, it is useful for speeding the response of a faster, repetitively

Figure 5-66. Output Drive Capabilities

		Line of output port capable of driving exactly one standard TTL input	Output of CMOS hex buffer with 5-V power (Motorola MC14050CP)
Logic 1 output	Minimum guaranteed source current with output pulled down to 2.4 V	40 μA	1.25 mA
Logic 0 output	Minimum guaranteed sink current with output pulled up to 0.4 V	1.6 mA	3.2 mA

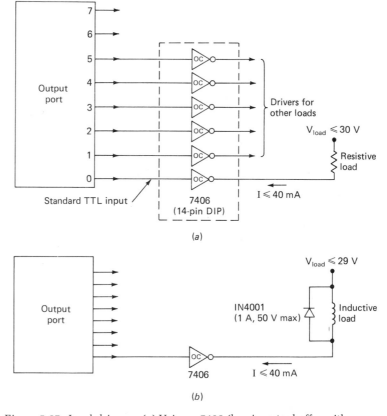

(a)

(b)

Figure 5-67. Load drivers. (a) Using a 7406 (hex inverter buffer with open-collector, high-voltage output) to turn on current to a resistive load with a logic 1 from the output port; (b) using a low-cost rectifier to protect the buffer from voltage surges occurring across an inductive load; (c) driving higher current loads; (d) driving even higher current loads; (e) 2N6038 Darlington power transistor. (Motorola Semiconductor Products, Inc.)

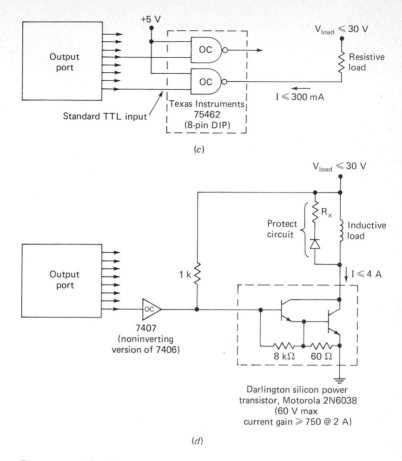

Figure 5-67. (*Continued*)

operating device like a stepper motor. The resistor R_x is selected so that

$$V_{load} + I_{load} \cdot R_x \leqslant \text{transistor breakdown voltage}$$

For driving ac loads, a *solid-state relay* provides megohms of isolation between the microcomputer circuitry and the ac voltage which could easily destroy that circuitry, if it could only reach into it. Many solid-state relays use a LED-phototransistor combination to achieve this isolation. The particularly small unit shown in Fig. 5-68 uses its dc input to turn on or off a 4-MHz oscillator so that a tiny transformer can provide the isolation. In either case, a breakdown voltage of 1500 V or so is achieved between input and output.

Zero voltage turn-on is a built-in feature of many solid-state relays (but not of the unit shown in Fig. 5-68). The ac line is monitored so that the current to an inductive load can be turned on at precisely that moment when the

(e)

Figure 5-67. (Continued)

voltage crosses through zero volts, thereby minimizing the generation of RFI (radio-frequency interference). A microcomputer-based instrument can use the circuit of Fig. 5-69 to provide zero-crossing detection for any number of solid-state relays not having this feature themselves. When it comes time to turn on any relay, we can call a subroutine which continually tests the flag labeled Polarity in Fig. 5-69, returning when its value changes. Alternatively, Polarity can be used under interrupt control.

In addition to the models of solid-state relays suitable for driving ac loads, other models are available for driving dc loads. These again provide the high degree of isolation between microcomputer circuitry and load circuitry afforded by a LED-phototransistor combination or by transformer coupling.

Position control within an instrument can be implemented with the combination of a synchronous motor and a few optoelectronic switches,

(a)

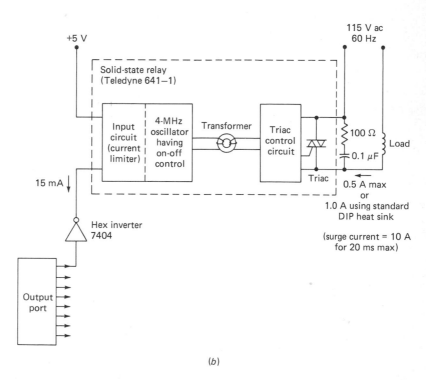

(b)

Figure 5-68. Solid-state relay. (Teledyne Relays.) (a) Device; (b) block diagram.

using the position-sensing scheme of Fig. 5-39. In fact, excellent quantization of position can be obtained with only a very rough encoder quantization, since the shaft of the synchronous motor rotates at a precisely known rate once it is up to speed. It is only necessary to wait a minimum amount of time after starting the motor before position can be precisely determined between quanta boundaries.

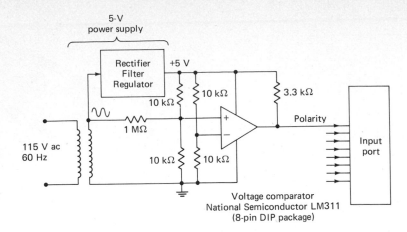

Figure 5-69. *Zero-crossing detection circuit.*

Synchronous motors come in a variety of sizes, speeds, and torque ratings. The 1-in.-diameter unit shown in Fig. 5-70 provides almost constant torque from start-up up to a synchronous speed of 1800 rpm. It is also available as a planetary gearmotor with an elongated package, available in speeds down to 0.05 rpm and torque ratings of up to 300 in.-oz.

Direct digital control of shaft position within an instrument can be efficiently achieved with a stepper motor, such as the 1-in.-diameter unit shown in Fig. 5-71. With the many manufacturers who provide them, stepper motors are available having a broad range of torque ratings, from a fraction of an inch-ounce for small units up to hundreds of inch-pounds for large units. They are also available in a broad range of step sizes, without gearing, from 90° down to 0.36° per step. With the addition of gearing, an arbitrary tradeoff between high sweep rate and high resolution and torque is possible.

In many applications, use is made of the fast start-stop capability of a stepper. If the dynamic torque of the load does not exceed that available from the motor, it can be started and stopped "on a dime." Typical stepping rates for various motors operated in this fashion range between 200 and 1000 steps per second. If the motor is gently accelerated up to its maximum stepping rate and decelerated to a stop, it can generally reach a speed of two to four times that specified for starting and stopping on a dime and still not miss a step.

Another useful feature of stepper motors is the accuracy of their stepping. For example, consider the motor of Fig. 5-71, which steps 24 steps per revolution. If it is stepped exactly 48 steps clockwise, it will turn exactly two revolutions. Then if it is stepped 48 steps counterclockwise, it will return to its exact starting position. In a *variable-reluctance* stepper motor, like that of Fig. 5-71, this happens because the rotor and stator have many teeth and slots which align themselves so as to minimize the magnetic reluc-

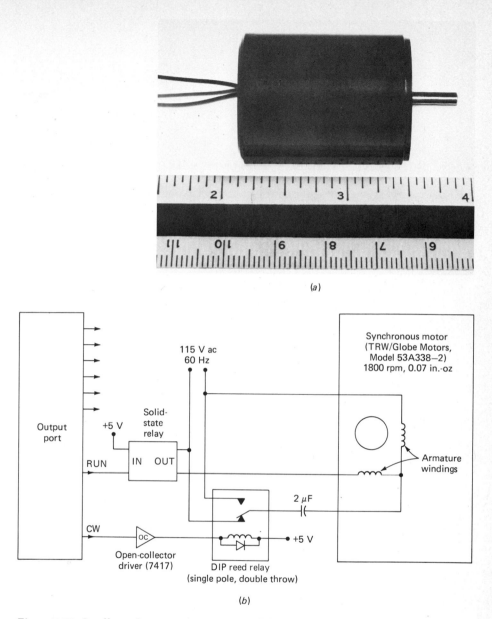

(a)

(b)

Figure 5-70. *Small synchronous motor.* (TRW/Globe Motors) (a) *Device;* (b) *drive circuit.*

tance in the field set up by the excitation current. In a *permanent-magnet stepper motor*, it happens because the permanent-magnet rotor aligns itself with the magnetic field set up in the stator by the excitation current. Consequently, although there is some error in the exact position held at each step position, this error does not accumulate as the motor steps along.

(a)

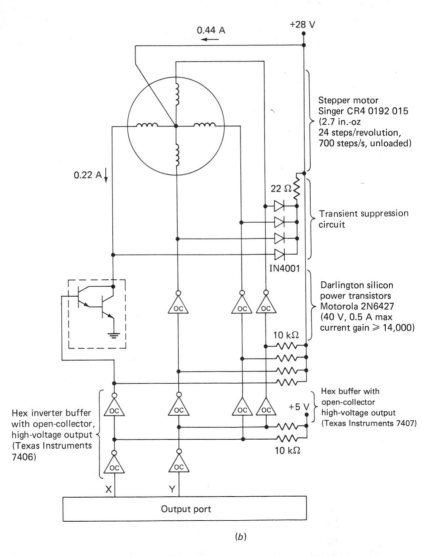

0.44 A

+28 V

0.22 A

22 Ω

Stepper motor
Singer CR4 0192 015
(2.7 in.-oz
24 steps/revolution,
700 steps/s, unloaded)

Transient suppression
circuit

IN4001

Darlington silicon
power transistors
Motorola 2N6427
(40 V, 0.5 A max
current gain ≥ 14,000)

OC OC OC

10 kΩ

Hex buffer with
open-collector
high-voltage output
(Texas Instruments 7407)

Hex inverter buffer
with open-collector,
high-voltage output
(Texas Instruments
7406)

OC OC OC OC

+5 V

10 kΩ

OC OC

X   Y

Output port

(b)

Figure 5-71. Stepper motor. (The Singer Company, Kearfott Division.)
(a) Device; (b) drive circuit; (c) stepping sequence.

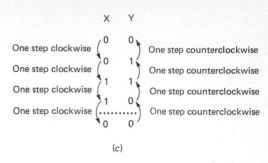

(c)

Figure 5-71. (Continued)

These two features of fast starting and stopping and of accurate stepping account for the use of stepper motors in a wide assortment of positioning applications. Plotters, printers, and optical instruments all use stepper motors to position a pen, print head, or optics. Each position corresponds to a discrete number of steps from a reference position. For example, if each step of the motor is translated into a 0.01-in. motion, moving 1.00 in. means taking 100 steps.

Incremental control such as this possesses the deficiency that if steps are ever missed, the instrument will be in error by that number of steps thereafter. This might occur if an inertial load is accelerated or decelerated too fast, if the device being driven by the motor runs into a stop or an obstacle, or if the motor is being stepped, and "coasts," when power is lost (even if the microcomputer employs power-standby capability for its register and RAM contents). In many applications, such a malfunction may occur so rarely, or with so little consequence, that the simplicity of stepper-motor positioning overrides this drawback. In addition, the same optoelectronic switch which might be used to provide an absolute reference position can also be used as a basis of self-testing for this kind of error using a scheme analogous to that of Prob. 5-13.

Stepper motors are driven by transistor switches, but the exact switching sequence depends on the specific motor used. The motor shown in Fig. 5-71 is reasonably typical in its drive circuitry. It uses a *bifilar-wound* stator, as shown schematically in Fig. 5-71b. The two vertical bifilar windings avoid the problem of having only one vertical winding in which the current must flow in either direction. Switching the current through one winding in either direction is difficult to achieve with transistor switches. In contrast, the bifilar windings permit current to be turned on (or off) in one winding while it is turned off (or on) in the other.

The actual sequencing of switching operations to make the motor step through four steps in a clockwise (or counterclockwise) direction is shown in Fig. 5-71c (where each step is 15°). If a RAM location is used to hold the two bits X and Y, which are presently driving the motor, then when a pro-

(a)

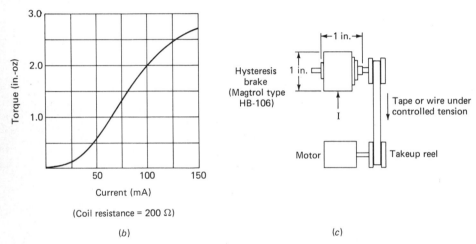

(b)   (c)

Figure 5-72. Hysteresis brake. (Magtrol, Inc.) (a) Device; (b) characteristic; (c) its use.

grammable timer says it is time to take the next step, its service routine can change this number appropriately and pack it out to the output port.

Many devices provide an output quantity proportional to an input voltage or current. For example, the miniature hysteresis brake shown in Fig. 5-72 can be used to produce a tension on a wire or tape which is roughly proportional to its input current. Significantly, the torque is virtually independent of the speed of the tape or wire.

To drive such devices, we can use a low-cost *digital-to-analog* (D/A) converter to provide a voltage or current proportional to a digital output. For example, an 8-bit D/A converter packaged in a 14-pin DIP package is shown in Fig. 5-73. It can be tied directly to an output port, providing a voltage between 0 and 10 V which is directly proportional to the contents of

Figure 5-73. Eight-bit D/A
converter. (Zeltex, Inc.)

the output port. Since the output of this unit requires 10 μs to settle to a
new value, its relatively slow speed (for a D/A converter) is fast enough for
most microcomputer-based instruments.

The output voltage of a D/A converter is typically limited to 0–5 V,
0–10 V, ± 5 V, or ± 10 V. The output current is typically limited to a few
milliamperes, which is hardly enough to drive any device other than a
cathode-ray-tube display. However, this problem is readily resolved using a
programmable power supply, such as the low-cost modular supply shown in
Fig. 5-74. This specific supply will accept the unipolar output of a D/A converter as an input and generate a unipolar dc voltage of up to 7 V (at a maximum of 2 A) which is proportional to this voltage and has an arbitrary proportionality factor. Alternatively, it can be connected to generate a unipolar
direct current of up to 2 A (at a maximum of 7 V) proportional to the input
voltage, again with an arbitrary proportionality factor. As a third alternative, both the current limit and the voltage limit can be programmed, so that
the mode of operation (that is, current-limited or voltage-limited) is determined by the load and yet precisely controlled.

In general, programmable power supplies will provide voltages up to
several thousand volts, and currents up to 100 A (but not in the same
supply!). If a programmable *bipolar* output is required, a unit to handle this
is available from at least some of the manufacturers of unipolar programmable supplies, albeit at a significantly higher cost than that required for a
unipolar supply. For example, Kepco's BOP36-1.5 modular bipolar power
supply is a true bidirectional power amplifier which can source or sink up to
± 36 V at up to ± 1.5 A.

Some instruments must generate an output-voltage waveform. This
can be generated algorithmically within the microcomputer and converted
into a voltage waveform with a D/A converter, provided that the microcomputer can keep up with the speed required. This scheme provides excellent
frequency and amplitude accuracy and is particularly simple to implement

Figure 5-74. Programmable modular power supply. (Kepco, Inc.)

for square, pulse, triangle, and sawtooth waveforms. For sinusoids, a waveform generator like Exar's XR-205 (packaged in a 16-pin DIP) permits modulation of both the amplitude and the frequency. The PC-board-mounted
frequency synthesizer of Fig. 5-75 uses phase-locked-loop control of
a frequency derived from a crystal oscillator to generate any frequency between 1 and 32 MHz, with a resolution of 500 Hz. It is controlled by a
BCD code input.

5-8 PRINTING

Many instruments can make excellent use of a built-in printer to provide
hard-copy output. For an instrument with a single output (for example, the
distance determined by a distance meter), a *numeric* printer like that of Fig.
5-76 can serve this purpose.

Of more general usefulness is a built-in *alphanumeric* printer. It can
provide a user with *labeled* outputs (for example, WEIGHT = 5.5LB), permitting it to be used in a variety of ways without confusion to the user.
Thus, it serves much the same purpose as the alphanumeric display of Fig.
5-64, but with the additional capability of providing multiple-line messages
and hard copy.

The manner in which a microcomputer interacts with the printer can

Figure 5-75. Frequency synthesizer. (Syntest Corp.)

be designed to be very simple. The printer mechanism can be embedded in suitable circuitry so that all character-decoding and timing requirements are handled by this circuitry. This is the approach taken by the TTL-compatible and modular numeric printer shown in Fig. 5-76. The BCD coding for an entire line is applied in parallel. Then a "print and advance" pulse tells the printer circuitry to print this data. A "busy" output is used under either

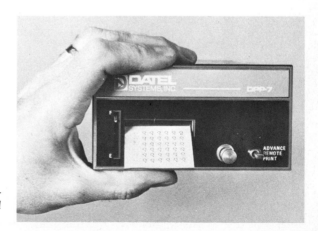

Figure 5-76. Modular seven-column numeric printer. (Datel Systems, Inc.)

flag control or interrupt control to inform the microcomputer when it can initiate the next line of printed output.

A more suitable interface for microcomputer control would include sufficient buffering in the printer electronics so that the successive characters to be printed in one line would be loaded in, one by one, much as was done with the alphanumeric display of Fig. 5-64. Then a "print and advance" pulse would cause this data to be printed and a "busy" output would signal when the printer is done.

While this circuitry makes it easy to use a printer, it is questionable whether such circuitry is cost-effective in a microcomputer-based instrument. In contrast with the display of Fig. 5-64, a printer has no requirement to be repeatedly refreshed. In addition, the printing events which must be timed are sufficiently slow so that they can be handled under interrupt control and still leave the microcomputer free to spend most of its time doing other things.

Using the philosophy of putting as much of the circuitry of an instrument as possible into the microcomputer, we end up trading off circuitry for ROM. The different pulses needed by the printer mechanism are generated directly on output ports, suitably buffered with the transistor drivers or optically coupled drivers discussed in the last section. In order to understand what this approach might involve, we need to know how a specific printer mechanism works.

The alphanumeric impact printer shown in Fig. 5-77a prints lines consisting of 21 alphanumeric characters, at a rate of about 1.2 lines per second. It has a character set consisting of the 42 characters shown in Fig. 5-77b. This figure is actually a linear representation of the print drum used in the printer and shown in cross section in Fig. 5-77c. It is continuously stepped through the 42 positions corresponding to the 42 characters once every 850 ms.

In order to print a letter P in column 5, we must wait until the letter P has been stepped into position behind the paper, at which time we must activate a hammer aligned over column 5. This strikes an inked ribbon against the paper, impressing it upon the raised letter P on the print drum and thereby printing a P on the paper in this column position. More generally, to print an entire line of characters, the hammer for each column must be actuated at just the right time to pick out and print the character for that column. Since a given character appears simultaneously in all columns, the hammers for every column having this character must be actuated simultaneously.

The timing for all these operations is provided by the detecting head T, shown in Fig. 5-77c. Its output, labeled "T pulses," is shown in Fig. 5-77d. It consists of exactly 84 pulses per revolution, with two pulses used to define a timing interval for each character. It is during this timing interval that a hammer must be actuated in each column in which that character is to be printed. Detecting head R, also shown in Fig. 5-77c, provides a "zero reference" for the T pulses. Its output, "R signal," is a wide pulse which occurs

(a)

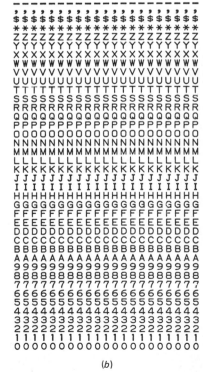

(b)

Figure 5-77. Twenty-one-column alphanumeric printer, Model AN-101F. (C. Itoh Electronics, Inc.) (a) Device; (b) character set; (c) schematic representation of timing and printing mechanisms; (d) timing diagram for printing; (e) timing diagram for paper feed and inked-ribbon feed; (f) microcomputer printer interface.

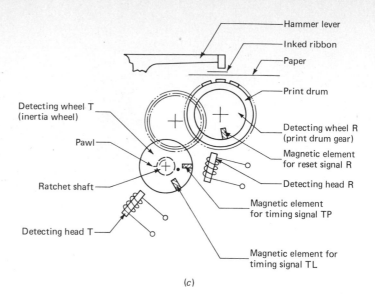

Detecting wheel T (inertia wheel)

Pawl

Ratchet shaft

Detecting head T

Hammer lever

Inked ribbon

Paper

Print drum

Detecting wheel R (print drum gear)

Magnetic element for reset signal R

Detecting head R

Magnetic element for timing signal TP

Magnetic element for timing signal TL

(c)

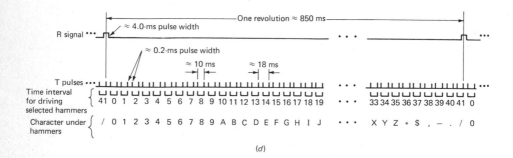

One revolution ≈ 850 ms

R signal ···

≈ 4.0-ms pulse width

≈ 0.2-ms pulse width

≈ 10 ms   ≈ 18 ms

T pulses ···

Time interval for driving selected hammers
{ 41 0 1 2 3 4 5 6 7 8 9 10 11 12 13 14 15 16 17 18 19 ··· 33 34 35 36 37 38 39 40 41 0

Character under hammers
{ / 0 1 2 3 4 5 6 7 8 9 A B C D E F G H I J ··· X Y Z * $, − . / 0

(d)

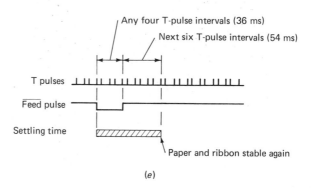

Any four T-pulse intervals (36 ms)

Next six T-pulse intervals (54 ms)

T pulses

Feed pulse

Settling time

Paper and ribbon stable again

(e)

Figure 5-77. (Continued)

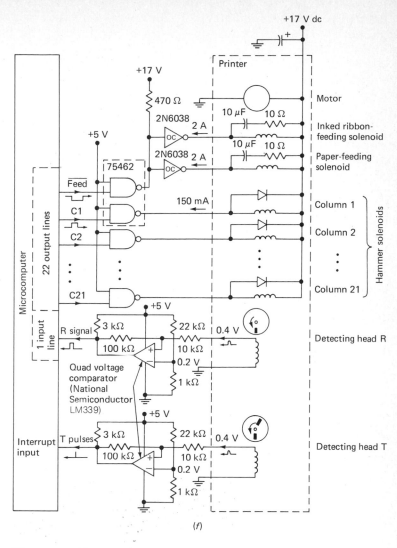

Figure 5-77. (Continued)

once per revolution, overlapping exactly one T pulse. It is truly a zero reference, since it is aligned with the pulse which occurs just before the two
pulses which define the timing interval for the zero character.

  After all the characters which are required for a complete line have
been printed, the paper is advanced to the next line and the inked ribbon is
advanced to a new position. This is accomplished with the single Feed
pulse shown in Fig. 5-77e. It is timed by turning it on at the start of any of

the T pulses and turning it off four T pulses later. Before beginning to print the next line, we must wait an additional six T pulses for the paper and ribbon to come to a halt.

Driving the 21 hammers and the solenoids for feeding paper and inked ribbon requires 22 output lines from the microcomputer, as shown in Fig. 5-77f. The drive circuitry was discussed in the last section. The manufacturer's recommended arc-suppression circuitry is shown.

Since the outputs of the two detecting heads are relatively low level signals (0.4 V minimum), the comparator circuits shown in Fig. 5-77f serve to amplify and square up these signals into proper logic levels. They include a hysteresis characteristic both to sharpen the edges of the output and to give immunity to noise on the input signals. The T pulses are used to provide interrupt control of the printer. In contrast, the R signal is monitored as a logic level on an input line each time a T pulse occurs.

Using interrupt control rather than flag control to drive the printer makes sense because the printer requires up to 84 responses to timing pulses to print all the characters of one line plus 10 responses to timing pulses to feed paper and ribbon, all in an interval of about 1 s. If a specific microcomputer can execute approximately 250,000 instructions in a second, then interrupt control will probably permit many other things to go on simultaneously during this 1-s interval. In fact, in their article referenced at the end of this chapter, Moore and Eidson show how the Motorola 6800 microcomputer can drive 16 columns of this printer under interrupt control using only 4 percent of the microcomputer's time servicing the printer.

A variety of approaches is possible for the manner in which the microcomputer software handles the hardware of Fig. 5-77f. We will assume that the specific microcomputer used is able to enable and disable a specific interrupt input, independent of whether other interrupt inputs remain enabled or disabled. As will be seen in the appendixes for specific microcomputers, this is a commonly available feature for a microcomputer having more than one interrupt input. An alternate approach would be to keep the interrupt input from the printer enabled all the time but to have the service routine do nothing when no printing is required.

The approach taken here will treat the printer in almost exactly the same way as the printer of Fig. 5-76 is treated. However, the desired characters to be displayed are first set up in an array in RAM rather than on output ports. The character codes used are shown in Fig. 5-78. These have been derived from Fig. 5-77b by assigning the hex code 00 to the numeral zero (which is the first character present under the column hammers after "R signal" provides a zero reference). Successive hex numbers are assigned to the characters which are successively present under the column hammers. In addition, the "blank" character is shown coded as 2A (hex) even though there is not actually a "blank" character on the print drum. As an example, Fig. 5-79 shows the contents of this printer array, called PARRAY, if the message to be printed is "AVERAGE IS 35.8."

Figure 5-78. Character Codes for Printer

Character to be printed	Character code (hex)	Character to be printed	Character code (hex)
0	00	M	16
1	01	N	17
2	02	O	18
3	03	P	19
4	04	Q	1A
5	05	R	1B
6	06	S	1C
7	07	T	1D
8	08	U	1E
9	09	V	1F
A	0A	W	20
B	0B	X	21
C	0C	Y	22
D	0D	Z	23
E	0E	*	24
F	0F	$	25
G	10	,	26
H	11	-	27
I	12	.	28
J	13	/	29
K	14	blank	2A
L	15		

The printer of Fig. 5-76 used a "busy" output to let the microcomputer know that the printer is still busy printing and advancing. We will do virtually the same thing, using a word in RAM labeled BUSY. As long as BUSY is nonzero, the printing and advancing operation is still going on.

The "print and advance" pulse required by the printer of Fig. 5-76 is replaced here by the instruction to enable interrupts from the "T pulses" input from the printer. In summary then, all that must be done, "consciously," to print a line is

1 Wait until BUSY equals zero, and then
2 Load PARRAY with the desired message, and then
3 Enable interrupts from the printer.

Everything else is done "subconsciously" by a succession of calls of the printer's interrupt service routine. The first call, after interrupts are enabled, sets BUSY to one. The last call occurs after the line has been printed

RAM contents	Meaning
0A	A
1F	V
0E	E
1B	R
0A	A
10	G
0E	E
2A	Blank
12	I
1C	S
2A	Blank
03	3
05	5
28	•
08	8
2A	Blank
2A	Blank
2A	Blank
2A	Blank
2A	Blank
2A	Blank

PARRAY → (points to first entry, 0A / A)

Figure 5-79. PARRAY, the array in RAM used by the printer's interrupt service routine.

and the paper has been advanced. It disables further interrupts and clears BUSY to zero.

When power is first turned on, the printer is initialized with the three steps shown in Fig. 5-80. Note the definition of POUT as consisting of the contents of 21 of the 24 lines of three 8-bit output ports. If a 4-bit microcomputer were employed instead of the assumed 8-bit microcomputer, we would use six output ports instead of three.

The printer's interrupt service routine PRINT must do the succession of jobs demanded by Fig. 5-77d, e, and f. In order to keep track of which job is to be done next, each time PRINT is entered, we can let the variable BUSY take on a succession of different values to serve as a mode, or control, or state variable. Thus at the beginning of the service routine, the value of BUSY is used as an offset into a table holding the addresses of BUSY0, BUSY1, BUSY2, etc., perhaps using the TBL2 subroutine of Sec. 2-8. This address is then loaded into the program counter to provide an indirect jump to the appropriate action to be taken, based upon the state of BUSY.

The PRINT routine has the six states shown in Fig. 5-81. First it waits in states BUSY0 and BUSY1 (that is, BUSY = 0 and BUSY = 1) for the zero reference provided by "R signal." When this occurs, the PRINT routine alternates, during the next 84 interrupts, between states BUSY2 and BUSY3.

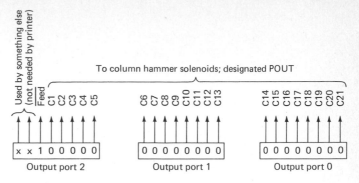

1 Initialize output ports as shown above.

2 Disable interrupts from printer.

3 Clear the RAM location labeled BUSY to zero.

Figure 5-80. *Printer initialization when power is first turned on.*

The BUSY2 state is used to turn off any column hammers which were actuated during a previous BUSY3 state. It is also used to decide which column hammers must be actuated when the next BUSY3 state occurs, temporarily storing this information in an array of three words in RAM called PTEMP. When "R signal" next occurs, all characters will have been printed. The paper and inked ribbon are now advanced by actuating the Feed output line. This should occur when PRINT is in the BUSY2 state. If, however, it occurs while PRINT is in the BUSY3 state, the proper number of "T pulses" has not been detected. The user can be told of the malfunction, perhaps using the self-test algorithm of Sec. 7-3.

If such a malfunction is not detected, then on its last entry into the BUSY2 state, when "R signal" equals one, the advancing of the paper and inked ribbon is initiated by clearing the output line Feed to zero. The variable labeled PCOUNT is used to count the next four interrupts (while PRINT is in the BUSY4 state) so that Feed will remain low for 36 ms, as specified in Fig. 5-77e. At the end of this time the paper and inked ribbon advance is turned off by setting Feed to one again. PCOUNT is now used to count through the next six interrupts (while PRINT is in the BUSY5 state), at which time the motion of the paper and ribbon will have settled out and the "print and advance" operation is complete.

The determination of which, if any, column hammers are to be actuated when the next BUSY3 state occurs is handled by the blocks cryptically labeled "Load PTEMP" and "POUT ← PTEMP" in Fig. 5-81. Their operation is expanded in Fig. 5-82. In Fig. 5-82a, the CPU's pointer to memory is initialized to PARRAY (that is, the address of the first word in PARRAY). Each word of the array initially holds the character code of the character to be printed in one column. During the first pass through this "Load PTEMP"

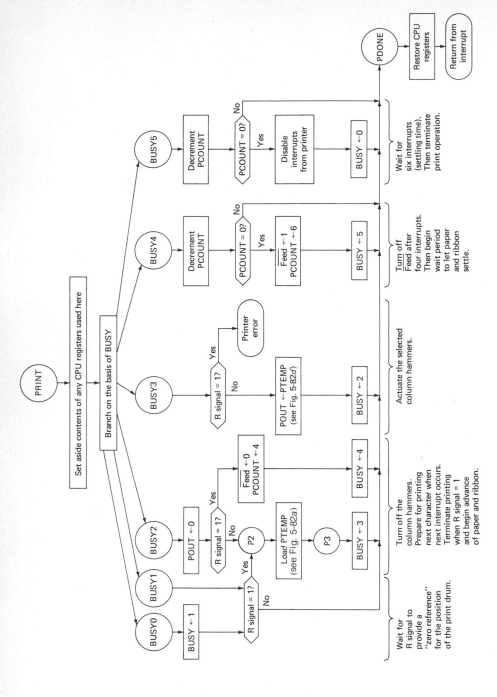

Figure 5-81. PRINT interrupt service routine.

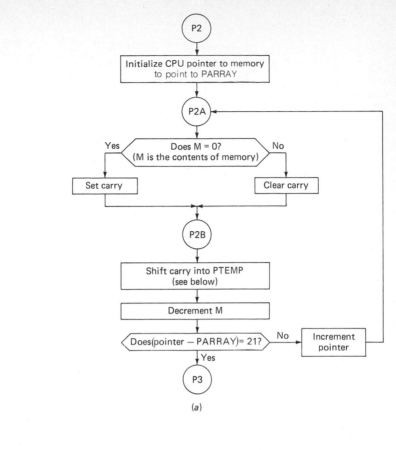

(a)

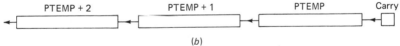

(b)

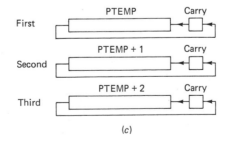

(c)

Figure 5-82. Expansion of algorithms alluded to in Fig. 5-81. (a) The operation Load PTEMP; (b) meaning of Shift carry into PTEMP; (c) actual implementation of Shift carry into PTEMP using "rotate left" instructions; (d) meaning of POUT ← PTEMP.

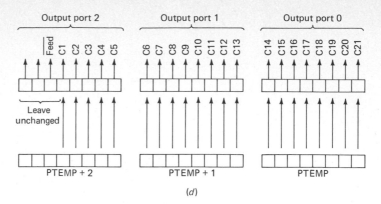

Figure 5-82. *(Continued)*

algorithm, while "R signal" = 1, a one will be shifted into the 3-byte array PTEMP for any columns which are to print a "zero" character. This operation is shown in Fig. 5-82b and c. In addition, each word of PARRAY is decremented so that the next time PRINT is entered while in the BUSY2 state, any words which initially held the character code for the numeral "one" will now contain a zero and cause the corresponding column hammer to be actuated. In this way, each of the 41 entries into PRINT, while in the BUSY2 state, picks up any characters in PARRAY coinciding with the character which will next be on the print drum beneath the column hammers.

This "print and advance" approach for handling the printer of Fig. 5-77 has the advantage of being conceptually simple. However, it suffers two disadvantages. First, if very much printing is to be done, then in effect the printer is used by the program under flag control (using BUSY as a flag) and each line requires the time taken by two revolutions of the print drum. Second, printed messages often consist of more than one line. It would be convenient if what was initiated was not an entire line, but rather an entire multiline message. These modifications are discussed in Probs. 5-25 and 5-27.

Before concluding this section, we will briefly consider the printer control approach taken by Rockwell for its PPS-4 and PPS-8 microcomputers. Rockwell, more than other microcomputer manufacturers, has supported its CPU chips with the development of dedicated controller chips for specific, generally useful, devices. As one example, we discussed the Rockwell floppy-disk controller chip in Sec. 4-4.

For printing with the 34-column impact printer shown in Fig. 5-83, Rockwell has developed two chips. One is a printer controller which can be loaded with all the characters for one line, followed by a command to advance the paper an arbitrary number of lines (if more than one line feed is de-

Figure 5-83. Thirty-four-column alphanumeric printer, Victor 130. (Victor Comptometer Corp.)

sired) when this line has been printed. Printing is then initiated by a "print and advance" command to this chip. Completion of this operation is determined by testing a "busy" flag in the controller. Once printing is initiated, no further CPU time is utilized to handle the printing. The timing required by the printer is derived by the controller chip from the microcomputer clock (which is connected to the controller chip).

The character generation required by the printer is derived from a "character generator" ROM chip provided by Rockwell. Each character consists of a dot array generated on a 9 × 7 matrix. Figure 5-84 illustrates the dot-matrix generation of the letter A. The character-generator chip permits the generation of any of 63 characters. As the print head moves across the paper, at each of the nine column positions for each character, the

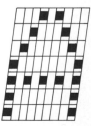

Figure 5-84. 9 × 7 matrix representation of the letter A

controller chip emits both a character code and a column number to the character-generator chip. The character-generator chip decodes these into drive signals for the seven printer solenoids, one for each of the seven row positions within that column, causing one column of the character to be impact-printed at a time.

Note that the process of setting up the line to be printed is not too different from that required for the printer of Fig. 5-77. The difference between the Rockwell approach and the one used previously resides instead in the lack of interrupts taking up CPU time and the lack of perhaps a page of ROM to store the interrupt service routine.

5-9 UARTS

A common means for transmitting characters between devices uses *asynchronous serial data transmission.* This approach was originated to provide reliable data transmission to and from electromechanical devices, such as teletypewriters. It has been extensively adopted for most low-data-rate applications (0 to 30 characters per second) as well as many medium-data-rate applications (30 to 500 characters per second), regardless of whether electromechanical devices are involved.

Because of this extensive use, semiconductor manufacturers have developed the *UART,* or *universal asynchronous receiver transmitter.* This is a single-chip LSI device which implements the asynchronous parallel-to-serial and serial-to-parallel conversions required to convert between the characters handled as words in a microcomputer and the data format used for serial data transmission. In this section, we will consider the characteristics of asynchronous serial data transmission. We will then consider a specific UART and its interactions with a microcomputer.

Each serial character consists of three (or optionally, four) parts:

1 A start bit
2 Five to eight data bits
3 An optional even or odd parity bit, for error-detection capability
4 One, one and a half, or two stop bits

For example, the format of a character made up of a start bit, 8 data bits, an even parity bit, and a stop bit is illustrated in Fig. 5-85a.

The fundamental feature of the asynchronous format is its ability to handle real-time data, with gaps of arbitrary length occurring between successive characters. At the end of each character, the line always goes high for the stop bit. It remains high with an arbitrary number of idling bits. Then the beginning of the next character is marked by the negative-going transition between the high idling bits and the low start bit.

When asynchronous serial data is transmitted at less than the maximum data rate, synchronization is straightforward, inasmuch as the re-

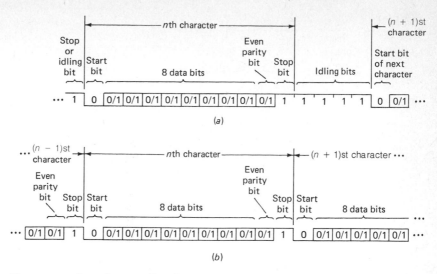

Figure 5-85. *Asynchronous data format.* (a) *Less than maximum data rate;* (b) *maximum data rate.*

ceiver resynchronizes at the beginning of each character, on the negative-going transition between the last idling bit and the start bit. On the other hand, asynchronous serial data transmission is often used to transmit long bursts of characters at the maximum data rate between two devices. For example, when a message is transmitted between a computer (or a microcomputer-based instrument) and a CRT terminal such as that of Fig. 1-17, the message begins (after a long string of idling bits), proceeds at the maximum rate with all the characters required by the display, and then stops (by generating nothing but idling bits again). The receiver initially synchronizes on the negative-going edge created by the start bit of the first character. Then the stop bit at the end of each character provides a well-defined time after which the receiver can look for a negative-going transition, knowing that it has been created by a start bit. The receiver resynchronizes on this edge, providing renewed synchronization to the transmitter with the start of each character.

The receiver portion of a UART will automatically check for synchronization by looking for logic 1 at the time when the stop bit should occur. If logic 0 ever occurs at this time, a *framing* error status bit is set. The microcomputer can check this status bit as part of its routine for reading each received character out of the UART. It can take appropriate action whenever a framing error occurs.

In order to facilitate its synchronization to received data, a UART uses an external clock having a period T_c given approximately by the relationship

$$T_d \approx K \cdot T_c \quad (K = 16, \text{ typically})$$

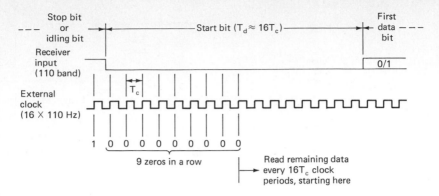

Figure 5-86. Receiver start-bit detection.

The *bit-time* of the data T_d is equal to the duration of any of the bits of a character (that is, the start bit, one of the data bits, etc.). The approximation in this relationship is due to using two distinct clocks, one in the transmitter and one in the receiver, whose frequencies are determined by the nominal bit-time of the data, as will be discussed in more detail shortly.

The approach used by a UART to synchronize on received data is shown in Fig. 5-86. Following the stop bit, or any number of idling bits, the receiver input is sampled with each rising edge of the external clock. By looking for nine consecutive zeros in a row (assuming $T_d \approx 16 \cdot T_c$):

1 "Glitches" on the receiver input are not able to initiate a false start.
2 The middle of the start bit is determined quite closely, providing an accurate time reference from which to sample the remaining data.

Following synchronization, the receiver input is sampled once every 16 clock periods, providing one sample per bit-time, centered quite closely to the middle of each bit-time, as shown in Fig. 5-87.

An asynchronous serial data link is properly defined between two devices when agreement is reached upon:

1 Each of the options listed earlier for the *format of a character* (for example, start bit, 8 data bits, even parity bit, and one stop bit)
2 The *baud* rate; that is, the rate at which data transmission takes place

To define baud rate, consider the case in which data is transmitted at a maximum rate of 10 characters per second. If each character is formatted so as to consist of 11 bits, as in the above example, then each character requires 11 bit-times. The baud rate in this case is

11 bit-times per character × 10 characters per second = 110 baud

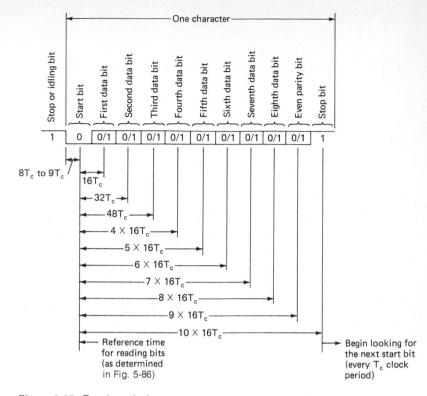

Figure 5-87. Receiver timing.

The bit-time T_d is the reciprocal of the baud rate:

$$T_d = \frac{1}{110 \text{ baud}} = 0.0091 \text{ second} = 9.1 \text{ milliseconds}$$

The baud rate is useful as a measure of the bandwidth required of the transmission channel, since it specifies the maximum modulation rate of a code (bits per second). Note that it is not the same as the data rate, which in this case is

8 data bits per character × 10 characters per second = 80 bits per second

Just as the UART automatically checks each character for a framing error, so it also automatically checks for a *parity* error, if a parity bit is included in the format. For example, if even parity is used, the transmitter selects the value of the parity bit in each character so as to make the total number of ones in the data bits and the parity bit be an even number. The receiver should likewise read an even number of ones among these bits, setting a *parity error* status bit if such is ever not the case. Again, the micro-

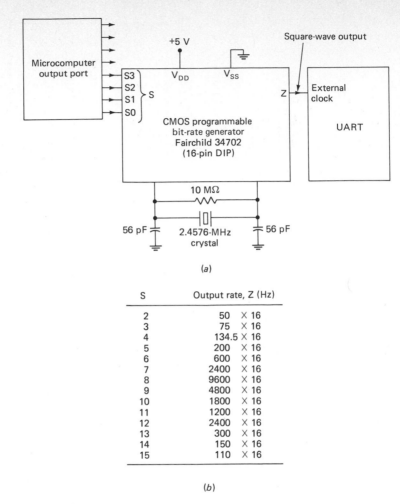

Figure 5-88. *UART external clock source (programmable).* (a) *Circuit;* (b) *output-rate selection.*

computer can check this status bit as part of its routine for reading each re-ceived character out of the UART. It can take appropriate action whenever a parity error occurs.

The external clock required by a UART can be provided for in several ways. If the baud rate is to be programmable, under microcomputer control, Fairchild's CMOS programmable bit-rate generator (34702), shown in Fig. 5-88a, is particularly convenient. It is packaged in a 16-pin DIP but, in addi-tion, requires the external crystal shown to form a 2.4576-MHz crystal oscil-lator from which the selected baud rate, times 16, is derived. It provides for all the commonly used baud rates, as shown in Fig. 5-88b.

For a fixed baud rate, the microcomputer's crystal clock can be divided

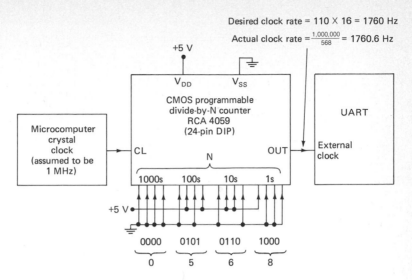

Figure 5-89. *UART external clock source (fixed).*

down to yield the required rate. Thus the circuit of Fig. 5-89 uses RCA's CMOS programmable divide-by-N counter (4059) to provide the desired rate. The output of this circuit is not a square wave but rather a pulse train in which the pulse width equals one clock period of the input. Consequently, while it will meet the pulse-width requirements of the specific UART to be discussed shortly, it might not do so for some other UART.

A UART includes both a receiver and a transmitter. It can receive data from one source and transmit data to another source at the same time. In fact, it is typical to have separate external clock inputs for these two halves of the UART so that even the baud rates can be different. On the other hand, typically the formats of the data (that is, number of data bits, etc.) in the two halves must be identical.

It is also typical to *double buffer* both the received data and the transmitted data. Thus, as illustrated in Fig. 5-90a, the received data is shifted into a Receive Shift Register, using a Receive Data Clock which has been synchronized to the data, as discussed previously. When the entire character, including parity bit (if present) and stop bit, has been received, two things happen:

1   The data bits are automatically transferred to a Receive Data Register.
2   The status bits are set and an interrupt request is sent to the CPU (assuming the UART is operating under interrupt control).

Once this transfer has taken place, the receiver begins looking for the next start bit in order to synchronize on, and shift in, the next character. Consequently, the CPU has all the time it takes to shift in the next character to

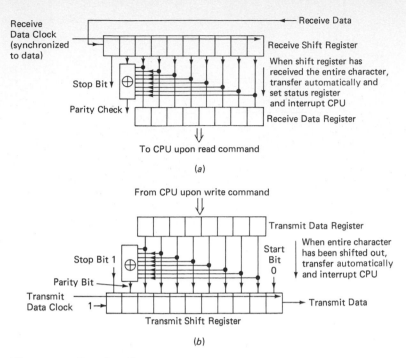

Figure 5-90. *Data handling in a UART.* (a) *Receive circuitry;* (b) *transmit circuitry.*

transfer the present character from the Receive Data Register to the CPU. Even at 9600 baud, this is about 1 ms. If the CPU does not meet this timing constraint, an *overrun error* status bit will be set. Without double buffering, the data would have to be transferred directly from the Receive Shift Register to the CPU after the stop bit of one character had been detected and before the first data bit of the next character was ready to be shifted into the Receive Shift Register.

As an example of a typical, flexible UART which includes circuitry to interface directly to a microcomputer, we will consider Motorola's 6850 Asynchronous Communications Interface Adapter, shown in Fig. 5-91. While this device also includes circuitry for controlling a modem (to transmit and receive data over telephone lines), we will ignore this capability in this section.

Referring to the general configuration of the Motorola 6800 microcomputer shown in Figs. A4-3 and A4-9 (in Appendix A4), we see that the UART hangs on the address bus/data bus structure in much the same manner as RAM chips or general I/O port chips. As pointed out in Appendix A4, the Motorola 6800 microcomputer design does not include the $\overline{\text{READ}}$ and $\overline{\text{WRITE}}$ signals discussed in Sec. 3-4. Instead, VMA · ϕ_2 serves as a timing pulse for both reading and writing, where VMA, valid memory address, in-

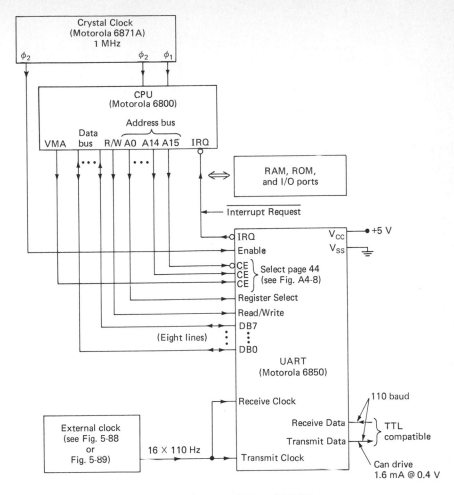

Figure 5-91. Interconnections between CPU and UART.

dicates to devices on the bus whether or not the present clock cycle is to be used by the CPU to access a device outside the CPU. The clock phase ϕ_2 is equal to logic 1 during the second half of the clock cycle, when all signals emanating from the CPU are stable.

The UART can gain the attention of the CPU with an interrupt request. Also, using the page-selection scheme discussed in conjunction with Figs. A4-8 and A4-9 and the connections shown in Fig. 5-91, the UART looks to the CPU like two memory addresses on page 44 (hex). With the Register Select input connected as shown, these can be considered to be addresses 4400 and 4401 (hex). Actually, the CPU interacts with the UART through four registers, two of which are read-only from the two addresses 4400 and 4401, and two of which are write-only to the same addresses, as shown in Fig. 5-92.

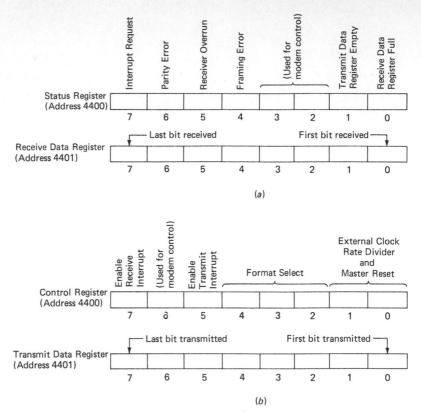

Figure 5-92. *Internal register addressing for Motorola's UART.* (a) *Read-only registers;* (b) *Write-only registers.*

The Control Register, which is modified by writing to address 4400 (hex), is used to set up the UART. As shown in Fig. 5-93, the UART is initialized by storing 00000011 into this address. This "Master Reset" clears the status register and aborts the transmission or reception of garbage because of initial random data in the registers upon power turn-on. Then, to set up for the format discussed previously and to cause an interrupt whenever a complete character has been received or transmitted, 10111001 is stored in this address.

When an interrupt occurs, the CPU will read the contents of address 4400, the Status Register, described in Fig. 5-94. If bit 7 is set, it is the UART which is requesting service (rather than some other device). Then by checking bits 0 and 1, the service routine can determine whether it was the receiver or the transmitter which caused the interrupt. If it was the transmitter, the next character to be transmitted is stored into address 4401. If it was the receiver, bits 4, 5, and 6 of the Status Register are checked and the appropriate error routine initiated if any are set. Otherwise, the received character is read from address 4401.

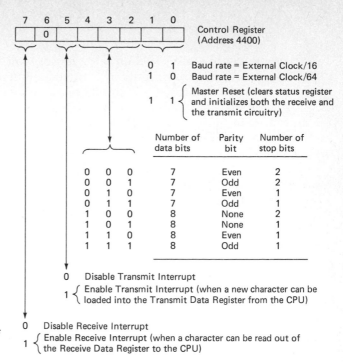

Figure 5-93. Function of Control Register bits.

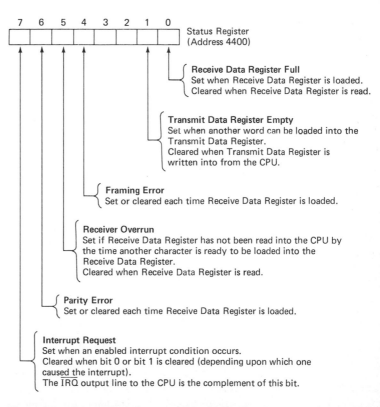

Figure 5-94. Setting and clearing of Status Register bits.

We will complete this section with a brief view of the use of *optoiso-lators* to couple inputs or outputs of a microcomputer-based instrument to other devices. An optoisolator is similar to a solid-state relay designed with a LED-phototransistor combination for dc loads. However, it is optimized for current gain and/or speed of response and is designed to drive logic rather than a heavy load. It is useful for coupling devices together which are aided by being electrically isolated from each other.

When the logic output of one device or instrument needs to drive the remote input of another, the circuit of Fig. 5-95 provides useful isolation. Even if a large dc or ac *common-mode* voltage V_1 exists between the grounds of the two units, the optoisolator ignores the voltage. This is useful

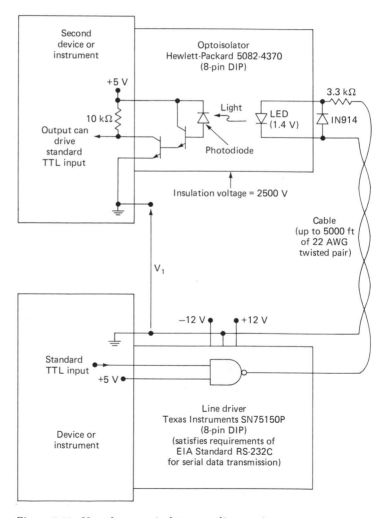

Figure 5-95. *Use of an optoisolator as a line receiver.*

for providing isolation for both the receiver input and transmitter output of a UART. It is also useful any time a common-mode voltage might otherwise cause problems in the transfer of logic levels between two devices, whether the problem is caused by power lines, telephone lines, or the shock hazard of medical equipment.

5-10   REMOTE INSTRUMENT CONTROL

Smart instruments, programmable calculators used as controllers, and the IEEE standard bus interface* together offer the opportunity of configuring automatic test systems (ATS) quickly and easily using off-the-shelf instruments. For example, Fig. 1-18 illustrates the simplicity of interconnecting instruments together in this way. What is not so apparent, but is nevertheless true, is the effectiveness of a programmable calculator, such as that of Fig. 5-96, for this job. Its language and its built-in functions make programming of an automatic test system straightforward. Whether the test results are printed out as messages on the calculator's printer or plotted on an X-Y plotter, the programming task is manageable by the same test engineer who has the problem of making the measurements. Alternatively, a minicomputer can be interfaced to the bus to serve as a controller.

The development of an interface bus *standard* represents a remarkable

* "IEEE Standard Digital Interface for Programmable Instrumentation," IEEE Standard 488-1975, is available at cost from IEEE Standards, 345 East 47 Street, New York, NY 10017. A brief overview is contained in "Condensed Description of the Hewlett-Packard Interface Bus," an 18-page booklet available from Hewlett-Packard Co. (-hp-Part no. 59401-90030).

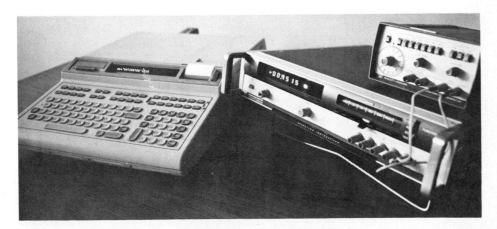

Figure 5-96. *Programmable calculator, shown on the left, can be used as a flexible controller for an automatic test system.* (Hewlett-Packard Co.)

Figure 5-97. Some ATS Instrument Possibilities

Stimulus	Measurement
Digitally programmable power supply	Digital multimeter
Frequency synthesizer	Digital voltmeter
Waveform generator	Electronic counter
Timing generator	Analog-to-digital converter
Digital word generator	Digital word detector
Programmable attenuator	Pulse detector
Multiphase clock	Pulse analyzer
Digital-to-analog converter	Time-interval meter
	Impedance bridge
	Phase-angle meter
	Distortion analyzer
	Analog scanner
	Digital comparator

feat begun within Hewlett-Packard and subsequently modified and accepted internationally by the instrument industry. It means that the best instruments for a specific measurement problem can be brought together into an automatic test system without regard to manufacturer. Some of the instrument possibilities are listed in Fig. 5-97.

The intent of this section is to explore the interface bus standard and its impact upon the design of a smart instrument. We will be particularly interested in the extent of the hardware needed if we wish to put as much of the workings of the interface into the software of the instrument's microcomputer. Inasmuch as we can only touch on the highlights of the standard here, the interested reader is referred to the standard itself and the references at the end of the chapter.

The IEEE interface bus standard includes standard cables and connectors, such as those shown in Fig. 5-98. The back of an instrument will include the mating connector (for example, Amphenol or Cinch Type 57 Microribbon connector) plus the designated pin connections shown in Fig. 5-99. In addition, the standard recommends that each of the signal lines shall be terminated with the resistive network and standard TTL logic shown in Fig. 5-100. All the signals on the interface cable are defined negative-true but are inverted to (or from) positive-true form by the bus-terminating circuitry.

The standard permits up to 15 instruments to be interconnected with a total cable length of up to 20 meters (m). For fewer instruments, the cable length is constrained to a maximum of 2 m of cable per instrument. The configuration of the cables is irrelevant, whether daisy-chained from one instrument to the next or, alternatively, connected in a "star" arrangement. If this cable-length constraint is met, the bus permits 8-bit bytes of data to be

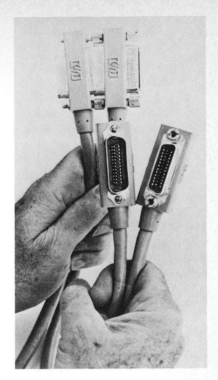

Figure 5-98. Standard interface bus cables. (Hewlett-Packard Journal.)

Figure 5-99. Standard Connector Pin Connections

Contact	Signal line	Contact	Signal line
1	DIO1	13	DIO5
2	DIO2	14	DIO6
3	DIO3	15	DIO7
4	DIO4	16	DIO8
5	EOI	17	REN
6	DAV	18	Ground, forming twisted pair with DAV
7	NRFD	19	Ground, forming twisted pair with NRFD
8	NDAC	20	Ground, forming twisted pair with NDAC
9	IFC	21	Ground, forming twisted pair with IFC
10	SRQ	22	Ground, forming twisted pair with SRQ
11	ATN	23	Ground, forming twisted pair with ATN
12	SHIELD (connect to earth ground)	24	Signal ground

Note: Each line from contacts 18–23 should be grounded in the instrument near the termination of the other wire of the twisted pair.

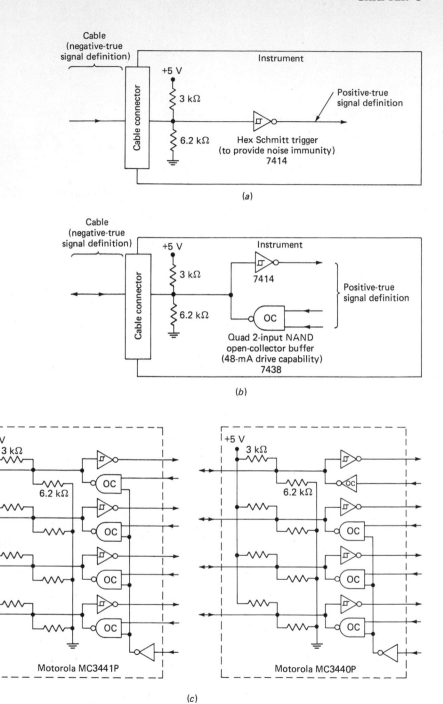

Figure 5-100. *Recommended termination of signal lines within an instrument.* (a) *Each unidirectional signal into the instrument;* (b) *bidirectional signals;* (c) *quad transceivers designed for this standard.*

transferred between instruments at rates of up to 250,000 bytes per second.

Each instrument hung on the bus must be capable of serving at least one of the following functions, which can be enabled or disabled at any time:

1   A *listener* must be capable of being enabled to receive data from other instruments (for example, a printer or a digitally programmable power supply).

2   A *talker* must be capable of being enabled to transmit data to other instruments (for example, a digital voltmeter transmitting its data output).

3   A *controller* does the enabling and disabling of talkers and listeners. It manages the overall activity on the bus, from initialization at start-up to handling interrupts from instruments. While it often enables itself as a talker or a listener, it can also relinquish both these roles, letting other instruments communicate among themselves.

An instrument can be designed to include the controller function as a means of providing specific options. For example, the selective level measurement set of Fig. 1-12 controls the optional printer shown by means of the interface bus, if it is included in the configuration of the instrument. On the other hand, the selective level measurement set itself can become a part of a larger automatic test system. In this case, it will have its role as bus controller taken away from it by a *system controller*.

The interface bus standard has been prepared in such a way that simple instruments (for example, a digitally programmable power supply which uses the bus *only* as a listener) can ignore many of the signals on the bus. That is, even though the bus can be used to provide sophisticated capability where it is desired, the needs of a simple instrument can be met with relatively simple bus hardware.

The interface bus consists of the 16 signal lines shown in Fig. 5-101. These are:

1   Five control lines, used for interface management. Four of these lines are driven by the controller to set up the other instruments on the bus as talkers or listeners. The fifth line, SRQ, is used by an instrument to interrupt the controller in order to request use of the bus.

2   Three handshake lines, used to ensure the valid transfer of data between a talker and any number of listeners. These also ensure the valid transfer of control information between the controller and all the other instruments.

3   Eight data lines, used for transferring data between a talker and its listeners while in the *data mode*. This mode is signaled by the controller with ATN = 0 (that is, a high output on the negative-true bus). These data lines are also used for transferring control information from the controller to all the other instruments while in the *command mode*, signaled by the controller with ATN = 1.

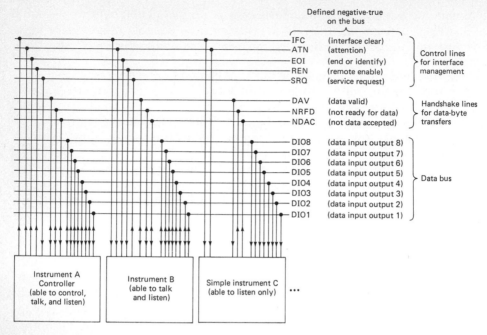

Figure 5-101. Signal lines on the interface bus.

Three handshake lines are used instead of the two discussed in Sec. 5-1 in order to provide proper handshaking with more than one listener. The open-collector buffer outputs of Fig. 5-100b are used to provide a mechanism for letting many listeners signal one talker (or the controller) when they have *all* accepted its data. As each listener accepts data, it stops pulling the NDAC (Not Data ACcepted) line low. When all listeners stop pulling NDAC low, the resistive load shown in Fig. 5-100, and found in each instrument, pulls NDAC up to 3.3 V. The talker uses this level as a signal that all listeners have accepted its data.

Now, the talker must let its (negative-true) DAV line go high to signal all listeners that it has seen their collective NDAC signal and to let them know that the data on the data lines is being changed (and is thus no longer valid). Now the talker must wait for all listeners to acknowledge that they have seen DAV go high (so that its subsequent lowering of DAV will have meaning to them). This acknowledgment is complete when all listeners have returned NDAC low and have stopped pulling NRFD (Not Ready For Data) low, letting the resistive load pull it up to 3.3 V.

The complete handshaking process is shown in Fig. 5-102a in the form of a timing diagram. The action required of the talker and each listener is shown in Fig. 5-102b. Note that the action of the talker is almost identical to the two-wire handshake of Sec. 5-1. Likewise, since each listener treats NRFD and NDAC as complements of each other, its implementation of the three-wire handshake is almost identical to a two-wire handshake. Of course, while in the data mode, any instruments which are disabled do not handshake at all. By not pulling any of the handshake lines low, they relinquish control of them.

Having seen the mechanism used for "handshaking" data and bus control information between instruments, we will now consider the control lines used by the controller to set up each use of the bus. The *interface clear* line IFC is used by the controller at any time, but particularly at start-up. The standard requires that all instruments on the bus initialize their use of the bus to an *idle* state within 100 μs after IFC is pulled low by the controller. This is not to say that the instrument itself must be initialized, but only its use of the bus. In this way, the controller can force the use of the bus by all instruments into a known idle state. The controller will go from there to configure the use of the bus as it sees fit. Because of the 100-μs response time required, a microcomputer-based instrument which implements much of the bus operation in software probably needs to use IFC as an interrupt input.

The *attention* line ATN is used by the controller to draw the distinction between the command mode (when ATN = 1, negative-true) and the data mode (when ATN = 0), as discussed earlier. The controller can come along

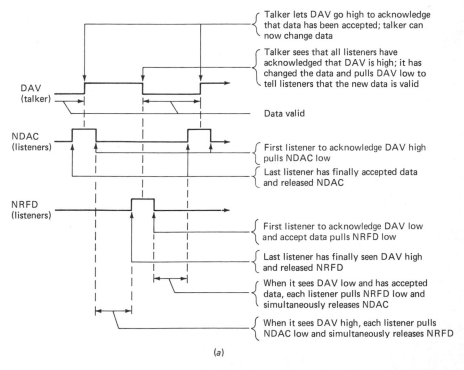

(a)

Figure 5-102. *Three-wire handshaking between one talker and several listeners.* (a) *Timing diagram;* (b) *flowchart.*

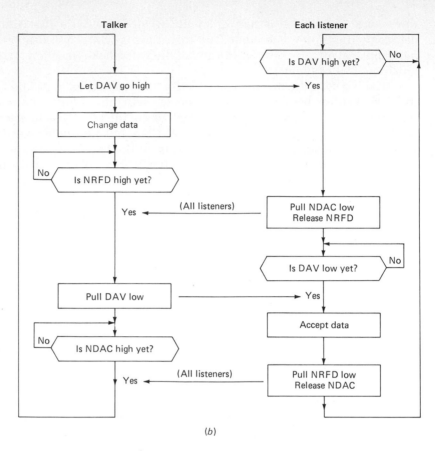

(b)

Figure 5-102. (Continued)

at any time and drive ATN low in order to change the use of the bus. For example, it can do this right in the middle of a handshaking operation for a
data transfer between a talker and a listener. The interface standard requires
all instruments to respond within 200 ns, indicating readiness to communicate with the controller. That is, the DAV and NRFD lines must go
high and the use of the data bus by a talker must be relinquished within this
brief time. This fast response permits the controller to obtain status information quickly from instruments equipped to provide it quickly (using a
"parallel poll" which does not employ handshaking). Instruments not so
equipped must not be permitted to block these fast queries by the controller.
Consequently, each instrument must provide enough hardware to handle
ATN automatically, without microcomputer intervention, to serve this end.

Beyond the above constraint, the interface standard puts no requirement upon how fast an instrument must respond to the controller while in
the command mode. Thus the controller will handshake with instruments

as it carries out its functions in the command mode. A microcomputer-based instrument may be slow to respond, particularly if it uses ATN under flag control rather than interrupt control. In spite of the slow response, the controller will not go on until all instruments have participated in the handshaking operation. Consequently, no demand of the controller is ever missed by any instrument on the bus.

The *end or identify* line EOI is used by the controller in conjunction with ATN to carry out a *parallel poll* of instruments equipped with the hardware to handle it. Up to eight instruments can participate in parallel polling, with each one assigned one line of the data bus. Then, when the controller drives EOI and ATN low simultaneously, an instrument can transmit one bit of status information to the controller on its assigned data bus line. The controller can use this facility to provide flag control of the instruments on the bus. Alternatively, it can use this facility to identify which instrument has interrupted the controller (using the SRQ line, to be discussed shortly). Parallel polling is the one means available to the controller to obtain information quickly from an instrument. The standard requires this response to take place within 200 ns after EOI and ATN go low. The circuitry of Fig. 5-103 illustrates how this can be set up with just an open-collector decimal decoder-driver plus a NAND gate. When the instrument is set up remotely, part of the setup information is the address to be used for parallel polling, which is transferred to the output port shown. The two Schmitt-trigger inverters are the ones already used to terminate the bus within the instrument, as shown in Fig. 5-100.

The EOI line can also be used in the data mode to give the talker a means of labeling the last, or "end," byte of data to be transferred. If this is done, the listener can monitor this bit, knowing that the transfer is complete when EOI = 1.

The *remote enable* line REN is used by the controller to disable the front-panel controls of selected instruments in order to operate them remotely. The controller must hold this line low *all the time* that remote control is desired. If it ever releases this line (that is, REN = 0, negative-true), the standard specifies that all instruments are to revert to local control within 100 μs. This might be initiated by an interrupt input into an instrument's microcomputer.

Remote control of each instrument is initiated by the controller by going to the command mode (ATN = 1) and driving REN low (REN = 1, negative-true). Then each instrument to be remotely controlled must be set up as a listener, at least momentarily. The standard uses this scheme so that an automatic test system can be set up with most of the instruments operated remotely, but perhaps one instrument operated locally from its front-panel controls.

The *service request* line SRQ gives the controller an interrupt input from the instruments on the bus. Any instrument can request service by pulling this line low, regardless of other activity taking place on the bus. The controller can then determine which instrument is requesting service

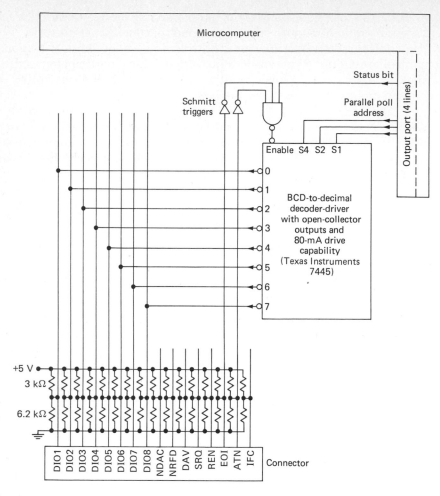

Figure 5-103. Parallel-poll circuitry.

either by preestablished ground rules (that is, by enabling only one instrument to interrupt at a time), by parallel polling as in Fig. 5-103, or by *serial polling.* Serial polling is carried out as a sequence of commands and requests for status information from one instrument after another. It is slower than parallel polling but permits any desired amount of status information to be transferred from an instrument to the controller, rather than just one bit. In addition, it can be implemented entirely in the software of an instrument.

To provide a commonly agreed upon language of commands from the controller, the IEEE standard includes an appendix (not accepted as standard) which assigns meaning to some specific words transferred from the controller over the data bus when ATN = 1 (that is, pulled low). Data bus line DIO8 is not specified by these commands. It could be used for a parity check on commands, if controller and instruments were set up with a common understanding of what was being done.

    If the controller puts

X	0	1	A5	A4	A3	A2	A1
(where			A5	A4	A3	A2	A1 ≠ 11111)

on the data bus as a command (that is, while pulling ATN low), then all instruments will handshake to accept this command. In addition, since this format represents listen addresses, the one instrument which has been set up with this listen address will respond by being a listener when ATN = 0 again. The command

X	0	1	1	1	1	1	1

is an unlisten command which "unlistens" all instruments which have previously been set up as listeners.

    The command

X	1	0	A5	A4	A3	A2	A1
(where			A5	A4	A3	A2	A1 ≠ 11111)

sets up a talk address. It also serves as an untalk command for any instrument not having this talk address which was previously set up as a talker. This feature automatically prevents having more than one talker at a time. In addition, the *untalk command*

X	1	0	1	1	1	1	1

"untalks" the previous talker without regard to which instrument it was.

    To avoid conflicting talk and listen addresses in an automatic test system made up of arbitrary instruments, the rear panel of each instrument can include a five-position DIP switch similar to that of Fig. 5-31. It provides an arbitrary value for A5 . . . A1 (other than 11111) and uses this value to form both the talk and the listen addresses for the instrument.

    Universal commands have the same effect upon all devices connected to the bus. For example, the *device clear* command

X	0	0	1	0	1	0	0

is used to force every instrument to an initial, or "clear," state. This initializes each instrument's total operation and not just its interface bus circuitry (which can be done with the IFC line, as discussed earlier).

    Addressed commands are acknowledged solely by devices which are presently set up to be listeners (when ATN goes high again). For example, the *group execute trigger* command

$$X \quad 0 \quad 0 \quad 0 \quad 1 \quad 0 \quad 0 \quad 0$$

initiates a simultaneous preprogrammed action by all listeners. It can be used to initiate the operation of all instruments involved in a specific test simultaneously.

As an example of the use of the interface bus in an automatic test system, we will consider one possible sequence:

1   Controller initializes the interface by pulling IFC low for at least 100 μs.
2   Controller initializes all instruments by handshaking out the "device clear" universal command.
3   Controller handshakes out the listen address for one instrument, while setting itself up as talker.
4   Controller goes to the data mode and handshakes out the setup data for this instrument.
5   Controller handshakes out the unlisten command.
6   Steps 3, 4, and 5 are repeated for each instrument until all instruments have been set up for the test.
7   Controller handshakes out the listen address for any instruments which need the "group execute trigger" addressed command in order to begin their function.
8   Controller handshakes out the "group execute trigger" command, initiating the test.
9   Controller handshakes out the unlisten command now that step 8 has been accomplished.
10   Controller handshakes out the talk address of the instrument which will be making a measurement during this test while setting itself up as a listener.
11   Controller lets ATN go high (data mode).
12   When the instrument set up as a talker completes its measurement, it handshakes its measurement results back to the controller.
13   The controller knows how many bytes of data to expect as measurement results from this instrument (or else it can look for the EOI signal discussed earlier). When it has received this data, it can use the data appropriately and then go on to set up another test.

We will conclude this section with one possible general-purpose circuit for coupling a microcomputer-based instrument to the standard interface bus, shown in Fig. 5-104. All the bus lines (except SRQ) are buffered into input ports through Schmitt triggers. In addition, the microcomputer is interrupted whenever:

1   REN goes high, so that the instrument can be returned to local control quickly.

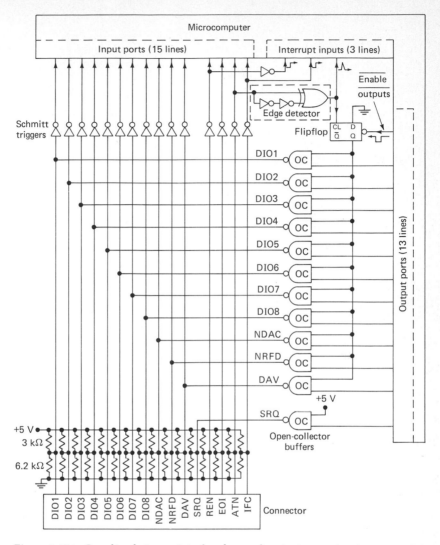

Figure 5-104. *Coupling between interface bus and an instrument's microcomputer.*

   2   IFC goes low, so that the interface circuitry can be initialized quickly.

   3   ATN changes, signaling a change from command mode to data mode, or vice versa.

The flipflop shown in Fig. 5-104 quickly and automatically disables all outputs to the interface bus whenever ATN changes. The third interrupt listed above is used to reenable any outputs which are appropriate as the new mode is entered.

5-11 SELF-TEST HARDWARE

In Sec. 7-3 we will develop an overall strategy whereby an instrument can carry out a sequence of tests on itself, both at start-up and unobtrusively during its ongoing operation. In this section, we will consider some of the hardware for implementing self-test communications with a user. We will also consider some of the specific tests which might be built into an instrument.

As discussed in Sec. 7-3, a self-test algorithm can begin by turning on all front-panel lights and displays, waiting for a keyswitch to be depressed, and then turning all lights and displays off. If this can be carried out, the user is assured that much of the instrument is working. In addition, the user gains confidence that if a malfunction is uncovered by subsequent self-test routines, the instrument can blink front-panel lights to signal this.

In order to provide diagnostic information to a user when a malfunction destroys the front-panel self-test communications just described, it is valuable to have a backup mechanism which depends upon very little more than a functioning CPU chip (and the ability to execute self-test routines). For example, an instrument built around the Intel 8080 microcomputer but which does not use its interrupt capability can use the INTE output pin of the CPU chip to drive a self-test annunciator light or buzzer, as shown in Fig. 5-105. This output indicates the state of the internal "interrupt enable" flip-flop. Consequently, the EI and DI instructions which set and clear this flip-flop can be used to drive this 1-bit output.

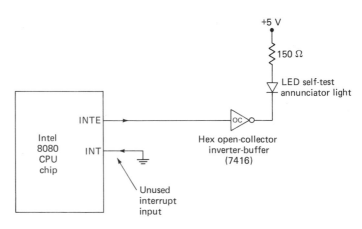

Turn on annunciator light by executing
an EI (enable interrupts) instruction

Turn it off by executing a DI
(disable interrupts) instruction

Figure 5-105. Driving a self-test annunciator from an otherwise unused output of a CPU chip.

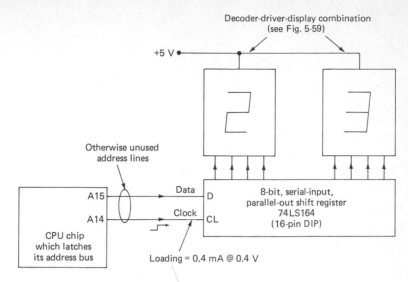

Figure 5-106. Compact display circuit.

Another possible source of output lines from the CPU chip is provided by address lines, if page decoding leaves some of these unused. For these to be usable directly, the CPU must *latch* the address outputs. That is, these outputs must only change from one valid address to the next valid address, without generating garbage in between. If this condition is met, so that no spurious pulses occur on the address lines, the compact arrangement of Fig. 5-106 uses two otherwise unused address lines to shift a two-digit diagnostic number out to a two-digit display. If these three chips are located on the printed-circuit board next to the CPU chip, they provide a highly reliable backup to a less reliable front-panel display of the same information.

The initial start-up sequence discussed earlier required a user to depress a front-panel keyswitch in order to tell the microcomputer to continue. If a malfunction forestalls this, it is extremely useful to have a small backup switch mounted on the printed-circuit board next to the CPU chip to serve as an alternative.

To keep the functioning of this switch from being blocked by other instrument malfunctions, again it is useful to look for an otherwise unused input into the CPU chip. For example, an instrument based upon the Fairchild F8 microcomputer can dedicate one of the 16 I/O lines on the CPU chip to this purpose. The Motorola 6800 microcomputer can have its "nonmaskable interrupt" input dedicated to this purpose if it is not otherwise being used. When a momentary-action switch causes an interrupt, the contents of one of the two accumulators in the CPU can be complemented to serve as a flag. Of course, this mechanism requires that the switch be used only when a malfunction has occurred and the instrument is dedicating itself solely to the self-test function.

The most valuable self-test which can be included in an instrument is one which provides an overall check of correct performance. For example, the distance meter of Fig. 1-4 includes a "push-to-test" check in which the instrument makes a simulated measurement (for which a target is unnecessary). The microcomputer exercises the electronic and optical systems, and the results of the simulated measurement are tested for proper operation of the circuitry and for system noise. If all tests are satisfactorily completed, all segments of the three-digit display are turned on, displaying 888. This also yields a check of the operation of the display. If any test fails, the display is flashed to warn the operator of the malfunction.

An instrument which can incorporate an overall self-test is valued for its ability to tell a user "I'm OK." On the other hand, if an instrument malfunctions, it is useful if the microcomputer can partition the instrument into "OK" versus "not OK" parts. This might mean isolating the malfunction to a specific printed-circuit board or to a specific subsystem (for example, printer control circuitry) which makes up part of a printed-circuit board.

The time to be thinking about specific self-tests is during the development of the specific capabilities of an instrument. We have done this to some extent in previous sections and in the end-of-chapter problems. For example, Prob. 5-13 takes the output of an incremental position encoder and forms an absolute address by counting quanta changes. At the same time, it sets an error flag if the calculated absolute position ever disagrees with the one fixed reference point available. This error flag will be picked up by the self-test algorithm of Sec. 7-3.

Since the instrument software depends upon the reliable use of ROM data, a self-test check might be carried out on this data. This is a particularly useful check in that a malfunction here can lead to peculiar behavior of the instrument, which might be difficult to track down. If a malfunction occurs, it is extremely helpful to know whether or not the software is being read out correctly to the CPU.

ROM address	ROM contents			
0	1	0	1	0
1	0	1	1	0
2	0	1	0	1
3	1	1	1	0
4	0	1	1	0
5	1	0	1	1
6	0	0	0	0
7	0	1	0	1	⟵ Check word
Check sum	1	1	1	1	⟵ Check sum

Figure 5-107. Formation of a check word.

Set pointer to memory to first address in ROM chip to be tested

Load CPU register 1 with the number of words in this ROM chip

(a)

A = complement of check sum

(b)

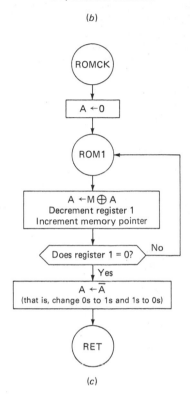

Figure 5-108. ROMCK, a ROM checking subroutine. (a) Parameters to be passed to ROMCK subroutine; (b) parameter to be returned by ROMCK subroutine; (c) flowchart.

(c)

Many error-detecting approaches have been proposed, and used, to obtain reliable data storage and data transmission under a variety of circumstances. The approach discussed here is particularly efficacious in translating a realistic set of ROM malfunction mechanisms (for example, a "dead" ROM; a shorted output line; a single erroneous bit) into a detected error. It is also easy to implement.

The approach requires that one word in each ROM (perhaps, but not necessarily, the last word) be set aside and not used in the instrument software. When the remainder of the contents of the ROM has been decided upon, this final "check word" is determined. As illustrated in Fig. 5-107 (for an 8 × 4 "example" ROM), each bit of the check word is selected so as to force "odd 1s parity" (that is, an odd number of 1s) in the corresponding column of the ROM contents. We will see that it is important that odd 1s parity

Figure 5-109. Summary of ROM Malfunction-Detection Capability

Type of malfunction	Probability of error detection	Explanation of probability
Dead ROM	1.000	For a ROM with an even number of words, all these cases will produce even 1s parity for any output lines which remain fixed for all addresses
Power disconnected from ROM	1.000	
Any number of output lines stuck at one or stuck at zero	1.000	
Two output lines shorted together	0.996 (assuming at least four ROMs are checked)	When one output line is pulling high and the other is pulling low, one of these outputs will be in error. Hence, shorted outputs will introduce random errors, giving a 0.50 chance that either output line produces even 1s parity and a 0.75 chance that one or the other output line will do so when one ROM is checked. Checking four ROMs, we have eight chances to err, giving $1- (0.5)^8 = 0.996$
Any number of address lines stuck at one or stuck at zero	1.000	If just one address line is stuck, only half of the addresses are accessed, each one twice. This will produce even 1s parity on all outputs. If more address lines are stuck, fewer addresses are accessed, but each one is accessed an even number of times, again producing even 1s parity on all outputs
Two address lines shorted together	0.996 (assuming 8-bit words)	When one address line pulls high and one pulls low, some addresses will never be read. This means that each output line has a 0.50 chance of producing even 1s parity. With eight output lines, we have $1- (0.5)^8 = 0.996$
A single bit in error anywhere in the ROM	1.000	It will produce even 1s parity in its bit position in the word
Any number of bits in error in just one word	1.000	Each bit in error will produce even 1s parity in its bit position in the word

be used rather than even 1s parity. Several of the error mechanisms arising when dealing with ROMs will be detected with odd 1s parity which would not be detected with even 1s parity. In a similar vein, we might be tempted to try to force the binary sum of all the words of a ROM to a fixed number, such as all 1s. Again, it has been found that several important error mechanisms go undetected when this is done.

To check the contents of each ROM, then, a parity check is made. A subroutine, ROMCK, to carry out this operation is shown in Fig. 5-108. It should return the complement of the "check sum" in the accumulator. Thus the accumulator will contain zero upon returning from a successful ROM check. A summary of the malfunction-detection capability achieved when this check is made upon all ROMs is given in Fig. 5-109.

An overall check on the operation of RAM cannot easily be carried out except at start-up. However, at start-up it is possible to load RAM locations with arbitrary contents and then read them out again. A stronger check re-

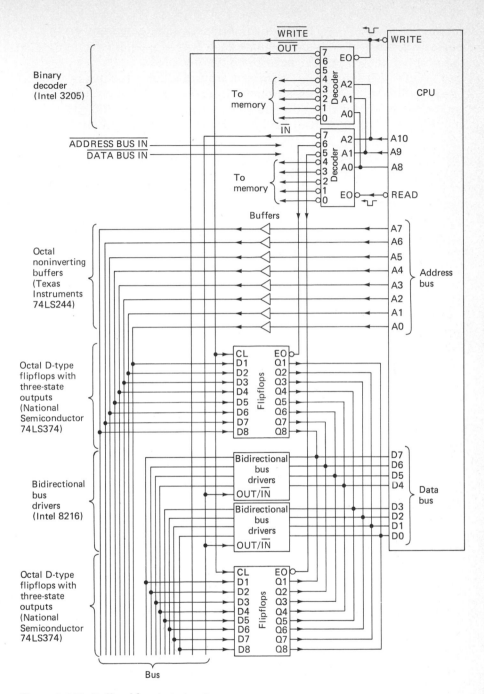

Figure 5-110. Buffered bus test circuit.

sults when all of RAM is first loaded with pseudorandom numbers and then, during a second pass, the content of each RAM location is compared with the number known to have been previously loaded.

Many instruments are organized around a bus structure in which the bus reaching out to devices is isolated from the CPU with buffers on address lines and bidirectional bus drivers on data lines, as in Fig. 5-9. With at least some ROM (holding start-up and self-test routines) located on the same PC board with the CPU and "inside" the buffering circuitry, it is possible to maintain a working microcomputer even when the bus (outside the buffering circuitry) malfunctions.

A test circuit for this buffered bus is shown in Fig. 5-110. Every time a write instruction is executed, either to memory or to an I/O device, the actual buffered address and data variables are latched into the 16 flipflops shown. These actual variables can be compared with the intended variables by reading from page 6 for the buffered address bus and page 5 for the buffered data bus.

A self-test routine can exercise the buffered bus with 32 separate tests. The first 16 tests consist of making each bus line in turn equal to one while all of the remaining 15 lines are equal to zero. The other 16 tests do just the opposite, driving each bus line in turn to zero while the remaining 15 lines are equal to one. If any lines are stuck at one, stuck at zero, or shorted together, this procedure will detect the offending lines.

We have considered how ROM, RAM, and buffered bus might be tested. As each major section of an instrument is considered (or each likely source of instrument malfunction), our job is to find a way to test for proper operation using as little extra hardware as possible. With ingenuity, we often require no extra hardware at all, as when a device signals proper operation by causing a detectable change to occur within a certain time.

PROBLEMS

5-1 Handshaking I/O control. For a specific microcomputer:

(a) Does the hardware include automatic handshaking capability for I/O control? This might be included on a general I/O chip.

(b) Can it be used for either flag control or interrupt control?

(c) What options are available?

(d) What must be done, if anything, to set up the capability during the initialization of an instrument?

5-2 Bus structure. For a specific microcomputer which uses general I/O ports or which has a variety of device controllers (for keyboards, displays, printers, etc.):

(a) Show the bus structure which can be used, labeling all I/O lines.

(b) Are interrupts possible? If so, how are these handled with the hardware of (a)?

(*c*) What is the dc drive capability and the capacitive drive capability of each device which can drive bus lines?

(*d*) Assuming that dc drive capability is the limiting factor, how many I/O ports or device controllers can be hung on the bus?

(*e*) Does the microcomputer hardware include a bus driver, or can that of Fig. 5-8 be used? If so, how does this affect your answers above?

5-3 I/O timing. For a specific microcomputer:

(*a*) Write an assembly language interrupt service routine having the flowchart of Fig. 5-11. In the "Take action . . ." block, execute an output instruction which, by outputting a fixed data byte to a specific address, will turn off the device and stop further interrupts. The main program can test LENGTH to determine when the array has been entirely transferred.

(*b*) Determine T_{MICRO1} and T_{MICRO}.

(*c*) Assuming this device is the only source of an interrupt, then at what maximum rate can it interrupt to initiate data transfers reliably?

(*d*) Make a flowchart for the steps needed in the main program to *initiate* the transfer of an array of data to or from this device.

5-4 I/O timing. For a specific microcomputer:

(*a*) Write an assembly language routine analogous to that of Prob. 5-3, but using flag control of the device. Use the flowchart of Fig. 5-14, but substitute automatic handshaking if that is a capability of the microcomputer.

(*b*) Determine T_{MICRO1} and T_{MICRO}.

(*c*) Assuming that interrupts are disabled, then at what maximum rate can data transfers take place (reliably)?

5-5 FIFOs. For a specific microcomputer, and using the elastic output port of Fig. 5-17, repeat Prob. 5-4 (*a*), (*b*), (*c*).

(*d*) At this maximum data transfer rate, how long can the microcomputer take to do other things after the FIFO is filled up and before DAC_{in} is tested again?

5-6 FIFOs. Using two FIFOs interconnected as in Fig. 5-16, can one of the handshaking lines interconnecting the two be used as a HALF-FULL indicator? Explain.

5-7 FIFOs. The discussion in the text uses the HALF-FULL output for interrupt control and the DAC_{IN} (or DAV_{OUT}) line for flag control. Explain why these roles would probably never be reversed.

5-8 Keyboard encoder. Some keyboard encoders employ an "N-key rollover" technique to handle the case of any number of keyswitches being depressed at the same time. The encoder scans the keys continuously, generating an output immediately upon detecting that a key is newly depressed, regardless of which other switches are depressed. Compare the performance resulting from this approach with that of the "two-key rollover" technique if

(a) One keyswitch is firmly depressed and in the process an adjacent keyswitch is also inadvertently depressed, to some extent.

(b) A fast succession of three keyswitch inputs occurs in which the second and third keyswitches are depressed before the first is released.

5-9 Keyboard encoder. Make a chart for a 22-key instrument, analogous to Fig. 5-27, so that the keyboard encoder will generate distinct outputs from 0 to 21 corresponding to each of these keys.

5-10 Keyboard reading. In their "M6800 Microprocessor Applications Manual" (referenced at the end of this chapter), Motorola suggests using their Peripheral Interface Adapter (PIA) to read a 16-keyswitch keyboard in a manner similar to that of Fig. 5-29. However, they use the configuration shown in Fig. P5-1a. The procedure shown in Fig. P5-1b and c takes advantage of the PIA's ability to set up each I/O line as either an input line or an output line independent of the remaining lines.

(a) Determine the number which will be generated in the accumulator A if the keyswitch in the lower right-hand corner of the keyswitch matrix is depressed.

(b) For the Motorola 6800 microcomputer, or any other specific microcomputer which can be operated in this way, show a flowchart and an assembly language routine for the "Obtain key code" step which will convert the contents of the accumulator into a number from 00 to 0F (hex). (If more than one key is depressed, convert to the key code for one of these keys.) Minimize ROM words.

5-11 Switch-programmed ROM. Show a specific example whereby an erroneous output can occur in the circuit of Fig. 5-33 if the diodes are omitted. That is, show an example of a specific address input and specific contents of specific thumbwheel switches which will lead to an erroneous reading of the addressed thumbwheel switch. Explain with the help of an equivalent circuit for this specific case.

5-12 Pulse-rate transduction. Using the approach of Figs. 5-45 and 5-46 and using a specific microcomputer:

(a) Write an assembly language routine to count pulses as fast as possible over a time interval T such that 2^{16} pulses will be counted if pulses occur continuously at this maximum rate f_{max}.

(b) What is this maximum rate f_{max}?

(c) What is this time interval T?

5-13 Incremental encoder. For an incremental encoder having outputs A, B, and Z as in Fig. 5-47a:

(a) Define any variables necessary and make a flowchart for obtaining an 8-bit binary encoding of position POS as measured from the zero reference point. Assume the encoder is used under flag control.

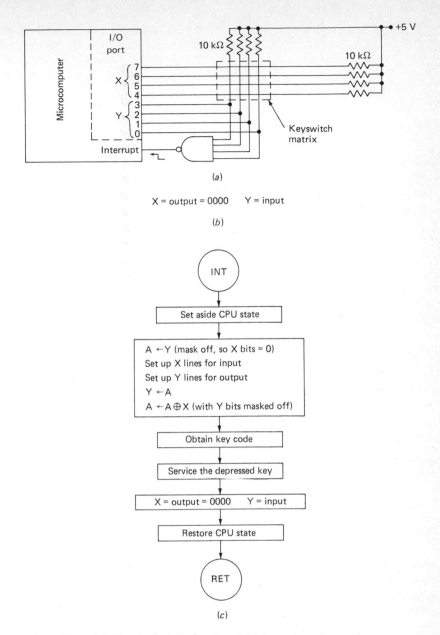

Figure P5-1. (a) Circuit; (b) initialization; (c) interrupt service routine.

When POS = 00 (hex) and new values of A and B indicate that POS should be decremented, keep POS at 00 but check that B = 0 and that A is changing from 0 to 1. Also when Z changes from 0 to 1, check that POS = 00. If one of these is *not* true, set a nonzero number into RAM at an address labeled ERR1, to serve as an error flag (which is used as discussed in Sec. 7-3). Any time Z = 1, clear POS to 00. When POS = 00 and Z = 0, do not increment POS if A changes from 1 to 0. (This handling of POS and Z permits the loosest possible tolerance on the position of the Z sensor.)

(b) Using a specific microcomputer, write an assembly language routine corresponding to this flowchart. Minimize ROM words.

5-14 Incremental encoder. Repeat Prob. 5-13, but change operation to interrupt control, using the circuit of Fig. 5-48a to generate an interrupt.

5-15 Seven-segment display. An all-CMOS alternative to Fig. 5-58 is shown in Fig. P5-2. However, it requires the addition of current-limiting resistors. In spite of being a CMOS device, the decoder-driver can drive up to 25 mA, even with a 5-V power-supply voltage. For 20 mA of drive current the typical output voltage is 3.75 V, and the worst-case output voltage is 3.40 V.

(a) Assuming a drop of 1.7 V across the LED segments, what should be the resistance of the current-limiting resistors in order to provide a "typical" current of 20 mA?

(b) With this value of resistance and the worst-case decoder-driver output voltage, what will be the current in the LED segments?

5-16 "Write-only memory" display circuit. The circuit of Fig. 5-60 buffers the data inputs to the 16 latch-decoder-driver-displays. If this buffering circuitry were removed, what would be the load on each of the data bus lines?

5-17 Multiplexed display. If the one-shot shown in Fig. 5-61 should ever malfunction just once, and not generate a pulse, consider the consequences.

(a) What would happen to the display? Would it miss one of its 1-ms refresh cycles or would it shut off from any further display? Explain.

(b) Could the $\overline{Q}$ output of the one-shot, used to generate the interrupt, be also used as a "self-test" input to the microcomputer to check for this malfunction periodically? How would the self-test routine ever detect that this malfunction has occurred? What might it do to try to correct for the malfunction?

5-18 Multiplexed display. The ultimate limit imposed upon the number of seven-segment LED displays which can be multiplexed from one BCD-to-seven-segment decoder is determined by the ratio of the maximum current which it can handle to the average current needed to provide an

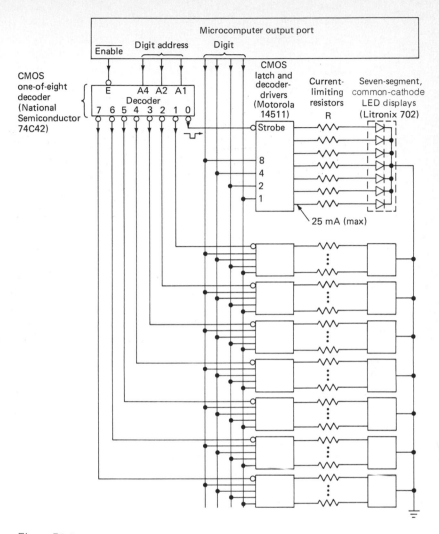

Figure P5-2.

adequately bright display. For example, Hewlett-Packard's 5082-7653 (red), 5082-7663 (yellow), and 5082-7673 (green) common-cathode units have a maximum current which depends upon the maximum pulse width, as shown in Fig. P5-3. These are high-efficiency displays, providing usable display brightness down to as low as 3 mA per segment.

(a) What is the maximum number of displays which can be multiplexed, still providing 3 mA of average current?

(b) What is the minimum rate at which the microcomputer can be

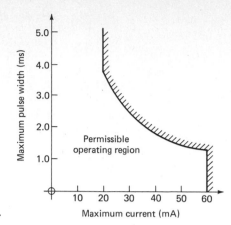

Figure P5-3.

interrupted to update the display (expressed in units of interrupts per second) under these circumstances?

(c) What is the minimum rate at which *each* digit is refreshed? Is it above the 20–50 refreshes per second rate at which the human eye stops detecting "flicker" and instead detects a continuous display?

(d) What is the maximum segment current?

(e) What is the maximum digit current?

5-19 Multiplexed display. For a specific microcomputer having interrupt capability:

(a) Write an assembly language interrupt service routine corresponding to the flowchart of Fig. 5-63b.

(b) Determine the time taken by this service routine.

(c) If an interrupt occurs every millisecond, what percentage of the CPU's time is taken up with refreshing the display?

5-20 Self-Scan display. The use of an alphanumeric display implies the storage of arrays of character strings in ROM to be displayed. Since the character coding of Fig. 5-64c requires only 6 bits, we can use the remaining 2 bits of each ROM word to help format the display, using the following ROM word structure

yyxxxxxx

where yy are the two format bits which are to be interpreted as follows:

yy	Meaning of xxxxxx
00	Use as a character code and display this character
01	Take next xxxxxx character codes from successive RAM locations pointed to by a pointer, RAMPT
10	Blank next xxxxxx display locations
11	Terminate any further entering of characters into the display

Using this structure, the ROM array to display FREQ = 15.6KHZ would look like

ROM word		Meaning	
Binary	Hex		
00000110	06	F	
00010010	12	R	
00000101	05	E	
00010001	11	Q	
00111101	3D	=	
01000010	42	1	(from RAM)
		5	(from RAM)
00101110	2E	.	
01000001	41	6	(from RAM)
00001011	0B	K	
00001000	08	H	
00011010	1A	Z	
11000000	C0	terminate	

(a) Make a flowchart for a subroutine DISP which has passed to it two pointers ROMPT and RAMPT and which updates the display of Fig. 5-64b with the message specified by the ROM array pointed to by ROMPT. Whenever the ROM word indicates that the next characters are to be taken from RAM, each of these characters is accessed using RAMPT, incrementing RAMPT after each access. Use flag control for handshaking with the display.

(b) For a specific microcomputer, write the assembly language subroutine.

5-21 **Zero-voltage turn-on.** For a specific microcomputer, write an assembly language subroutine ZERO which tests an external flag consisting of the Polarity output of the circuit of Fig. 5-69. The subroutine is to hang up in a wait loop until a newly read value of Polarity differs from the previously read value, at which time a return from the subroutine is executed. If this does not occur within $\frac{1}{40}$ s, set a nonzero value in the memory location labeled ZERROR and then return from the subroutine anyway. ZERROR can be used as an error flag by the self-test routine discussed in Sec. 7-3 to indicate a malfunction in the circuit of Fig. 5-69.

5-22 **Synchronous-motor position quantization.** Use the nonzero value of a RAM variable labeled LTOR to indicate left-to-right motion. Then assume that an interrupt service routine has already been written to take the position encoder output of Fig. 5-39 (and using an edge-detector circuit consisting of one-half of the circuit of Fig. 5-48a) and update a variable INCHES each time a quanta boundary is crossed. The motor can be assumed to be started and stopped only when one of the limit switches is being detected. Furthermore, the motor can be assumed to be up to synchronous speed by the time the first edge is detected from the position encoder, representing INCHES = 0 or 7, depending upon the direction of the motion.

Assume that the motor causes quanta boundaries to be crossed every 128 ms and that each quantum is to be divided into 64 parts, with a binary variable labeled PARTS.

(a) Flowchart the changes required in this service routine so that PARTS will be initialized to either 00111111 or 00000000 when an interrupt occurs, depending upon whether LTOR does, or does not, equal zero when an interrupt occurs. Furthermore, reinitialize a programmable timer at this time. The timer is to generate an interrupt every 2 ms. (Assume that tolerances are such that whenever quanta boundaries are crossed, and an interrupt occurs, PARTS will have been counted up to exactly 00111111 or down to exactly 00000000.)

(b) Using the structure exemplified in Fig. 3-49, describe what is needed so that the programmable timer can update PARTS appropriately. Then at any time when PVALID is nonzero, INCHES and PARTS provide a measure of absolute position (where PVALID is a flag saying the position encoder has crossed the first quanta position from either limit switch).

5-23 **Stepper-motor position controller.** Linear position is to be quantized into 256 parts by the discrete positions of a stepper motor. An optoelectronic switch SPOS is used with a mask having only one boundary, which is located midway between the 127th and 128th quanta defined by the stepper. One 8-bit word in RAM is labeled ACTPOS and is used to denote the actual position controlled by the stepper. Furthermore, when power is turned on, the stepper is stepped until the optoelectronic switch crosses its boundary, at which point ACTPOS is initialized to either 01111111 or 10000000, so that the most significant bit of ACTPOS is the same as the output of the optoelectronic switch SPOS.

Define any variables necessary and make a flowchart for the service routine for a programmable timer dedicated solely to this stepper and which causes an interrupt every 4 ms (or so). Do not use the TIMER subroutine of Sec. 3-9 but instead proceed so that the worst-case execution time of the service routine is as short as possible. The service routine is to compare the contents of a RAM location holding the desired position, labeled POS, with the actual position ACTPOS. If these are equal, a word in RAM labeled PVALID is set equal to a nonzero value as a flag indicating that POS represents the actual position. If POS and ACTPOS are not equal, PVALID is cleared to zero and a step is taken in the direction to move ACTPOS toward POS. Assume that this requires a clockwise step if POS is larger than ACTPOS.

Monitor the optoelectronic switch output SPOS and set a nonzero value in the memory location labeled PERROR if SPOS and the most significant bit of ACTPOS ever differ. PERROR can be used as an error flag by the self-test routine discussed in Sec. 7-3 to indicate a malfunction in stepping by the stepper motor.

This problem permits an arbitrary position to be set into POS. Then under interrupt control, the stepper will step to this position. The flag PVALID indicates when this position has been achieved.

5-24 Printing. For a specific microcomputer:

(*a*) Implement the PRINT interrupt service routine of Fig. 5-81. Minimize ROM words.

(*b*) Determine the worst-case (that is, highest) percentage of time taken by the printer from the moment interrupts are enabled until the final return from interrupt has taken place.

5-25 Printing. Make all the following flowchart modifications to the PRINT interrupt service routine of Fig. 5-81 so that the printer has a faster response, while still operating in a "print and advance" mode. In this modification, called PRINTF, interrupts from the printer are enabled *all* the time the instrument is in use.

(*a*) Let BUSY0 be a do-nothing state, so that if PRINTF is entered with BUSY = 0, it will return with BUSY = 0, having done nothing more than to handle PCHAR, as discussed·next.

(*b*) Define a variable PCHAR which is equal to the character code of the next character into position under the column hammers. Upon entering PRINTF, clear PCHAR to zero if "R signal" equals one. Otherwise, increment PCHAR during every other interrupt.

(*c*) Define a variable PNUM which is initially set equal to the number of characters to be printed (that is, 21 minus the number of blanks), and which is decremented each time a one is shifted into PTEMP in the algorithm of Fig. 5-82*a*. When BUSY2 is entered (in Fig. 5-81) and PNUM = 0, use this to terminate printing and to begin advancing the paper.

(*d*) To initiate printing, set BUSY equal to one (rather than enable interrupts). However, use the means needed in (*b*) to increment PCHAR during every other interrupt so as to decide whether to go to BUSY2 during this interrupt or the next one. Remember that BUSY3 must occur at the beginning of each interval when columns are to be actuated and BUSY2 must terminate each of these intervals. Refer to Fig. 5-77*d* for the definition of these timing requirements.

5-26 Printing. For a specific microcomputer:

(*a*) Implement the PRINTF interrupt service routine of Prob. 5-25.

(*b*) Determine the average percentage of time taken by the interrupt service routine when no printing is being done (that is, when BUSY equals zero).

(*c*) Determine the worst-case (that is, highest) percentage of time taken by the printer from the moment when BUSY is set to one until the final return from interrupt (during which BUSY has been cleared to zero again) has taken place.

5-27 Printing. In this problem, we will modify the PRINTF interrupt service routine of Prob. 5-25, resulting in the flowchart for an interrupt service routine to print multiline messages PRINTM. Instead of initiating a print operation by loading PARRAY with the message for one line, we will use a variation of the approach used in the DISP subroutine of Prob. 5-20. PRINTM will have two pointers passed to it. One, ROMPT, points to a character string in ROM which includes both the fixed characters to be printed and information to help format the printed output. The other, RAMPT, points to RAM, to pick up any variable data in the message. Consequently, we will want to store in ROM not only the character strings to be printed but also format information telling the printer to do such things as print characters taken from RAM, go to the next line and continue printing, skip some lines, and terminate printing.

Since the coding of the 42 characters of the printer requires only 6 bits, we can use the remaining 2 bits of each ROM word to help format the display, using the ROM word structure shown in Fig. P5-4a and b. When $yy = 00$ or 01, we will use the character coding shown in Fig. 5-78.

(a)   yyxxxxxx

yy	Meaning of xxxxxx
0 0	Use as a character code for the next character to be printed in this line
0 1	Take the next x x x x x x character codes from successive RAM locations pointed to by a pointer RAMPT
1 0	Blank the next x x x x x x columns in this line
1 1	If x x x x x x = 0 x x x x x, then fill out this line with blanks; print it; advance x x x x lines; continue
	If x x x x x x = 1 x x x x x, then fill out this line with blanks; print it; advance x x x x lines; stop further printing

(b)

AVERAGE☐☐☐☐35.8
STD.☐DEV.☐☐☒5.5
(blank line)
(c)   (blank line)

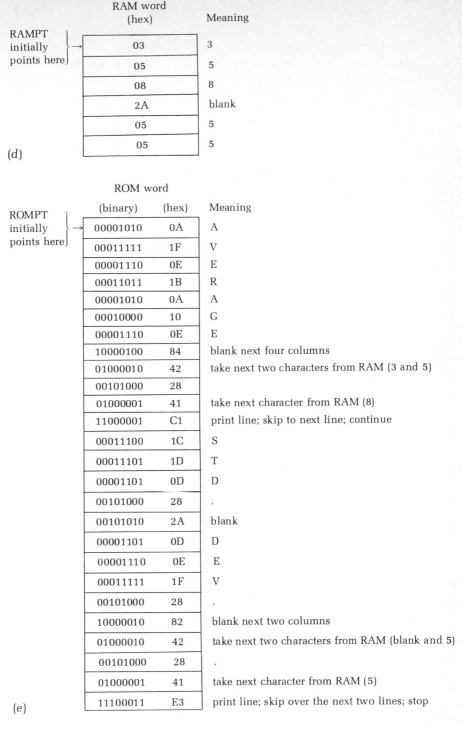

RAM word
(hex)   Meaning

RAMPT
initially →
points here

RAM word (hex)	Meaning
03	3
05	5
08	8
2A	blank
05	5
05	5

(d)

ROM word

(binary)   (hex)   Meaning

ROMPT
initially →
points here

(binary)	(hex)	Meaning
00001010	0A	A
00011111	1F	V
00001110	0E	E
00011011	1B	R
00001010	0A	A
00010000	10	G
00001110	0E	E
10000100	84	blank next four columns
01000010	42	take next two characters from RAM (3 and 5)
00101000	28	
01000001	41	take next character from RAM (8)
11000001	C1	print line; skip to next line; continue
00011100	1C	S
00011101	1D	T
00001101	0D	D
00101000	28	.
00101010	2A	blank
00001101	0D	D
00001110	0E	E
00011111	1F	V
00101000	28	.
10000010	82	blank next two columns
01000010	42	take next two characters from RAM (blank and 5)
00101000	28	.
01000001	41	take next character from RAM (5)
11100011	E3	print line; skip over the next two lines; stop

(e)

Figure P5-4. (a) ROM word structure; (b) interpretation of the format bits yy; (c) two-line message, where □ is a blank character specified in ROM and ⊠ is a blank character specified in RAM; (d) RAM array required for this message; (e) ROM array required for this message.

An example of a two-line message, together with the RAM and ROM arrays needed to generate it, is shown in Fig. P5-4c, d, and e. To initiate this printed message, first BUSY is checked to determine if it equals zero, indicating that the printer's interrupt service routine has completed its last job. If not, we must wait to use the printer. When finally BUSY = 0, the two pointers RAMPT and ROMPT must be set up as shown in Fig. P5-4d and e, and the RAM array set up using exactly the format shown in Fig. P5-4d. Then BUSY is set equal to one.

(a) Define any variables needed to implement this algorithm and describe their role.

(b) Develop the flowchart for the algorithm, together with any little explanatory notes which are helpful, like those of Fig. 5-81.

5-28 Printing. Repeat Prob. 5-26 for the PRINTM interrupt service routine of Prob. 5-27.

5-29 Asynchronous serial data transmission. Given the format options for a serial character listed at the beginning of Sec. 5-9 (that is, 5 to 8 data bits, etc.) and assuming a 110 baud rate, determine:
(a) The maximum possible data rate
(b) The minimum possible data rate

5-30 Asynchronous serial data transmission. Assuming the serial format of Fig. 5-87, the receiver start-bit-detection mechanism of Fig. 5-86, and the 110×16-Hz crystal-clock-derived (that is, extremely accurate) UART external clock source of Fig. 5-88, determine:
(a) The maximum baud rate of the transmitter which will never produce a framing error due to a difference between transmitter and receiver clock frequencies.
(b) The minimum baud rate of the transmitter which will likewise never produce a framing error.

5-31 UARTs. If a UART operating at 9600 baud did not double buffer the data received, as in Fig. 5-90, how long would a microcomputer have, to respond to an interrupt and read out the received data, before an overrun error occurred?

5-32 UARTs. Consider some UART other than the Motorola unit discussed in the text.
(a) How is it connected to a CPU?
(b) What registers does it contain which are accessible to the CPU, how are they used, and how are they accessed?
(c) What serial format options are available?
(d) What particularly useful features does it have which Motorola's does not have?
(e) What particularly useful features of Motorola's unit does it not have?

5-33 UARTs. Construct the flowchart of the interrupt service routine used to service the UART discussed in the text. Assume that the transmitter's ongoing job is to transmit the array pointed to by the pointer stored in TPOINT and TPOINT + 1 and that the complete array will have been transmitted when the number stored in TNUM has been counted down to zero. Likewise, use RPOINT, RPOINT + 1, and RNUM for the receiver. If the receiver detects an error, cause a jump to the appropriate address FRAME, PARITY, or OVRUN, but do not actually flowchart these error routines.

5-34 UARTs. Using the algorithm of Prob. 5-33:

(a) What must the microcomputer do to initiate the transmission of an array of 128 words starting at the beginning of page 2?

(b) What must it do to initiate the reception of an array of 32 words to be put into RAM starting at the beginning of page 3?

(c) Assuming that both these uses have the same baud rate and serial format, is there any dependence between the two operations? Explain.

5-35 Optoisolators. Optoisolators are useful as line receivers for high data rates. For example, while the unit of Fig. 5-95 is suggested for data rates up to 300 kilobits per second, Hewlett-Packard's 5082-4364 dual optoisolator (in an 8-pin DIP) lists "typical" data rates of 10 megabits per second with a specified input current of 5.0 mA. While a single-ended driver (like that of Fig. 5-95) may be fine for many applications, for transmission over long distances or in very noisy environments a balanced system should be used. In Application Note 939, "High Speed Optically Coupled Isolators," Hewlett-Packard suggests the circuit shown in Fig. P5-5.

(a) With worst-case specifications on line driver output voltages of 1.8 V (high output) and 0.5 V (low output) when the output current is 40 mA, determine the worst-case dc input current to the optoisolator. Assume zero cable resistance and 1.5 V across the LED.

(b) With typical specifications of 3.3 and 0.22 V under the same circumstances, determine the typical dc input current to the optoisolator.

(c) The optoisolator lists a typical specification for current gain of 600 percent under one set of circumstances. What is the minimum current gain required for the input current of (a) to drive the output into saturation (0.5 V), given the 330-Ω load resistor shown?

(d) Repeat (c) with the results of (b).

5-36 Remote instrument control. As suggested in Sec. 5-10, options for a microcomputer-based instrument can often be handled with software in ROM together with no hardware other than that required for the standard interface bus. The implication of this situation for the future

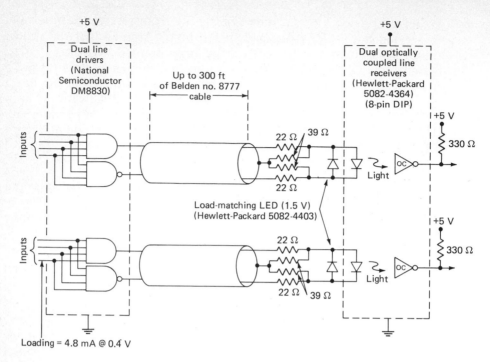

Loading = 4.8 mA @ 0.4 V

Figure P5-5.

will be the development of "dumb" peripherals which have as their only input the interface connector plus a DIP switch to program a talk and/or listen address.

(a) Describe a peripheral device which you can envision fitting into this mold (other than the printer already discussed).

(b) What interactions with the bus would you envision for this device, if as much of the complexity of using the device as possible were deferred to the microcomputer-based instrument at the other end of the interface bus?

5-37 Remote instrument control. Repeat Prob. 5-36 with a description of a "dumb" instrument or device developed for use with a programmable calculator and other instruments in order to put together automatic test systems. Again, the intent is to come up with a product idea made possible by the interface bus. Suggest something other than one of the possibilities of Fig. 5-97.

5-38 Remote instrument control. Instrument C shown in Fig. 5-101 is able to listen only. It is intended to have limited capability, using only two of the interface bus control lines. Actually, all signal lines of the bus would be terminated in the resistive circuit of Fig. 5-100.

(a) Explain why *no* instrument can get along without the IFC line.

(b) Repeat (a) for the ATN line.

(c) Of the instruments of Fig. 5-97, which might be listeners only? Qualify your answers for specific instruments, if necessary, so as to make this possible.

(d) Repeat (c) for talkers only.

5-39 Remote instrument control. By setting itself up as a listener, the controller can terminate the transfer of data bytes between two other instruments cleanly. It can take the bus back into the command mode, without inadvertently catching the two instruments in the middle of a handshake (with data possibly transferred). Make a flowchart for the controller's operation to do this if it knows that the last data byte from the talker will include the EOI ("end") signal.

5-40 Remote instrument control. Repeat Prob. 5-39 when it is the controller itself which is the talker.

5-41 Remote instrument control. For setting up which instruments in an automatic test system are to be operated locally from their front-panel controls and which are to be operated remotely from a programmable calculator, the appendix (nonstandard, but suggested) of the IEEE interface bus standard includes a "go to local" addressed command which returns responding devices to local control. Describe a situation for which the remote/local enabling mechanism described in the text is inadequate and which needs the "go to local" addressed command to achieve a desired instrument configuration.

5-42 Remote instrument control. Construct flowcharts for the following three interrupt service routines to go along with the circuit of Fig. 5-104, assuming the microcomputer includes *vectored* interrupt capability:

(a) Following a rising edge on REN.

(b) Following a falling edge on IFC.

(c) Following any edge on ATN.

5-43 Self-test. For a specific microcomputer, what possibilities exist:

(a) For obtaining an unused output from the CPU chip?

(b) For obtaining an unused input to the CPU chip?

In each case, indicate what normal capability is lost if a self-test input or output to the CPU chip is made available in this way.

5-44 Self-test. A subtle input to the CPU chip might be obtained if a switch on the CPU's printed-circuit board were used to change the microcomputer's clock frequency. For example, the Fairchild F8 microcomputer can easily be switched between a standard 2.0-MHz crystal clock and a slower RC-controlled clock.

(a) If this were done for a specific microcomputer, how might the change in frequency be detected (so as to serve as an input)?

(b) Can you do this entirely within the CPU chip?

(c) If not, can you do this using only the CPU chip plus external circuitry not otherwise used by the microcomputer (and therefore independent of its malfunction)?

(d) If not, how would you do this so as to involve as little of the microcomputer's capability as possible?

5-45 Self-test. (a) For a specific 8-bit microcomputer, make a flowchart and write an assembly language subroutine which will take the two BCD digit content of the accumulator and put it out to the display of Fig. 5-106 with a sequence of write instructions (or other instructions which affect the address lines). The "data" bit should be stable on the rising edge of the "clock" bit.

(b) If the particular microcomputer used does not latch its address outputs, and therefore emits spurious pulses on the address lines, add appropriate gating on the "clock" line of Fig. 5-106 so as to eliminate this problem.

5-46 Self-test. Under certain adverse conditions, EPROMs have been known to "drop" one or more bits.

(a) Under what circumstances would this lead to a detected malfunction using the ROM-checking scheme proposed in the text?

(b) Conversely, what error patterns would go undetected?

5-47 Self-test. Consider the following check which can be made on RAMs at any time. One word in each RAM chip is set aside for self-testing. During one test, only one RAM is accessed. The test consists of writing a word having a single one (that is, with zeros in the other bits) into the self-test address within one RAM chip and then reading it back out and comparing the result. Successive tests put the single one into every bit position in this word and then do the same for all other RAM chips. Of the types of malfunctions listed (for ROMs) in Fig. 5-109, which ones will be detected for RAMs using this test?

5-48 Self-test. For a specific microcomputer, and minimizing ROM words, make a flowchart and write an assembly language subroutine for the "buffered bus" self-test scheme described in conjunction with Fig. 5-110. The subroutine is to return with the carry bit set if a malfunction is detected. In addition, it is to return four words to the calling program: ADD1, ADD0, DATA1, and DATA0. Whereas the carry bit is to be set if *any* error is detected, each of these words has a one in a bit position only if the one different bit of each test were changed. Thus, an address of 10000000 returned as 00000000 would result in the most significant bit of ADD1 being set to one. On the other hand, if 10000000 were returned as 11000000, none of the four words would be affected (but a note would be made to set the carry bit upon returning from the subroutine).

REFERENCES

An unusually thorough and diverse discussion of I/O devices, their interconnections to a microcomputer, and the timing considerations and service routines involved is contained in the "M6800 Microprocessor Applications
Manual" which can be purchased in paperback from distributors of Motorola products or in hardcover from the McGraw-Hill Book Company.

The variety of keyboard switches available is discussed by S. Davis,
Keyswitch and Keyboard Selection for Computer Peripherals, *Computer Design*, March 1973, pp. 67–79.

An excellent discussion of the operation of the alphanumeric printer
shown in Fig. 5-77, as well as the detailed development of the Motorola 6800
assembly language service routine to drive it, is presented by A. Moore and
M. Eidson, Printer Control: A Minor Task for a Fast Microprocessor, *Electronic Design*, Dec. 6, 1974, pp. 74–83.

The operation of Motorola's UART is described in more detail in their
"M6800 Microprocessor Applications Manual" and also in Motorola Appli-
cation Note AN-754, "Device Operation and System Implementation of the
Asynchronous Communications Interface Adapter (MC6850)."

Examples of the use of optoisolators for the isolation of power lines,
medical equipment, and telephone lines are given in Hewlett-Packard Application Note 951-1, "Applications for Low Input Current, High Gain Optically Coupled Isolators."

Insights into the IEEE Interface Bus Standard through state-diagram
descriptions of its functioning are provided by D. E. Knoblock, D. C.
Loughry, and C. A. Vissers, Insight into Interfacing, *IEEE Spectrum*, May
1975, pp. 50–57.

Some of the considerations which arise when an automatic test system
is configured around the standard interface bus are discussed by D. W. Ricci
and P. S. Stone, Putting Together Instrumentation Systems at Minimum
Cost, *Hewlett-Packard Journal*, January 1975, pp. 5–11.

HARDWARE
AND SOFTWARE
DEVELOPMENT

6-1 THE HIGH ROAD VERSUS THE LOW ROAD

A benefit of attending a technical meeting or seminar which attracts designers of microcomputer-based instruments occurs as these designers compare
how they developed their instruments. It can come as a revelation to one
designer, used to having extensive development tools available, that another
designer has created a "smart" instrument with almost no development
tools. In this section, we will look at some of these possibilities.

In Fig. 1-19, we considered some of the design steps involved in the
development of an instrument. If the input and output devices of the instrument (for example, printer, display, keyboard, actuators, and transducers) require any design work themselves, this must be carried out, including the
circuitry to interface them to the microcomputer. A helpful step at this
stage is to check the operation of each device and its interface circuitry, independent of the rest of the system. If a device can be operated meaning-
fully "by hand," a simple, low-cost approach is to single-step the device
through its different modes of operation using switches patched to inputs
and LEDs patched to outputs, as shown in Fig. 6-1.

Ultimately, each device must operate under control of the microcom-

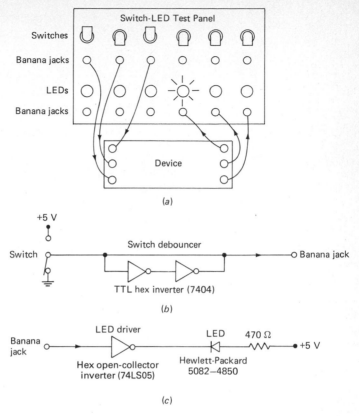

Figure 6-1. Device testing by single-stepping. (a) Connections for single-step testing; (b) switch circuit; (c) LED circuit for testing TTL circuitry.

puter. This testing need not wait upon all final decisions concerning the microcomputer structure which will be used in the instrument. It can be done with a standard prototyping board, like that of Fig. 6-2, having clock, CPU, EPROM, RAM, and I/O. Alternatively, it can be achieved by simply interconnecting clock, CPU, one EPROM, and enough I/O ports and interrupt capability to handle each device, one at a time, as in Fig. 6-3. This approach permits the device to be tested in real time, if that is important. By taking advantage of the reprogramming capability of the EPROM, the designer need not get deeply involved in software at this stage. Instead, the device is checked a little at a time, reprogramming the EPROM for each test.

To ascertain proper operation during each test, one approach is to repeat the test over and over again in an endless loop. An oscilloscope can be used if a test requires looking at only one or two variables at a time, as in Fig. 6-4a. The test routine can include the generation of a pulse on one line of an

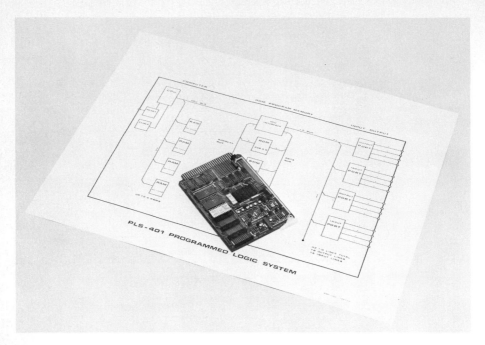

Figure 6-2. Standard prototyping board. (Pro-Log Corp.)

output port to serve as a trigger input to the oscilloscope. In this way, the time of each event in the test is referenced to the one instruction in the loop which initiates the pulse.

By connecting a display to the microcomputer, the microcomputer it-self can serve as the test instrument, as in Fig. 6-4b. The display might be a decimal display which will be part of the finished instrument, or it might be the LEDs of Fig. 6-1. For a simple test, like whether a device handshakes properly or not, the test routine can display a one or a zero (or turn a LED on or off) to indicate the result. The microcomputer is an even more valuable

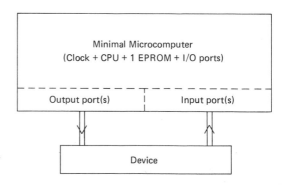

Figure 6-3. Device testing under microcomputer control.

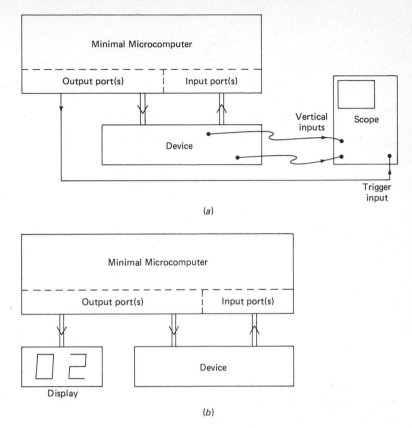

Figure 6-4. Testing a device. (a) Setup for oscilloscope testing; (b) setup for self-testing.

test instrument for detecting whether proper timing relationships exist between unsynchronized events. For example, if proper operation depends upon event 1 terminating before event 2 begins, the microcomputer can initiate the event over and over again, looking to see if event 1 and event 2 ever overlap in time and incrementing the display if they do.

The approaches discussed so far for testing devices represent the "low road," or low-cost approach, to this design step. Alternatively, we can travel the "high road" and expedite the same result with equipment produced by the microcomputer manufacturer. For example, Motorola's EXORciser, shown in Fig. 6-5, permits a designer to obtain a working Motorola 6800 microcomputer, configured with an arbitrary amount of RAM and I/O ports, and easily connect it to the devices it is to control. It contains a ROM program which can load a user program, like one of the test routines discussed earlier, from a terminal like that of Fig. 6-6, into RAM and then execute the test. It (temporarily) avoids the use of EPROMs, permitting quick

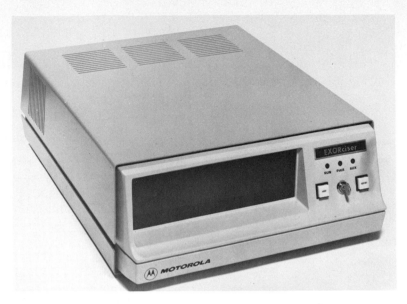

Figure 6-5. Motorola's EXORcisor.   (Motorola Semiconductor Products Inc.)

Figure 6-6. Silent 700® programmable data terminal.   (Texas Instruments Inc.)

changes in programs by entering new ones from the terminal. Furthermore, it provides a variety of debugging functions, like stepping through a program while printing out the contents of the CPU's registers. When the program counter gets to a preselected address, the EXORciser can stop executing further instructions or, alternatively, can generate a pulse to trigger an oscilloscope.

Because many of the hardware-debugging problems of a microcomputer-based instrument involve the *relationships* among many signals during successive clock periods, it is often difficult to track down the source of a problem by looking at one or two signals on an oscilloscope. An unusually capable tool, designed specifically for this purpose, is the logic-state analyzer. While the unit shown on the left of Fig. 6-7 is designed for use with the Motorola 6800 microcomputer, other microcomputers can be debugged with other models. Not the least of its features is its circuit-probing ability. One probe clips directly onto the CPU chip. In addition, eight more probes can sense conditions anywhere else. These probes can attach to the adjacent pins of an integrated circuit or adjacent posts of a wire-wrap board.

This analyzer can trigger upon any combination of address information, data bus information, and information on the eight probes. It displays addresses, instructions in mnemonic form, and binary data from the probes over a "window" of 64 memory cycles (or about 20 to 30 successively executed instructions). It has the powerful capability of triggering on a malfunction and being able to look backward in time for up to 64 memory cycles to see how the fault was arrived at. Alternatively, the window can be delayed for up to 65,472 memory cycles after the trigger condition. Once the logic-state analyzer has pinned down the *time of occurrence* of a fault, it can

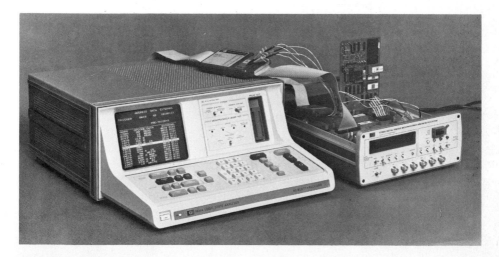

Figure 6-7. Logic-state analyzer. (Hewlett-Packard Co.)

generate a trigger pulse to an oscilloscope, thus providing waveform information if this is necessary to diagnose the *cause* of the fault.

Two other modes of operation of this instrument are worth noting. The instrument can determine the time taken between any two events, each of which is identified in the same versatile manner as is used for triggering the display. It can also single-step or slowly scan (at a rate of several instructions per second) through a program.

In its use of a keyboard and CRT to enter and display setup information, this instrument is an outstanding example of smart instrument design. The user "fills in the blanks" of a "menu" for the setup desired. By automatically blanking those portions of the menu which are irrelevant to the setup, the instrument does not confuse the user with a multitude of unused options. In this way the designers have provided the novice with an easy-to-use instrument and the experienced user with a variety of sophisticated options.

If there is some disparity in the approaches taken by designers in tackling the problems of putting together a system's hardware, this is dwarfed by the disparity in the approaches taken to software development. At the low-cost end of the scale, a designer can take assembly language programs and assemble them by hand into object code (that is, the 1s and 0s, or the hexadecimal equivalent, which form the EPROM contents). To a designer who has always had this step done by an assembler program in a computer, it is almost unbelievable that this is a viable alternative. Yet, in spite of its tediousness, some microcomputer-based instruments have actually been designed in just this way, with the designers claiming that the time taken in assembling, and reassembling, has not been an overriding factor in the development time for the instrument. But, it is tedious.

A fundamental problem arises for the designer who wishes to use the microcomputer itself for debugging software. For this debugging, the ability to view the program counter, accumulator, carry bit, address pointer(s), and other CPU scratchpad registers is a vital necessity. The problem arises because there is no way in which we can connect displays to these registers directly, since they reside deep within the CPU chip.

One "minimal" approach, shown in Fig. 6-8, requires a microcomputer which:

1   Incorporates a maskable interrupt.
2   Permits access to the return address of an interrupt routine.

The displays shown are the hexadecimal displays discussed in Sec. 5-6 and configured to look like RAM addresses or else connected to an output port. The microcomputer includes one EPROM which contains an interrupt service routine to help with debugging. This is shown as a *separate* EPROM so that it need not be reprogrammed every time the program under test is reprogrammed.

This approach permits *single-stepping* through the program under test.

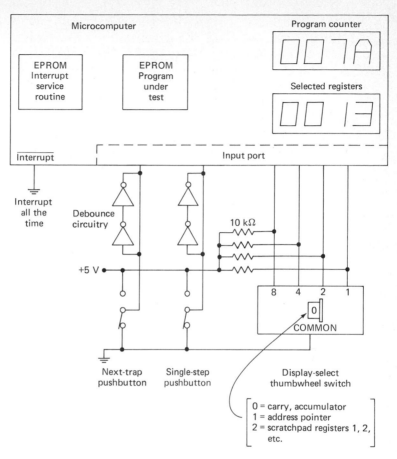

Figure 6-8. *Software debugging within the microcomputer.*

However, it does not employ a normal single-step circuit, since this does not solve the problem of displaying internal registers. Instead, it spends most of its time in an interrupt service routine, returning to the program under test once each time a "single-step" push button is depressed. The CPU's Enable Interrupt flipflop remains disabled while in the interrupt service routine. By enabling interrupts again upon exit, we hope to execute exactly one instruction of the program under test before entering the interrupt service routine again. If tying the Interrupt input low does not accomplish this, the interrupt service routine can generate a pulse on an output line just before returning to the program under test. This can trigger a one-shot, whose output then stays high until the middle of the first instruction of the program under test. By driving the Interrupt input from this one-shot output, the CPU will be interrupted again after executing this one instruction of the program under test.

The interrupt service routine is flowcharted in Fig. 6-9. It checks the

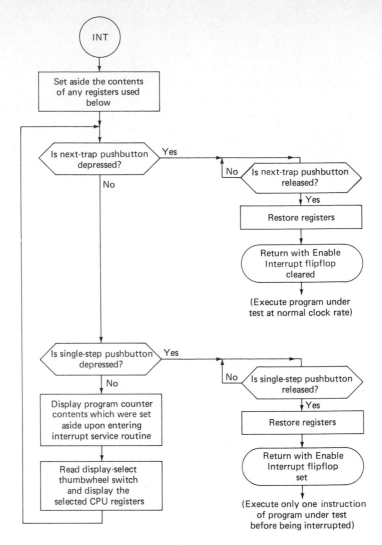

Figure 6-9. Interrupt service routine.

"next-trap" push button, and if this is depressed and then released, it returns to the program under test with further interrupts disabled. It will continue to execute instructions at the normal clock rate until "trapped" by an
enable interrupt instruction. Consequently, in preparing the program to be
tested, at least one point, and perhaps several points, should be used to initiate single-stepping by inserting an enable interrupt instruction at these
points. To skip to the following enable interrupt instruction, it is only necessary to depress and release this push button again.

Once the interrupt service routine is entered, if neither the "next-trap" nor the "single-step" push button is depressed, the CPU will remain in the interrupt service routine, displaying the program-counter contents set aside upon entering the service routine (which is the *next* instruction to be executed) as well as the CPU registers selected with the "Display select" thumbwheel switch. Note that changing this thumbwheel switch immediately changes the display to the appropriate registers, permitting the user to look at any CPU registers while remaining at one instruction.

In contrast to the previous approach, having a disk operating system available as a design tool takes the maximum burden off the designer. The floppy-disk-based computer shown in Fig. 6-10 provides a relatively low-priced vehicle for this design approach. It permits a user to create and edit an assembly language program with ease, to assemble it, to simulate and debug the operation of the microcomputer, and to transfer object code either to a PROM programmer (like that of Fig. 1-10) or to a manufacturer's hardware development unit (like that of Fig. 6-5).

Developing software involves interactions between all these steps. Being able to manage them all "under the one roof" of a (fast) disk operating system, controlled from a (fast) CRT terminal drastically simplifies the interactions. As an example of the interactions, a typical design iteration involves developing some new assembly language code as a file in the computer, assembling it, using the diagnostic error messages from the assembler

Figure 6-10. Floppy-disk-based computer system. (Digital Equipment Corp.)

to go back and edit the file, assemble again, simulate* it to debug its operation, go back and edit the original file to remove flaws discovered in simulation, assemble and simulate again, go back and append this newly developed assembly language code into the rest of the instrument software already developed, assemble and simulate again, try it on the hardware-development unit, and iterate once more.

A disk operating system is a development tool which benefits by not being dedicated to a specific microcomputer in the same sense as a hardware-development unit must be. Using its Fortran compiler, it can accept any assembler and simulator written in Fortran for a specific microcomputer. To update the facility for a different microcomputer means obtaining (or writing) an assembler and simulator for that microcomputer. The ability to edit a file and the ability to transfer data to a teletype-like device are inherent capabilities of the disk operating system itself.

Hand assembly followed by software debugging on the setup of Fig. 6-8 represents one extreme approach toward software development. A disk-based computer represents the other extreme. In addition, there are several "middle-ground" alternatives. Most manufacturers provide cross-assembler† and simulator facilities through one of the time-sharing services available over a telephone line. This is probably the easiest way to get started. It requires a terminal ranging anywhere from a teletype, through that of Fig. 6-6, to that of Fig. 1-15. Since both the designer and the time-sharing service can maintain files of assembly language programs, these can be debugged and edited without actually sending entire programs over the telephone line each time they are used. Only the edited changes need be transmitted. On the other hand, the useful output at some stage in the development process is the object code emitted by the assembler. If punched paper tape is avoided in favor of the cassette-tape unit of Fig. 6-6 or the floppy-disk unit of Fig. 1-15, this transfer can be speeded up.

Speed is more important in simulation because it is such an interactive process. Typically, we want to call the simulator, enter our file name, enter commands to the simulator to load some of the CPU registers and RAM locations as desired, and then tell the simulator to begin executing instructions while providing a *trace* (that is, a printout of the CPU register contents) after each one. On the basis of the results, we will decide what to do next.

Some microcomputer manufacturers provide hardware, based upon their microcomputer, for "complete system development." This will usually include a resident-assembler‡ either in ROM or as a program which must be loaded into RAM before assembling can take place. The tricky step

---

* Discussed in Sec. 6-6.
† A cross-assembler for a microcomputer is an assembler which has been prepared to run on another machine, like the disk operating system.
‡ A resident-assembler converts an assembly language program to object code using the same machine which the assembly language describes.

Figure 6-11. Intel's 8080 Microcomputer Development System. (Intel Corp.)

is to provide the kind of software debugging flexibility *within* the microcomputer that a simulator provides when run on another computer. Having a trace of CPU registers during the execution of successive instructions printed out, or shown on a CRT display, is more helpful than simply seeing the contents of the address bus and data bus displayed in lights on a front panel of a minicomputer-like device built up from microcomputer components.

Intel's Microcomputer Development System for their 8080 microcomputer is built up around the 8080, but it does not suffer from this dependence. Rather, it is configured into a floppy-disk-operating system with CRT display, line printer, PROM programmer, and an "In-Circuit Emulator," as shown in Fig. 6-11. The software can be developed as in any disk operating system. Then the hardware can be prototyped using standard CPU, RAM, ROM, and I/O boards available from Intel or with hardware configured specifically for the instrument. Intel, with their In-Circuit Emulator, provides the ability to remove the actual 8080 CPU chip from this hardware and replace it with their emulator. The emulator consists of a buffered 8080 CPU chip which can drive the instrument but which can also be started, stopped, and interrogated by the disk operating system. Consequently, debugging the hardware of an 8080-based instrument is greatly facilitated.

6-2 OVERALL SOFTWARE ORGANIZATION: BREAKING DOWN COMPLEXITY

The first step in developing the software for an instrument is to avoid being overwhelmed. We might begin by listing, rather quickly and crudely, what we expect of the instrument in order to obtain an overall perspective. The list of Fig. 6-12 can be used as a starter.

Next, we might associate with each of these items some idea of the cir-

Figure 6-12. Starter List for Describing the Capabilities of an Instrument

List and describe instrument inputs and outputs.

Describe any algorithmic processes which are likely to play a predominant role in the development.

Is self-test capability to be included? What overall checks can be designed into the instrument?

Is automatic calibration to be included? Roughly, what is involved in doing this?

Is remote control to be an included feature? What control and data inputs and what data outputs does this imply?

Is power-standby capability required? How is the instrument to start up again when power is restored?

cumstances under which they take place (for example, only at start-up; periodically; in response to an input). For periodic events controlled by the microcomputer, what are reasonable limits on the period of control (that is, how often is too often and how slow is too slow)? For external events to which the microcomputer must respond, how quickly must the response occur? For any events requiring a fast response, must other functions go on at the same time or can the CPU monitor the event under flag control using a "wait loop"?

With this information, we can sort out control inputs which can be handled under flag control from those to be handled under interrupt control. If DMA capability is needed, will it idle the CPU more than a negligible amount?

A rough flowchart of the overall system operation can now be made. Our goal here is to indicate the different kinds of functions which must be included, perhaps using a structure like that of Fig. 6-13. The final initialization routines will include both functions which we can identify now and a variety of others which will become apparent only as the software is developed (like initializing a RAM address used in an algorithm). The growth of this list of initialization requirements as the software development proceeds does not complicate the design process at all.

A more significant consideration concerns the times T_{MIN} and T_{MAX} shown in Fig. 6-13 and which are dictated by our earlier considerations. However, we have three means for fitting the things to be done by the instrument into this structure if it turns out that this time constraint is not going to be met. A task which does not have to be completed immediately can be completed a little at a time, during successive passes around the loop. It is only necessary to set aside some parameters which indicate where we are in the task so that during the next pass we can pick up again. Second, any input which is not being tested sufficiently often can be tested more than once within the loop. Third, if neither of these approaches can resolve the

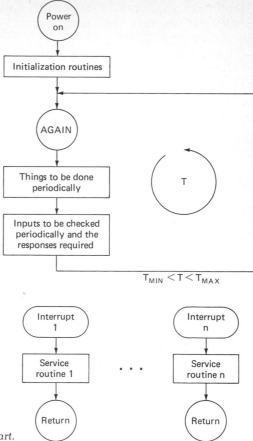

Figure 6-13. Starter for an overall flowchart.

problem of responding sufficiently fast to a certain input, it can be changed
from flag control to interrupt control.

Recognizing that whatever we have done to this point is likely to grow
more complex as we actually get involved in the software development, we
can begin that development with the outline of Fig. 1-22. If register-
management decisions are to be made (as discussed in the next section), this
is the time to make them. Then we can begin almost anywhere if we take
the precaution to develop specific capabilities as well-defined subroutines.
"Well-defined" is used here in the sense of documenting how parameters
are passed to and from a subroutine and what registers are changed during
execution of the subroutine, as in Fig. 2-22.

If we want to postpone the development of any general software tools
which we will need, as indicated in Fig. 1-22, we should at least *define* their
operation as a subroutine so that we can call them. Then, in checking out a
routine which uses one of these tools (like a table-driver subroutine), we can

"fake" the response of the unwritten subroutine by substituting a simpler subroutine. It need only return parameters that will satisfy the routine being tested, but little else.

6-3 REGISTER MANAGEMENT

We will use the term *register management* to signify all decisions concerning how CPU registers are to be utilized. If we do not do this at the outset, it will probably require some undoing to do it later.

Some decisions are built into the hardware and consequently have already been made for us by the manufacturer. For example, the RCA COSMAC CPU has 16 scratchpad registers R0, . . . , RF each 16 bits long. However, if DMA operations are anticipated, R0 should be set aside and not generally used, since the hardware will look to this register for an address pointer during a DMA operation. Similarly, the Intel 8008 CPU has seven scratchpad registers, any one of which can be generally used as the source of an operand or the destination of a result. However, two of these (registers H and L) form the only pointer to memory. There are two risks when using the CPU registers casually in the development of algorithms. These arise when data is manipulated solely within the CPU, and no attention is paid to the problem of getting the data into these registers at the outset and moving it out when done. At the very least, this may entail extra shuffling around of the data. At worst, if we have filled up *all* scratchpad registers with derived results, we will have left ourselves no means for forming a pointer to RAM to move these results out. In this case, the algorithm must be rewritten, moving results out before all scratchpad registers have been filled.

One decision encompassed by the term register management occurs when we take a generally useful scratchpad register and set it aside for a specific purpose. For example, if an interrupt occurs in an Intel 8008-based instrument, we will want to set aside the contents of at least some of the CPU's scratchpad registers in order to use these registers in the interrupt service routine. In Sec. 3-7, we discussed the problem of forming a pointer when all CPU registers are in use. A minimum hardware solution to the problem requires setting aside two of the scratchpad registers (such as registers D and E) solely for use by interrupt service routines. Then when an interrupt occurs, the contents of the H and L registers are moved to registers D and E, a pointer is formed to RAM in registers H and L, and registers A, B, C, D, and E can be moved out to RAM. The process is reversed at the end of the service routine. However, unless we make this register-management decision at the outset, we are likely to write routines which use all seven available CPU registers. A late decision will mean rewriting these routines.

Some microcomputers avoid register-management problems by not having any scratchpad registers at all. Thus the Motorola 6800 CPU has two accumulators, an index register, and a stack pointer, each of which is too valuable in its own right to be set aside for some special purpose.

One register-management decision, for a microcomputer having quite a few scratchpad registers, concerns the use of scratchpad registers by a subroutine. If we prepare software on the assumption that between *every* subroutine call and its corresponding return, the contents of all scratchpad registers have been changed, as in Fig. 6-14a, then we will avoid building a potential source of trouble into the software. In contrast, consider Fig. 6-14b, in which the subroutine leaves registers B, C, and D unchanged during its execution. If an operand is used both before the subroutine and again afterward, but not by the subroutine itself, the strong temptation arises to maintain it in register B, C, or D during the subroutine execution. The risk arises if at some future time we decide to modify the subroutine. If, in so doing, we change the contents of the register which holds this operand, we will introduce a "bug" into the program. With our documentation of subroutines, we can avoid this problem by avoiding the use of registers which are listed as being unused, when we make changes to a subroutine.

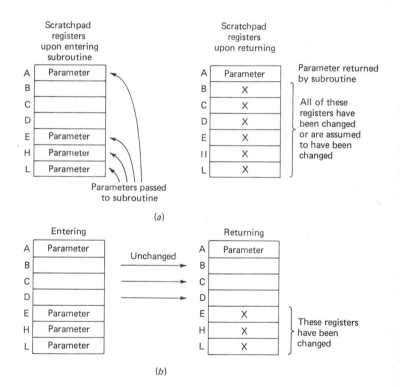

Figure 6-14. Subroutine register management. (a) Safe assumption of register usage by a subroutine; (b) potential source of future trouble.

6-4 THE PROCESS OF ASSEMBLY

Assembly language permits us to develop software using a mnemonic for each instruction instead of the 1s and 0s which the CPU understands. It also permits us to represent addresses in RAM and ROM with address labels. The process of assembly (whether done by a resident-assembler, by a cross-assembler, or by hand) consists largely of translating the mnemonics and address labels of the assembly language *source program* into the *object code* of the microcomputer.

A *two-pass assembler* carries out the translation by going through the source program, from beginning to end, twice. During the first pass, the assembler creates a *symbol table* consisting of one entry for each address label together with its actual address in RAM or ROM. During the second pass, it creates the object code. By assembling in two passes, the assembler can deal with the source program a line at a time.

To create a symbol table, the assembler first initializes an *address counter* to address 0000 (hex). If the source program begins with an ORG assembler directive,* the address associated with this directive is loaded into the address counter. Then, as the assembler looks at each line of the source program, if that line begins with an address label, the label is entered into the symbol table together with the contents of the address counter. Next, the mnemonic is used to access an *instruction list* and extract a parameter LENGTH which tells how many bytes there are in the instruction. This number is added to the address counter to form the address of the next instruction. In this way, the assembler works its way through the source program, a line at a time, forming successive entries in the symbol table.

The process of forming a symbol table during the first pass is illustrated in Fig. 6-15a. The assembler treats the assembler directives ORG and END differently from the remaining mnemonics. It makes no access to the instruction list, shown in Fig. 6-15b, in these two cases. Instead, it loads the address counter in response to ORG, and it terminates the first pass of assembly in response to END. Otherwise, it proceeds line by line, updating the address counter (using the instruction list entries shown in Fig. 6-15b) and making additions to the symbol table. It uses the REG (register) and OP (operand) fields only if necessary to determine the number of bytes in an instruction.

During the second pass, the assembler has a more involved task. To process each instruction, it again uses the mnemonic to enter the instruction list, shown in complete form in Fig. 6-16. It ignores LENGTH and extracts the four parameters CODE, BYTE1, BYTE2, and BYTE3.

The number BYTE1 is used by the assembler to decide how to form the first byte of the instruction. For example, if BYTE1 = 1, the first byte of the

---

* Defined in Fig. 2-32.

Figure 6-15. First Pass of Assembly

| | | | | Address counter | | Addition to symbol table when line is processed | |
| | Source program | | | Before starting line | After finishing line | | |
ADD	MNE	REG	OP			Label	Address
	ORG		0100	0000	0100		
TIMER	DCR	C		0100	0101	TIMER	0100
	JNZ		TIMER	0101	0104		
	DCR	B		0104	0105		
	JNZ		TIMER	0105	0108		
	MVI	C	H'5A'	0108	010A		
TIM1	DCR	C		010A	010B	TIM1	010A
	JNZ		TIM1	010B	010E		
	RET			010E	010F		
	END						

(a) Assembling, line by line

MNEMONIC	LENGTH
DCR	1
JNZ	3
MVI	2
RET	1

(b) Part of the instruction list

Figure 6-16. Format of Complete Instruction List

MNEMONIC	LENGTH	CODE	BYTE1	BYTE2	BYTE3
DCR	1	05	3	0	0
JNZ	3	C2	1	2	2
MVI	2	06	3	1	0
RET	1	C9	1	0	0

.
.
.

(other instruction mnemonics)

instruction might be the two-hex-digit number CODE with no further modi-fication. On the other hand, if BYTE1 = 3, then perhaps the first byte of the instruction is formed by adding a constant to CODE which depends upon the entry in the REG (register) field of the instruction. For each value of BYTE1, the assembler will have a different routine for forming the first byte of the in-struction. After the first byte is formed, it is emitted by the assembler, together with its address, and the address counter is incremented.

If BYTE2 = 0, this is a 1-byte instruction. Since the assembler is done with this instruction, it can proceed to the next one. Otherwise, the as-sembler uses the value of BYTE2 to enter a routine which will form the sec-ond byte of the instruction. This might be the two-hex-digit number in the OP (operand) field of the instruction if BYTE2 = 1. Or it might be the lower half of a four-hex-digit number in the OP field if BYTE2 = 2. After forming the second byte of the instruction, it is emitted by the assembler together with its address, and once again the address counter is incremented. The third byte, if there is one (that is, if BYTE3 does not equal zero) is formed in similar fashion.

As the assembler proceeds, it will generate output in two forms. It will generate addresses and object code on paper tape, cassette tape, or floppy disk in a form which can be used by a PROM programmer or a hardware or software simulator. It will also generate a printout or display like that of Fig. 6-17, giving the user a listing of both the source program and the object code together with *diagnostics* if errors in the source program are detected (for example, "Mnemonic is not valid;" "Operand is missing;" "END state-ment is missing").

Figure 6-17. Assembler Listing (Intel 8080 Object Code)

Address counter	Object code: Byte number			Source program				
	1	2	3	ADD	MNE	REG	OP	Comments
00 00					ORG		0100	
01 00	0D			TIMER	DCR	C		
01 01	C2	00	01		JNZ		TIMER	
01 04	05				DCR	B		
01 05	C2	00	01		JNZ		TIMER	
01 08	0E	5A			MVI	C	H'5A'	
01 0A	0D			TIM1	DCR	C		
01 0B	C2	0A	01		JNZ		TIM1	
01 0E	C9				RET			
					END			

6-5 HIGH-LEVEL LANGUAGES

Designers of microcomputer-based instruments are divided in their advocacy of assembly language versus a high-level language (like Algol, or Intel's PL/M) for developing software. A high-level language simplifies and accelerates the development of the software in that each statement in a high-level language represents many statements in assembly language. It makes functions such as multiplication easy to use because they have already been prepared by the person who wrote the compiler which translates the high-level language instructions into object code for a specific microcomputer.

The main argument favoring software development in assembly language is one of efficiency in the number of ROM words required to hold the total instrument software. Also, if I/O timing is "close," the software needed to handle this timing can be controlled more directly in assembly language. In addition, the availability of a general-purpose computer as a development tool is not *required* to assemble software prepared in assembly language whereas one is a necessity to compile a high-level language.

Some of the advantages of a high-level language can be attained without forsaking the advantages of assembly language programming. In particular, if we implement each algorithm with a subroutine, and if the number and location of parameters required by the subroutine are *passed* to the subroutine, then the algorithm's implementation will be available any time it is needed throughout the development of an instrument and for subsequent instruments.

As an example of the alternative, if we want to add two 6-digit decimal numbers X and Y in an 8-bit microcomputer, we could prepare a subroutine to which *no* parameters are passed. It would go to addresses X and Y in RAM and add the numbers, digit by digit, until all six digits have been added. However, when next we desired to add two decimal numbers, we would need another subroutine, almost identical to the first. Not only is this inefficient, but in modifying the first subroutine, we would need to refresh ourselves on its operation to assure ourselves of its correct operation when modified to form the new routine.

In contrast, we might pass parameters N, P1, and P2 to the subroutine, where N is the number of digits to be added while P1 and P2 are pointers to the numbers to be added. In this way we will have solved the problem of decimal addition once and for all. We might even go a step further and represent signed numbers in such a way that they can be added with the same subroutine. We also might have two entry points into the subroutine, one for addition and one for subtraction, if most of the steps of the two operations can be made the same.

Designers using the same microcomputer sometimes get together to share such generally useful subroutines. This has been a strong impetus for the creation of "users groups" of specific minicomputers, and it likewise makes sense for the users of a specific microcomputer. These generally useful subroutines available to us when developing instrument software represent very useful tools. Furthermore, because of the specific nature of the instruments which we design, we may find that some of the subroutines which we develop are useful to us again and again whereas they may be of little use to a designer of a different class of instruments. With our subroutines, we approach the ease of using a high-level language. Furthermore, it is a customized high-level language, especially suited to our needs.

In contrast, a compiler language like Intel's PL/M provides an effective software-development tool to us almost immediately, with the effectiveness built into the structure of the language. A compiler language has the following advantages over an assembly language:

1   It permits faster, more concise, software development.
2   It automatically, and flawlessly, manages all decisions on register use and parameter passing.
3   It provides the designer with a language which is especially well suited to implementing and describing algorithms.
4   It leads to software which is close to being "self-documenting."
5   It permits software development to be carried out independently of the specific microcomputer used (provided that for each specific microcomputer of interest, a compiler exists for this compiler language to translate it into the microcomputer's object code).

Software development with a compiler language is accelerated not only because each line of instructions compiles into many lines of object code. In addition, because the compiler manages all decisions on how, when, and where data must be moved, we are freed of a significant mental burden and can concentrate fully upon the algorithm itself. For example, if we want to normalize the 8-bit binary output of a linear transducer TR which falls in the range

$$TRMIN < TR < TRMAX$$

then the PL/M statement

$$TRNORM = SCALE * (TR - TRMIN)/(TRMAX - TRMIN)$$

will compute a 16-bit value for TRNORM. It does so without our having to think about CPU registers and how they will be used to obtain TRNORM. It does so with an expression that "looks like" the algorithm much more than does the assembly language equivalent. Thus it is easy to create the expression, and the result is close to being self-documenting. That is, very few additional words are needed to clarify what the algorithm does.

In an effort to be both useful and efficient for microcomputer-based instrument design applications, PL/M includes some built-in procedures which facilitate this work. For example, the statement

CALL TIME (15)

will be compiled into a wait loop which will last for $15 \times 0.1 = 1.5$ ms.

A user of PL/M can combine arithmetic statements, tests, and operations upon arrays into *procedures* (that is, subroutines) in order to implement an arbitrary algorithm as a modular unit, of general applicability. If the result turns out to be particularly inefficient (as might happen with a bit-packing procedure, for example), then PL/M permits an alternative. An object code subroutine can be assembled from an assembly language source program in conjunction with an object code main program compiled from a PL/M source program. While the final program has to be patched together, nevertheless this provides a solution to what might otherwise be a sticky problem.

In the future it would seem that more and more microcomputer software will be developed using compiler languages. Four factors will foster this trend:

1 Floppy-disk-based development systems will drop in cost and become more readily available. This will provide the fast, interactive capability and the compiling capability which together maximize the efficacy of this design approach.

2 Compiler languages will be developed, and features added, which attune them more and more to the needs of the instrument designer. Just as each new microcomputer tends to incorporate the best features which have appeared in other recent microcomputers, so successive "generations" of compilers will tend to pick up features. This is especially true since a feature (for example, a special, built-in procedure) adds nothing to the final object code unless it is used. Therefore, it makes sense to include a variety of these features. Microcomputer manufacturers will have every incentive to develop compilers with unusual features to promote the acceptance of their microcomputer.

3 Microcomputer architecture, at least for some manufacturers, will probably change radically from an accumulator-type organization to a stack-type organization to improve the efficiency of compilation of block-structured compiler languages like PL/M. At least some of the effectiveness which the Burroughs B5700 and B6700 computers* achieve in handling programs written in Algol should rub off on microcomputers. In particular, the awkwardness displayed in passing parameters to a subroutine and handling them within the subroutine should give way to data transfers directly to a stack (including load

* See the book by Organick referenced at the end of the chapter.

immediates) followed by operations carried out on operands addressed within the stack.

4   ROM and PROM chips are ever decreasing in cost. In contrast, the cost of a designer's time is ever increasing in cost. As a consequence, the use of a high-level language will make economic sense for an ever-increasing number of instrument and device designs.

6-6   SOFTWARE SIMULATION

When developing software, some "internal" routines operate primarily within the microcomputer itself, with very little I/O. Other routines involve extensive external interactions to drive the instrument's input and output devices. A software simulator, implemented as an interactive facility, is far and away the best design tool available for debugging "internal" routines. It can also debug external routines, but its operation becomes cumbersome to use if the simulator is forever stopping with requests for data, to respond to the execution of an input instruction.

An interactive software simulator is available for most microcomputers through time-sharing services. Significantly faster interaction is provided by a disk operating system, like that of Fig. 6-10.

A simulator is a program which simulates the operation of a microcomputer, including CPU, RAM, ROM, I/O ports, and interrupt inputs. It permits a user to load an object code program for the microcomputer into ROM, initialize CPU registers and RAM locations as desired, and then begin executing instructions. A "trace line" of the contents of the CPU registers can be displayed (or printed) after every instruction. Alternatively, some simulators cause a trace line to be displayed after the execution of the instruction in a specified address. The running of a program can be halted after the execution of a specified instruction (or a specified number of instructions, depending upon the simulator). The contents of those portions of RAM affected by the program can be displayed. Then operation can begin again from this point. Whenever output instructions are executed, the data emitted on the output port can be displayed.

Using a simulator is quite simple. To give an idea of what is involved in using a simulator, we will consider some of the capabilities of Motorola's simulator for their 6800 microcomputer. The simulator program is first called up with a RUN MPSSIM command. It will begin by asking for the object code's file name for the program to be simulated, to which we might respond, MYFILE. If we want to have the simulator execute 20 (hex) instructions, beginning at address 0100, and displaying a trace line of all CPU registers after the execution of each instruction, we enter

SR P0100.T20

which gives two commands to the simulator, separated by a period. The SR

(Set Register) command is used to "set" the contents of any CPU registers to any desired values. In this case we are only setting P, the program counter, to address 0100. The T (Trace) command says to execute the next 20 (hex) instructions, including a trace line after each. After executing these instructions, the simulator waits for our next command which might be

$$DM\ 0031,8$$

to Display Memory. The contents of the eight consecutive locations beginning at address 0031 will be displayed. Next, we might command the simulator with

$$SM\ 0031,0,0,0,0,0,0,99,0.SR\ P0100.T20$$

which will repeat the same routine executed before, but with a different initialization. Instead of starting with all zeros in RAM, this time location 0037 is set to 99 by the SM (Set Memory) command.

Some simulators include a trap command, which terminates the execution of further instructions when a specific instruction address is reached. This, together with a display of clock cycles since the last command, permits an easy and exact determination of how long it will take the microcomputer to execute a certain segment of a program. For this purpose, the simulator can be run without generating trace lines for each instruction, drastically speeding up its response.

PROBLEMS

6-1 Single-step testing. Using the switch-LED test panel of Fig. 6-1 to test the "switch-programmed ROM" circuit of Fig. 5-33, how would you check that:

(a) The three-state inverters work correctly?

(b) The decoder works correctly?

(c) Each thumbwheel and DIP switch (and its diodes) works correctly?

6-2 Device testing. Construct a flowchart for a simple algorithm to test the handshaking response times of the FIFO of Fig. 5-15 using the approach of Fig. 6-4a. Note that the oscilloscope wants to have the same events occur over and over again. Note also that the FIFO does not handshake on both input and output unless the FIFO is partially full.

6-3 Device testing. Construct a flowchart for an algorithm to determine the contact-bounce time of the mechanical keyswitches of a keyboard using the circuit of Fig. 6-4b. Assume that all switches are connected in parallel as shown in Fig. P6-1, and determine the time from the moment a logic 0 is detected until its final $1 \rightarrow 0$ transition occurs, mea-

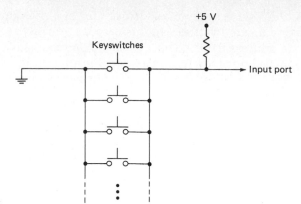

Figure P6-1.

sured from 0.1 to 9.9 ms. Generate the output using a two-digit 8421 BCD code and updating the display each time a new key is depressed.

6-4 **Logic-state analyzer.** Using the ability of the logic-state analyzer of Fig. 6-7 to capture one-shot events and to look backward in time, describe how you might determine how a specific microcomputer behaves when power is turned on. Does it flail the devices connected to the address bus or to output ports? What test program in the microcomputer would facilitate this test?

6-5 **Software debugging.** For a specific microcomputer, will the circuit of Fig. 6-8 work as shown? That is, can the $\overline{\text{Interrupt}}$ input line be tied low and have the microcomputer execute just one instruction after returning from a service routine (during which interrupts were disabled) and before being interrupted again?

6-6 **Software debugging.** For a specific microcomputer, modify the circuit of Fig. 6-8 using a one-shot (like that of Fig. 3-44) in the manner suggested in the text. List the last steps of the service routine including restoring the accumulator and a pointer to memory and then determine the required pulse width of the one-shot as well as the tolerance on this pulse width.

6-7 **Software debugging.** Both push buttons in Fig. 6-8 are shown debounced. Is this necessary in each case? That is, what would be the effect of contact bounce occurring at each of these inputs? What would be the effect of contact bounce on the thumbwheel-switch outputs?

6-8 **Software debugging.** The interrupt service routine of Fig. 6-9 tests each push-button switch for being first depressed and then released. Is this really necessary? That is, what would be the effect in each case if the push button were only tested to see if it is depressed?

6-9 **Software debugging.** For a specific microcomputer, construct a flow-chart and an assembly language routine for the two blocks at the

bottom of Fig. 6-9 which control the register display of Fig. 6-8. Minimize ROM words. Also list the coding you have used for the thumbwheel switch to determine which registers are to be displayed.

6-10 Instrument organization. Consider the design of an instrument
which is to carry out the indirect measurement of distance, as in Fig.
1-5. It has two transducers. The distance transducer shown is started
with a $\overline{\text{Start}}$ (⎍) pulse and returns a Ready signal which can be read
as a flag in the most significant bit position of the three-state outputs.
When Ready = 1, the distance is available as a 16-bit binary number
with the all-1s output corresponding to a distance of 1000.0 ft. It is
read out in two parts, as controlled by the two enable inputs. Make an
assumption, and state it, concerning how the microcomputer is set up
to address the four control inputs shown in Fig. P6-2.

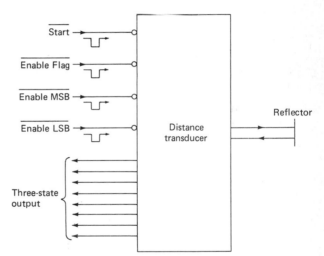

Figure P6-2.

The angular measure is provided by an incremental shaft-angle
encoder with two outputs A and B which generate a Gray code output
as the shaft is rotated. Assume these are used under interrupt control,
using the circuit of Fig. 5-48. Also assume that the resolution of the
encoder is such that one revolution of the encoder generates 2^{14} counts.

The instrument has two push buttons, as specified in the text in
conjunction with Fig. 1-5. One enters a new P1 measurement and the
other enters successive P2 measurements (to be used with the P1 measurement previously obtained). These are operated under flag control.

The display is a four-digit decimal display from 000.0 to 999.9 ft.
Assume that the displays are connected to the CPU so as to look like
two RAM addresses, that they include latches, and that they are coded
in BCD code (as discussed in Sec. 7-4).

(a) Make a flowchart for the instrument organization, showing all the kinds of things you can think of that must be done. Assume subroutines for cosine, squaring, square-rooting, and binary-to-BCD conversion (that is, do not get involved here with these).

(b) With the transducers described, what is the worst-case resolution in distance attainable, given exact calculating capability? This should be somewhat smaller than the 0.1-ft resolution of the display. Is it?

6-11 Assembling by hand. (a) For a specific microcomputer other than the Intel 8080, write an assembly language subroutine beginning at (hex) address 01 00. It is to count a variable 16-bit binary number (which has been passed to it) down to zero, count a fixed 8-bit binary number down to zero, then return, just as has been done in Fig. 6-15 using the Intel 8080.

(b) Construct the first three columns of the instruction list of Fig. 6-16 for the instructions used in your subroutine.

(c) Generate the symbol table for your subroutine, using the procedure of Fig. 6-15 and showing the contents of the address counter *before* each line is processed.

(d) Generate the object code and show it in an assembler listing for your subroutine, analogous to that of Fig. 6-17.

6-12 Assembling by hand. Repeat Prob. 6-11 for a subroutine beginning at address 01 00 which decrements an 8-bit binary number (whose value is less than 100) down to zero while at the same time incrementing a two-digit BCD code number (see Sec. 7-4) up from zero. When the binary number (which was passed to the subroutine) reaches zero, the BCD number will have a value equal to the original value of the binary number. Thus we will have implemented a (slow, but simple) binary-to-BCD conversion routine. Return the BCD result in the register which contained the binary number.

6-13 Macro assembler. Describe what modifications are needed in the assembler procedure of Sec. 6-4 if macro-defining capability, as described in Sec. 2-10, is to be included. Does it matter whether macro definitions are placed at the beginning or the end of the program? Can assembling still be carried out in just two passes?

6-14 High-level language. Using a specific compiler language, write a routine to pack the lower 2 bits of an 8-bit variable A together with the upper 6 bits of another 8-bit variable B into a third variable C.

6-15 High-level language. (a) For a specific compiler language, what features do you find which have been incorporated especially for "smart" instrument design work, like the TIME procedure discussed in the text?

(b) What features do you find which have been incorporated to provide agility when compiled for a (4-bit or an 8-bit) microcomputer? For example, PL/M requires variables to be declared as either 8-bit variables or 16-bit variables, two values which can be conveniently handled in an 8-bit microcomputer.

6-16 Software simulation. For a specific software simulator:

(a) What options are available for generating trace lines?

(b) What options are available for "trapping" (that is, halting at a certain address)?

(c) How are the contents of CPU registers and RAM locations changed?

(d) Can the format of a trace line be chosen by the user? Does it include "time," to provide a measure of actual CPU running time? Can it include a RAM address?

REFERENCES

A good description of Intel's versatile hardware and software debugging MDS system is provided by the pair of articles by W. Davidow, The Coming Merger of Hardware and Software Design, and R. Garrow, S. Hou, J. Lally, and H. Walker, Microcomputer Development System Achieves Hardware-Software Harmony, *Electronics*, May 29, 1975, pp. 91–102.

For a four-color rendition of the operation of a computer designed for the efficient compilation and execution of block-structured languages, see E. I. Organick, *Computer System Organization: The B5700/B6700 Series*, Academic, New York, 1973.

7
ALGORITHMIC
PROCESSES

Interspersed throughout the previous chapters have been a variety of algorithmic processes aimed at serving the needs of a specific device (for example, a printer) or optimizing the use of a specific microcomputer capability (for example, programmable timers). The careful implementation of these algorithmic processes represents a major step in the smooth development of an instrument.

As an example, consider the printer control algorithm of Sec. 5-8. It results in a combined hardware-software facility which interacts with the remaining instrument software through only three things: a BUSY flag, an array in RAM into which the characters for one printed line must be loaded, and the enabling of interrupts from the printer. In addition, the time it takes to service the printer's interrupt service routine must be considered in relation to other demands for quick response by the microcomputer which might occur at the same time. But this is all. The software interface between the printer and the remaining instrument software has thus been made both *well defined* and *simple*.

Our approach to the development of the software for an instrument is to divide and conquer. Just as for the printer, we facilitate the overall software development to the extent that we not only define appropriate subsystems but also create well-defined and simple software interfaces to these sub-systems.

In this chapter we will consider further examples of algorithmic processes. We will strive for simple software interfacing, regardless of whether the algorithm has a "global" or a "local" impact upon the remaining instrument software.

7-1   KEYBOARD PARSING

Keyboard parsing is a systematic means for organizing the responses of an instrument to *sequences* of keyswitch inputs. For example, to set up a 0.615-V output amplitude for the waveform generator of Fig. 5-23, the keys are depressed as follows:

AMPL

6

1

5

MULT

1

The generator expects the output amplitude to be expressed in the form

$$0.0F \times 10^{-M} \text{ volts}$$

or

$$0.FS \times 10^{-M} \text{ volts}$$

or

$$F.ST \times 10^{-M} \text{ volts}$$

where F, S, and T are the first, second, and third keys depressed *after* the AMPL key is depressed, while M is the digit key depressed *after* the MULT key is depressed.

The amplitude of the output of this instrument can be thought of as one *setup parameter* of the instrument. The function of a keyboard parser is divided into two parts. It must

1   Interpret sequences of keyswitch inputs for each setup parameter.
2   Execute an action routine for each keyswitch input (which is dependent upon the keyswitch inputs which preceded this input).

A *keychart* provides a means for visualizing the keyswitch input sequences used for each setup parameter. As shown in Fig. 7-1 for the amplitude setup parameter of the waveform generator, a keychart includes *state boxes* to keep track of keyswitch input sequences, and *keyswitch paths* between state

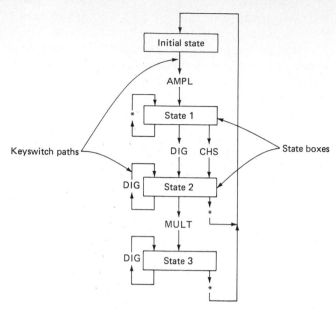

Figure 7-1. Keychart for the amplitude setup parameter.

boxes. We begin entering data for a setup parameter in an *initial state*. When the AMPL keyswitch is depressed, the state of the keyboard parser changes to state 1. When a key is next depressed, Fig. 7-1 shows that if it is one of the 10-digit switches, represented by DIG, or if it is the CHange Sign (CHS) keyswitch, then the state of the parser changes to state 2. For any other keyswitch input (represented by *), the parser remains in state 1, locked up and accepting only a digit key or the CHS key (Wavetek's function generator may handle this differently, but that is immaterial for the purposes of developing a keyboard parsing routine).

Associated with each keyswitch path will be an *action routine*. For example, the action routine which occurs when the parser is in state 1 and a digit key is depressed (taking the parser to state 2) consists of shifting the number represented by the digit key into the least significant digit position of the RAM addresses holding output amplitude information.

When developing an instrument, sometimes we are not sure of how best to handle all the alternative ways for entering each setup parameter. For example, the alternative keychart of Fig. 7-2 never hangs up when an extraneous key is depressed in the middle of the amplitude setup sequence. Instead, the parser returns to the initial state. Also, the function of the change sign key CHS has been redefined. A significant feature of the keyboard parsing routine which we will develop is that it is a *table-driving* routine. All the decisions concerning keyswitch paths to be used and action routines to be executed will simply involve entering state numbers and ac-

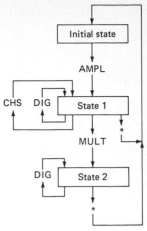

Figure 7-2. Alternative keychart for the amplitude setup
parameter.

*Signifies other keyswitch input

tion routine numbers into a table.   A change in the keychart only requires
changing entries in a table.

As a vehicle for developing the keyboard parsing routine, Fig. 7-3 illustrates the keychart for one possible definition for the keyboard of the waveform generator shown in Fig. 5-23.   The waveform generator includes eight
setup parameters for amplitude, frequency, function (sine, square, triangle,
ramp), offset, mode (continuous, triggered, gated), unit (a number used for
identification under remote control), on, and off.

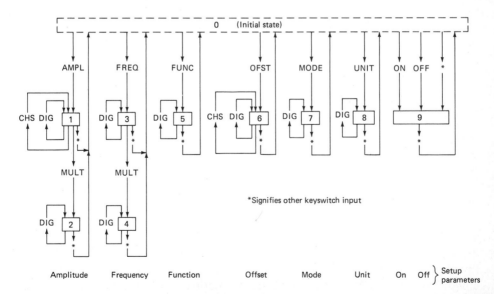

Figure 7-3. Keychart of a waveform generator.

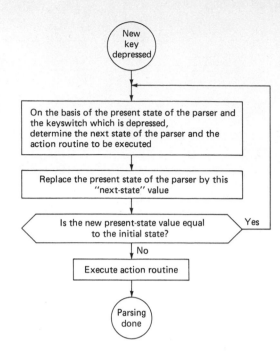

Figure 7-4. Flowchart of keyboard parsing routine.

The initial state is shown, dotted in, in Fig. 7-3, to accentuate its nature as a "pseudostate." Whenever we have finished keying in a value for one setup parameter, such as amplitude, we begin the next setup parameter with a new function key, such as FUNC. We do not really want the parser to go, and stay, in the initial state (state 0), since this would necessitate depressing the FUNC key again to get it to go to state 5. Rather, as shown in Fig. 7-4, the parsing routine will use its present state and the depressed keyswitch to determine its next state. *If* this state is the initial state, it begins again, using this as the present state together with the depressed keyswitch. While this procedure adds a cumbersome twist to the algorithm, it drastically reduces the size of the table which stores the keychart information by permitting OTHER inputs (represented by * in Fig. 7-3) instead of requiring the listing, for example, of all the keyswitch paths from state 2 to states 1, 3, 5, 6, 7, 8, and 9.

The heart of the keyboard parser routine is the *parser state table*, shown in Fig. 7-5 for the keychart of Fig. 7-3. The action routines are described in Fig. 7-6. The remainder of this section describes how to get into this table and use its contents to update the state of the parser and to get to the appropriate action routine. Figure 7-7 is a listing of the variables we will use.

The parser state table is entered using two parameters PREST and FNKY. PREST is the present state of the parser (stored at a location in RAM labeled PREST). FNKY is a functional keycode derived from the actual keycode of the key which is depressed. By translating the actual keycode into two parameters FNKY and NUMB, we can categorize related keys with the

Figure 7-5. Parser State Table

	Keyswitch	Next state	Action routine number
Present state = 0	AMPL	1	0
	FREQ	3	0
	FUNC	5	0
	OFST	6	0
	MODE	7	0
	UNIT	8	0
	ON	9	1
	OFF	9	2
	*	9	0
Present state = 1	CHS	1	3
	DIG	1	4
	MULT	2	0
	*	0	0
Present state = 2	DIG	2	5
	*	0	0
Present state = 3	DIG	3	6
	MULT	4	0
	*	0	0
Present state = 4	DIG	4	7
	*	0	0
Present state = 5	DIG	5	8
	*	0	0
Present state = 6	DIG	6	9
	CHS	6	A
	*	0	0
Present state = 7	DIG	7	B
	*	0	0
Present state = 8	DIG	8	C
	*	0	0
Present state = 9	*	0	0

same value of FNKY to steer them all to the same action routine and next state. NUMB is used by the action routines to draw a distinction between keys having the same value of FNKY. We will illustrate the use of this feature with an example based upon a waveform generator which labels keyswitches quite differently from the generator we have been discussing.

Figure 7-6. Brief Description of Action Routines

Action routine	Function
ACT0	Do nothing
ACT1	Enable output
ACT2	Disable output
ACT3	Change the sign of the amplitude setup parameter
ACT4	Shift digit into the amplitude setup parameter
ACT5	Use digit as an amplitude multiplier, shifting the number entered, through successive ACT4 action routines, an appropriate number of places
ACT6	Shift digit into the frequency setup parameter
ACT7	Do action similar to ACT5 on the frequency setup parameter
ACT8	Load digit into the function setup parameter
ACT9	Load digit into the offset setup parameter
ACTA	Change sign of the offset setup parameter
ACTB	Load digit into the mode setup parameter
ACTC	Load digit into the unit setup parameter

Figure 7-7. Variables Defined for Use in the Keyboard Parser Routine

Variable	Definition
PREST	Present state, a number stored in RAM and used to enter the parser state table
FNKY	Functional keycode, derived from the keycode of the depressed keyswitch (in a manner described in the text) and used to enter the parser state table
NUMB	Numerical value derived from a keycode (used with digit keys and sometimes with other keys, as described in the text)
FNKYT	Functional keycode entry in the parser state table against which FNKY will be matched
NEXST	Next state, a number extracted from the parser state table and used to update PREST
ARNO	Action routine number, a number extracted from the parser state table and used as a pointer to the desired action routine

Example 7-1. Develop FNKY and NUMB values for a waveform generator with ten digit keys, four waveform keys (sine, square, triangle, ramp), two level keys (amplitude, rms), etc.

Figure 7-8. Use of FNKY and NUMB

Actual keyswitch labeling	Actual hex keycode	FNKY	NUMB
0	00	1	0
1	01	1	1
2	02	1	2
3	03	1	3
4	04	1	4
5	05	1	5
6	06	1	6
7	07	1	7
8	08	1	8
9	09	1	9
SINUSOID	0A	2	0
SQUARE	0B	2	1
TRIANGLE	0C	2	2
RAMP	0D	2	3
AMPLITUDE	0E	3	0
RMS	0F	3	1

One possibility is shown in Fig. 7-8, where all digit keys have been assigned FNKY = 1, all wave form keys have been assigned FNKY = 2, and both level keys have been assigned FNKY = 3. Regardless of which digit key is depressed, the parser will jump to a single action routine determined by its present state PREST and its functional keycode FNKY. The action routine will use NUMB as required.

In like manner, if any of the four waveform keys are depressed, one action routine (determined by the values of PREST and FNKY) will be executed. It will use NUMB as a parameter to draw a distinction between different waveforms.

The rationale behind this use of functional keycodes instead of actual keycodes is to minimize

1   Entries in the parser state table
2   The need for separate action routines for similar functions

This discussion raises an interesting human engineering point. Is it "better" to use four waveform keys (so that the user sees words like sine, square, triangle, and ramp) as discussed here or, alternatively, to have one FUNC (function) key which must be followed by the entry of a digit to denote the same information? For an instrument with many options, such as that of Fig. 5-23, the latter choice avoids an excessive proliferation of keys. Furthermore, the user does not really have to remember which waveform goes with which digit, since the setup display indicates the result of any choice, permitting a user to get to the desired choice by trial and error.

For the keyboard of the waveform generator of Fig. 5-23, we might define the FNKY, FNKYT, and NUMB as in Fig. 7-9, leading to the coded form of the parser state table shown in Fig. 7-10. To enter this table, we need to translate the present state variable PREST into one of the addresses PST0, PST1, PST2, ... The parser entry table shown in Fig. 7-11 serves this

Figure 7-9. Definitions of FNKY, FNKYT, and NUMB for the Waveform Generator

Keyswitch labeling	FNKY	NUMB
0	1	0
1	1	1
2	1	2
3	1	3
4	1	4
5	1	5
6	1	6
7	1	7
8	1	8
9	1	9
AMPL	2	0
FREQ	3	0
FUNC	4	0
OFST	5	0
MODE	6	0
UNIT	7	0
CHS	8	0
MULT	9	0
ON	A	0
OFF	B	0

FNKYT is defined identically to FNKY except that ∗ is coded as 0.

Figure 7-10. Parser State Table in Coded Form

Address label	FNKYT	NEXST	ARNO
PST0	2	1	0
	3	3	0
	4	5	0
	5	6	0
	6	7	0
	7	8	0
	A	9	1
	B	9	2
	0	9	0
PST1	8	1	3
	1	1	4
	9	2	0
	0	0	0
PST2	1	2	5
	0	0	0
PST3	1	3	6
	9	4	0
	0	0	0
PST4	1	4	7
	0	0	0
PST5	1	5	8
	0	0	0
PST6	1	6	9
	8	6	A
	0	0	0
PST7	1	7	B
	0	0	0
PST8	1	8	C
PST9	0	0	0

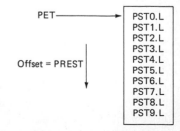

Figure 7-11. Parser entry table. PST0.L *is the lower byte of the full address* PST0.

purpose when used with the table-driver subroutine TBL1 of Sec. 2-8. PET is used as the base address of the table and PREST as the offset into it. It is assumed that the parser state table will be aligned to fall entirely within one page. If this page address is designated PST0.H (where H signifies the higher byte of the full address PST0), the full address can be formed by appending the selected entry taken from the parser entry table to PST0.H.

Once the parser entry table has been used to set up the memory pointer to PSTi, the parser state table must be entered looking for either of two conditions:

1   The end of table PSTi, indicated in Fig. 7-10 by the terminating character 0
2   A match between FNKY and FNKYT

The MATCH subroutine of Fig. 7-12 serves this purpose. It is entered with PSTi in the CPU's memory pointer and with the variable FNKY located in either a CPU scratchpad register or a RAM memory location, whichever is more appropriate for the microcomputer being used.

The MATCH subroutine also makes use of the two fixed parameters shown in Fig. 7-12b, which are determined by the structure of the parser state table and which therefore can be defined at the time of assembly. Since each entry of the parser state table shown in Fig. 7-10 can be stored in two (8-bit) bytes, PBYTES would equal two for this example. To provide a general understanding of the use of the parser state table, we will break each entry into three fields, as shown in Fig. 7-12c:

1   FNKYT is packed into the six most significant bits of the first byte.
2   NEXST is packed into the next five bits, that is, into the two least significant bits of the first byte and the three most significant bits of the second byte.
3   ARNO is packed into the five least significant bits of the second byte.

With this division of each entry of the parser state table, we can define the two fixed parameters of Fig. 7-12b as shown in Fig. 7-12d. Then, to simplify the MATCH subroutine, it is convenient to redefine FNKY, aligning it to the position at which FNKYT is packed in the table. This is shown in Fig. 7-12e. Finally, the MATCH subroutine is shown in Fig. 7-12f. It will return with the CPU's memory pointer P (which points to the operand labeled M in Fig. 7-12f) pointing to the selected entry in the parser state table.

The keyboard parser unpacks this entry to form NEXST and ARNO, the two values in the parser state table we have been seeking. Using this table-driving approach, the general flowchart of Fig. 7-4 becomes the more specific flowchart of Fig. 7-13.

To execute the appropriate action routine, the action routine number ARNO must be translated into the address of the corresponding action routine (ACT0, ACT1, ACT2, . . .) listed in Fig. 7-6. The action pointer table

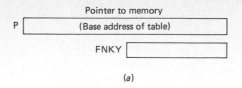

Pointer to memory

P | (Base address of table)

FNKY |

(a)

Variable	Definition
PBYTES	Number of bytes per entry in the parser state table
MASK	Used to select the bits in each entry which are involved in the match

(b)

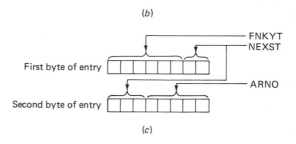

FNKYT
NEXST

First byte of entry

ARNO

Second byte of entry

(c)

ADD	MNE	REG	OP
PBYTES	EQU		2
MASK	EQU		B'11111100'

(d)

FNKY of Fig. 7-9

(e)

Figure 7-12. MATCH subroutine, for entry into the parser state table. (a) Parameters passed to MATCH subroutine by calling program; (b) parameters used by MATCH subroutine which are specified at the time of assembly; (c) example of the packing of each entry in the parser state table; (d) definition of PBYTES and MASK for the above example; (e) new definition of FNKY so as to be aligned with FNKYT taken from the parser state table; (f) flowchart of the subroutine.

MATCH

A ← M AND MASK
(that is, keep only the bits of FNKYT)

Does A = 0?
(that is, are we at the terminating character?) — Yes

No

Does A ⊕ FNKY = 0?
(that is, does FNKYT = FNKY?) — Yes

No

Add PBYTES to the memory pointer P

RET

(f)

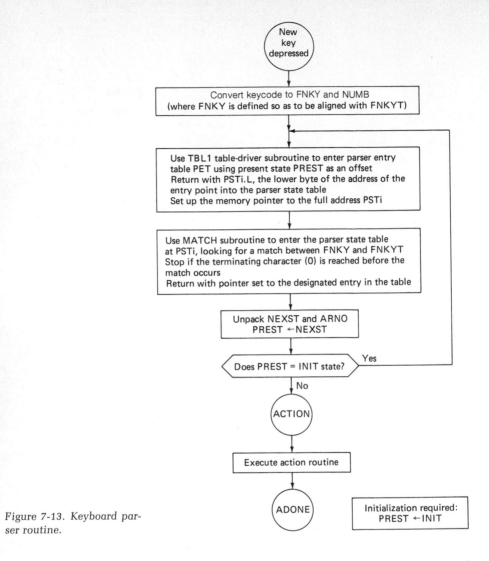

New
key
depressed

Convert keycode to FNKY and NUMB
(where FNKY is defined so as to be aligned with FNKYT)

Use TBL1 table-driver subroutine to enter parser entry
table PET using present state PREST as an offset
Return with PSTi.L, the lower byte of the address of the
entry point into the parser state table
Set up the memory pointer to the full address PSTi

Use MATCH subroutine to enter the parser state table
at PSTi, looking for a match between FNKY and FNKYT
Stop if the terminating character (0) is reached before the
match occurs
Return with pointer set to the designated entry in the table

Unpack NEXST and ARNO
PREST ←NEXST

Does PREST = INIT state?   Yes

No

ACTION

Execute action routine

ADONE

Initialization required:
PREST ←INIT

Figure 7-13. Keyboard parser routine.

of Fig. 7-14 is used by the table-driver subroutine TBL2 for this purpose,
with ACTPT as a base address and ARNO as an offset. The parser uses the
resulting address ACTi in a jump indirect instruction to jump to the action
routine itself. Every action routine then terminates with an unconditional
jump to an address ADONE to finish up the operation of the keyboard parser.

This procedure is illustrated in Fig. 7-15. ACT0 is the "do nothing"
action routine, causing a jump to ADONE. Note that two action routines
(such as ACT1 and ACT2 shown) can be combined, for efficiency, if they end
in a common part.

There are several steps we can take to make this section of the keyboard
parser more efficient in its use of ROM. If all action routines fit on a single

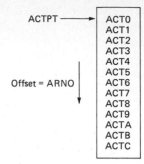

Figure 7-14. *Action pointer table ACTPT.*   (Two bytes per entry to hold a full address)

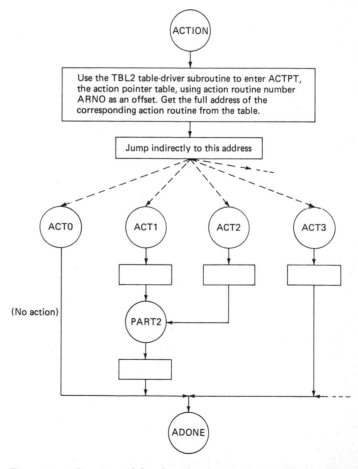

Figure 7-15. *Structure of the algorithm for executing action routines.*

page of ROM, then the action pointer table need only include the address within the page. The parser can append this address to the known page address. In fact, if all but one or two of the action routines fit on one page, it is probably more efficient to use an action pointer table which assumes all action routines are on one page. Then, unconditional jump instructions can be included on this page to any action routines residing on other pages.

This section of the keyboard parser can also be made more efficient for microcomputers which can call a subroutine indirectly. Then each action routine can conclude with a one-byte subroutine return instruction. Both these modifications are illustrated in Fig. 7-16.

If the keyboard parser routine is used with a keyboard encoder which interrupts the CPU when a new key is depressed, the service routine need only set aside the CPU registers, execute the algorithm of Figs. 7-13 and 7-16, restore the CPU registers, and return to the program which was inter-

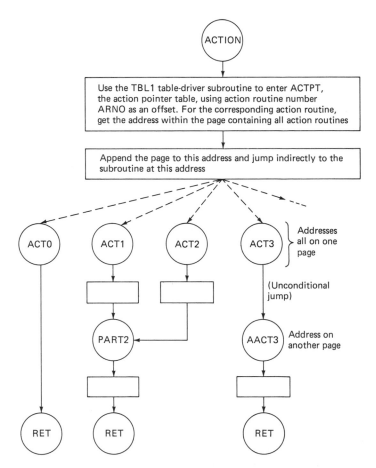

Figure 7-16. Somewhat more efficient structure for the algorithm which executes action routines.

rupted by the keyboard. If the keyboard parser routine is used with the "minimum hardware" circuit of Fig. 5-29, it represents the bottom block of Fig. 5-30.

In developing the software for an instrument, it is convenient to be able to assemble *everything*, tables included. Furthermore, when some tables contain the addresses corresponding to address labels, it is convenient to be able to list these table contents using the symbolic address labels rather than the absolute addresses. Then when software modifications change some of these absolute addresses, the tables need not to be changed, but only reassembled. Some assemblers permit DW (define word) and DB (define byte) (both of which were defined in Fig. 2-32 for our purposes) to be used to assemble an address label into a full address and the lower byte of a full address, respectively. To avoid any ambiguity, we will use the LB and LBL directives defined in Fig. 7-17 for this purpose. Also LBH picks out the page portion of an address label.

A problem arises when a table is *packed* together using fields for each entry which may be of arbitrary length. We will define two more assembler directives TBF and TB to handle this problem. The TBF directive (implicitly) designates how many bytes in ROM will be used for each table entry. It also (explicitly) designates how the hex characters in the operand field of TB directives are to be packed together to form these bytes in ROM. Using these directives, the three tables used by the keyboard parser routine (that is,

Figure 7-17. Assembler Directives for Table Formation

Mnemonic	Function
LB	This LaBel directive interprets the operand as an address label. It will be assembled into the corresponding full address (2 bytes) which that label represents
LBL	This LaBel, Lower-byte directive interprets the operand as an address label. It will be assembled into the lower byte of the corresponding full address which that label represents
LBH	This LaBel, Higher-byte directive interprets the operand as an address label. It will be assembled into the upper byte (that is, page address) of the corresponding full address which that label represents
TBF	This TaBle Format directive interprets the operand as a sequence of hex digits, separated by spaces. Each digit designates the number of bits to be reserved in the assembled word for the corresponding hex digits in any TB directives which follow this TBF directive (until another TBF directive occurs)
TB	This TaBle directive is used to specify the successive fields of a table in hex form, with at least one space between successive fields. It will be interpreted and assembled in light of a preceding TBF directive

Figure 7-18. Keyboard Parser Tables

ADD	MNE	REG	OP			Comments
*						
*						Tables for keyboard parser
*						
	ORG		0100			Start tables at beginning of page 01
	TBF		6	5	5	Format for parser state table
PST0	TB		2	1	0	Parser state table
	TB		3	3	0	
	TB		4	5	0	
	TB		5	6	0	
	TB		6	7	0	
	TB		7	8	0	
	TB		A	9	1	
	TB		B	9	2	
	TB		0	9	0	
PST1	TB		8	1	3	
			.			
			.			
			.			
PST8	TB		1	8	C	
PST9	TB		0	0	0	
*						
PET	LBL		PST0			Parser entry table
	LBL		PST1			
	LBL		PST2			
	.		.			
	.		.			
	.		.			
	LBL		PST9			
*						
ACTPT	LBL		ACT0			Action pointer table
	LBL		ACT1			
	LBL		ACT2			
	.		.			
	.		.			
	.		.			
	LBL		ACTC			

the parser state table, PET, and ACTPT) take on the form shown in Fig. 7-18. Note that the TBF directive says that the following TB directives will have three fields each and that they are to be packed into 6 bits, 5 bits, and 5 bits, respectively, resulting in the use of 2 bytes of ROM for each entry (that is, each TB directive).

Because so much of this section has been concerned with variations in the way the keyboard parsing algorithm might be implemented, it is probably worthwhile to review what this table-driving approach achieves. First, it divorces the "action routine" part of handling a keyboard from the "interpreting sequences of keyswitch inputs" part, thereby fostering the development of the action routines as a separate entity. If efficiencies can be achieved by finding common parts among action routines, developing the action routines as a separate step in the design process will help. Every bit as important, our thinking while trying to handle keyswitch input sequences is not cluttered by action-routine thoughts. Finally, and most valuable, the parser state table puts all the sequencing decisions in one place. The structure permits changes and additions to be made in these sequencing decisions simply by changing or adding entries in a table.

7-2   REAL-TIME PROGRAMMING

The commonly used means for keeping track of time in a microcomputer-based instrument is to interrupt the microcomputer periodically with a signal whose frequency is sufficiently accurate for the purposes of the instrument. For example, if a display of hours, minutes, and seconds is required, an interrupt signal can be derived from the ac power line, as in Fig. 7-19a. The service routine for this interrupt appropriately counts the RAM locations containing "hours," "minutes," "seconds," and "sixtieths of a second."

For measuring time intervals (for example, to generate a 50-ms pulse on one line of an output port), the same approach can be used if it is satisfactory to divide time into sixtieth-of-a-second intervals. A faster rate can be obtained if a crystal clock (perhaps the microcomputer clock) is counted down with a scaler, as in Fig. 7-19b, to interrupt at a rate which yields the resolution needed and yet does not cause the microcomputer to spend an excessive amount of time servicing the interrupts.

A *real-time clock* used in this way can provide the equivalent of a juggler's capability for keeping a sequence of events all going on at the same time. Furthermore, no confusion arises even if the events are unsynchronized to each other (for example, when driving a stepping motor and a printer at the same time). With the starting and stopping of each event occurring at the time of one of the interrupts, the service routine need only count the contents of one register per event down to zero to keep track of when next to start or stop that event, as shown in Fig. 7-20. In this figure, T1FLG is an internal flag (that is, the zero or nonzero contents of a word in RAM) used to turn this updating capability on and off. TIM1 is another word in RAM used to time the event. It is initialized before setting T1FLG, and reinitialized as appropriate in the "Update event 1" block of Fig. 7-20.

A programmable timer (discussed in Sec. 3-9) is an example of another approach to this same problem. It could be used in this same way, pro-

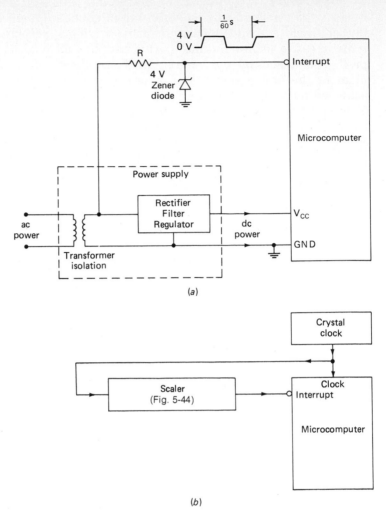

Figure 7-19. Real-time clock circuits. (a) Deriving time from the power line frequency; (b) deriving time from the microcomputer clock.

ducing interrupts at fixed time intervals which are then counted to determine when to update any one of several events. However, with the ability to vary the time interval between interrupts and to be turned on and off, a programmable timer does the equivalent of Fig. 7-20 for one event (at a time) directly, saving both software and CPU time.

A third approach for providing real-time control of events consists of constraining the software so that, in spite of branches and loops, the time interval between two specific points in a program remains constant. To base the entire software for an instrument upon this philosophy puts great strain upon designer (the person) and designee (the instrument) alike. Thus, if the

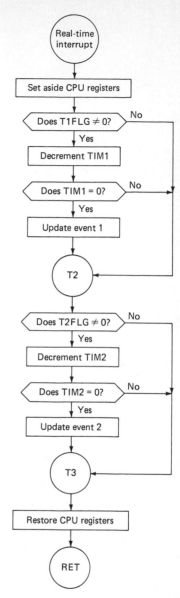

Figure 7-20. Juggling real-time events.

software is organized as in Fig. 6-13, we are constraining T to be constant. If we permit interrupts, we must compensate for the time taken by each interrupt. We might do this as in Fig. 7-21 by incrementing a counter once during each interrupt and then using, or bypassing, a wait loop in the main program which compensates for the time taken by the interrupt service routine.

Direct memory access can be handled in a similar way if it is satisfac-

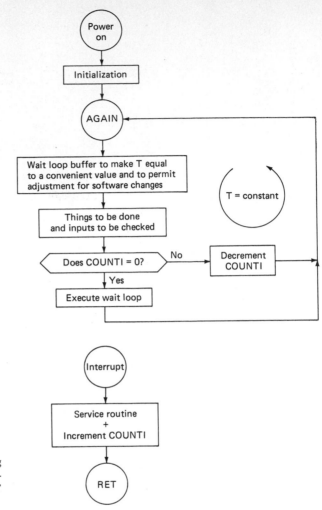

Figure 7-21. Compensating for the time taken by an interrupt in order to maintain T constant.

tory to maintain the *average* value of T precisely equal to T. The number of clock cycles required for the complete DMA transfer is a known quantity, permitting compensation.

Using this approach, each branch will (usually) require the introduction of a wait loop to keep time constant regardless of which branch is taken, as in Fig. 7-22. Obviously, we cannot cope with a branch whose time of execution depends upon the data being manipulated.

It is this tediousness of calculating (or measuring through simulation) the duration of each branch in a program and compensating for differences, as in Fig. 7-23, which accounts for the vanishingly small number of apostles for this technique. On the other hand, this is a valuable technique for handling events which involve short intervals of time (for example, less than

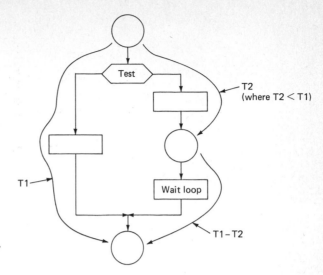

Figure 7-22. Compensating for alternate branches.

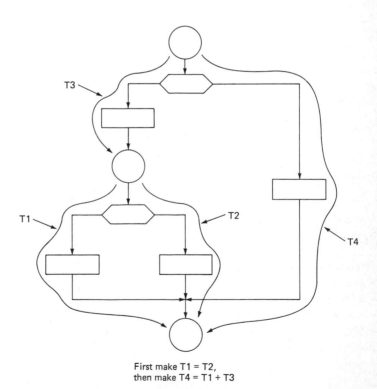

First make T1 = T2,
then make T4 = T1 + T3

Figure 7-23. Compensating for multiple branches.

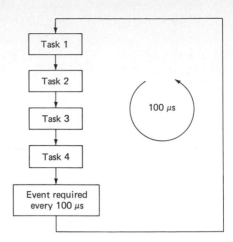

Figure 7-24. Providing real-time control for
short time intervals during which the CPU must
do more than wait.

100 μs) and during which we want to carry out other tasks. For short time
intervals, the time required by an interrupt technique to set aside and restore
CPU registers becomes significant. Alternatively, a wait loop provides a
"do nothing" time delay. If our job, at some time in the operation of an instrument, is to execute four short tasks repetitively followed by an event
which is required every 100 μs, then setting up a loop as shown in Fig. 7-24
makes sense. If any of the tasks involve branches, these can be compen-
sated.

7-3   SELF-TEST*

In Sec. 5-11, we considered some of the kinds of tests which an instrument
might execute to test itself. In this section, we will consider the philosophy
of self-test and then develop an overall self-test algorithm. Self-test capability, the ability of an instrument to check itself and to report that all is, or is
not, well in certain respects, has been with us for some time. A limited
amount of self-test capability comes easily, as with the addition of a parity
check on the data read from a paper-tape reader. Computer-based systems
provide the opportunity for more extensive self-testing. However, it is only
with the advent of microcomputers that we have both the relatively tight
coupling inherent in a self-contained instrument and the ever-present, flexible testing capability inherent in the instrument's microcomputer.

By self-test we mean the ability of an instrument to exercise itself extensively, periodically, and unobtrusively. This exercising will automatically take place when power is turned on, as well as periodically during
normal instrument operation. The user becomes aware of the self-testing
going on within the instrument only if a malfunction occurs.

---

* This section is based on a paper presented by the author at a March 1974 "Microcomputers: Fundamentals and Applications" 3-day short course held at The Polytechnic of
  Central London and directed by Dr. Gerald D. Cain.

In contrast, some instruments have been designed around a "push-to-test" capability in which the instrument is not exercised except under command of the user. Depressing a push button or keyswitch initiates testing. At the completion of testing, a go—no go lamp indicates the status of the instrument.

Push-to-test is a somewhat simpler approach to implement than self-test. There is no difficulty with finding a suitable time when the instrument can be tested and at the same time not interfere with normal operation. The intent of this section is to illuminate a systematic approach which will permit extensive self-testing, which will not interfere with normal instrument operation, and which is quite straightforward to implement.

By permitting the instrument to exercise itself during normal operation, the user is confident that it is operating properly and in calibration throughout its use, not just at start-up. Under those circumstances in which measurements come out wrong, the user is confident that the problem resides elsewhere than in the instrument.

For the approach taken here, we assume that there are some front-panel annunciator lights (that is, on-off lights) or decimal displays which can be blinked if the microcomputer detects a malfunction. Alternatively, if there are no displays at all (as is the case for the "two-push-button" automatic objective refractor of Fig. 1-6), and if we choose not to add a self-test light, an acoustical annunciator, such as that of Fig. 7-25, mounted inside the instrument can alert the user of a malfunction.

We also assume that the instrument has a keyboard or at least one push-button switch. Following a malfunction, we want to be able to communicate with the microcomputer, and any keyswitch or push-button switch will do. Under such circumstances the microcomputer can forego the normal keyswitch meanings and accept any keyswitch input as a signal from the user to continue in its self-test routine.

Finally, a decimal display is needed to give the user two digits of diagnostic information. If the instrument uses a front-panel multiple-digit dis-

Figure 7-25. Acoustical annunciator. (Projects Unlimited Inc.)

play for its normal operation, this can be "borrowed" by the self-test algorithm in the event of instrument malfunction. For an instrument with no front-panel display, it can be mounted inside the instrument, ready for use when a malfunction occurs and service is required.

Actual testing begins with an initial test which is distinct from the remaining tests in that it is executed only when power is first turned on and never again. This initial test must turn on all the front-panel lights, assuring the user that this minimal capability works, that all lights work, and that in the event of any subsequent malfunctions, the user can be signaled. The user then depresses any keyswitch or push-button switch. If the microcomputer can detect this, it turns off the front-panel lights, signaling this ability and ending further self-test interactions with the user unless an instrument malfunction is actually detected. This initial test procedure is illustrated in Fig. 7-26.

We now come to the heart of the self-test algorithm, consisting of self-test subroutines TSTi and a self-test number TNUM which will be used to point to one of these subroutines via a test pointer table TSTPT, as shown in Fig. 7-27. We will assume that the operation of the instrument is cyclic, as in Fig. 6-13, and that enough time is left over at the completion of each cycle to permit a single self-test subroutine to be executed. This will require that the duration of each test be constrained so as to assure

$$T < T_{MAX}$$

for the execution time of one cycle of operation, as discussed in conjunction with Fig. 6-13.

All these self-test subroutines will be called, one after another, before normal instrument operation begins. Because each one will also be called at the completion of each cycle of operation, this puts a constraint on the

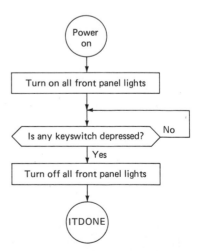

Figure 7-26. Initial test.

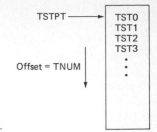

Figure 7-27. Test pointer table TSTPT.

manner in which each test can be implemented. For example, a test which exercises RAM can write into arbitrary RAM addresses only initially. Other tests may be executed only at certain times, which are independent of the cyclic structure of the software. For example, if an instrument includes a bidirectional incremental encoder with a zero reference, such as that of Fig. 5-47, then an opportunity for self-testing arises, when the instrument is not otherwise busy, by moving until the zero reference point is attained. In doing this, the incremental encoder should have counted back to position zero. If this has not happened, a malfunction has occurred which should be signaled to the user.

Our way of handling tests such as these which cannot be executed after an arbitrary cycle of operation will be to execute them whenever appropriate and to set a flag TFLGi if an error is detected (that is, store a nonzero number in a RAM location TFLGi) as in Fig. 7-28a. Then the self-test routine TSTi (which is executed when TNUM selects this test) does not actually carry out the test but only tests the flag TFLGi as in Fig. 7-28b.

A "single-test" subroutine STEST, shown in Fig. 7-29, handles the process of getting to the subroutine TSTi (pointed to by TNUM), executes it, and determines if a malfunction has been detected. The MALF parameter passed back to STEST by TSTi might use the CPU's carry bit or accumulator for this purpose. If a malfunction has been detected, the entire front-panel display is turned off except for the two-digit decimal equivalent of TNUM, called TNUMD, which is flashed to the user as a signal that a malfunction has occurred. The test number TNUMD serves as a diagnostic number for the user. By depressing any keyswitch, the user can restore normal operation to see if other diagnostics occur or to see if the original malfunction occurs again.

Finally, whether or not a malfunction has been detected, TNUM is incremented in preparation for the next test. It is incremented both as a binary number (TNUM) and as a decimal number (TNUMD). This use of two values permits the test pointer table TSTPT to be entered with a binary number in order to keep the table compact. Handling the decimal value at all could be avoided if the front panel included a two-digit hexadecimal display.

The overall system operation including self-test is shown in Fig. 7-30. It executes all tests initially and one test per cycle during normal operation.

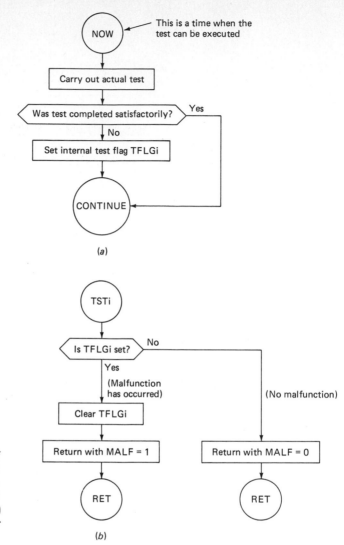

Figure 7-28. Handling of tests which can be carried out only at certain times. (a) Test carried out as part of normal operation; (b) self-test subroutine for this test.

7-4 NUMBER REPRESENTATION

The instruction sets of most microcomputers are organized to execute arithmetic instructions on 4-bit or 8-bit *binary* numbers, depending on the word length of the microcomputer. Often, this is exactly what we want. On the other hand, the occasion frequently arises where it is useful to express

1 Numbers having an arbitrary length
2 Decimal numbers
3 Signed numbers

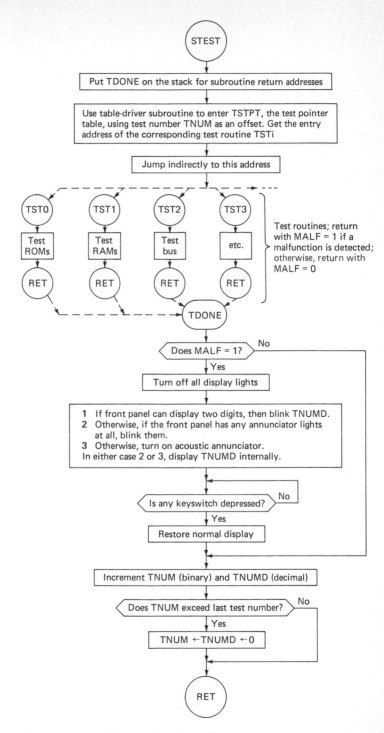

Figure 7-29. Single-test subroutine STEST.

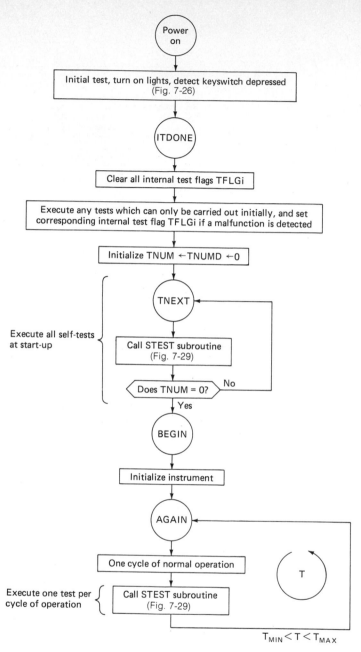

Figure 7-30. *Overall system operation including self-test.*

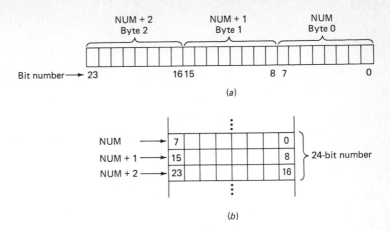

Figure 7-31. *Handling numbers having an arbitrary length.* (a) *24-bit number;* (b) *its representation as a RAM array NUM of 3 bytes in an 8-bit-word-length microcomputer.*

To store, and operate upon, numbers having a length which is longer than the word length of the microcomputer, we can think of the successive *bytes** of the number as forming an array in memory, as in Fig. 7-31. If we set up a pointer to NUM, we can access the number, a byte at a time, by incrementing the pointer between accesses. If we want to operate upon corresponding bytes in two arrays, we can either use two pointers or an index register, as was discussed in conjunction with Figs. 2-6 and 2-7. We must take care to handle any carrying or borrowing occurring between bytes.

Decimal numbers are handled in a microcomputer using a *BCD*, or binary-coded-decimal, code. Each digit is coded by its 4-bit binary equivalent, as shown in Fig. 7-32. If a variable requires 10 digits for its expression, we can handle it in the form of a 5-byte array, with each byte consisting of two digits, as in Fig. 7-33. Many microcomputers include a decimal adjust instruction which permits BCD numbers to be added with a binary add instruction followed by a decimal adjust instruction. We will discuss this further in the next two sections.

A *2s-complement* code is normally used to represent signed numbers for operations in which a binary code, rather than a BCD code, seems most appropriate. It permits some arithmetic operations to be implemented on signed numbers easily. In this code, the most significant bit of a number

---

* The term "byte" is used in this section to mean the number of bits of data upon which the microcomputer instructions operate. In our examples, we will assume 8-bit bytes. The modification for 4-bit bytes is straightforward.

Digit value	BCD coding
0	0000
1	0001
2	0010
3	0011
4	0100
5	0101
6	0110
7	0111
8	1000
9	1001

(a)

Decimal number	BCD coding
23	00100011
99	10011001
1892	0001100010010010

(b)

Figure 7-32. BCD code. (a) Coding of each digit; (b) BCD coding of some decimal numbers.

represents the sign of the number, as shown in Fig. 7-34a and b. This *sign bit* S codes the sign as follows:

$$S = \begin{cases} 0 & \text{for positive numbers and for zero} \\ 1 & \text{for negative numbers} \end{cases}$$

For positive numbers, a binary coding is used, subject to the constraint that the most positive number which can be coded, for a given number of bytes, has a 0 in the most significant bit of the most significant byte, and 1s every-

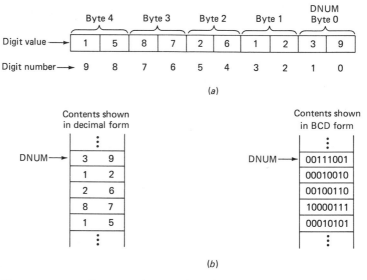

Figure 7-33. Handling a 10-digit number. (a) 10-digit number; (b) its representation as a RAM array DNUM of 5 bytes in an 8-bit-word-length microcomputer.

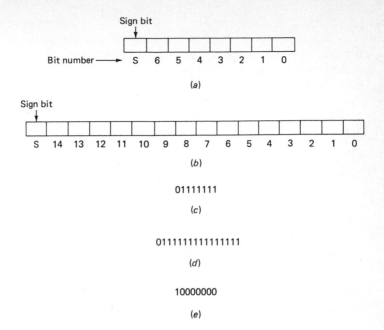

Figure 7-34. 2s-complement code.   (a) 1-byte numbers; (b) 2-byte numbers; (c) most positive 1-byte number, +127; (d) most positive 2-byte number, +32767; (e) most negative 1-byte number, −128; (f) coding for 1-byte numbers.

where else, as shown in Fig. 7-34c and d. Negative numbers are coded in "2s-complement" form. For 1-byte (8-bit) numbers this means that the magnitude of the negative number is subtracted from 2^8. Thus the 2s-complement representation of -3 is

$$
\begin{array}{rl}
2^8 = & 100000000 \\
-3 = & -\underline{00000011} \\
& 11111101
\end{array}
$$

The coding for 1-byte numbers is shown in Fig. 7-34f.
   To obtain the magnitude of a negative number N, expressed in 2s-complement code, we can subtract N from zero, neglecting the borrow which occurs. Alternatively, we can complement all the bits of N and increment the result, if this is easier to implement.

Example 7-2. Obtain the magnitude of the following negative number N, expressed in 2s-complement code, using the subtraction method.

$$N = 10110101$$

Subtracting from zero gives

neglect borrow ←

$$
\begin{array}{rl}
& 00000000 \\
N = & \underline{10110101} \\
\text{magnitude of } N = & 01001011
\end{array}
$$

which is the binary equivalent of decimal 75. This approach works because it provides the same 8-bit result as subtraction from 2^8.

Example 7-3. Obtain the magnitude of the same negative number using the "complement and increment" approach.

$$
\begin{array}{rl}
N = & 10110101 \\
& 01001010 \quad \} \text{ complement} \\
\text{magnitude of } N = & 01001011 \quad \} \text{ increment}
\end{array}
$$

This approach is based upon subtraction from $2^8 - 1 = 11111111$, which results in all bits being complemented:

$$
\begin{array}{rl}
& 11111111 \\
N = & \underline{10110101} \\
& 01001010
\end{array}
$$

But since we subtracted from $2^8 - 1$ instead of 2^8, we need to correct this difference by adding one to the result.

Signed BCD numbers can be dealt with using a *10s-complement* code. This code has properties for signed BCD numbers which are analogous to the properties of 2s-complement code for signed binary numbers. If we wish to deal with three-digit numbers, we will append one more digit to represent a sign. The coding employed by this *sign digit* SD is

$$SD = \begin{cases} 0000 & \text{for positive numbers and for zero} \\ 1001 & \text{for negative numbers} \end{cases}$$

A 10s-complement number can be handled in the form of an array, as in Fig. 7-35.

For positive numbers, a BCD coding is used, to which the sign digit is appended. Negative numbers are coded in "10s-complement" form. For 2-byte numbers (that is, sign plus three digits), this means that the magnitude of the negative number is subtracted from 10^4. Thus, the 10s-complement representation of -75 is

$$\begin{array}{r} 10^4 = 10000 \\ -75 = -0075 \\ \hline 9925 \end{array}$$

The most positive and most negative numbers which can be coded in this form are shown in Fig. 7-36a and b. The coding for 2-byte numbers, in general, is shown in Fig. 7-36c.

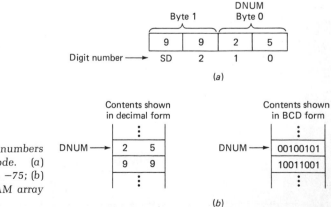

Figure 7-35. Signed BCD numbers using 10s-complement code. (a) Sign + three-digit number, −75; (b) its representation as a RAM array DNUM of 2 bytes.

BCD form ⟶ 0000100110011001

Decimal form ⟶ 0 9 9 9

(a)

BCD form ⟶ 1001000000000000

Decimal form ⟶ 9 0 0 0

(b)

Number coded	10s complement code
+999	0999
⋮	⋮
+3	0003
+2	0002
+1	0001
0	0000
−1	9999
−2	9998
−3	9997
⋮	⋮
−1000	9000

Figure 7-36. 10s-complement code. (a) Most positive 2-byte number, +999; (b) most negative 2-byte number, −1000; (c) coding for 2-byte numbers.

(c)

Obtaining the magnitude of a negative number N, expressed in 10s-complement code, can be carried out by decimally subtracting N from zero and neglecting the borrow which occurs. Alternatively, we can subtract each digit (including the sign) from nine and add one to the result, using decimal addition.

Example 7-4. Obtain the magnitude of the following number N, expressed in 10s-complement code, using the subtraction method.

$$N = 9925$$

Subtracting from zero gives

neglect borrow⤦
0000
N = 9925
magnitude of N = 0075

Example 7-5. Obtain the magnitude of the same negative number using the "subtract from nines and increment" approach.

$$
\begin{array}{r}
9999 \\
N = \underline{9925} \\
0074 \\
\text{magnitude of } N = 0075
\end{array}
\begin{array}{l}
\Big\} \text{ subtract each digit from nine} \\
\Big\} \text{ increment}
\end{array}
$$

This approach offers the advantage, over the previous approach, that borrows between digits never occur. As a consequence, the "subtract each digit from nine" step can be carried out using a binary subtraction instruction.

For display purposes, as well as for decimal multiplication and division, it is useful to define a *sign-plus-BCD-magnitude* code in which the sign digit remains the same but the other digits have been changed, for negative numbers, from 10s-complement form to the corresponding magnitude form. This coding is illustrated in Fig. 7-37.

The sign of a signed number, whether expressed in 2s-complement

Figure 7-37. Coding of 2-Byte Numbers Expressed in Sign-plus-BCD-Magnitude Code

Number coded	Sign-plus-BCD-magnitude code
$+999$	0999
.	.
.	.
.	.
$+3$	0003
$+2$	0002
$+1$	0001
0	0000
-1	9001
-2	9002
-3	9003
.	.
.	.
.	.
-999	9999

code, 10s-complement code, or sign-plus-BCD-magnitude code, can be determined by testing the most significant bit of the most significant byte of the number. For an 8-bit microcomputer, this assumes that signed BCD numbers consist of a sign digit plus an *odd* number of digits, in order to put the sign digit into the most significant digit position of the most significant byte. Even if we only needed a sign-plus-six-digits code, we would use a sign-plus-seven-digits code in order to put the sign digit into this position. Some microcomputers permit a direct test of this most significant bit, calling it the "sign bit" or the "S" flag. While this designation is appropriate when we are dealing with signed numbers, that does not preclude the use of this S flag for other purposes. Thus, in Sec. 3-6, we discussed reading an external flag into the most significant bit position of an input port so that we could facilitate its testing.

7-5 BINARY ↔ BCD CONVERSION

In this section, we will concern ourselves with the conversion between two unsigned numbers (that is, positive numbers). NUM and NUMD identify the binary number and the BCD number, respectively, which are involved in the conversion. We will assume that the result of the conversion does not overflow; that is, the variable representing the result consists of enough bytes to forestall this possibility. This is a condition which is usually under our control as we define the variables involved in an instrument design.

Often we choose to operate upon numbers in binary form because the operations which we wish to carry out can be implemented most directly in this form. At the same time, numbers are most conveniently expressed by the user of an instrument in decimal form, whether entering data on a keyboard or reading a display or printed output.

In Fig. 7-29, we *generated* a number in both forms TNUM and TNUMD in order to avoid a subsequent conversion. This provides a simple solution when the generation of both forms is easy to carry out.

Sometimes, even if the generation is easy, we might choose to avoid this alternative because of the times involved. For example, the self-test procedure makes no use of TNUMD until a malfunction is detected. The time taken for self-test during each cycle of normal operation could have been minimized if only TNUM were formed. Then, in the event of a malfunction, and when there is plenty of time, TNUMD could be obtained by conversion from TNUM.

Because incrementing and decrementing are the simplest operations which can be carried out in a microcomputer having no decimal adjust instructions, we will first consider a technique of conversion by counting. The technique is relatively slow. On the other hand, this is often irrelevant since, as in the last example, we probably need only to convert to interact with an even slower user of an instrument.

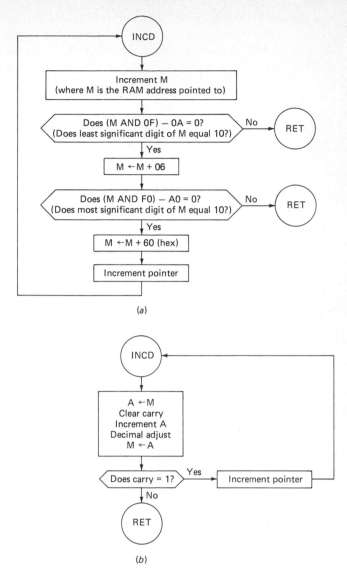

Figure 7-38. Subroutine for incrementing a BCD number in an 8-bit microcomputer. (a) Algorithm; (b) same algorithm implemented with the help of a decimal adjust instruction.

The subroutine of Fig. 7-38a will increment a BCD number consisting of any (even) number of digits stored in the RAM of an 8-bit microcomputer. The algorithm is structured on the assumption that it will never be called when the number consists of all nines, which would produce an overflow. With this assumption, the algorithm is self-stopping without being told the number of bytes making up the number. The subroutine expects that the CPU's pointer to RAM has been set up to point to the least significant byte of the number to be incremented. It begins by incrementing the first byte of the number. It is finished unless the least significant digit has been incremented from nine to ten (A in hex code). By masking off this digit and comparing it with A, the subroutine decides whether further action is needed. If so, adding six to this least significant digit, using binary addition, will cause it to change to zero and also increment the second digit. For example, if M has been incremented from 29 to 2A, adding 06 produces a result of 30:

$$
\begin{array}{ll}
\text{hex} & \text{binary} \\
\overbrace{2A} = \overbrace{00101010} \\
+\ \underline{06} = \underline{00000110} \\
30 = 00110000
\end{array}
$$

In like manner, the most significant digit of this byte can now be checked. If it equals A, it must be corrected and the next byte of the number incremented. This continues until all digits which must be incremented have been.

Figure 7-38b illustrates the power of a decimal adjust instruction in simplifying a BCD algorithm. After incrementing the accumulator A, the decimal adjust instruction converts the result back to BCD form. If A = 99 before incrementing, A = 00 and carry = 1 after incrementing and decimal adjusting. For any other value of A before incrementing, the carry bit will equal zero after incrementing and decimal adjusting, thus terminating the algorithm.

To convert a binary number NUM to its decimal equivalent NUMD, we can use the BTOD subroutine shown in Fig. 7-39a, which is based upon the INCD subroutine just discussed. As implied by Fig. 7-39b, we require almost as many instructions in passing parameters to the subroutine as there are in the subroutine itself. Because of this, it is a good example of an algorithm which might not be prepared as a general-purpose subroutine if it is called at only one point in the software. Instead, it could be written so as to access the variables involved in the conversion directly.

A faster binary-to-BCD algorithm is available for microcomputers which include the decimal adjust instruction discussed earlier, which corrects a binary sum of two BCD numbers into a BCD result. The algorithm begins with an expression of the binary number NUM as a function of its binary bits:

$$
\text{NUM} = b_7 \times 2^7 + b_6 \times 2^6 + b_5 \times 2^5 + b_4 \times 2^4 + b_3 \times 2^3
$$
$$
+\ b_2 \times 2^2 + b_1 \times 2^1 + b_0
$$

where, for convenience, NUM is shown as a 1-byte number of 8 bits. NUM can be reexpressed as

$$
\text{NUM} = (((((b_7 2 + b_6)2 + b_5)2 + b_4)2 + b_3)2 + b_2)2 + b_1)2 + b_0
$$

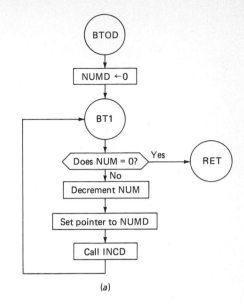

(a)

Parameter	Meaning
NUM	Address label of the binary number
NBIN	Number of bytes in NUM
NUMD	Address label of the BCD number
NDEC	Number of bytes in NUMD

(b)

Figure 7-39. BTOD, a subroutine for binary-to-BCD conversion by counting. (a) Algorithm; (b) parameters which must be passed to this subroutine.

If the operation within each one of the nested parentheses is executed in BCD code, this produces an iterative algorithm for forming NUMD:

$$NUMD = ((((((b_7 2 + b_6)2 + b_5)2 + b_4)2 + b_3)2 + b_2)2 + b_1)2 + b_0$$

where, again, $b_7, \ldots, b_0$ are the bits of NUM.

The algorithm for converting NUM, consisting of NBIN bytes, into NUMD, consisting of NDEC bytes, is shown in simplified form in Fig. 7-40a. Both NBIN and NDEC are assumed to have been chosen so that an error overflow in the formation of NUMD cannot occur. If NBIN = 2, meaning that the binary number NUM consists of 2 bytes, or 16 bits, then a variable INDEX = 16 is formed. This will cause the operation within successive pairs of brackets,

$$(NUMD \times 2 + b_i)$$

to be executed 16 times, where the array NUMD is used to accumulate the re-

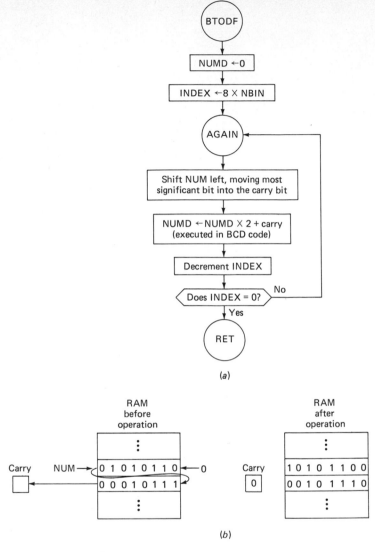

(a)

(b)

Figure 7-40. Fast binary-to-BCD conversion subroutine BTODF. (a) Algorithm; (b) definition of the "shift NUM left" operation; (c) algorithm in more detail.

sult. Each of the successive values of b_i can be obtained by shifting all bits of all bytes of NUM one position to the "left," toward the most significant bit position and shifting this most significant bit into the carry bit, as shown in Fig. 7-40b. This might be implemented as a subroutine which moves successive bytes to the accumulator, shifts them, and then returns them to memory. Executing the step

$$\text{NUMD} \leftarrow \text{NUMD} \times 2 + \text{carry}$$

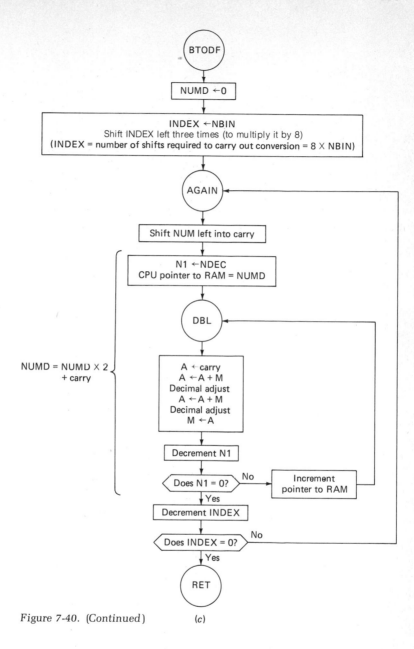

Figure 7-40. (Continued)   (c)

in BCD code, using binary addition followed by decimal adjust instructions
in order to implement BCD addition, is shown in Fig. 7-40c.

   The conversion from BCD code to binary code can be carried out using
a counting scheme analogous to that of Fig. 7-39 for binary-to-BCD conversion. It would count the BCD number down to zero and the binary number
up from zero to the converted value. The scheme of Fig. 7-41 is a variation

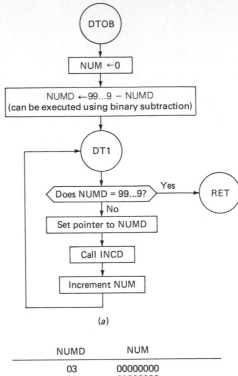

(a)

NUMD	NUM
03	00000000
96	00000000
97	00000001
98	00000010
Stop → 99	00000011 ← Result

Figure 7-41. DTOB, a subroutine for BCD-to-binary conversion by counting. (a) Algorithm; (b) example, for NUMD = 03, NUM = 00000011.

(b)

on this approach which permits it to utilize the same INCD subroutine used in Fig. 7-39 to increment a BCD number. Instead of counting the BCD number down to zero, it is first subtracted from all nines and then counted up to all nines. The subtraction from all nines can be carried out using binary subtraction instructions because subtraction from all nines does not propagate borrows between digits.

A faster algorithm for BCD-to-binary conversion, analogous to that of Fig. 7-40, requires the division of a BCD number by 2. Division of a binary number by 2 can be implemented simply by shifting the number one place to the right. Unfortunately, BCD division by 2 cannot be implemented in the same way. Even following the shift by a normal decimal adjust instruction (designed to follow a binary addition of BCD numbers) does not help.

A subroutine to implement this operation can shift the number to the right and then subtract 3 from any resulting digit which is equal to or greater than 8, as illustrated by the example of Fig. 7-42. That this procedure works

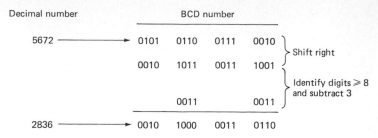

Figure 7-42. *Example of BCD division by 2 by shifting and then subtracting 3 from any digit which is equal to or greater than 8.*

is a consequence of the "weights" associated with the bits of binary numbers

$$\ldots \quad 128 \quad 64 \quad 32 \quad \circled{16} \quad 8 \quad 4 \quad 2 \quad 1$$

as compared with the weights associated with the bits of BCD numbers

$$\ldots \quad 80 \quad 40 \quad 20 \quad \circled{10} \quad 8 \quad 4 \quad 2 \quad 1$$

Shifting a 1 to the right from the encircled bit position does indeed produce division by 2 for a binary number because the resulting bit will have a weight of 8. For the BCD number, the correct weight is 5 (that is, $\frac{10}{2}$), not 8. Subtracting 3, when there is a 1 in this bit position, provides the required correction.

To understand the rationale behind the complete conversion algorithm, consider that we have the same number *already* expressed in both BCD and binary form:

$$\text{NUMD} \quad \text{and} \quad \text{NUM}$$

If the number is even, both NUMD and NUM will have a zero in their least significant bit position, whereas if the number is odd, both will have a one there. Consequently, the least significant bit of the binary number is equal to the least significant bit of the BCD number and can be obtained directly. Next, both NUMD and NUM can be divided by 2, discarding the remainders (which had to be equal by the previous discussion). NUMD and NUM must again be equal in value (but coded differently) and therefore have identical least significant bits. But the least significant bit of NUM, now, was the second bit of NUM originally. Since we want to determine all the bits of NUM, given NUMD, we can obtain the successive bits of NUM, least significant bit first, by repeatedly dividing NUMD by 2 and collecting the least significant bit of each result.

This algorithm is shown in Fig. 7-43. It assumes that NUM has been chosen to be large enough to hold the converted binary number so that an

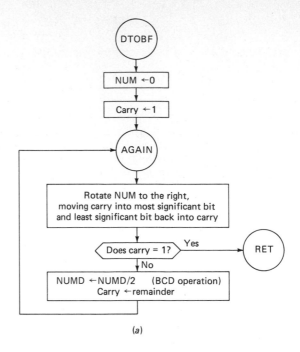

(a)

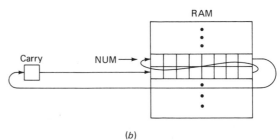

Figure 7-43. Fast BCD-to-binary
conversion. (a) Algorithm; (b) definition of Rotate NUM to the right
operation.

(b)

overflow error does not occur. As the successive bits of NUM are formed,
they are shifted into NUM from the CPU's carry bit. By setting this up as a
"rotate" operation, as shown in Fig. 7-43, we can use a little trick to iterate
around the loop 8 × NBIN times (where NBIN is again the number of 8-bit
bytes making up NUM) without actually setting up and using the variable
INDEX of Fig. 7-40. Instead, we first clear NUM to all zeros and then rotate a
1 into the most significant bit of NUM from the carry bit. This is followed
by the successive bits of the binary result. We want to keep rotating until
the least significant bit of the binary result has shifted all the way down to
the least significant bit position of NUM. When that has happened, the 1
which was originally rotated into NUM will be rotated back into the carry
bit, and since NUM was originally all zeros, this will be the *first* time when
carry = 1 after a rotate operation.

7-6 ADDITION AND SUBTRACTION

A routine to handle addition, or subtraction, on multibyte numbers can be broken down into two parts. The first part is the execution of the operation on one byte of each number, with CPU pointers having already been set up to point to each byte involved. The execution must handle the carry from the operation on the previous byte (or be suitably initialized for the operation on the first byte). The second part of the routine consists of the handling of the pointers so that the operation is carried out on all the corresponding bytes of both numbers. Structures to do this with indexed addressing or doubly indirect addressing are shown in Figs. 2-6 and 2-7.

In this section we will concentrate on the first step, recognizing that the actual implementation of the second step is very dependent upon the addressing alternatives available within a specific microcomputer. We will find that the algorithms for addition and subtraction can be handled byte by byte in this way, independent of which byte is being operated upon, including the byte which includes a sign bit (or sign digit). Furthermore, if we wish to operate upon single-byte numbers, an algorithm which we have developed for each byte of a multibyte number is the algorithm needed for the single-byte number, once we have initialized appropriately.

We require that the number of bytes chosen to hold each variable be sufficient so that overflow errors never occur. For example, we will never add the decimal numbers 3167 + 8950 and try to store the decimal result in two 8-bit bytes. When designing a specific instrument, we can usually assure this.

The development of a multibyte algorithm in this way involves incrementing or decrementing a counter (and/or pointers) followed by a test to detect when the last bytes have been processed. If these increment or decrement operations affect the carry bit, the carry from one byte to the next must be set aside. Most microcomputers (for example, Intel 4004/4040 and 8008/8080, Motorola 6800, RCA COSMAC, Rockwell PPS-4 and PPS-8) recognize the value of leaving the carry bit unchanged during an increment instruction, thus facilitating all operations on multibyte operands.

Because the arithmetic instructions of a microcomputer operate on a single byte, an addition or subtraction subroutine for handling multibyte numbers must cope with the carries occurring between each byte. This is facilitated by having an add with carry instruction, which adds the carry bit plus the accumulator plus the addressed operand, forming the result in the accumulator and the carry bit. Addition of each byte of a binary number requires nothing more than this add with carry instruction plus instructions to move data to and from memory. Figure 7-44 illustrates the implementation of the complete multibyte addition subroutine for the Intel 8080 microcomputer. Binary subtraction requires only a subtract with borrow instruction, where the carry bit serves as a borrow bit for subtraction. A multibyte subtraction subroutine for the Intel 8080 would be identical to

Register-pair B and C points to FIRST number
Register-pair H and L points to SECOND number
Register D equals the number of bytes in each number

(a)

Sum is returned in memory location which held FIRST number

(b)

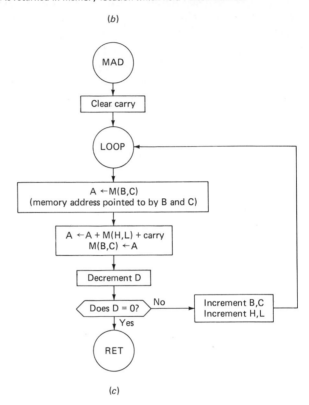

(c)

ADD	MNE	REG	OP	Comments
MAD	XRA	A		Clear carry bit (exclusive-OR A with A)
LOOP	LDAX	B		Load byte of FIRST
	ADC	M		Add byte of SECOND with carry
	STAX	B		Store result at FIRST
	DCR	D		Decrement D
	RZ			Return if zero (that is, if D = 0)
	INX	B		Increment B, C pointer
	INX	H		Increment H,L pointer
	JMP		LOOP	

(d)

Figure 7-44. Multibyte addition subroutine MAD for the Intel 8080 micro-computer. (a) Parameters passed to subroutine; (b) parameters returned by subroutine; (c) flowchart of MAD; (d) assembly language subroutine.

that of Fig. 7-44 but with the ADC instruction replaced by a SBB (subtract with borrow) instruction.

Some microcomputers do not include a subtract instruction. In this case, the subtraction can be implemented by first complementing all the bits of the subtrahend S (that is, the number subtracted from the minuend) and adding one to the result. Then this number is added to the minuend. To understand why this works, note that for 2-byte numbers, as far as the 16 least significant bits are concerned,

$$M - S = M - S + 2^{16}$$

These are the only bits we care about. Therefore,

$$M - S = M - S + (2^{16} - 1) + 1$$
$$= M + [[(2^{16} - 1) - S] + 1$$

But the expression $2^{16} - 1$ is equal to 16 1s, and subtraction of a binary number from all 1s simply complements all the bits of the binary number. Thus the bracketed term represents the subtrahend after all bits have been complemented, and by adding this to the minuend together with an initial carry, we get the desired difference.

The value of the 2s-complement representation of numbers is that it permits us to add, or subtract, signed numbers as if they were unsigned numbers. The results will be correct, expressed in 2s-complement code. Consequently, the algorithms which we have just finished discussing are the algorithms for adding and subtracting numbers expressed in 2s-complement code. The sign bits take care of themselves.

Example 7-6. Add $+5$ to -3, expressed in 2s-complement code, using 2 bytes for each number.

Referring back to Fig. 7-34f, we have

	ignore carry	C = 1	C = 0
(+5)	00000000 ←	00000101	
+ (−3)	11111111	11111101	
(+2)	00000000	00000010	

Example 7-7. Add -5 to $+3$, expressed in 2s-complement code, using 2 bytes for each number.

		C = 0	C = 0
(−5)		11111111 ←	11111011
+ (+3)		00000000	00000011
(−2)		11111111	11111110

Example 7-8. Add -5 to -3, expressed in 2s-complement code, using 2 bytes for each number.

```
          ignore carry        C = 1        C = 0
 (−5)            11111111←    11111011
+ (−3)           11111111     11111101
 (−8)            11111111     11111000
```

Example 7-9. Subtract -3 from $+5$, expressed in 2s-complement code, using 2 bytes for each number.

```
          ignore carry        C = 1        C = 0
 (+5)            00000000←    00000101
− (−3)           11111111     11111101
 (+8)            00000000     00001000
```

Or, we can complement the subtrahend and add one:

```
                    C = 0          C = 1
          00000000←    00000101
          00000000     00000010
          00000000     00001000
```

The addition of BCD numbers is greatly facilitated by the availability of a decimal adjust instruction. As a specific example of its operation, consider the DAA (decimal adjust accumulator) instruction available with the Intel 8080 microcomputer. Whenever 2 bytes are added using a normal, binary add instruction, *two* carry bits are affected, as shown in Fig. 7-45a. The normal carry bit is set if a carry out of bit 7 occurs. At the same time the *auxiliary carry* bit is set if a carry from bit 3 to bit 4 occurs. For binary operations, the auxiliary carry is ignored. In fact, the only instructions which ever look at the auxiliary carry bit are the DAA instruction and an instruction to push all the status flags (that is, Carry, Zero, Sign, Parity, and Auxiliary Carry) onto the stack, which is useful during an interrupt.

The execution of a DAA instruction decimally adjusts the accumulator as shown in Fig. 7-45c. It corrects a binary addition, but *not* a binary subtraction, of 10s-complement numbers into a 10s-complement result.

Example 7-10. Illustrate the addition of the 1-byte decimal numbers 19 and 48.

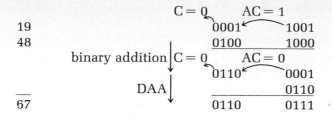

$$
\begin{array}{cc}
& C=0 \qquad AC=1 \\
19 & 0001 \qquad 1001 \\
48 & 0100 \qquad 1000 \\
\text{binary addition} \downarrow & C=0 \qquad AC=0 \\
& 0110 \qquad 0001 \\
\text{DAA} \downarrow & \underline{\qquad\qquad 0110} \\
\overline{67} & 0110 \qquad 0111
\end{array}
$$

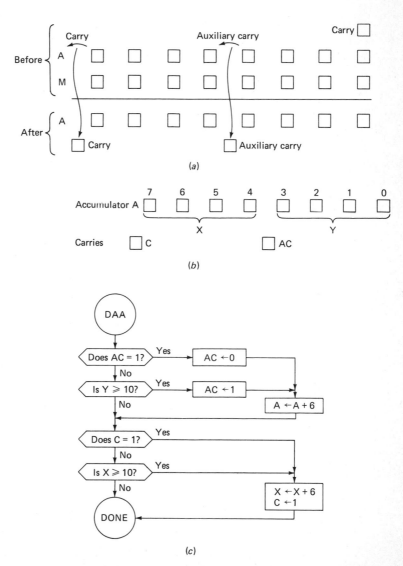

Figure 7-45. Intel 8080 DAA instruction. (a) Effect of binary addition upon carry and auxiliary carry bits; (b) definition of X, Y, A, C, and AC; (c) operation.

Example 7-11. Illustrate the addition of the 1-byte decimal numbers 27 and 35.

$$C = 0 \qquad AC = 0$$

```
                                 0010       0111
27
35                               0011       0101
        binary addition  C = 0        AC = 1
                                 0101       1100
             DAA                            0110
___                              _____
62                               0110       0010
```

Example 7-12. Illustrate the addition of the 2-byte decimal numbers 0957 and 1968.

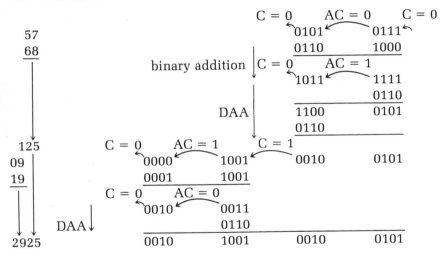

Example 7-13. Illustrate that the DAA instruction does *not* provide proper correction for the subtraction of the 1-byte decimal numbers 35 − 27.

$$C = 0 \qquad AC = 1$$

```
                                 0011       0101
35
27                               0010       0111
        binary subtraction  C = 0      AC = 1
                                 0000       1110
             DAA                            0110
___                              _____
08    ≠                          0001       0100
```

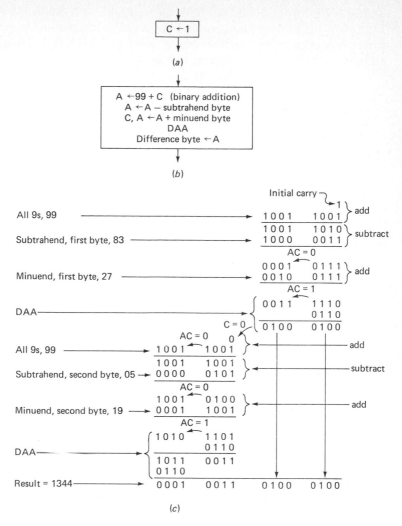

Figure 7-46. BCD subtraction. (a) Initialization; (b) operation on each byte; (c) 2-byte example, $1927 - 0583 = 1344$.

A subroutine for the BCD addition of multibyte numbers can be obtained from the corresponding subroutine for a binary addition of multibyte numbers. A DAA instruction is inserted immediately following the instruction which adds each pair of bytes as binary numbers. Thus the Intel 8080 subroutine of Fig. 7-44 can be converted to a multibyte BCD addition subroutine by inserting a DAA instruction immediately after the ADC instruction.

In contrast, a BCD subtraction must be construed into an addition so that the proper correction can be applied. The procedure, shown in Fig. 7-46, is analogous to that discussed earlier for binary subtraction by complementing the subtrahend and adding. Here we add one to all nines (using binary addition) and then subtract the subtrahend using binary subtraction. This step can be done using binary subtraction because no borrows between digits ever occur. The minuend byte is then added and the result is decimal adjusted. An example is given in Fig. 7-46c.

The addition and subtraction of signed BCD numbers expressed in 10s-complement code uses exactly these same routines. The sign digits take care of themselves.

Example 7-14. Add the 1-byte 10s-complement numbers $+5$ and -3.

$$
\begin{array}{llcc}
 & & C = 0 & AC = 0 \\
(+5) & & 0000 & 0101 \\
+\,(-3) & & 1001 & 0111 \\
 & \text{binary addition} \; \Big|\; C = 0 & AC = 1 \\
 & & 1001 & 1100 \\
 & & & 0110 \\
 & \Big|\, C = 1 & & \\
 & \text{DAA} \; \Big| & 1010 & 0010 \\
 & & 0110 & \\
(+2) & & 0000 & 0010 \\
\end{array}
$$

7-7 MULTIPLICATION, DIVISION, AND REENTRANT SUBROUTINES

In this section we will consider the binary multiplication of two 1-byte numbers to produce a 2-byte result. We will also consider the binary division of a 2-byte number by a 1-byte number to produce a 1-byte result. We will develop the algorithms using a specific microcomputer, the Motorola 6800, in order to exhibit its means for implementing reentrant subroutines.

A *reentrant* subroutine is one which can be used in both a main program and an interrupt service routine. If the subroutine is being executed in the main program when an interrupt occurs, we must not permit any of the data being used in the main program to be destroyed when the interrupt service routine executes the same subroutine upon different parameters. To avoid this problem, a reentrant subroutine can only access data

1   Held in CPU scratchpad registers
2   Addressed indirectly via a pointer in the CPU whose absolute address was set up *before* the subroutine was entered
3   Addressed directly in RAM or ROM if that data is only read (and not changed)

In other words, a subroutine is not reentrant if it directly addresses a RAM location (or sets up a pointer to an absolute address in RAM) and then writes data into that location. However, it can *increment* a pointer within the subroutine.

These rules are relatively easy to abide by with a microcomputer having quite a few scratchpad registers and pointers, such as the Intel 8080. When an interrupt occurs, the contents of these registers and the status flags (carry, zero, etc.) are pushed onto the stack, thereby removing them from the destructive manipulations of the interrupt service routine. At the completion of the service routine, these registers are restored and the operation of the interrupted program picks up again in exactly the same state as when it left off.

For a microcomputer such as the Motorola 6800 which does not employ CPU scratchpad registers, care must be taken with the registers which it does have in order to produce reentrant subroutines. The technique used is to pass parameters to a reentrant subroutine either through the two accumulators or by putting them in RAM and setting up the index register as a pointer to them. We will see two alternative ways that RAM can be used in conjunction with a reentrant subroutine in the remainder of this section.

Binary multiplication of two 8-bit numbers produces a 16-bit result. The procedure is analogous to the usual pencil-and-paper technique of decimal multiplication except that accumulation is carried out after the multiplicand is multiplied by each bit of the multiplier, as illustrated with an example in Fig. 7-47. The process is also simpler than decimal multiplication because each bit of the multiplier can equal only 0 or 1 instead of any value between 0 and 9. If the multiplier bit equals 0, the accumulator is unchanged; if 1, then the multiplicand is suitably aligned with the accumulator

```
Multiplicand ─────────────────────────────────  1 1 0 0 0 0 0 1
Multiplier ──────────────────────────────────  0 1 0 1 0 0 1 1

Initial value of accumulator ──────────  0 0 0 0 0 0 0 0 0 0 0 0 0 0 0 0
                                         1 1 0 0 0 0 0 1
                                         ─────────────────────────────
                                         0 0 0 0 0 0 0 0 1 1 0 0 0 0 0 1
                                                         1 1 0 0 0 0 0 1
                                         ─────────────────────────────
                                         0 0 0 0 0 0 1 0 0 1 0 0 0 0 1 1
                                                     0 0 0 0 0 0 0 0
                                         ─────────────────────────────
                                         0 0 0 0 0 0 1 0 0 1 0 0 0 0 1 1
                                                 0 0 0 0 0 0 0 0
                                         ─────────────────────────────
                                         0 0 0 0 0 0 1 0 0 1 0 0 0 0 1 1
                                             1 1 0 0 0 0 0 1
                                         ─────────────────────────────
                                         0 0 0 0 1 1 1 0 0 1 0 1 0 0 1 1
                                           0 0 0 0 0 0 0 0
                                         ─────────────────────────────
                                         0 0 0 0 1 1 1 0 0 1 0 1 0 0 1 1
                                         1 1 0 0 0 0 0 1
                                         ─────────────────────────────
                                         0 0 1 1 1 1 1 0 1 0 0 1 0 0 1 1
                                         0 0 0 0 0 0 0 0
                                         ─────────────────────────────
Product ─────────────────────────  0 0 1 1 1 1 1 0 1 0 0 1 0 0 1 1
```

Fig. 7-47. Example of binary multiplication.

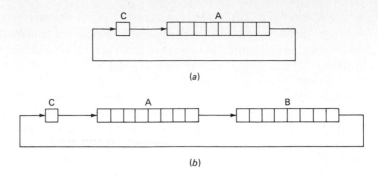

(a)

(b)

Figure 7-48. Motorola 6800 ROR (rotate right) instruction.   (a) ROR A;
(b) effect of the sequence of ROR A followed immediately by ROR B.

and then added to it.   Notice that each addition only affects, at most, the 8 bits aligned with the multiplicand plus the 1 bit to the left of it.

Implementing this procedure with the Motorola 6800 is facilitated by its two accumulators A and B and its ROR (rotate right) instruction, which can be executed on either accumulator, as in Fig. 7-48a.   By executing ROR A followed by ROR B, we rotate the 17-bit register made up of the carry bit and A and B to the right, as in Fig. 7-48b.   We will use this 17-bit register to accumulate the product.   However, since we also need to test successive bits of the multiplier, we can combine both functions by initially loading the multiplier into the B register and only using the nine remaining bits (C and A) for the accumulator, as in Fig. 7-49a.   Each successive rotate instruction will discard a bit of the multiplier and add a bit to the length of the accumulator.

An example of the multiplication process is illustrated in Fig. 7-49b, where each iteration is represented by a pair of rows.   The first row in each pair tests the bit of the multiplier which has been shifted into the carry bit and either adds the multiplicand into A or leaves A unchanged.   The second row in each pair rotates C, A, B right.   Note that the multiplier is represented by the bits to the right of the crossed-out zeros.

A flowchart for the multiplication subroutine is shown in Fig. 7-49c. Since the subroutine has the multiplicand and the multiplier passed to it in the A and B accumulators, it first moves the multiplicand out of the CPU and onto the stack.   Because it must iterate nine times, a counter, called COUNT, is also initialized to nine and pushed onto the stack.   Next, the carry bit C and accumulator A are cleared.   The C, A, and B registers now look like the top row of Fig. 7-49b.   Nine iterations around the loop carry out the steps corresponding to the successive rows in Fig. 7-49b, at which point COUNT = 0 and the iteration stops.   Because 2 bytes (the multiplicand and COUNT) were pushed onto the stack at the beginning of the subroutine, the return address from the subroutine no longer resides at the top of the stack. Incrementing the stack pointer twice rectifies this.

The assembly language program of Fig. 7-49d is a direct translation of the flowchart. The TSX (transfer stack pointer to index register) permits subsequent instructions to address data in the stack. For example, the byte of data residing on the top of the stack, COUNT, is accessed using indexed addressing, with 0,X in the operand field of the instruction. The next byte down in the stack (that is, the multiplicand) is addressed with 1,X. At the end of the subroutine, COUNT and the multiplicand must be removed from the stack so that the return instruction will pop the subroutine return address back into the program counter. If the accumulator were not being used to hold the product of the multiplication, we could pop the stack twice to achieve this. Instead, we simply increment the stack pointer twice, using the INS instructions shown. This leaves COUNT and the multiplicand in RAM, but in locations just above the top of the stack whose contents will be replaced during subsequent subroutine calls or push instructions.

The process of binary division is illustrated in Fig. 7-50, using the same numbers which were involved in the multiplication example. It requires that the most significant byte of the dividend be less than the divisor in order

Multiplicand, initially in accumulator A, is pushed onto stack
Multiplicand = 11000001
Multiplier is in accumulator B
Multiplier = 01010011
Accumulator A and the carry bit are cleared

(a)

	C	A	B
Initial conditions	0	00000000	01010011
Because C = 0, do nothing	0	00000000	01010011
Rotate C,A,B right	1	00000000	00101001
Because C = 1, add multiplicand to A	0	11000001	00101001
Rotate C,A,B right	1	01100000	10010100
Because C = 1, add multiplicand to A	1	00100001	10010100
Rotate C,A,B right	0	10010000	11001010
Because C = 0, do nothing	0	10010000	11001010
Rotate C,A,B right	0	01001000	01100101
Because C = 0, do nothing	0	01001000	01100101
Rotate C,A,B right	1	00100100	00110010
Because C = 1, add multiplicand to A	0	11100101	00110010
Rotate C,A,B right	0	01110010	10011001
Because C = 0, do nothing	0	01110010	10011001
Rotate C,A,B right	1	00111001	01001100
Because C = 1, add multiplicand to A	0	11111010	01001100
Rotate C,A,B right	0	01111101	00100110
Because C = 0, do nothing	0	01111101	00100110
Rotate C,A,B right	0	00111110	10010011

16-bit product

Figure 7-49. Binary multiplication in the Motorola 6800. (a) Initial conditions; (b) example of the multiplication process; (c) flowchart; (d) reentrant assembly language subroutine.

(b)

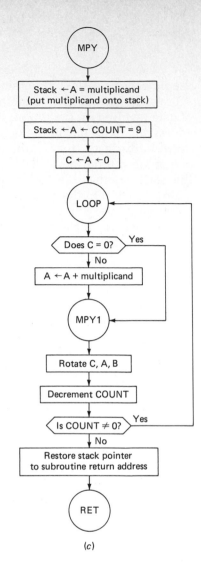

(c)

ADD	MNE	REG	OP	Comments
NINE	EQU		9	Define initial value of COUNT
COUNT	EQU		0	Define location of COUNT on stack
MLTD	EQU		1	Define location of multiplicand on stack
MPY	PSH	A		Push multiplicand onto stack
	LDA	A	#NINE	Load immediate, the initial value of COUNT
	PSH	A		Push COUNT onto stack
	TSX			Load index register from stack pointer
	CLR	A		Clear A and C
LOOP	BCC		MPY1	Branch to MPY1 if carry is clear
	ADD	A	MLTD,X	Add multiplicand to A
MPY1	ROR	A		Rotate C,A,B right
	ROR	B		
	DEC		COUNT,X	Decrement COUNT
	BNE		LOOP	Branch to LOOP if COUNT ≠ 0
	INS			Increment stack pointer twice so that it
	INS			points to the subroutine return address
	RTS			Return from subroutine

Figure 7-49. (Continued)   (d)

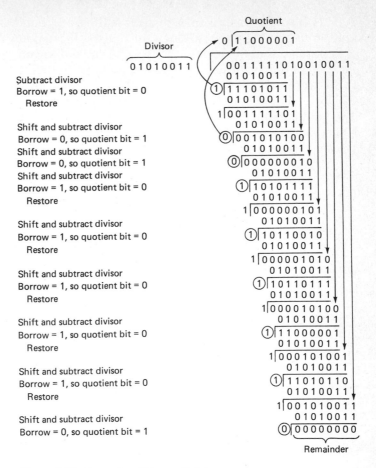

Figure 7-50. *Example of binary division.*

for a correct 1-byte quotient to result. If this is not true, the result will require more than 1 byte and will not be correct. The subroutine we will
develop will return carry = 1 in the latter case, signifying that the divisor
and dividend need to be shifted relative to each other before division is tried
again.

This "restoring" division algorithm tries to subtract the divisor from
the dividend. If an underflow occurs (C = 1), the quotient bit is zero. In
this case, the dividend is restored by adding the divisor to the dividend. If
underflow does not occur (C = 0), the quotient bit is one and the subtraction
was proper. Then, in either case, the divisor and dividend are shifted relative to each other and the procedure iterated again. After nine iterations, division terminates. The first iteration provides a quotient bit which should
equal zero if the most significant byte of the dividend is less than the divisor.
The subroutine will terminate with this bit shifted into the carry bit to provide the test mentioned previously. The remaining eight iterations produce
the eight bits of the quotient.

This subroutine assumes that the calling program has set up the index register to point to the location of the divisor, located anywhere in RAM. It also assumes that the location of the divisor is followed immediately by the location of the 2 bytes of the dividend, which in turn is followed by a spare RAM word which will be used by the subroutine as a counter, called COUNT. These parameter-passing assumptions are shown in Fig. 7-51a. The quotient and the remainder will be returned in accumulators B and A, respectively, as listed in Fig. 7-51b.

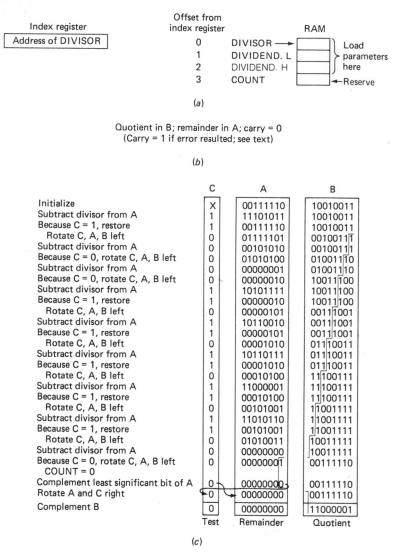

Figure 7-51. Binary division in the Motorola 6800. (a) Initial conditions; (b) conditions upon return; (c) example of the division process; (d) flowchart; (e) reentrant assembly language subroutine.

Just as for multiplication, the division algorithm uses the 17-bit register made up of the carry bit and accumulators A and B, which can be rotated together, this time to the left. After each subtraction, or subtraction plus restoration, the carry bit is equal to the complement of the quotient bit. By rotating this into accumulator B, we end up with the complement of the quotient in accumulator B. The subroutine can complement accumulator B just before returning in order to pass the quotient, and not the complement of the quotient, back to the calling program.

The flowchart for this algorithm is shown in Fig. 7-51d. After COUNT is initialized to nine, for nine iterations, the dividend is brought into accumulators A and B. The "restoring" division algorithm is then iterated nine

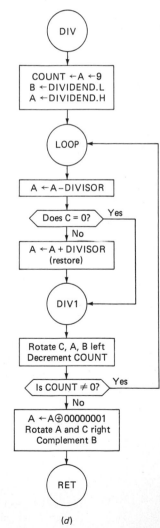

Figure 7-51. (Continued)   (d)

ADD	MNE	REG	OP	Comments
NINE	EQU		9	Define initial value of COUNT
DVR	EQU		0	Define indexed location of DIVISOR
DVDL	EQU		1	Define indexed location of DIVIDEND.L
DVDH	EQU		2	Define indexed location of DIVIDEND.H
COUNT	EQU		3	Define indexed location of COUNT
LSB	EQU		00000001B	Define LSB to select the least significant bit
DIV	LDA	A	#NINE	Load immediate, the initial value of COUNT
	STA	A	COUNT, X	COUNT ←A ←9
	LDA	B	DVDL, X	Load accumulators with the 16-bit dividend
	LDA	A	DVDH, X	
LOOP	SUB	A	DVR, X	Subtract divisor from A
	BCC		DIV1	Branch to DIV1 if carry is clear
	ADD	A	DVR, X	Restore dividend
DIV1	ROL	B		} Rotate C, A, B left
	ROL	A		
	DEC		COUNT, X	Decrement COUNT
	BNE		LOOP	Branch to LOOP if COUNT ≠ 0
	EOR	A	#LSB	Complement LSB of A using immediate data
	ROR	A		Rotate A and C right
	COM	B		Complement B to get quotient
	RTS			Return from subroutine

Figure 7-51. (Continued)   (e)

times, resulting in nine quotient bits, all in complemented form. The first bit is in the least significant bit of accumulator A. It is complemented and rotated right to put this bit into the carry bit to align the remainder properly in accumulator A. Then accumulator B is complemented and the subroutine returns to the calling program.

The reentrant assembly language subroutine is shown in Fig. 7-51e. In accessing the divisor, dividend, and COUNT, it uses indexed addressing in order to be reentrant. While this was not evident in the flowchart, it is easy enough to handle in the assembly language subroutine.

PROBLEMS

7-1 Keychart. (a) Modify the keychart of Fig. 7-3 so that after depressing a parameter keyswitch such as AMPL or MODE, which must be followed by at least one digit, all other parameter keyswitches are locked out until a digit key *has* been depressed.

(b) How many states does this lead to?

(c) How many bits are required in the binary number which codes this state information?

7-2 Keychart. For an instrument available to you (or for which you have descriptive information) which uses a keyboard input, describe the interactions with a keychart.

7-3 Keychart. Construct the keychart for a specific four-function calculator available to you. If your four-function calculator has a special function slide switch, then:

(a) Treat each keyswitch as if it were two keyswitches (for example, +ON and +OFF instead of just +).

(b) Construct two keycharts, one for each position of the slide switch.

(c) Describe how these two approaches would affect the implementation of the keyboard parser.

7-4 **Action routines.** For one of the applications which you have described with a keychart in Prob. 7-1, 7-2, or 7-3, make a listing of action routines needed analogous to the listing in Fig. 7-6.

7-5 **Parser state table.** For the application which you dealt with in Prob. 7-4, construct a parser state table analogous to that of Fig. 7-5.

7-6 **Functional keycodes.** For the application of Prob. 7-5, define functional keycodes analogous to those of Fig. 7-9. Try to combine similar parameters into the same value of FNKY and then describe briefly how the action routine will use NUMB. That is, what are the differences required within the action routine for different values of NUMB? Modify your solutions to Probs. 7-4 and 7-5 to reflect these combinations.

7-7 **Setup parameters.** Consider a specific instrument (not necessarily designed with keyswitch inputs, or even digital inputs) for which you have a user's manual or a sales brochure. List each setup parameter of the instrument and describe the range and resolution of its value. Note that some setup parameters may be either grouped together or listed separately, analogous to the difference between keyswitches used for Fig. 7-3 versus those of Fig. 7-8. Explain any choices of this nature and show which you would group together with the same functional key code (FNKY) if you were redesigning the instrument for a keyboard input.

7-8 **Action routines.** (a) Describe, with flowcharts, how you might organize the action routines for an instrument such that when the instrument is initialized, an annunciator light for one setup parameter is blinked slowly (0.5 Hz), telling the user that this parameter has not yet been set up. Sequence the user through all setup parameters in this way, until when all parameters have been entered, no lights remain blinking.

(b) Does your "blinking" algorithm require any special initialization?

7-9 **Coded form of parser state table.** For the application of Prob. 7-6, translate the (modified) parser state table of Prob. 7-5 into coded form analogous to that of Fig. 7-10.

7-10 **Keyboard parser routine.** For a specific microcomputer, write an assembly language keyboard parser routine based upon the flowcharts of Figs. 7-13 and 7-16 (or Fig. 7-15, if Fig. 7-16 cannot be implemented on this microcomputer). Assume that the parser state table is entirely on page PST0.H and that the parser entry table contains only addresses on this page. On the other hand, assume that action routines can be anywhere and that the action pointer table contains full addresses.

7-11 Time display. Assuming the structure of a specific microcomputer, construct the flowchart for an interrupt service routine which will update RAM memory locations labeled SECONDS, MINUTES, and HOURS, recycling every 24 hours. Interrupts occur every sixtieth of a second. Assume the availability of a subroutine INCD which increments the two-digit number stored in RAM at the location pointed to by the CPU's pointer.

7-12 Real-time interrupt. Assume that circuitry like that of Fig. 7-19b provides an interrupt every 0.5 ms:

(a) Describe how you would modify the service routine of Fig. 7-20 so that the first timer (represented by T1FLG and TIM1) turns off any positive pulses being generated on output port 5 (page 5 of "memory").

(b) Describe how you would generate a 10-ms positive pulse on the least significant bit of output port 5.

(c) What constraint does this approach impose upon the pulses which can be generated on the output lines of this output port?

7-13 Real-time interrupt. Modify the solution to Prob. 7-12 so that upon initiating either a positive or a negative pulse on any of the output lines of output port 5, a mask word OMASK is updated with a 1 in the bit position corresponding to the output line to be pulsed and 0s everywhere else. Then when the pulse is to be turned off, under interrupt control, this output line is complemented, leaving the other output lines unchanged.

7-14 Real-time compensation. For a specific microcomputer, if an interrupt service routine takes 100 clock cycles, show the assembly language program steps to compensate for this, as in Fig. 7-21 from the "Does COUNTI = 0?" test to the instruction labeled AGAIN. Does the test require the same number of clock cycles to execute whether the test is answered one way or the other? If not, take this into account.

7-15 Real-time compensation. For a specific microcomputer, show the wait loop assembly language instructions ending in an unconditional jump for $T_1 - T_2$ equal to each of the following number of clock cycles. As-

sume that an unconditional jump takes UJ clock cycles. Use as few
ROM words as possible in each case.

(a) UJ + 1	(e) UJ + 5
(b) UJ + 2	(f) UJ + 6
(c) UJ + 3	(g) UJ + 20
(d) UJ + 4	(h) UJ + 30

7-16 Self-test. In self-testing the contents of the ROMs of an instrument,
we wish to have distinct values of TNUM for each page of ROM. On
the other hand, we will use only one subroutine ROMTEST to test all of
these. ROMTEST will look at TNUM to decide which ROM to address
for its test. Assume ROM pages are 0, 1, 2, 3, 4, 5. Also assume
TNUM = 4, 5, 6, 7, 8, 9 for these tests. For a specific microcomputer,
describe how to organize this as efficiently as possible.

7-17 Self-test. For a specific microcomputer, write the assembly language
subroutine STEST corresponding to the flowchart of Fig. 7-29. Assume that the blinking of TNUMD is carried out by a programmable
timer so that we need only get it started.

7-18 Binary code. Express each of the following binary numbers in terms of
their decimal equivalents:

(a) 00001101	(d) 11000000
(b) 01000000	(e) 11111111
(c) 10000000	

7-19 BCD code. Express each of the following decimal numbers in BCD
code as a 2-byte number (using 8-bit bytes):

(a) 1486	(c) 349
(b) 0	(d) 37

7-20 BCD code. Express each of the following BCD code numbers in terms
of their decimal equivalents:

(a) 01011000	(c) 10010000
(b) 00001001	(d) 0001010001111000

7-21 2s-complement code. Express each of the following numbers as a
1-byte (8 bits) number using both a 2s-complement representation and
its hexadecimal equivalent:

(a) +1	(c) +13
(b) −1	(d) −13

7-22 2s-complement code. If each of the following 2s-complement numbers
represents a number N, find N + 1 as a 2s-complement number:

(a) 00011011
(b) 10011011

CHAPTER 7

7-23 2s-complement code. Find the binary magnitude of each of the following 2s-complement numbers using the subtraction method:

(a) 11100111
(b) 10111111
(c) 11000000

7-24 2s-complement code. Repeat Prob. 7-23 using the "complement and increment" method.

7-25 10s-complement code. If each of the following 10s-complement numbers represents a number N, find N + 1 as a 10s-complement number:

(a) 0000000001011000
(b) 1001000001011000

7-26 10s-complement code. Find the BCD magnitude of each of the following 10s-complement numbers using the subtraction method:

(a) 1001000010000010
(b) 1001010101111001
(c) 1001010101110000

7-27 10s-complement code. Repeat Prob. 7-26 using the "subtract from nines and increment" method.

7-28 10s-complement code. For a specific microcomputer, develop a flowchart and an assembly language subroutine which will convert a number from 10s-complement code to sign-plus-BCD-magnitude code or vice versa. Assume NDEC is a variable which has been passed to the subroutine representing the number of bytes making up the number. Also assume that the CPU pointer has been set up to point to the first byte of the number to be converted. The result of the conversion is to replace the original number.

7-29 Binary-to-BCD conversion. For a specific microcomputer, write an assembly language subroutine for each of the following, minimizing the number of ROM words required. Indicate how each subroutine expects parameters to be passed to it.

(a) The INCD subroutine defined in Fig. 7-38b if the microcomputer has a decimal adjust instruction. Otherwise implement that of Fig. 7-38a.

(b) The BTOD subroutine of Fig. 7-39.

(c) The BTODF subroutine of Fig. 7-40.

(d) The BTODF subroutine of Fig. 7-40, but modified as discussed in conjunction with Fig. 7-43 to eliminate the INDEX variable.

7-30 BCD-to-binary conversion. Repeat Prob. 7-29 for each of the following:

(a) The DTOB subroutine of Fig. 7-41. Assume the availability of the subroutine INCD.

(b) A subroutine HALF which executes the bottom block of Fig. 7-43a.

(c) The DTOBF subroutine of Fig. 7-43.

7-31 Multibyte addition. For a specific microcomputer, and minimizing the number of ROM words required, write an assembly language subroutine with two entry points, called BAD and DAD, for the addition of 2s-complement and 10s-complement multibyte numbers, respectively. Use a structure based on Fig. 7-44, but upon entry to BAD, set BINARY = 1, whereas upon entry to DAD, clear BINARY = 0. Then branch where necessary by testing BINARY to obtain the right algorithm in each case. When you are done, determine how many *extra* ROM words were necessary over the number required for a subroutine which does only the DAD function.

7-32 Multibyte binary addition and subtraction. Repeat the idea of Prob. 7-31 to add or subtract multibyte 2s-complement numbers. Call the subroutine entry points ADDB and SUBB, and use the variable ADDIT to draw a distinction between the two processes, where needed.

7-33 Decimal adjust instruction. For a specific microcomputer having a decimal adjust instruction, is its operation identical to that described in Fig. 7-45? If not, describe with a flowchart (or truth table) exactly what it does. Also, describe its uses, if it does other than just correct the binary sum of BCD numbers into a BCD result.

7-34 10s-complement subtraction. For a specific microcomputer, and minimizing the number of ROM words required, write an assembly language subroutine DSUB for the subtraction of 10s-complement multibyte numbers. Indicate how the subroutine expects parameters to be passed to and from it.

7-35 Reentrant subroutines. For a specific microcomputer, list all the ways you can think of to pass parameters to and from a subroutine so that it will be reentrant.

7-36 Binary multiplication. For a microcomputer other than the Motorola 6800, write a MPY assembly language reentrant subroutine analogous to that of Fig. 7-49. Indicate how parameters are passed to and from the subroutine.

7-37 Binary division. Repeat Prob. 7-36, but with the DIV subroutine of Fig. 7-51.

7-38 Numerical scaling. In developing any numerical algorithm for an instrument, it is worthwhile to consider how the algorithm will be used. For example, in developing the algorithm to scale the CRT display for the instrument of Fig. 1-12, the design engineer Kevin Bradford was faced with the computation

$$V_{out} = \frac{V_{in} - V_{min}}{V_{max} - V_{min}} \times 256$$

In this computation, V_{in}, V_{max}, and V_{min} are BCD values, while V_{out} is to be the 8-bit binary output to the D/A converter which drives the CRT.

It appears that the generation of each point on the display requires BCD subtraction, BCD-to-binary conversion, and division. In actual fact, many values of V_{in} are used with fixed values for V_{max} and V_{min}. Consequently, the "smart" algorithm incorporates an initialization phase during which the BCD division by two algorithm of Fig. 7-42 can be repeatedly applied to $V_{max} - V_{min}$, generating the eight BCD numbers

$$\frac{V_{max} - V_{min}}{2}, \frac{V_{max} - V_{min}}{4}, \ldots, \frac{V_{max} - V_{min}}{256}$$

Then each time V_{out} is to be determined, these eight values are used in a "binary chop" on $V_{in} - V_{min}$, with each one contributing one bit to the binary result.

We can illustrate the algorithm with an example. If $V_{max} = 3192$ and $V_{min} = 2234$, then $V_{max} - V_{min} = 958$ and the eight values are 479, 239, 119, 59, 29, 14, 7, and 3. Subsequently, if $V_{in} = 2816$, then $V_{in} - V_{min} = 582$ and the binary chop gives

$$
\begin{array}{rl}
582 > 479 & \longrightarrow 1 \\
-479 & \\
\hline
103 < 239 & \longrightarrow 0 \\
103 < 119 & \longrightarrow 0 \\
103 > \ 59 & \longrightarrow 1 \\
-\ 59 & \\
\hline
44 > \ 29 & \longrightarrow 1 \\
-\ 29 & \\
\hline
15 > \ 14 & \longrightarrow 1 \\
-\ 14 & \\
\hline
1 < \ \ 7 & \longrightarrow 0 \\
1 < \ \ 3 & \longrightarrow 0
\end{array}
$$

That is, $V_{out} = 10011100$.

(a) For a specific microcomputer, and assuming the availability of the HALF subroutine of Prob. 7-30b, write an assembly language subroutine PSCALE which accepts the n-byte BCD numbers VMAX and VMIN, which forms VMAX − VMIN, and which carries out eight successive divisions by 2. The result is to be stored in an array called CHOP. It consists of eight n-byte BCD numbers, beginning with (VMAX − VMIN)/2. SCBYT is a parameter to be passed to HALF and

PSCALE (and to SCALE in the next part) which designates the number of bytes involved in the computations. It must not be changed by any of the subroutines. Minimize the number of ROM words used in PSCALE.

(b) Write an assembly language subroutine SCALE which forms the 8-bit binary output VOUT using each of the eight values of CHOP in a binary chop on VIN − VMIN. Minimize the worst-case execution time of the SCALE subroutine. Also determine the average execution time of the SCALE subroutine, if this is different.

REFERENCES

An excellent presentation of a variety of arithmetic algorithms for binary, BCD, and signed numbers is given by Y. Chu, *Digital Computer Design Fundamentals,* chaps. 1 and 2, McGraw-Hill, New York, 1962.

An example of an excellent sixteen-bit-binary-to-BCD conversion algorithm prepared for the Intel 8080 is presented by J. A. Tabb and M. L. Roginsky, μP Algorithms Make BCD-Binary Conversions Super-Fast, *EDN,* January 5, 1977, pp. 46–50. An efficient BCD-to-sixteen-bit-binary conversion algorithm prepared for the Motorola 6800 is presented by B. E. Allen, A BCD-to-Binary Conversion Scheme, *EDN,* April 5, 1977, p. 135.

See the user's manual or the programming manual provided by the manufacturer of a specific microcomputer. A study of specific algorithms presented there will provide quick insights not only into the algorithms themselves but also into the little tricks used to implement them efficiently on that specific microcomputer.

APPENDIXES

CHARACTERISTICS OF SPECIFIC MICROCOMPUTERS

In these appendixes, the register structure and instruction set of selected microcomputers will be described. A limited amount of information will also be included on the hardware structure of the CPU, a general I/O chip, how the CPU interacts with ROM, RAM, and I/O chips, and how it implements interrupt capability.

APPENDIX A1

INTEL 4004

The Intel®4004 chip set* was the first commercially available microcomputer, introduced in 1971. It is still a viable choice for the many applications in which the need for small physical size and low cost are combined with relatively simple algorithms to be implemented in the software. The microcomputer chips are all packaged in 16-pin dual-in-line packages (DIPs) except for the general I/O chip, which is a 28-pin DIP. While the 4004 chip set requires more chips to construct a minimum configuration microcomputer than, say, the Fairchild F8's two-chip minimum, this is offset by the small size of the chips (that is, 16-pin DIPs versus 40-pin DIPs).

Being the first microcomputer chip set available, the 4004 does not have some of the features found in later microcomputers. For example, it does not permit interrupts. Also, its stack is limited to four registers, one of which is the program counter. Thus subroutines can be nested only to three levels. Finally, the instruction set seems rather simple and the addressing of operands rather awkward in comparison with more recent microcomputers.

---

* Designated the MCS-4® chip set by Intel.

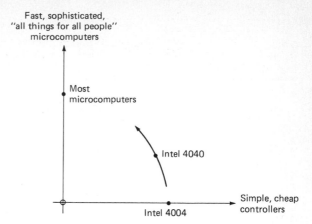

Figure A1-1. Two dimensions of microcomputer design philosophy.

Intel has moved in the direction of rectifying these weaknesses* by introducing the 4040 CPU chip. However, quite a few designers of smart instruments view the growth in microcomputer capability as being almost entirely in the dimension of speed and sophistication. The dimension required for simple instrument control has not seen the same proliferation of new microcomputers. This viewpoint is illustrated in Fig. A1-1.

As shown in Fig. A1-2, the 4004 CPU includes a 4-bit accumulator (A), sixteen 4-bit scratchpad registers (0, . . . , 15), a carry bit (C), a test or external flag bit (T), an address stack containing the 12-bit program counter and up to three subroutine return addresses, and in effect, an 11-bit pointer used to access RAM and I/O ports. In actuality, only the upper 3 bits of this pointer are located in the CPU chip. The other 8 bits are located in each chip containing RAM and I/O ports, being transferred there with a send register control (SRC) instruction, to be discussed shortly. The sixteen 4-bit scratchpad registers are also identified by some instructions as register-pairs, using the register-pair labeling shown in Fig. A1-3.

The ROM chip (Intel 4001), shown in Fig. A1-4, includes not only a 256 × 8 ROM but also one 4-bit I/O port. When the ROM chip is mask-programmed by Intel, not only are the 256 words of ROM specified, but also a 4-bit ROM page address (used to distinguish each ROM chip from up to 15 other ROM chips), and the function of each line of the I/O port (that is, whether input or output, and whether positive-true or negative-true).

The RAM chip (Intel 4002), shown in Fig. A1-5, is configured into four "registers," each of which contains sixteen 4-bit "main memory characters" and four 4-bit "status characters." The distinction between these types of characters lies in the way they are addressed by the instruction set, as we will discuss shortly. This chip also includes a 4-bit output port, for which

---

* Weaknesses only for applications needing these features.

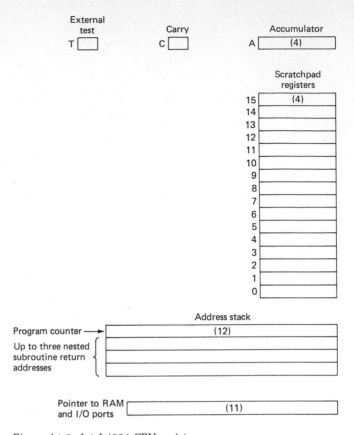

Figure A1-2. Intel 4004 CPU registers.

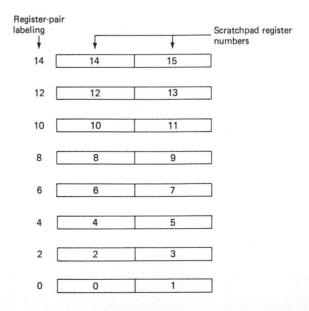

Figure   A1-3. CPU   scratchpad
register-pairs.

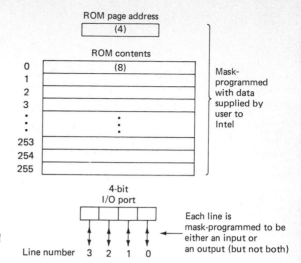

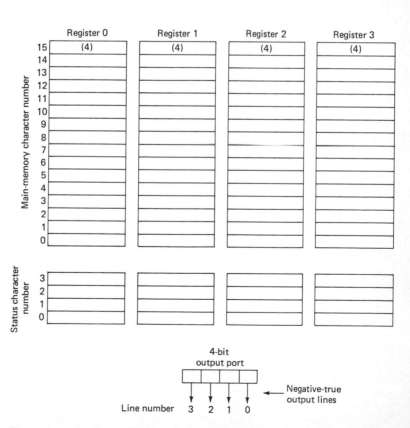

Figure A1-4. Intel 4001 ROM and I/O port.

Figure A1-5. Intel 4002 RAM and output port.

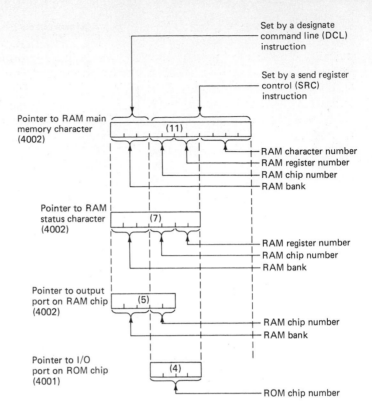

Figure A1-6. Use of pointer by RAM and I/O ports.

each line is defined negative-true (that is, a logic 1 is a lower voltage than a logic 0). The 4004 microcomputer permits up to 16 RAM chips to be connected to the CPU and addressed with no extra chips required for page decoding.

The pointer which selects a RAM main memory character, a RAM status character, an output port on a RAM chip, and an I/O port on a ROM chip is shown in Fig. A1-6. Two instructions, designate command line (DCL) and send register control (SRC), set up this one pointer, which is used in any of the four ways shown. If four or fewer RAM chips are used in an instrument, the DCL instruction is unnecessary. Otherwise, the RAM chips are selected in groups of four by loading the accumulator as follows and then executing a DCL instruction:

Accumulator contents	Select RAM chips
0000	0, 1, 2, 3
0001	4, 5, 6, 7
0010	8, 9, 10, 11
0100	12, 13, 14, 15

The SRC instruction takes the contents of one of the eight register-pairs of Fig. A1-3 and sends it out to each RAM and ROM chip to set up the remaining 8 bits of the pointer of Fig. A1-6. Thus, to point to RAM chip 5, register 3, main memory character 6, the accumulator is loaded with 0001, a DCL instruction is executed, a register-pair (say, register-pair 14) is loaded with 01110110, and then a SRC 14 instruction is executed. As shown in Fig. A1-6, this sequence also selects the four status characters associated with register 3 in RAM chip 5, as well as the output port on RAM chip 5, as well as the I/O port on ROM chip 7.

The 4004 instruction set is given in Fig. A1-7. In the register field, R is a generic label standing for any one of the 16 CPU scratchpad registers. P stands for any one of the eight CPU register-pairs of Fig. A1-3. In the operand field, I represents the decimal equivalent of a 4-bit "immediate" operand. W represents the decimal equivalent of an 8-bit immediate operand. L represents an address label. If the instruction requires the address to be on the same page as the present instruction but it is not, the assembler will generate an error diagnostic.

The effect of each instruction upon the carry bit is listed in the third column from the right using the symbolism

—	No effect
↕	Set or cleared, depending upon the result of the instruction
1	Set
0	Cleared

Each instruction's execution time is indicated by the "Cycles" column in Fig. A1-7. Since the 4004 microcomputer can operate with any clock period between 1.35 and 2.00 μs and since the CPU's operation for each byte of an instruction is multiplexed over eight clock cycles (as shown in Fig. 3-32), each instruction requires a multiple of $8 \times 1.35 = 10.8 \ \mu$s (minimum) to $8 \times 2.00 = 16.0 \ \mu$s (maximum) to execute. An instruction like DCL which lists cycles = 1 in Fig. A1-7 will thus take 10.8 to 16.0 μs to execute. An instruction like JUN which lists cycles = 2 requires 21.6 to 32.0 μs.

The number of 8-bit bytes taken up in ROM to store each instruction is listed in the column labeled "Bytes." Note that no instruction requires more than 2 bytes, in contrast to many other microcomputers which use up to 3 bytes. This is a direct result of only addressing memory and I/O ports indirectly, first setting up a pointer in one of the register-pairs and then selecting this pointer with an SRC instruction (as well as extending the pointer to larger memory arrays with a DCL instruction).

Several of the 4004 instructions require further comment. The transfer carry subtract (TCS) instruction loads the accumulator with either nine or ten, depending upon whether the carry bit equals zero or one. This is useful in forming the 10s complement of a decimal number in order to carry out decimal subtraction using the "complement and add" algorithm of Sec. 7-6.

Figure A1-7. Intel 4004 Instruction Set

Operation	MNE	REG	OP	Description	Carry	Bytes	Cycles
Set pointer	DCL			Pointer.H ⟵ A (see text)	−	1	1
	SRC	P		Pointer.L ⟵ P (see text)	−	1	1
Move	LD	R		A ⟵ R	−	1	1
	XCH	R		A ⟷ R	−	1	1
	RDM			A ⟵ M	−	1	1
	RD0			A ⟵ Selected status character 0	−	1	1
	RD1			A ⟵ Selected status character 1	−	1	1
	RD2			A ⟵ Selected status character 2	−	1	1
	RD3			A ⟵ Selected status character 3	−	1	1
	RDR			A ⟵ Selected ROM input port	−	1	1
	WRM			M ⟵ A	−	1	1
	WR0			Selected status character 0 ⟵ A	−	1	1
	WR1			Selected status character 1 ⟵ A	−	1	1
	WR2			Selected status character 2 ⟵ A	−	1	1
	WR3			Selected status character 3 ⟵ A	−	1	1
	WRR			Selected ROM output port ⟵ A	−	1	1
	WMP			Selected RAM output port ⟵ A	−	1	1
Move, immediate	LDM		I	A ⟵ I	−	1	1
	FIM	P	W	P ⟵ W	−	2	2
Move, indirect	FIN	P		Register-pair P ⟵ Contents of ROM address on present page pointed to by register-pair 0	−	1	2
Increment	IAC			A ⟵ A + 1	↕	1	1
	INC	R		R ⟵ R + 1	−	1	1
Decrement	DAC			A ⟵ A − 1	↕	1	1
Set carry	STC			C ⟵ 1	1	1	1
Clear carry	CLC			C ⟵ 0	0	1	1
Complement carry	CMC			C ⟵ $\bar{C}$	↕	1	1
Transmit carry and clear	TCC			A ⟵ 000C; C ⟵ 0	0	1	1
Transfer carry subtract	TCS			A ⟵ 10C$\bar{C}$; C ⟵ 0	0	1	1
Clear both	CLB			A ⟵ 0000; C ⟵ 0	0	1	1
Complement A	CMA			A ⟵ $\bar{A}$	−	1	1
Keyboard process	KBP			A ⟵ function of A (see text)	−	1	1

The keyboard process (KBP) instruction is useful for translating a one-out-of-four code into a binary number, as follows:

A (before)	A (after)
0000	0000
0001	0001
0010	0010
0100	0011
1000	0100
Anything else	1111

Figure A1-7. (*Continued*)

Operation	MNE	REG	OP	Description	Carry	Bytes	Cycles
Add	ADD	R		A ← A + R + C	↕	1	1
	ADM			A ← A + M + C	↕	1	1
Decimal adjust	DAA			Correct BCD addition	↕	1	1
Subtract	SUB	R		A ← A − R − C	↕	1	1
	SBM			A ← A − M − C	↕	1	1
Rotate all left	RAL			(C ← A rotate diagram)	↕	1	1
Rotate all right	RAR			(C → A rotate diagram)	↕	1	1
No operation	NOP			PC ← PC + 1	−	1	1
Jump unconditional	JUN		L	PC ← L (full address)	−	2	2
if C = 0	JCZ		L	PC ← L (same page) if C = 0	−	2	2
if C = 1	JCO		L	if C = 1	−	2	2
if A = 0	JAZ		L	if A = 0	−	2	2
if A ≠ 0	JAN		L	if A ≠ 0	−	2	2
if T = 0	JTZ		L	if T = 0	−	2	2
if T = 1	JTO		L	if T = 1	−	2	2
Jump indirect	JIN	P		PC ← Contents of register-pair P (on same page)	−	1	1
Increment R, jump if result = 0	ISZ	R	L	R ← R + 1; if result ≠ 0 then jump to L (on same page)	−	2	2
Jump to subroutine	JMS		L	Stack ← PC; PC ← L (full address)	−	2	2
Return from sub.	BBL		I	PC ← Stack; A ← I	−	1	1

R = register   = 0, 1, 2, 3, . . . , 15
P = register-pair = 0, 2, 4, 6, . . . , 14
I = 4 bits of immediate data
W = 8 bits of immediate data
L = address label representing an 8- or 12-bit address
M = selected main memory character (selected by pointer)

This is useful in encoding the output of a keyboard, where only one key is depressed at a time.

The decimal adjust (DAA) instruction looks for a 5-bit result of 10 or greater in the carry and accumulator. If such is not the case, the instruction changes nothing; otherwise 6 is added to the accumulator to obtain the BCD equivalent of this 5-bit binary number, leaving the carry bit set.

The conditional jump instructions depend directly upon the contents of the carry bit, the accumulator, and the external flag bit T. This last is defined negative-true, so that a low voltage on the $\overline{\text{TEST}}$ input pin on the CPU chip represents logic 1 while a high input represents logic 0.

In returning from a subroutine with a BBL (branch back and load) instruction, a variable cannot be passed back to the calling routine in the accumulator. The accumulator will be loaded with immediate data.

The circuitry of a 4004 microcomputer can use special prototyping chips to permit standard EPROMs to be used in place of the mask-

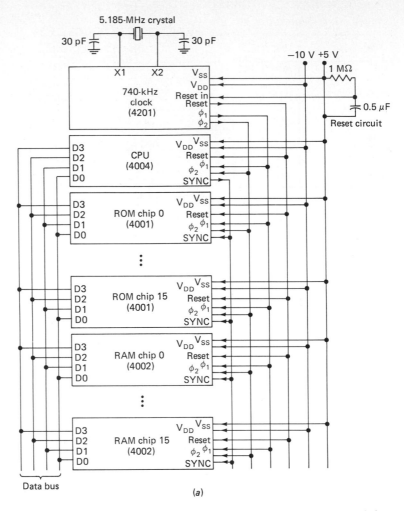

Figure A1-8. Intel 4004 microcomputer. (a) Power, reset, clock, and data bus connections; (b) chip selection and I/O lines.

programmed 4001 ROMs during instrument development. Thus, the board shown in Fig. 6-2 can be used for prototyping 4004-based instruments and includes up to four pages of EPROM (1024 eight-bit words), four RAM chips (320 four-bit words), five output ports (20 lines), and four input ports (16 lines).

The circuitry of a 4004 microcomputer is shown in Fig. A1-8. The two clock phases ϕ_1 and ϕ_2 are used by every chip. The SYNC output of the CPU chip is used to synchronize all ROM and RAM chips to the eight-clock-cycle period used to fetch and execute each byte of each instruction. The reset signal from the clock chip is just the output of a Schmitt trigger which

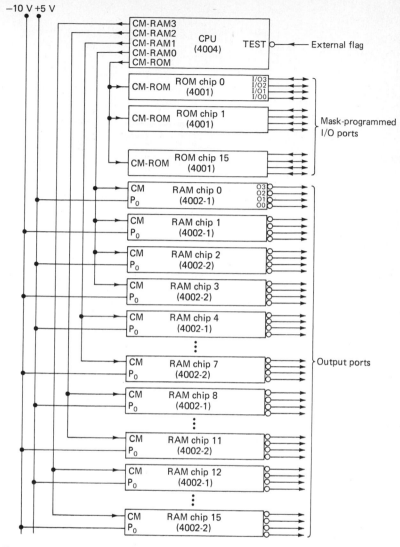

Figure A1-8. (Continued)   (b)

squares up the output of the RC time constant reset circuit shown. It automatically clears all flipflops in all chips. Consequently the CPU will look for its first instruction in ROM address 000 (hex).

The CPU transfers all addresses and data over the 4-bit data bus (D3, D2, D1, D0) to RAM, ROM, and I/O ports. The CPU's CM-ROM line goes to all ROM chips to distinguish them from RAM chips. As mentioned earlier, the chip number for each ROM chip is mask-programmed into the chip and requires no special external connections for page selection.

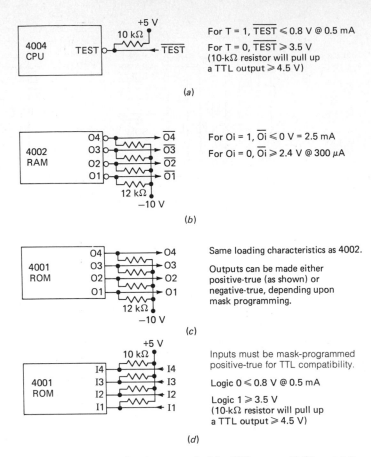

Figure A1-9. *External resistors needed for TTL compatibility.* (a) External flag input to the CPU; (b) RAM output port; (c) ROM output port; (d) ROM input port.

    In contrast, the RAM chips are selected in groups of four by the four lines CM-RAM0, CM-RAM1, CM-RAM2, and CM-RAM3 from the CPU chip. It is these lines which are handled by the designate command line (DCL) instruction discussed earlier. The 2-bit address for each chip in each group of four is implemented by having the most significant bit of the address mask-programmed (giving rise to a 4002-1 chip if that bit is a zero and a 4002-2 chip if that bit is a one). The least significant bit of the address is hard-wired by tying the P_0 input to either $+5$ V or -10 V, as shown in Fig. A1-8b. The result is an extremely compact microcomputer structure involving only 16-pin DIPs and having very regular wiring between the chips.

    For TTL compatibility, the I/O ports need the addition of the resistors shown in Fig. A1-9. For CMOS compatibility (with CMOS power equal to $+5$ V and 0 V), the resistors can be omitted from both input and output lines.

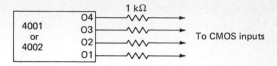

Figure A1-10. Protection resistors between output port and CMOS inputs.

However, outputs may drop below 0 V. To protect the CMOS inputs from
excessive current in this case of out-of-range input voltage, resistors can be
inserted, as shown in Fig. A1-10.

Intel's 4265 General Purpose Programmable I/O Device contains 16
positive-true I/O lines in a 28-pin DIP package. It is available mask-
programmed with either of two chip-select addresses; the 4265-2 can replace
any of the 4002-2 chips of Fig. A1-8 having address 2, 6, 10, or 14; the 4265-3

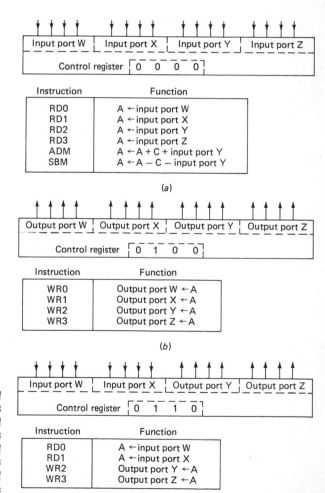

Figure A1-11. Use of the Intel
4265 as four I/O ports. (a) 16
(positive-true) input lines and
access instructions; (b) 16
(positive-true) output lines and
access instructions; (c) 8
(positive-true) input lines and
8 (positive-true) output lines
and access instructions.

can replace any of the 4002-2 chips of Fig. A1-8 having address 3, 7, 11, or 15. Then DCL and SRC instructions are used to set up a pointer to the chip just as if it were a RAM chip.

Because it contains only I/O ports, the normal instructions for interacting with the RAM addresses in the 4002 chip have been redefined for use when this chip is selected. The chip contains a 4-bit control register whose contents determine which one of 14 possible modes of operation will be used. The 4265 chip is initialized to the desired mode when power is turned on to the microcomputer by first setting up the CPU's pointer to this chip, loading the accumulator with the number to be transferred to the 4265's control register, and then executing a WMP instruction to transfer the accumulator contents to this control register. Three possible modes of operation are shown in Fig. A1-11 in which all four ports are configured as I/O ports. Each instruction shown transfers 4 bits of data between the accumulator and one of the I/O ports. In addition, when either port Y or Z, or both, is configured as an output port, it is possible to set or clear individual output lines on these ports by the following procedure:

1 Set up the pointer to select the desired 4265 chip (which takes the address of the 4002 RAM chip it replaces).
2 Load the accumulator, as shown in Fig. A1-12.
3 Execute a WRM instruction.

Figure A1-12. Bit-Manipulation Operations

Accumulator contents	Action which will occur when a WRM instruction is executed	
0 0 0 0	Clear	Bit 0 of output port Y
0 0 0 1	Set	
0 0 1 0	Clear	Bit 1 of output port Y
0 0 1 1	Set	
0 1 0 0	Clear	Bit 2 of output port Y
0 1 0 1	Set	
0 1 1 0	Clear	Bit 3 of output port Y
0 1 1 1	Set	
1 0 0 0	Clear	Bit 0 of output port Z
1 0 0 1	Set	
1 0 1 0	Clear	Bit 1 of output port Z
1 0 1 1	Set	
1 1 0 0	Clear	Bit 2 of output port Z
1 1 0 1	Set	
1 1 1 0	Clear	Bit 3 of output port Z
1 1 1 1	Set	

The 4265 offers a variety of other modes of operation, in addition to the three shown in Fig. A1-11. Unfortunately for applications in which handshaking is a requirement, as discussed in Sec. 5-1, none of these modes offers *automatic* handshaking. Instead, the handshaking inputs must be unpacked from one of the input ports and tested. The handshaking outputs can take advantage of the bit-manipulation operations of Fig. A1-12.

APPENDIX A2

FAIRCHILD F8

The description of the F8 register structure is facilitated by postponing a discussion of the pointer to memory (the data counter DC) and the CPU registers which interact with it (H and Q). In addition, while the CPU contains an array of 64 eight-bit scratchpad registers, some of these are dedicated to specific functions (that is, registers 9 through 15) and are designated by letter names (that is, J, H, K, and Q). The CPU registers can then be represented as in Fig. A2-1. These include an 8-bit accumulator (A), five internal flag flipflops (IE, O, Z, C, S) which together form the 5-bit status register (W), a temporary status storage register (J), nine 8-bit directly addressed scratchpad registers (0, . . . , 8) one of which (8) we will set aside to store a stack pointer, 48 eight-bit indirectly addressed scratchpad registers for which we will use *octal* addresses (20, . . . , 77) and which are accessed by means of the 6-bit pointer (the indirect scratchpad address register ISAR), a 16-bit program counter (PC0), and two other 16-bit registers (PC1 and K) used as temporary storage for the program-counter contents during subroutine calls and returns and during interrupts. Actually, while it is convenient to think of PC0 and PC1 as residing in the CPU, this is not really the case. Instead, they are duplicated in each chip containing ROM or interfacing to ROM, as discussed later in this appendix.

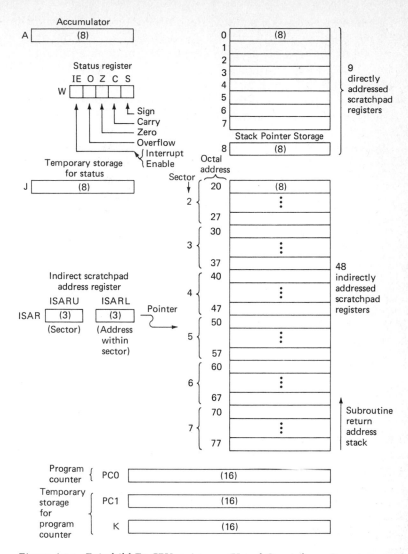

Figure A2-1. Fairchild F8 CPU registers. (H and Q not shown.)

Of the internal flags, the interrupt enable flipflop IE is set and cleared under program control using EI and DI instructions. It is automatically cleared when power is first turned on and when an interrupt occurs, disabling interrupts in either case until an EI instruction is subsequently executed. The overflow bit is set (cleared) by certain instructions to indicate that an operation on 2s-complement numbers (see Sec. 7-4) has (has not) overflowed. The zero bit Z is set (cleared) by certain instructions when the 8-bit result of an operation equals (does not equal) zero. The carry bit C is the normal carry resulting from arithmetic operations on 8-bit numbers.

The sign bit S is made equal to the complement of the most significant bit of the result of certain operations. (Note that this is just the opposite of the definition of the sign bit used by some other microcomputers.)

The F8 has an unusually extensive and powerful scratchpad register structure built into its CPU. It is sufficient to permit many instruments to be designed without requiring any additional RAM at all. In order to handle multibyte numbers and arrays within a loop structure, we need to be able to set up a pointer to the address of each operand and increment or decrement the pointer for successive passes through the loop. The 6-bit indirect scratchpad address register ISAR is used as this pointer. Its 3 upper bits, ISARU, designate a "sector" of the scratchpad. Each sector consists of the eight addresses designated by the 3 lower bits, ISARL. Because of this division of the scratchpad into 8-byte sectors, it is convenient to use octal addressing for the portion of the scratchpad which is accessed with indirect addressing.

To operate upon two multibyte numbers, as was done in the multibyte addition subroutine of Fig. 7-44, it is only necessary to align corresponding bytes so that they have the same ISARL addresses. The ISARU can be independently loaded to change the pointer from one number to the other, as illustrated in Fig. A2-2a. Furthermore, the F8 provides the three modes of indirect addressing listed in Fig. A2-2b so that the pointer can be automatically incremented or decremented, if desired, at the completion of an instruction. For example, Fig. A2-2c shows how the add instruction AS can use this facility to change the pointer. Note that only the lower bits, ISARL, of the pointer are affected by the increment or decrement operation.

While it is possible to use a separate counter to count iterations through a loop in order to determine when an operation on multibyte numbers is done, the F8 includes a test for ISARL = 7. Consequently, multibyte numbers should be aligned so that the bytes are accessed at successively increasing addresses within one sector and with the last byte located in address 6. Then, after the last byte is operated upon, ISARL will have been incremented to 7 and a test for this will terminate further iterations. This is illustrated in Fig. A2-2a for 3-byte numbers. Alternatively, the bytes can be accessed at successively decreasing addresses within one sector, with the last byte located in address 0, as in Fig. A2-2d. After the last byte has been operated upon, ISARL will have been decremented down through 0 and back to 7, and a test of this will terminate further iterations.

The F8 instruction set is given in Fig. A2-3 (except for those instructions involving the memory pointer DC, which will be discussed later). Immediate instructions have their operand designated as I(3), I(4), I(8), or I(16) to indicate the extent of the immediate data involved. For example, the instruction LISU is a 1-byte instruction in which 3 of the 8 bits of the instruction hold the 3-bit number to be loaded into ISARU.

As noted at the bottom of Fig. A2-3, the register which can be associated with some instructions is indicated with the generic label R. Thus

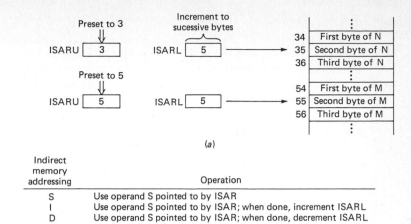

(a)

Indirect memory addressing	Operation
S	Use operand S pointed to by ISAR
I	Use operand S pointed to by ISAR; when done, increment ISARL
D	Use operand S pointed to by ISAR; when done, decrement ISARL

(b)

ADD	MNE	REG	OP	Comments
	AS	S		A ← A + S
	AS	I		A ← A + S; ISARL ← ISARL + 1
	AS	D		A ← A + S; ISARL ← ISARL − 1

where S is the scratchpad register pointed to by ISAR

(c)

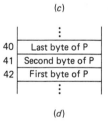

(d)

Figure A2-2. Use of ISAR, the indirect scratchpad address register. (a) Accessing corresponding bytes of two arrays; (b) three modes of indirect addressing; (c) examples of addition instruction using each mode of indirect addressing; (d) location of an array to take advantage of the test for ISARL = 7 to terminate iterations.

the add instruction AS can access any of the 9* directly addressed scratchpad registers 0, . . . , 8 as well as any of the 48† indirectly addressed scratchpad registers pointed to by ISAR and using the automatic increment or decrement facility discussed in conjunction with Fig. A2-2b.

The execution time of each instruction is given as a number of

* Actually, it can also directly access register J (which is register 9) as well as the upper and lower halves of H (10 and 11).
† Actually, ISAR can be used to access any of the 64 scratchpad registers.

Figure A2-3. Fairchild F8 Instruction Set

Operation	MNE	REG	OP	Description	Optional inc. or dec. of pointer (ISAR)	Bytes	Cycles	Flags O Z C S
Move pointer	LR	IS,A		ISAR ← A		1	1	– – – –
	LR	A,IS		A ← ISAR		1	1	– – – –
Load pointer, immediate	LISU		I(3)	ISARU ← I		1	1	– – – –
	LISL		I(3)	ISARL ← I		1	1	– – – –
Move	LR	A,R		A ← R	x	1	1	– – – –
	LR	R,A		R ← A	x	1	1	– – – –
Move, I/O ports	INS		I(4)	A ← Input Port I		1	2/4	0 ↔ 0 ↔
	IN		I(8)	A ← Input Port I		2	4	0 ↔ 0 ↔
	OUTS		I(4)	Output Port I ← A		1	2/4	– – – –
	OUT		I(8)	Output Port I ← A		2	4	– – – –
Load, immediate	LI		I(8)	A ← I		2	2.5	– – – –
	LIS		I(4)	A ← 0I (hex) (clear upper hex digit)		1	1	– – – –
Increment	INC			A ← A + 1		1	1	↔ ↔ ↔ ↔
Decrement	DS	R		R ← R − 1	x	1	1.5	↔ ↔ ↔ ↔
Clear	CLR			A ← 0		1	1	– – – –
Complement	COM			A ← $\overline{A}$		1	1	0 ↔ 0 ↔
Add carry	LNK			A ← A + C		1	1	↔ ↔ ↔ ↔
Add, binary	AS	R		A ← A + R	x	1	1	↔ ↔ ↔ ↔
	AI		I(8)	A ← A + I		2	2.5	↔ ↔ ↔ ↔
Add, decimal	ASD	R		A ← A + R (see text)	x	1	2	↔ ↔ ↔ ↔
AND	NS	R		A ← A AND R	x	1	1	0 ↔ 0 0
	NI		I(8)	A ← A AND I		2	2.5	0 ↔ 0 0
Exclusive-OR	XS	R		A ← A ⊕ R	x	1	1	0 ↔ 0 0
	XI		I(8)	A ← A ⊕ I		2	2.5	0 ↔ 0 0
OR (inclusive)	OI		I(8)	A ← A OR I		2	2.5	0 ↔ 0 0
Compare	CI		I(8)	$\overline{A}$ + I + 1 (A not changed)		2	2.5	↔ ↔ ↔ ↔

Description	Mnemonic	Operand	Operation	Bytes	Cycles				
Shift left one place	SL	1	(shift diagram: A → 0)	1	1	0	↕	0	↕
Shift left four places	SL	4		1	1	0	↕	0	↕
Shift right one place	SR	1		1	1	0	↕	0	1
Shift right four places	SR	4	$0 \rightarrow$	1	1	0	↕	0	1
Jump, unconditionally	JMP	I(16)	PC0 ← I	3	5.5	—	—	—	—
Branch relative, uncond.	BR	I(8)	PC0 ← PC0 + I	2	3.5	—	—	—	—
if carry	BC	I(8)	if C = 1	2	3.5	—	—	—	—
if no carry	BNC	I(8)	if C = 0	2	3.5	—	—	—	—
if zero	BZ	I(8)	if Z = 1	2	3.5	—	—	—	—
if not zero	BNZ	I(8)	if Z = 0	2	3.5	—	—	—	—
if plus	BP	I(8)	if S = 1	2	3.5	—	—	—	—
if minus	BM	I(8)	if S = 0	2	3.5	—	—	—	—
if no overflow	BNO	I(8)	if O = 0	2	3.5	—	—	—	—
if ISARL = 7	BR7	I(8)	if ISARL = 7	2	2.5	—	—	—	—
if true	BT	I(3),I(8)	if $I_2Z + I_1C + I_0S = 1$	2	3.5	—	—	—	—
if false	BF	I(4),I(8)	if $I_3O + I_2Z + I_1C + I_0S = 0$	2	3.5	—	—	—	—
Jump, indirect	LR	P0,Q	PC0 ← Q	1	4	—	—	—	—
Call to subroutine	PI	I(16)	PC1 ← PC0; PC0 ← I	3	6.5	—	—	—	—
Call to subroutine, indirect	PK		PC1 ← PC0; PC0 ← K	1	4	—	—	—	—
Return from subroutine	POP		PC0 ← PC1	1	2	—	—	—	—
Store top of stack	LR	K,P	K ← PC1	1	4	—	—	—	—
Move	LR	A,X	A ← X } where X =	1	1	—	—	—	—
	LR	X,A	X ← A } KU or KL	1	1	—	—	—	—
Load top of stack	LR	P,K	PC1 ← K	1	4	—	—	—	—
Disable interrupts	DI		IE ← 0	1	2	—	—	—	—
Enable interrupts	EI		IE ← 1	1	2	—	—	—	—
Store status register	LR	J,W	J ← W	1	1	—	—	—	—
Restore status register	LR	W,J	W ← J	1	2	↔	↔	↔	↔
No operation	NOP		PC0 ← PC0 + 1	1	1	—	—	—	—

R = 0,1,2,3,4,5,6,7,8,S,I,D

Direct address

Indirect address, pointed to by ISAR

"cycles." Depending upon the crystal-clock frequency used, each cycle can take anywhere between 2.0 and 40 μs. Since each "cycle" takes four clock periods, a 2.0-MHz crystal provides the 2.0-μs "cycle" time, permitting a one-cycle instruction like AS to be executed in 2.0 μs. The INS input instruction lists 2/4 cycles, with the 2 applying to input ports located on the CPU chip and the 4 applying to all other input ports.

An instruction can affect each flag flipflop in any one of four ways:

–	No effect
↕	Set or cleared, depending upon the result of the instruction
1	Set
0	Cleared

The effect upon the four flags which can be tested (O, Z, C, and S) is listed for each instruction in the right-hand column of Fig. A2-3.

Input and output instructions are available in two forms, IN and OUT on the one hand and INS and OUTS on the other. This permits microcomputer configurations having up to eight I/O ports to use the 1-byte INS and OUTS instructions using the circuit configuration to be discussed in conjunction with Fig. A2-7. Larger configurations can use the 2-byte IN and OUT instructions to access the remaining I/O ports.

The arithmetic instructions require some explanation. Arithmetic operations upon multibyte numbers are severely complicated because the instruction set has neither an add with carry instruction nor the ability to set the carry bit directly, as required by the algorithm of Fig. 2-11, which could otherwise be used to propagate carries between bytes. In their "Guide to Programming," Fairchild suggests a six-instruction sequence whose sole purpose is to solve this problem. However, this sequence involves the use of the J register, which also serves to provide temporary storage of the status register W during interrupts. Consequently use of the suggested approach complicates every interrupt service routine (or alternatively, requires the disabling and reenabling of interrupts before and after multibyte arithmetic operations). Rather than delve into the details of alternative solutions to this problem, we may perhaps assume that Fairchild will introduce an updated F8 CPU chip having an add with carry instruction.

The F8 does not include a subtract instruction. Therefore, it is necessary to carry out binary subtraction using the "complement and increment" algorithm discussed in Sec. 7-6.

BCD addition of multibyte numbers is carried out a byte (two digits) at a time using the following two-instruction sequence in place of the AS instruction required in a multibyte binary addition routine. First, the hexadecimal number 66 is added to one of the BCD bytes which has been moved to the accumulator. Then the BCD content of a scratchpad register is added to this using the decimal add instruction ASD:

ADD	MNE	REG	OP	Comments
	AI		H'66'	Always precedes ASD for BCD addition
	ASD	I		BCD add the scratchpad register pointed to by ISAR to the accumulator; increment ISARL

The F8 permits unconditional jumps to anywhere in memory using the 3-byte JMP instruction of Fig. A2-3. On the other hand, the 2-byte unconditional and conditional branch instructions use relative addressing to jump to any address up to 128 locations forward or 127 locations back from the address of the branch instruction's second byte. To do this, the second byte of a branch instruction is used as a 2s-complement number (see Sec. 7-4) and added to the contents of the program counter to form the new program-counter contents. Actually, we do not care how the address is formed, since we simply label the address to which the program should branch and the assembler will compute the proper offset, issuing a diagnostic-error message if the address is out of range.

Not only can the F8 test each of the internal flags C, Z, S, or O individually, but also it can test for combinations of these flags. Thus the branch on true instruction BT includes two items in its operand field. The first item is an octal number having a value of 0 to 7. The assembler interprets this as a 3-bit binary number $I_2I_1I_0$ and uses these bits to decide which of the internal flags to test, causing a branch to take place if

$$I_2Z + I_1C + I_0S = 1$$

For example, the instruction

$$BT \qquad 3,ALPHA$$

is interpreted by representing 3 as the 3-bit binary number 011. Thus this branch instruction will branch to the address labeled ALPHA if either C or S equals one. In similar fashion, the branch if false instruction

$$BF \qquad 3, ALPHA$$

will branch to ALPHA if C *and* S both equal *zero*.

Subroutine calls and returns are complicated in the F8 by the lack of a built-in stack pointer. For any subroutine SUB which will not itself call another subroutine (and which will not be disturbed by an interrupt) the instruction

$$PI \qquad SUB$$

will serve as a call to it, while

$$POP$$

will serve as a return from it. More generally, when we want to nest subroutines and also when we want to design an instrument which interacts with one or more devices under interrupt control, we can implement a stack structure either in the CPU's scratchpad registers or in RAM. An approach which can be used in conjunction with the scratchpad registers is illustrated in Fig. A2-4.

Because nested subroutines form such a fundamental tool for breaking down the complexity of the software of an instrument into manageable pieces, it would seem likely that an updated version of the F8 CPU chip will eventually become available in which a stack pointer is implemented in the scratchpad registers. The incentive to do this arises from the 74 μs it takes the F8 to execute a subroutine call which puts the return address on a stack and the 37 μs it takes to return from the subroutine. In contrast, the Intel 8080 and the Motorola 6800 with their automatic stack-handling capability require 13.5 and 14 μs, respectively, to execute both a call and a return.

The definition of an automatic stack-handling capability in the F8 is complicated somewhat because some users will want the stack itself located

ADD	MNE	REG	OP	Comments
	LI		63	A ⟵ address of highest scratchpad register
	LR	8,A		Stack pointer contents = Register 8 ⟵ A

(a)

ADD	MNE	REG	OP	Comments
	PI		SUB1	PC1 ⟵ PC0; PC0 ⟵ SUB1

(b)

ADD	MNE	REG	OP	Comments
SUB1	LR	K,P		K ⟵ PC1
	PI		CALL	PC1 ⟵ PC0; PC0 ⟵ CALL
	.			⎫
	.			⎬ instructions of SUB1 subroutine
	.			⎭
	JMP		RET	PC0 ⟵ RET

(c)

Figure A2-4. *Implementing a stack in the scratchpad registers of the F8. (a) Initialization of stack pointer at start-up; (b) to call a subroutine SUB1; (c) first two instructions of any subroutine are used to call the stack-handling routine CALL while the last instruction of any subroutine is a jump to the stack-handling routine RET; (d) subroutine CALL (12 bytes, 20 cycles); (e) routine RET (10 bytes, 13 cycles); (f) registers which cannot be used for parameter passing during subroutine calls and returns using this stack structure; (g) CPU scratchpad registers dedicated to this stack structure for subroutines nested n levels deep.*

ADD	MNE	REG	OP	Comments
CALL	DI			Disable interrupts and set aside K and PC1
	LR	A,8		A ⟵ stack pointer, SP (stored in Register 8)
	LR	IS,A		ISAR ⟵ A
	LR	A,KU		A ⟵ upper byte of K
	LR	D,A		Stack ⟵ A; decrement SP
	LR	A,KL		A ⟵ lower byte of K
	LR	K,P		K ⟵ PC1
	EI			Enable interrupts again
	LR	D,A		Stack ⟵ A; decrement SP
	LR	A,IS		Save ISAR (SP)
	LR	8,A		in Register 8
	PK			Return by PC0 ⟵ K

(d)

ADD	MNE	REG	OP	Comments
RET	LR	A,8		A ⟵ stack pointer (SP)
	LR	IS,A		ISAR ⟵ SP
	LR	A,I		Increment SP to top of stack
	LR	A,I		A ⟵ stack; increment SP
	LR	KL,A		KL ⟵ A
	LR	A,S		A ⟵ stack
	LR	KU,A		KU ⟵ A
	LR	A,IS		A ⟵ ISAR = SP
	LR	8,A		Register 8 ⟵ SP
	PK			PC0 ⟵ K

(e)

A
ISAR
K

(f)

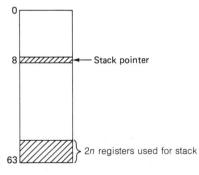

(g)

Figure A2-4. (Continued)

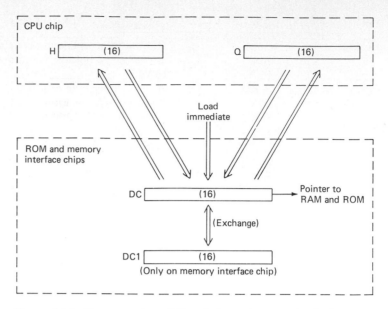

Figure A2-5. Memory pointer DC and the registers with which it can
transfer a full address.

in the scratchpad registers while others will want it in RAM. This could be
resolved by having two call instructions CALS and CALR, letting users who
want the stack to be located in the scratchpad registers use the former instruction while users who want the stack to be located in RAM would use
the latter instruction. In like manner, two return instructions RETS and
RETR could be implemented.

For accessing tables and arrays in ROM and for using F8 microcomputer configurations which include more RAM than is available in the
scratchpad registers, the F8 has the memory pointer* register DC, shown in
Fig. A2-5. This register is repeated in each chip containing mask-
programmed ROM and in the chip which interfaces to standard memory
chips, as will be discussed shortly. Consequently operations upon arrays
are expedited because each instruction accessing memory need not transfer
this pointer from the CPU chip to the desired memory chip.

The instructions which manipulate the DC memory pointer and which
use it to access memory are listed in Fig. A2-6. Typically, DC will be set up
to point to the beginning of an array using the 3-byte DCI instruction to load
it with the "immediate" address which is contained in the second and third
bytes of the instruction. Alternatively a variable address can be formed in
the H register in the CPU and then transferred from there to DC. Subsequent
to this, each of the instructions which access data with DC automatically in-

_____
* Called the data counter by Fairchild.

Figure A2-6. Instructions Used in Accessing Memory

Operation	MNE	REG	OP	Description	Bytes	Cycles	Flags O Z C S
Load DC, immediate	DCI		I(16)	DC ⟵ I	3	6	– – – –
Load H with a	LR	10,A		HU ⟵ A (load upper byte)	1	1	– – – –
variable address*	LR	11,A		HL ⟵ A (load lower byte)	1	1	– – – –
Move DC	LR	DC,Q		DC ⟵ Q	1	4	– – – –
	LR	DC,H		DC ⟵ H	1	4	– – – –
	LR	Q,DC		Q ⟵ DC	1	4	– – – –
	LR	H,DC		H ⟵ DC	1	4	– – – –
	XDC			DC ⇌ DC1	1	2	– – – –
	LR	A,Y		A ⟵ Y ⎱ where Y = QU or QL	1	1	– – – –
	LR	Y,A		Y ⟵ A ⎰	1	1	– – – –
Add to DC	ADC			DC ⟵ DC + A	1	2.5	– – – –
Move, memory	LM			A ⟵ M; Increment DC	1	2.5	– – – –
	ST			M ⟵ A; Increment DC	1	2.5	– – – –
Add, binary	AM			A ⟵ A + M; Increment DC	1	2.5	↕ ↕ ↕ ↕
Add, decimal	AMD			A ⟵ A + M; Increment DC	1	2.5	↕ ↕ ↕ ↕
				(similar to ASD)			
AND	NM			A ⟵ A AND M; Inc. DC	1	2.5	0 ↕ 0 ↕
Exclusive-OR	XM			A ⟵ A ⊕ M; Increment DC	1	2.5	0 ↕ 0 ↕
OR (inclusive)	OM			A ⟵ A OR M; Increment DC	1	2.5	0 ↕ 0 ↕
Compare	CM			A̅ + M + 1; Increment DC	1	2.5	↕ ↕ ↕ ↕
				(A not changed)			

M = indirect address, pointed to by DC.
* Since HU and HL are actually the directly addressable scratchpad registers 10 and 11, they can be manipulated by any of the instructions of Fig. A2-3 which involve the generic register label R (by substituting 10 or 11 for R).

crement DC (which is the rationale behind the name "data counter" given by Fairchild to this pointer). To facilitate operations upon two arrays, as when two multibyte numbers are added together, each pointer can be set aside and subsequently restored, using the H, Q, and DC1 registers shown in Fig. A2-5.

The compact circuit configuration of Fig. A2-7 provides one approach to the implementation of an F8 microcomputer. For it to be feasible, all RAM requirements must be met by the CPU scratchpad registers alone. While this configuration could use an RC circuit to set the clock rate, the crystal control shown permits full advantage to be taken of the built-in programmable timers. These provide for the generation of signals by the microcomputer with the proper timing characteristics needed by assorted I/O devices, as discussed in Sec. 3-9.

The CPU chip includes a power-on detect circuit, requiring no external circuitry, which clears the program counter PC0 and the interrupt enable flipflop IE when power is turned on. All other initialization is then carried out under program control. The CPU chip also includes an External Reset input, not shown in Fig. A2-7, which permits push-button control of the initialization process, at the discretion of a user.

The F8 microcomputer configuration of Fig. A2-7 consists solely of the

460

APPENDIX A2

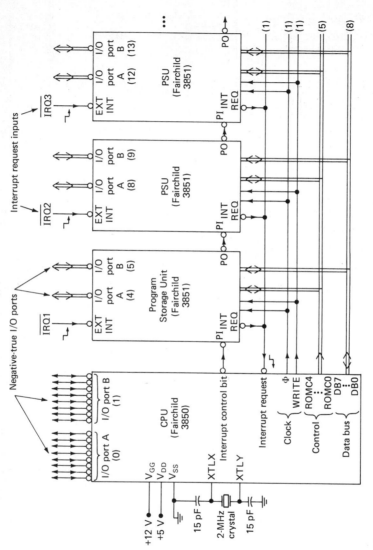

Figure A2-7. Fairchild F8 microcomputer configuration using mask-programmed chips.

CPU chip plus as many Program Storage Units (PSUs) as are needed to handle ROM and I/O requirements.   Each Program Storage Unit chip includes:

1   A 1024 × 8 ROM for program storage
2   Two 8-bit I/O ports
3   An external interrupt line
4   A programmable timer (discussed in Sec. 3-9)
5   Registers PC0, PC1, and DC

It is specified by the following mask-programmed information:

1   The contents of the 1024 × 8 ROM.
2   A 6-bit chip select code which, together with the 10-bit address input to the chip, form full 16-bit addresses for each memory location on the chip.
3   A 6-bit I/O port select code which can be distinct from the chip select code.   This specifies the addresses of the two I/O ports on each PSU as well as the address of an interrupt control register and a programmable timer.   The relationship between the I/O port select code and the addresses of these registers is shown in Fig. A2-8.   Note that no PSU chip should be assigned I/O port select code = 0, since the corresponding addresses are reserved for the I/O ports on the CPU chip.
4   A 16-bit interrupt address vector having a zero in bit 7.   When the programmable timer generates an interrupt,* the CPU will execute the equivalent of a PI, call to subroutine, instruction to this address.   When the external interrupt line generates an interrupt,* the CPU will execute the equivalent of a PI instruction to this address plus 128 (corresponding to having a one in bit 7).
5   A specification of one of three alternative I/O configurations.   The standard pull-up configuration provides the same I/O port specifications as for those on the CPU chip.   The output characteristics are shown in Fig. 3-10.   For use as an input port, the output latches must first be cleared by clearing the accumulator and then executing an OUTS or OUT instruction to this port (making the negative-true output lines go high).   This provides an input which is internally pulled up, providing good TTL compatibility.   A device driving this input low must override this pull-up, requiring a maximum of 1.6 mA at 0.4 V, the same as a standard TTL input.

The interrupt control register in each PSU chip is used to select whether the programmable timer or the external interrupt line is to be enabled.   This selection is made by loading the accumulator with a 0, 1, or 3

---

* Which requires that the interrupt enable flipflop in the CPU be set.

Figure A2-8. Port Select Codes and the Addresses They Specify

PSU I/O port select code (mask-programmed)	"I/O port" address	Chip type	Meaning of port address	Accessed by one-byte instructions	Accessed by two-byte instructions
(Reserved for CPU)	0	CPU	I/O port A	INS 0 OUTS 0	
	1		I/O port B	INS 1 OUTS 1	
1	4	PSU	I/O port A	INS 4 OUTS 4	
	5		I/O port B	INS 5 OUTS 5	
	6		Interrupt control	OUTS 6	
	7		Programmable timer	OUTS 7	
2	8	PSU	I/O port A	INS 8 OUTS 8	
	9		I/O port B	INS 9 OUTS 9	
	10		Interrupt control	OUTS 10	
	11		Programmable timer	OUTS 11	
3	12	PSU	I/O port A	INS 12 OUTS 12	
	13		I/O port B	INS 13 OUTS 13	
	14		Interrupt control	OUTS 14	
	15		Programmable timer	OUTS 15	
4	16	PSU	I/O port A		IN 16 OUT 16
	17		I/O port B		IN 17 OUT 17
	18		Interrupt control		OUT 18
	19		Programmable timer		OUT 19
			. . .		
63	252	PSU	I/O port A		IN 252 OUT 252
	253		I/O port B		IN 253 OUT 253
	254		Interrupt control		OUT 254
	255		Programmable timer		OUT 255

Figure A2-9. Meaning of Interrupt Control Register Contents in the PSU and SMI Chips

Interrupt control register contents	Meaning for this chip
0	Disable interrupts
1	Enable external interrupts
3	Enable programmable timer interrupts

and then executing an OUTS or OUT instruction to the address of the interrupt control register. The possibilities are listed in Fig. A2-9.

The interrupt structure of the F8 is both powerful and flexible. A negative-going edge on any of the external interrupt inputs ($\overline{IRQ1}$, $\overline{IRQ2}$, etc.) shown in Fig. A2-7 will cause a negative-going edge on the Interrupt Request input to the CPU chip if:

1   The PSU chip receiving this external interrupt input has its interrupt control register contents set equal to 1 to enable external interrupts, and if
2   The CPU's interrupt enable flipflop is set, and if
3   No PSU located closer to the CPU chip in the "priority daisy chain" is simultaneously trying to interrupt. This daisy chain is defined by the $\overline{PI}$ (priority in) and $\overline{PO}$ (priority out) connections shown in Fig. A2-7.

The CPU will then

1   Execute the equivalent of a PI, call to subroutine, instruction using the interrupt address vector, plus 128, which is mask-programmed into the PSU chip.
2   Clear its interrupt enable flipflop, disabling further interrupts. Interrupts can be enabled again under program control at the end of the interrupt service routine. In order to permit the reenabling of interrupts and yet at the same time get back to the interrupted routine before a PSU waiting to interrupt is permitted to do so, the F8 does not acknowledge interrupts after any of the following instructions: EI, PK, PI, POP, JMP, OUT, OUTS, and LR W,J.

In order to add flexibility to the structure of Fig. A2-7, Fairchild has two other chips which we will discuss. The Fairchild 3861 Peripheral I/O (PIO) chip looks essentially like a 3851 Program Storage Unit without Rom. The other mask-programmed options are available in a limited number of alternatives in the 3861. This chip permits the expansion of I/O ports, interrupt inputs, and programmable timers. It also makes these capabilities

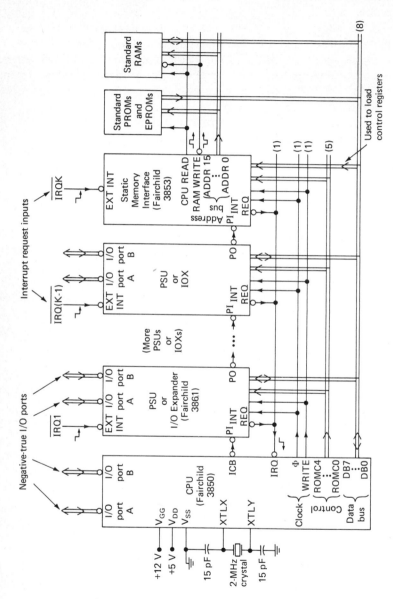

Figure A2-10. Flexible Fairchild F8 microcomputer configuration.

available as standard parts, with no mask-programming charges imposed upon the designer.

The Fairchild 3853 Static Memory Interface (SMI) chip establishes the conventional address bus/data bus structure discussed in Sec. 3-4 for the F8 microcomputer. While this is certainly necessary when the RAM requirements exceed the RAM requirements of the CPU, it is also desirable for prototyping microcomputer configurations which will eventually end up using only the CPU chip and PSU chips. In addition, it permits an F8 microcomputer to take advantage of standard devices having good features (for example, EPROMs and I/O ports having automatic handshaking capability).

The Static Memory Interface chip includes:

1   Address, read, and write lines which, together with the CPU's data bus, make up the address bus/data bus structure
2   An external interrupt line and a programmable vectored interrupt address
3   A programmable timer
4   Registers PC0, PC1, DC, and DC1

So as to be an off-the-shelf device, the internal registers used for initializing the operation of the SMI chip are assigned fixed "I/O port" addresses and loaded using OUTS instructions. Thus the microcomputer configuration of Fig. A2-10 has six of its I/O port addresses preassigned by Fairchild for use by the CPU chip and the SMI chip. These are shown in Fig. A2-11. The remaining I/O port addresses are assigned as in Fig. A2-8, subject to the constraint that the I/O port select code of 3 cannot be used, since this would conflict with the SMI chip.

Figure A2-11. Preassigned I/O Port Addresses for the Microcomputer Configuration of Fig. A2-10

"I/O port" address	Chip type	Meaning of port address	Accessed by 1-byte instructions
0		I/O port A	INS 0
			OUTS 0
	CPU		
1		I/O port B	INS 1
			OUTS 1
12		Interrupt vector, upper byte	OUTS 12
13		Interrupt vector, lower byte	OUTS 13
	SMI		
14		Interrupt control	OUTS 14
15		Programmable timer	OUTS 15

The interrupt control register contents of the SMI chip are defined identically to those for the PSU chip, listed in Fig. A2-9. The programmable timer has been described in Sec. 3-9. Because the number loaded into the programmable timer does not relate in a simple way to the time until it will produce an interrupt, the F8 assembly language includes an operand representation to handle this problem. With the maximum clock rate (set with a 2.0-MHz crystal), the timer counts every 15.5 μs. The operand representation T'100' will be converted by the assembler into the 8-bit number which must be loaded into the programmable timer in order to generate an interrupt after

$$100 \times 15.5 = 1550 \ \mu s = 1.55 \ ms$$

The largest time duration available corresponds to T'254' and is just under 4 ms. Larger time intervals are obtained by counting a specific number of interrupts, as discussed in Sec. 3-9. As an example of the manner in which a 1.55-ms time interval would be initiated by the programmable timer in the SMI chip of the F8 configuration of Fig. A2-10, the following sequence could be used:

ADD	MNE	REG	OP	Comments
	LI		T'100'	A ⟵ 100 × 15.5 μs
	OUTS		15	Set timer
	LI		3	⎫ Enable timer interrupt
	OUTS		14	⎭

The programmable timer can be turned off by loading it with FF (hex):

ADD	MNE	REG	OP	Comments
	LI		H'FF'	A ⟵ FF (hex)
	OUTS		15	Turn off timer

Alternatively, it can be turned off by disabling it.

When the programmable timer generates its interrupt, the F8 will jump to the service routine whose address has been previously loaded into the interrupt vector register, addressed as in Fig. A2-11. As discussed previously, bit 7 of this address must equal zero. Other than this, the address is arbitrary.

Neither the F8 configuration of Fig. A2-7 nor that of Fig. A2-10 included bidirectional bus driver circuitry. However, for large configurations which might otherwise present loading problems, the F8 chips include the necessary outputs (not shown in either figure) to control this circuitry.

APPENDIX A3

INTEL 8080

As shown in Fig. A3-1, the Intel® 8080 CPU has one 8-bit accumulator (A), six 8-bit scratchpad registers (B, C, D, E, H, L), five internal flag flipflops (S, Z, P, C, AC) which form the contents of a flag register, a 16-bit program counter (PC), a 16-bit stack pointer (SP), and an interrupt enable flipflop (IE). Of the internal flags, the sign bit S is set by certain instructions when the most significant bit of the result of an operation equals one. It is cleared if it equals zero. C is the normal carry bit, while AC is an auxiliary carry used with BCD operations, as discussed in Sec. 7-6. The zero bit Z is set (cleared) by certain instructions when the 8-bit result of an operation equals (does not equal) zero. The parity bit P is set (cleared) if the 8-bit result of an operation includes an even (odd) number of ones. The interrupt enable flipflop IE is set and cleared under program control using EI and DI instructions. It is automatically cleared when the CPU is reset and when an interrupt occurs, disabling further interrupts until IE = 1 again.

The H and L registers serve as the high and low bytes of a full 16-bit pointer to memory. The contents of this memory address, designated M, can be used as an operand for many instructions.

Many instructions involve the CPU register-pairs shown in Fig. A3-2 and designated PSW, B, D, and H. PSW, the processor status word, designates the accumulator A and the flag register.

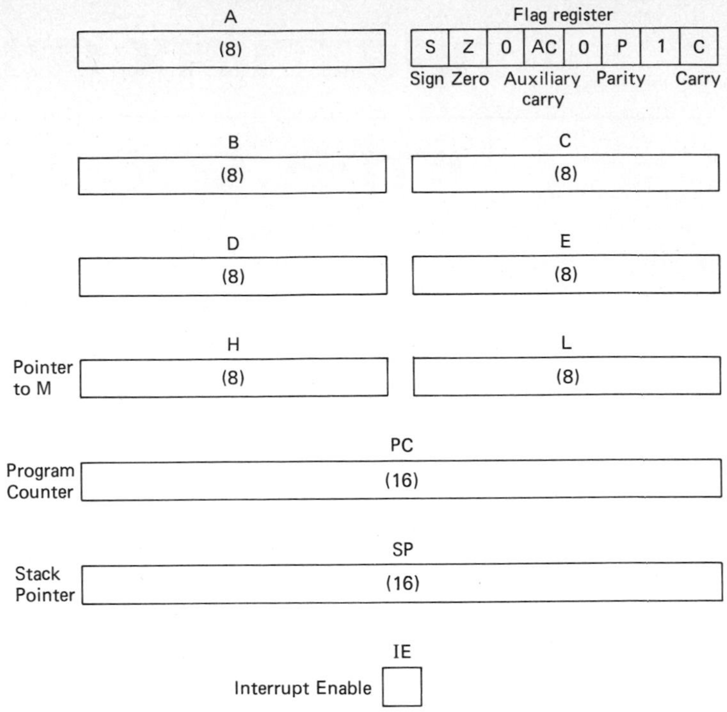

A
(8)

Flag register

| S | Z | 0 | AC | 0 | P | 1 | C |

Sign Zero Auxiliary Parity   Carry
carry

B
(8)

C
(8)

D
(8)

E
(8)

Pointer
to M

H
(8)

L
(8)

PC

Program
Counter

(16)

SP

Stack
Pointer

(16)

IE

Interrupt Enable

Figure A3-1. Intel 8080 CPU registers.

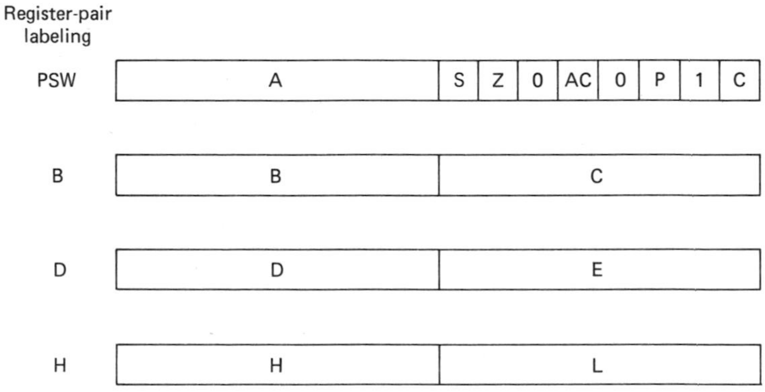

Register-pair
labeling

PSW | A | S | Z | 0 | AC | 0 | P | 1 | C |

B | B | C |

D | D | E |

H | H | L |

Figure A3-2. CPU register-pairs.

The 8080 instruction set is given in Fig. A3-3. The registers or register-pairs which can be associated with specific instructions are indicated with generic labels. Thus the single-byte source of an operand used by an instruction is labeled S, but the actual register name used by the instruction is A, B, C, D, E, H, L, or M. The generic label D stands for the destination register which is to be loaded with the result of the operation. As

shown at the bottom of Fig. A3-3, D stands for any one of these same registers A, B, C, D, E, H, L, or M. In like manner, X stands for any of the three
register-pairs B (that is, registers B and C), D, or H or for the stack pointer SP.
Immediate instructions have operands labeled I for a single-byte operand
and W for a double-byte operand. The latter are 3-byte instructions having
the form

Operation code	(first byte of instruction)
W.L	(second byte of instruction)
W.H	(third byte of instruction)

where W.L and W.H stand for the lower and upper bytes of W, respectively.

The execution time of each instruction is given as a number of clock
cycles. The 8080's clock can operate with any clock period between 0.5 and
2.0 μs. Operating at the maximum clock rate, the 8080 will execute the
STAX instruction in $0.5 \times 7 = 3.5 \mu$s. Some instructions, such as MOV, list
two numbers, 5(7). The 5 applies as long as the registers selected are CPU
registers. The 7 applies if the selected register is M. Thus in this case, accessing RAM or ROM requires two extra clock cycles.

Conditional subroutine calls and returns list two execution times (for
example, 11,17 cycles for a conditional subroutine call). The shorter time
applies if the test fails and the call or return does not take place.

An instruction can affect each flag flipflop in any one of four ways:

—	No effect
↕	Set or cleared, depending upon the result of the instruction
1	Set
0	Cleared

The effect upon the four flags which can be tested (that is, C, Z, S, P) is listed
for each instruction in the right-hand column of Fig. A3-3.

The 8080 uses a stack, located in RAM, to handle subroutine return addresses automatically during subroutine call and return instructions.
During an interrupt, any of the CPU register-pairs desired can be set aside
onto the stack with a PUSH instruction and subsequently restored with a
POP instruction. In fact, any time data must be temporarily set aside to free
up a CPU register, a PUSH instruction provides a 1-byte instruction for
doing this.

In preparing the software for an instrument, enough words in RAM
must be set aside for use by the stack so that when data or return addresses
are pushed onto the stack, this data does not write over other data stored in
RAM. Since the 8080 *decrements* the stack pointer as it pushes successive
words onto the stack, the stack pointer must be initialized, when power is
turned on, to the *highest* address set aside for the stack. This can be done
with an LXI SP instruction, to load this address as immediate data into the
stack pointer.

When 2 bytes of data are pushed from two CPU scratchpad registers

Figure A3-3. Intel 8080 Instruction Set

Operation	MNE	REG	OP	Description	Bytes	Cycles	Flags C Z S P
Move	MOV	D,S		D ⟵ S	1	5(7)	— — — —
	STAX	Z		M(Z) ⟵ A	1	7	— — — —
	LDAX	Z		A ⟵ M(Z)	1	7	— — — —
	STA		W	M(W) ⟵ A	3	13	— — — —
	LDA		W	A ⟵ M(W)	3	13	— — — —
	IN		I	A ⟵ Device I	2	10	— — — —
	OUT		I	Device I ⟵ A	2	10	— — — —
Move, register-pair	PUSH	Y		Stack ⟵ Y	1	11	— — — —
	POP	Y		Y ⟵ Stack	1	10	(PSW)
	SHLD		W	M(W + 1,W) ⟵ HL	3	16	— — — —
	LHLD		W	HL ⟵ M(W + 1,W)	3	16	— — — —
	SPHL			SP ⟵ HL	1	5	— — — —
	PCHL			PC ⟵ HL	1	5	— — — —
Exchange, reg. -pair	XCHG			HL ⟷ DE	1	4	— — — —
	XTHL			Stack ⟷ HL	1	18	— — — —
Move, immediate	MVI	D	I	D ⟵ I	2	7(10)	— — — —
	LXI	X	W	X ⟵ W	3	10	— — — —
Increment	INR	D		D ⟵ D + 1	1	5(10)	— ↕ ↕ ↕
	INX	X		X ⟵ X + 1	1	5	— — — —
Decrement	DCR	D		D ⟵ D − 1	1	5(10)	— ↕ ↕ ↕
	DCX	X		X ⟵ X − 1	1	5	— — — —
Set carry	STC			C ⟵ 1	1	5	1 — — —
Complement carry	CMC			C ⟵ C̄	1	4	↕ — — —
Complement A	CMA			A ⟵ Ā	1	4	— — — —
Add	ADD	S		A ⟵ A + S	1	4(7)	↕ ↕ ↕ ↕
	ADI		I	A ⟵ A + I	2	7	↕ ↕ ↕ ↕
Double add	DAD	X		HL ⟵ HL + X	1	10	↕ — — —
Add with carry	ADC	S		A ⟵ A + S + C	1	4(7)	↕ ↕ ↕ ↕
	ACI		I	A ⟵ A + I + C	2	7	↕ ↕ ↕ ↕
Decimal adjust	DAA			Correct BCD addition	1	4	↕ ↕ ↕ ↕
Subtract	SUB	S		A ⟵ A − S	1	4(7)	↕ ↕ ↕ ↕
	SUI		I	A ⟵ A − I	2	7	↕ ↕ ↕ ↕
Subtract with borrow	SBB	S		A ⟵ A − S − C	1	4(7)	↕ ↕ ↕ ↕
	SBI		I	A ⟵ A − I − C	2	7	↕ ↕ ↕ ↕
AND	ANA	S		A ⟵ A AND S	1	4(7)	0 ↕ ↕ ↕
	ANI		I	A ⟵ A AND I	2	7	0 ↕ ↕ ↕
Exclusive-OR	XRA	S		A ⟵ A ⊕ S	1	4(7)	0 ↕ ↕ ↕
	XRI		I	A ⟵ A ⊕ I	2	7	0 ↕ ↕ ↕
OR (inclusive)	ORA	S		A ⟵ A OR S	1	4(7)	0 ↕ ↕ ↕
	ORI		I	A ⟵ A OR I	2	7	0 ↕ ↕ ↕
Compare	CMP	S		A-S (A not changed)	1	4(7)	↕ ↕ ↕ ↕
	CPI		I	A-I (A not changed)	2	7	↕ ↕ ↕ ↕
Rotate left into carry	RLC				1	4	↕ — — —
Rotate right into carry	RRC				1	4	↕ — — —
Rotate all left	RAL				1	4	↕ — — —
Rotate all right	RAR				1	4	↕ — — —
Enable interrupts	EI			Set IE flipflop	1	4	— — — —
Disable interrupts	DI			Clear IE flipflop	1	4	— — — —
Halt	HLT			Stop	1	7	— — — —

Figure A3-3. (*Continued*)

Operation	MNE	REG	OP	Description	Bytes	Cycles	Flags C Z S P
Jump unconditionally	JMP		W	PC ⟵ W	3	10	– – – –
if carry	JC		W	if C = 1	3	10	– – – –
if no carry	JNC		W	if C = 0	3	10	– – – –
if zero	JZ		W	if Z = 1	3	10	– – – –
if not zero	JNZ		W	if Z = 0	3	10	– – – –
if minus	JM		W	if S = 1	3	10	– – – –
if plus	JP		W	if S = 0	3	10	– – – –
if parity even	JPE		W	if P = 1	3	10	– – – –
if parity odd	JPO		W	if P = 0	3	10	– – – –
Call subroutine	CALL		W	Stack ⟵ PC; PC ⟵ W	3	17	– – – –
	RST		N	(see text)	1	11	– – – –
if carry	CC		W	if C = 1	3	11,17	– – – –
if no carry	CNC		W	if C = 0	3	11,17	– – – –
if zero	CZ		W	if Z = 1	3	11,17	– – – –
if not zero	CNZ		W	if Z = 0	3	11,17	– – – –
if minus	CM		W	if S = 1	3	11,17	– – – –
if plus	CP		W	if S = 0	3	11,17	– – – –
if parity even	CPE		W	if P = 1	3	11,17	– – – –
if parity odd	CPO		W	if P = 0	3	11,17	– – – –
Subroutine return	RET			PC ⟵ Stack	1	10	– – – –
if carry	RC			if C = 1	1	5,11	– – – –
if no carry	RNC			if C = 0	1	5,11	– – – –
if zero	RZ			if Z = 1	1	5,11	– – – –
if not zero	RNZ			if Z = 0	1	5,11	– – – –
if minus	RM			if S = 1	1	5,11	– – – –
if plus	RP			if S = 0	1	5,11	– – – –
if parity even	RPE			if P = 1	1	5,11	– – – –
if parity odd	RPO			if P = 0	1	5,11	– – – –

Registers: D or S = A,B,C,D,E,H,L,M
Register-pairs: X = B,D,H,SP   Y = B,D,H,PSW   Z = B,D

onto the stack, the high-order byte goes on first and then the low-order byte. Also, the stack pointer is decremented *before* each data transfer. Consequently, the stack pointer always points to the last byte of data entered onto the stack, and not to the address into which the next byte is to go. This is useful to know if data within the stack is to be accessed in the following way. First, the HL register-pair is preset to the depth of the byte to be accessed within the stack. For example, it is preset to zero to access the byte on top of the stack, one to access the next byte, and so forth. Then the content of the stack pointer is added to the content of the HL register-pair using a DAD SP instruction. M, the address pointed to by H and L, is then the desired byte in the stack.

In addition to the 3-byte unconditional and conditional call subroutine instructions, the 8080 includes a 1-byte RST (restart) instruction which requires an operand, N, set to one of the eight values 0, . . . , 7. In response to this instruction, the CPU will execute an unconditional subroutine call to one of the following eight hex addresses on page zero: 00, 08, 10, 18, 20, 28, 30, or 38.

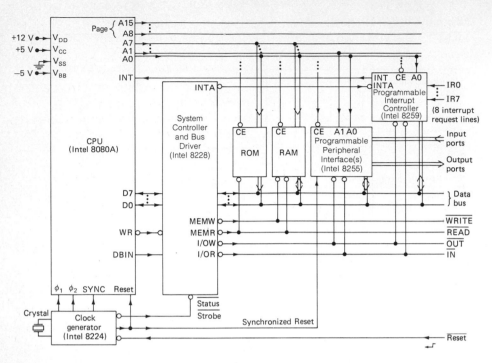

Figure A3-4. *Intel 8080 microcomputer configuration.*

The circuitry of an 8080 microcomputer is shown in Fig. A3-4 including CPU chip, clock chip, a system controller chip, an interrupt chip, RAM, ROM, and I/O. The system controller chip derives memory and I/O read and write pulses from a status word emitted by the CPU on the data bus when a Status Strobe timing pulse from the clock chip occurs. The timing of these read and write pulses is determined by DBIN and $\overline{\text{WR}}$, respectively. The configuration of Fig. A3-4 does not show the DMA control lines. However, it does show the $\overline{\text{Reset}}$ input, which is synchronized to the clock in the clock chip. Resetting the CPU at start-up forces address 00 00 into the program counter, and continues to do so until $\overline{\text{Reset}}$ goes high again. In addition, the Interrupt Enable flipflop is cleared, disabling interrupts initially. The other CPU registers are not cleared.

Page selection is facilitated by having IN and OUT instructions which are distinct from memory reference instructions. The second byte of an IN or OUT instruction is treated as immediate data, giving an 8-bit device address. This address is put out by the CPU as both a page (A15, . . . , A8 address lines) and as an address within a page (A7, . . . , A0 address lines), permitting the number of devices which can be driven without buffers to be larger than it otherwise would be. Because only an IN (OUT) instruction will cause the $\overline{\text{IN}}$ ($\overline{\text{OUT}}$) line to be pulsed, the addresses used for I/O chips can coincide with memory addresses without causing any ambiguity. Consequently, one Programmable Interrupt Controller (PIC) and five Programmable Peripheral Interfaces (PPI), each of which has a single Chip Enable ($\overline{\text{CE}}$) input, can be decoded without special decoding circuitry if the addresses shown in Fig. A3-5 are used. Each Programmable Peripheral Interface requires four addresses to access its internal registers while the Programmable Interrupt Controller requires two addresses. This internal register addressing is handled with address lines A0 and A1, as shown in Fig. A3-4.

The Programmable Interrupt Controller (Intel 8259), shown in Fig. A3-4, permits up to eight devices to interrupt the CPU, each with its own interrupt request line. It can be expanded to handle up to 64 devices by interconnecting up to nine chips (one master and eight slaves). It is designed to be used with the 8080A CPU chip. If instead, the original 8080 chip is used, then each interrupt service routine must include instructions to increment its return address twice.

When power is turned on, the Programmable Interrupt Controller can be initialized into any of several modes of operation. For example, the "fully nested priority mode" is set up (for eight or fewer inputs) by transferring two successive bytes of setup data from the accumulator to the PIC with two OUT instructions to device FB (assuming the device-selection scheme of Fig. A3-5, and making address line A0 equal to one). This provides 16 bits of setup data which are shifted into the PIC, 8 bits at a time. Not only do these 16 bits of setup data select the fully nested priority mode of operation, they can also select an arbitrary page which will be used to hold the entry addresses for the service routines to be called by each interrupt request line. Then if interrupts are enabled, a rising edge on interrupt request line IR0 will cause a subroutine call to be executed to address 00 on the selected page. The remaining seven interrupt request lines, IR1, . . . , IR7, can be set up to vector to addresses 04, 08, 0C, 10, 14, 18, and 1C on the selected page. The four words of ROM allotted to each interrupt request line are enough to

Figure A3-5. Intel 8080 I/O Device Selection

Device	A7	A6	A5	A4	A3	A2	A1	A0	Hex addresses	$\overline{\text{CE}}$ tied to
				Binary addresses						
PIC	1	1	1	1	1	0	1	x	FA, FB	A2
PPI 1	1	1	1	1	0	1	x	x	F4, F5, F6, F7	A3
PPI 2	1	1	1	0	1	1	x	x	EC, ED, EE, EF	A4
PPI 3	1	1	0	1	1	1	x	x	DC, DD, DE, DF	A5
PPI 4	1	0	1	1	1	1	x	x	BC, BD, BE, BF	A6
PPI 5	0	1	1	1	1	1	x	x	7C, 7D, 7E, 7F	A7

hold a JMP instruction to the remainder of the service routine, which can thus reside anywhere in ROM.

When an interrupt occurs, the Programmable Interrupt Controller makes the interrupt (INT) line to the CPU go high. If interrupts are enabled, the CPU will respond at the end of the present instruction cycle by disabling further interrupts. During the next instruction cycle, the CPU causes the Interrupt Acknowledge ($\overline{\text{INTA}}$) line to go low. The PIC responds to $\overline{\text{INTA}}$ by automatically clearing the one flipflop out of eight which was set by a rising edge on an interrupt request line and which caused the interrupt request to the CPU. The PIC also places the first byte of a CALL instruction on the data bus, followed in the next two fetch cycles by the full address of the appropriate service routine.

If, during execution of the interrupt service routine for a particular device, higher-priority interrupts are to be reenabled, the accumulator can be loaded with a word which will disable this and lower-priority interrupt lines. Then an OUT instruction can be executed to address FA (making address line A0 equal to zero) to transfer this word into a Request Latch Mask Register in the PIC. An enable interrupt (EI) instruction is now executed. If another interrupt occurs, the service routine for the interrupting device can read the contents of the Request Latch Mask Register into the CPU with an IN instruction to address FA and push this mask onto the stack. At the end of the service routine the mask can be restored to the PIC so that the interrupt service routine which was interrupted will pick up again with the same mask that it had when it was interrupted.

Intel's general I/O port chip, their Programmable Peripheral Interface (PPI), has the general structure shown in Fig. A3-6. The Reset input makes all ports look like input ports when power is first turned on. The two least significant address bits A1 and A0 are used to address one of four registers internal to the selected PPI, as shown in Fig. A3-7a. Each I/O port can be set up under program control to be either an input port or an output port. In addition, each half of port C can be set up for either input or output. To set up all 24 lines as three general-purpose I/O ports, the accumulator is loaded with the word shown in Fig. A3-7b, and then an OUT instruction is executed, addressing the Mode Control register (A1 A0 = 1 1). For example, to set up all ports of the PPI selected with the A7 address line as output ports, first

$$A \leftarrow 10000000$$

Then an OUT instruction is executed to device

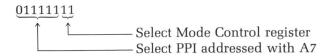

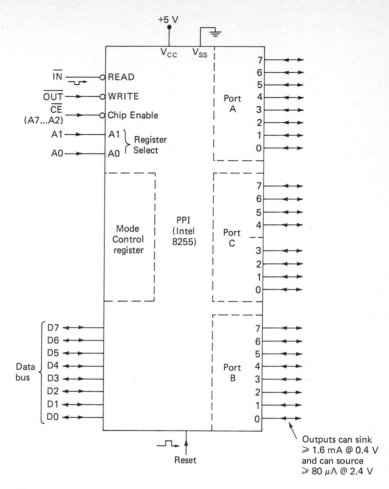

Figure A3-6. *Intel 8255, Programmable Peripheral Interface.*

Subsequent to this, an OUT instruction to device

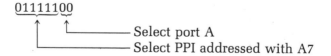

will load the contents of the accumulator into output port A of this PPI.

In addition to being able to transfer data between the accumulator and port C (using address A1 A0 = 1 0), those lines of port C which have been set up as outputs can be individually set and cleared, as shown in Fig. A3-7c. For example, to set bit six of port C of the PPI selected with the A7 address line (previously set up as an output line), first

A1	A0	Addressed register	
0	0	I/O port A	(read or write)
0	1	I/O port B	(read or write)
1	0	I/O port C	(read or write)
1	1	{ Mode Control { Output port C bit set/reset	(write only) (write only)

(a)

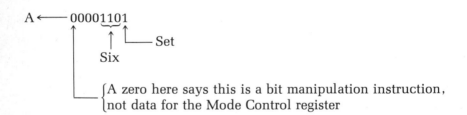

Figure A3-7. *Control of Programmable Peripheral Interface. (a) Addressing of PPI registers; (b) word to be written into Mode Control register to set up three I/O ports (addressed with A1 A0 = 1 1); (c) output word format used for setting or resetting an individual output line of port C (addressed with A1 A0 = 1 1).*

(b)

(c)

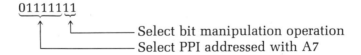

A zero here says this is a bit manipulation instruction, not data for the Mode Control register

Then an OUT instruction is executed to device

01111111

Select bit manipulation operation
Select PPI addressed with A7

The Programmable Peripheral Interface can also be set up so that some of the lines of port C provide automatic handshaking with the devices transferring data to or from ports A and B, as discussed in Sec. 5-1, for either flag control or interrupt control. Both ports A and B can be set up as input ports, with the handshaking lines shown in Fig. A3-8a. For example, to set up the

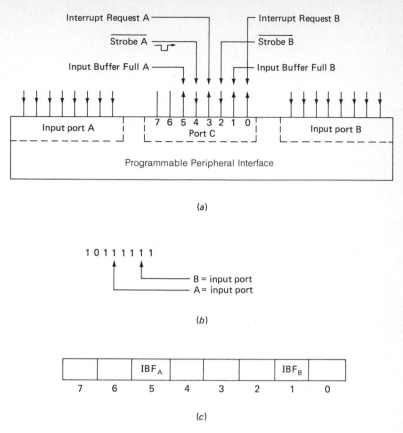

(a)

(b)

(c)

Figure A3-8. Handshaking mode for input ports. (a) Automatic handshaking on input ports A and B; (b) word to be written into Mode Control register to set up input ports A and B for automatic handshaking (addressed with A1 A0 =1 1); (c) read port C (A1 A0 = 1 0) for flag control to determine if a data word has been strobed into either port A or port B (look at bits 5 and 1).

PPI selected with the A7 address line in this way, first

$$A \leftarrow 10111111$$

Then an OUT instruction is executed to device

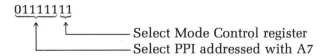

In this mode, the data on the port A input is *latched* into an input buffer when the device driving it puts a negative $\overline{\text{Strobe A}}$ pulse into line 4 of port C. This permits the data to change thereafter without being lost. When a $\overline{\text{Strobe A}}$ pulse occurs, line 5 of port C, which serves as an "Input Buffer Full, A" (IBF$_A$) flag, is automatically set. For flag control, port C is read in to the accumulator using an IN instruction from device

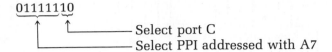

and bit 5 can be tested. If it equals 1, data has been entered into the port A input buffer which can be read into the accumulator with an IN instruction from device

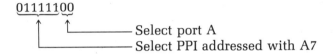

Not only does this IN instruction transfer data from the port A input buffer to the accumulator, it also clears the IBF$_A$ flag automatically, to serve notice that the input port is ready for more data. Automatic handshaking for input port B operates in the same way, using line 2 of port C as a $\overline{\text{Strobe B}}$ input for a negative pulse and line 1 as an IBF$_B$ flag.

To set up both ports A and B as output ports having automatic handshaking, consider that the PPI selected with the A6 address line is used for this purpose. As shown in Fig. A3-9, we first load

$$A \leftarrow 10101101$$

Then an OUT instruction is executed to device

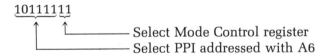

Data is transferred from the accumulator to output port A with an OUT instruction to device

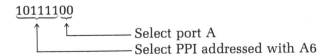

The execution of this OUT instruction will automatically clear the Output Buffer Empty, A (OBE$_A$) flag. When the device connected to output port A accepts this data, it signals the microcomputer with a negative pulse on the

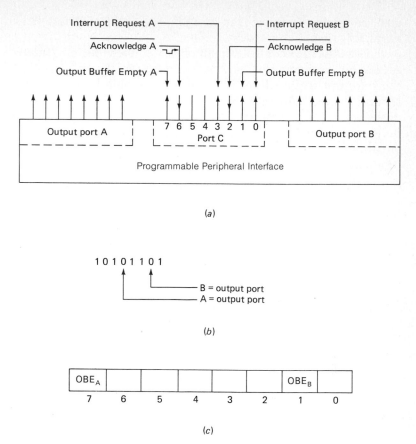

(a)

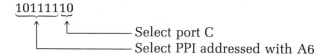

Figure A3-9. Handshaking mode for output ports. (a) Automatic handshaking
on output ports A and B; (b) word to be written into Mode Control register to set
up output ports A and B for automatic handshaking (addressed with A1 A0 =
1 1); (c) read port C (A1 A0 = 1 0) for flag control to determine if a data
word has been accepted from either port A or port B (look at bits 7 and 1).

Acknowledge A handshaking input, which automatically sets the OBE$_A$ flag.
This flag can be tested to determine when the device is ready for more data
by using an IN instruction from device

10111110
— Select port C
— Select PPI addressed with A6

and testing bit 7. If it equals 1, the data has been accepted from output port
A and the next word of data can be loaded into output port A from the accumulator. Automatic handshaking for output port B operates in the same

way, using line 1 of port C as an OBE_B flag and line 2 as an Acknowledge B input for a negative pulse.

For interrupt control, line 3 of port C provides an "Interrupt Request, A" output, as shown in Figs. A3-8a and A3-9a. It can be used to drive one of the interrupt request lines of the Programmable Interrupt Controller. It is set and cleared automatically when the handshaking takes place which was described for flag control. Similarly, line 0 of port C provides an "Interrupt Request, B" output, as shown in the same figures. These interrupt outputs are almost identical in operation to the corresponding handshaking outputs (that is, Input Buffer Full and Output Buffer Empty). They differ in that the rising edge which causes an interrupt does not occur until the *trailing* edge of the handshaking input (that is, $\overline{\text{Strobe}}$ or $\overline{\text{Acknowledge}}$) occurs. In contrast, the handshaking output goes high in response to the *leading edge* of the handshaking input.

APPENDIX A4

MOTOROLA 6800

As shown in Fig. A4-1, the 6800 CPU includes two 8-bit accumulators (A, B), a 16-bit index register (X), six internal flag flipflops (H, I, N, Z, V, C) located in a condition code (CC) register, a 16-bit program counter (PC), and a 16-bit stack pointer (SP). Most of the internal flags are identical to those of the Intel 8080, with the following correspondence in names:

Motorola 6800		Intel 8080	
C	(Carry)	C	(Carry)
H	(Half carry)	AC	(Auxiliary carry)
Z	(Zero)	Z	(Zero)
N	(Negative)	S	(Sign)

The I flag serves as an interrupt mask bit, or interrupt disable. Thus, when I = 1, (maskable) interrupts are disabled. The overflow flag V is set when an overflow occurs during a 2s-complement addition or subtraction operation.

The 6800 instruction set is given in Fig. A4-2. If the register involved in an instruction is labeled A(B), either accumulator A or accumulator B can be designated for use with the instruction. The columns marked

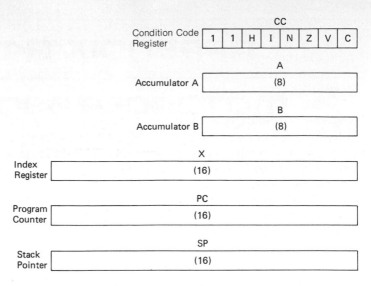

Figure A4-1. Motorola 6800 CPU registers.

"Bytes/Cycles" indicate how many bytes make up an instruction and how many clock cycles are required to execute the instruction for each appropriate addressing mode. For example, an LDA A instruction loads accumulator A from memory. The memory location employed can be the second byte of the instruction (immediate addressing), it can be an operand on page zero, it can be located anywhere with a full address, or it can be obtained using indexed addressing (that is, by adding the second byte of the instruction to the contents of the index register to form a pointer to the desired address).

If the operand is identified by an address label, the assembler will look to see if that address label has been assigned to page zero. This will be true of *all* RAM addresses for instruments requiring less than 256 words of RAM. If a label has been assigned to page zero (and if page zero addressing is listed in Fig. A4-2 for that instruction), a 2-byte instruction will be used. Otherwise a 3-byte full address instruction will be used. The first byte of the instruction draws the distinction between which addressing mode is to be used by the CPU.

Both the unconditional jump instruction JMP and the jump to subroutine instruction JSR employ either a full address or an indexed address. The unconditional branch instruction BRA and all the conditional branch instructions (for which the test is true) jump to an address formed as follows. The second byte of the instruction is treated as a 2s-complement number (see Sec. 7-4) and added to the contents of the program counter to form the new program-counter contents. At the time of the addition, the program counter points to the next instruction, so that the offset is referenced to that address.

Actually, we do not care how the address is formed, since we simply label the address to which the program should jump and the assembler will compute the proper offset. If this offset is outside the range of -125 bytes to $+129$ bytes of the branch instruction, the assembler will inform us with a diagnostic-error message.

The 6800's clock can operate with any clock period between 1.0 and 10 μs. At the maximum clock rate, the LDA A instruction will take 2, 3, 4, or 5 μs to execute, depending upon the addressing mode used.

One-byte instructions (for example, TAB, PSH A) use operands which are implied by the instruction itself. These are listed in the first "Bytes/Cycles" column of Fig. A4-2.

Those flag bits of the condition code which can be tested are shown in the right-hand column of Fig. A4-2. The effect of each instruction upon these flags is coded in the same way as was done in previous appendixes. The encircled numbers point to clarifying comments listed at the bottom of the figure, on page 486.

The 6800 uses a stack, located in RAM, to handle subroutine return addresses automatically during subroutine call and return instructions. During an interrupt, all the CPU registers (except the stack pointer) are automatically pushed onto the stack. The servicing of an interrupt can be speeded up by executing a wait for interrupt instruction WAI which puts all the CPU registers on the stack and then halts. When the interrupt occurs, the seven clock cycles needed to move the CPU registers onto the stack will have already taken place.

Just as for the Intel 8080, enough words in RAM must be set aside for the stack so that use of the stack will never write over other data stored in RAM. When data is pushed onto the stack, the data is *first* moved, and *then* the stack pointer is *decremented*. Consequently, when power is first turned on, the stack pointer must be initialized to the highest address reserved for the stack. Notice that the TSX instruction loads the stack pointer contents, plus one, into the index register. While this instruction does not change the stack pointer contents, it does load the index register with a pointer into the stack. Because of the "plus one," an indexed instruction such as LDA A 0,X will load the byte on the top of the stack into accumulator A. Deeper bytes in the stack are accessed accordingly.

The circuitry of a 6800 microcomputer is shown in Fig. A4-3 including CPU chip, clock chip, RAM, ROM, and I/O. The dual-in-line clock chip, shown in Fig. A4-4, includes both the crystal and drive circuitry. Motorola's microcomputer design does not include the $\overline{\text{READ}}$ and $\overline{\text{WRITE}}$ signals discussed in Sec. 3-4. Instead, VMA $\cdot$ ϕ_2 serves as a timing pulse for both reading and writing, where VMA, valid memory address, indicates to devices on the bus whether or not the present clock cycle is to be used by the CPU to access ROM, RAM, or I/O. If not, the CPU will put garbage onto the address bus and let the data bus float. By disabling ROM, RAM, and I/O when VMA $= 0$, these chips will ignore the garbage. The

Figure A4-2. Motorola 6800 Instruction Set

Operation	MNE	REG	Description	One-byte	Immediate	Page zero	Full	Indexed	C	Z	N	V
Move	LDA	A(B)	A ← M		2/2	2/3	3/4	2/5	—	↕	↕	0
	STA	A(B)	M ← A			2/4	3/5	2/6	—	↕	↕	0
	TAB		B ← A	1/2					—	↕	↕	0
	TBA		A ← B	1/2					—	↕	↕	0
	PSH	A(B)	Stack ← A	1/4					—	—	—	—
	PUL	A(B)	A ← Stack	1/4					—	—	—	—
	CLR		M ← 00				3/6	2/7	0	1	0	0
	CLR	A(B)	A ← 00	1/2					0	1	0	0
	LDX		X ← M		3/3	2/4	3/5	2/6	—	↕	①	0
	LDS		SP ← M		3/3	2/4	3/5	2/6	—	↕	①	0
	STX		M ← X			2/5	3/6	2/7	—	↕	①	0
	STS		M ← SP			2/5	3/6	2/7	—	↕	①	0
	TXS		SP ← X − 1	1/4					—	—	—	—
	TSX		X ← SP + 1	1/4					—	—	—	—
	TPA		A ← CC	1/2					—	—	—	—
	TAP		CC ← A	1/2					↕	↕	↕	↕
Increment	INC		M ← M + 1				3/6	2/7	—	↕	②	②
	INC	A(B)	A ← A + 1	1/2					—	↕	②	②
	INX		X ← X + 1	1/4					—	—	—	—
	INS		SP ← SP + 1	1/4					—	—	—	—
Decrement	DEC		M ← M − 1				3/6	2/7	—	↕	③	③
	DEC	A(B)	A ← A − 1	1/2					—	↕	③	③
	DEX		X ← X − 1	1/4					—	—	—	—
	DES		SP ← SP − 1	1/4					—	—	—	—
Set carry	SEC		C ← 1	1/2					1	—	—	—
Clear carry	CLC		C ← 0	1/2					0	—	—	—
Set overflow	SEV		V ← 1	1/2					—	—	—	1
Clear overflow	CLV		V ← 0	1/2					—	—	—	0
Complement	COM		M ← $\overline{M}$				3/6	2/7	1	↕	↕	0
	COM	A(B)	A ← $\overline{A}$	1/2					1	↕	↕	0

Operations	Mnemonic		Boolean/Arithmetic Operation	Implied	Immediate	Direct	Extended	Indexed	H	I	N	Z	V	C
Add	ADD	A(B)	A ← A + M		2/2	2/3	3/4	2/5	↕	•	↕	↕	↕	↕
	ABA		A ← A + B	1/2					↕	•	↕	↕	↕	↕
Add with carry	ADC	A(B)	A ← A + M + C		2/2	2/3	3/4	2/5	↕	•	↕	↕	↕	↕
Decimal adjust acc. A	DAA		Correct BCD addition	1/2					•	•	↕	↕	↕	④
Subtract	SUB	A(B)	A ← A − M		2/2	2/3	3/4	2/5	•	•	↕	↕	↕	↕
	SBA		A ← A − B	1/2					•	•	↕	↕	↕	↕
Subtract with carry	SBC	A(B)	A ← A − M − C		2/2	2/3	3/4	2/5	•	•	↕	↕	↕	↕
Negate	NEG		M ← 00 − M				3/6	2/7	•	•	↕	↕	②	⑤
	NEG	A(B)	A ← 00 − A	1/2					•	•	↕	↕	②	⑤
AND	AND	A(B)	A ← A AND M		2/2	2/3	3/4	2/5	•	•	↕	↕	0	•
Exclusive-OR	EOR	A(B)	A ← A ⊕ M		2/2	2/3	3/4	2/5	•	•	↕	↕	0	•
OR (inclusive)	ORA	A(B)	A ← A OR M		2/2	2/3	3/4	2/5	•	•	↕	↕	0	•
Compare	CMP	A(B)	A − M		2/2	2/3	3/4	2/5	•	•	↕	↕	↕	↕
(only flags are affected)	CBA		A − B	1/2					•	•	↕	↕	↕	↕
	TST		M − 00				3/6	2/7	•	•	↕	↕	0	0
	TST	A(B)	A − 00	1/2					•	•	↕	↕	0	0
	CPX		X − (M, M + 1)		3/3	2/4	3/5	2/6	•	•	①	↕	①	•
	BIT	A(B)	A AND M		2/2	2/3	3/4	2/5	•	•	↕	↕	0	•
Rotate left	ROL		C ⟵ [b7 ⟵ ⋯ ⟵ b0] ⟵ C (M, A, or B)				3/6	2/7	•	•	↕	↕	⑥	↕
	ROL	A(B)		1/2					•	•	↕	↕	⑥	↕
Rotate right	ROR		C ⟶ [b7 ⟶ ⋯ ⟶ b0] ⟶ C (M, A, or B)				3/6	2/7	•	•	↕	↕	⑥	↕
	ROR	A(B)		1/2					•	•	↕	↕	⑥	↕
Arithmetic shift left	ASL		C ⟵ [b7 ⟵ ⋯ ⟵ b0] ⟵ 0 (M, A, or B)				3/6	2/7	•	•	↕	↕	⑥	↕
	ASL	A(B)		1/2					•	•	↕	↕	⑥	↕
Arithmetic shift right	ASR		b7 ⟶ [b7 ⟶ ⋯ ⟶ b0] ⟶ C (M, A, or B)				3/6	2/7	•	•	↕	↕	⑥	↕
	ASR	A(B)		1/2					•	•	↕	↕	⑥	↕
Logic shift right	LSR		0 ⟶ [b7 ⟶ ⋯ ⟶ b0] ⟶ C (M, A, or B)				3/6	2/7	•	•	0	↕	⑥	↕
	LSR	A(B)		1/2					•	•	0	↕	⑥	↕
Set interrupt mask	SEI		I ← 1	1/2					—	—	—	—	—	—
Clear interrupt mask	CLI		I ← 0	1/2					—	—	—	—	—	—
No operation	NOP		PC ← PC + 1	1/2					—	—	—	—	—	—

(Continues)

Figure A4-2. (Continued)

Operation	MNE	Description	One-byte	Relative	Full	Indexed	Flags C Z N V
Jump unconditionally	JMP	PC ⟵ M			3/3	2/4	– – – –
Branch unconditionally	BRA	PC ⟵ PC + M		2/4			– – – –
if carry set	BCS	if C = 1		2/4			– – – –
if carry clear	BCC	if C = 0		2/4			– – – –
if equal zero	BEQ	if Z = 1		2/4			– – – –
if not equal zero	BNE	if Z = 0		2/4			– – – –
if minus	BMI	if N = 1		2/4			– – – –
if plus	BPL	if N = 0		2/4			– – – –
if overflow set	BVS	if V = 1		2/4			– – – –
if overflow clear	BVC	if V = 0		2/4			– – – –
if ≥ zero	BGE	if N ⊕ V = 0		2/4			– – – –
if > zero	BGT	if Z + (N ⊕ V) = 0		2/4			– – – –
if ≤ zero	BLE	if Z + (N ⊕ V) = 1		2/4			– – – –
if < zero	BLT	if N ⊕ V = 1		2/4			– – – –
if higher	BHI	if C + Z = 0		2/4			– – – –
if lower or same	BLS	if C + Z = 1		2/4			– – – –
Jump to subroutine	JSR	Stack ⟵ PC; PC ⟵ M			3/9	2/8	– – – –
Branch to subroutine	BSR	Stack ⟵ PC; PC ⟵ PC + M		2/8			– – – –
Software interrupt	SWI	Stack ⟵ PC,X,A,B,CC; I ⟵ 1; PC ⟵ M	1/12				– – – –
Wait for interrupt	WAI	Stack ⟵ PC,X,A,B,CC; halt	1/9				– – – –
Return from subroutine	RTS	PC ⟵ Stack	1/5				– – – –
Return from interrupt	RTI	CC,B,A,X,PC ⟵ Stack	1/10				↔ ↔ ↔ ↔

Notes on flags (set flag if test is true; otherwise clear flag):

① Does bit 15 = 1?   ④ Is most significant digit greater than nine? (Do not clear if previously set)
② Does result = 10000000?   ⑤ Does result = 00000000?
③ Does result = 01111111?   ⑥ Does N ⊕ C = 1?

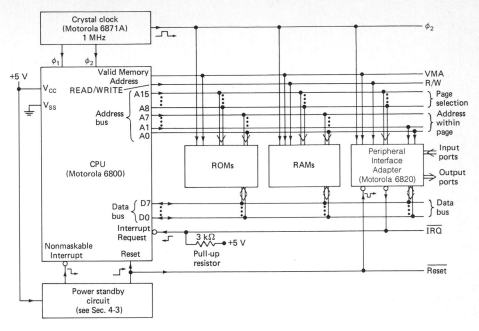

Figure A4-3. Motorola 6800 microcomputer configuration.

"Read/Write" (R/W) signal, which lasts an entire clock cycle, is used with RAM and I/O chips to indicate whether reading or writing is to occur when VMA · ϕ_2 occurs. If R/W = 1, reading is to occur. The Motorola ROM, RAM, and I/O chips include enough chip enable inputs to permit many systems to be implemented with no extra page-decoding circuitry, perhaps using the page-selection scheme of Fig. 3-26.

The 6800 has three interrupt inputs: Reset, Nonmaskable Interrupt, and Interrupt Request. A rising edge on the Reset input sets the interrupt mask flag I to disable interrupts appearing on the Interrupt Request input. Then the CPU loads the program counter with the contents of addresses FFFE and FFFF, as shown in Fig. A4-5. Obviously, the microcomputer hardware must be organized so that a ROM chip is selected as page FF.

Figure A4-4. Crystal clock for the Motorola 6800 microcomputer. (Motorola, Inc.)

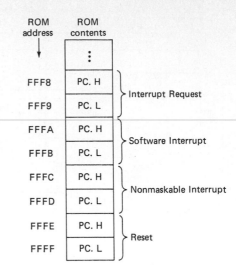

where PC. H = the high-order byte to be loaded into the program
          counter when the specific interrupt occurs

PC. L = the low-order byte to be loaded into the program
          counter when the specific interrupt occurs

Figure A4-5. Memory map for inter-
rupt vectors.

Furthermore, the desired interrupt vectors must be programmed into the
top addresses on this page.

A falling edge on the Nonmaskable Interrupt (NMI) input interrupts
the CPU at the end of the instruction currently being executed. It puts all
the CPU registers onto the stack, sets I = 1, and then jumps to the address
pointed to by the contents of addresses FFFC and FFFD. Because it
cannot be turned off under program control, the NMI input is appropriate
to use if power failure is to be detected, as shown in Fig. A4-3. However,
if not used in this way, it can be used as a high-priority vectored interrupt
input.

A falling edge on the Interrupt Request (IRQ) input produces much
the same response, using the contents of addresses FFF8 and FFF9 to load
the program counter. However, if the interrupt mask flag I is set, the interrupt is ignored.

The software interrupt instruction SWI is a 1-byte subroutine call to
the address stored in locations FFFA and FFFB. Unlike normal subroutine calls, it automatically pushes the CPU registers onto the stack and sets
I = 1. In order to return from the service routine for this or one of the other
interrupts, it is necessary to use the return from interrupt instruction RTI,
which restores the CPU registers from the stack. If IRQ inputs were enabled before the interrupt occurred (I = 0), they will be enabled again
after the RTI instruction, when the condition code register is restored.

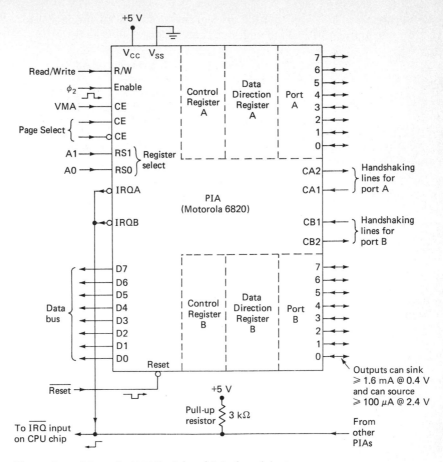

Figure A4-6. *Motorola 6820 Peripheral Interface Adapter.*

Motorola's general I/O chip is their Peripheral Interface Adapter (PIA), shown in Fig. A4-6. It is reset with a low signal on the $\overline{\text{Reset}}$ input, which clears all bits of all registers. This makes both ports look like input ports initially. The setup of each port and its handshaking lines are determined by the bits in its Control Register and its Data Direction Register. Thus each line of each port can be set up as an output (input) by writing a one (zero) into the corresponding bit position of its Data Direction Register.

To access any of the six registers of the PIA, the chip must be selected and enabled. The Enable input is, in effect, just another chip enable (CE) input. However, all changes which take place within the PIA are initiated by the Enable input, so the other inputs should all be stable when the enable pulse occurs. Therefore, the Enable input is tied to ϕ_2.

The use of the PIA is complicated because only two inputs RS1 and

RS0 are used to select which of six registers are to be accessed. At *any* time, either of the control registers can be accessed, as follows:

RS1	RS0	Register accessed
0	1	Control Register A
1	1	Control Register B

That is, Control Register A has address 01 on the page selected for this PIA, while Control Register B has address 03. The state of bit 2 of each control register is used to determine which of the other registers are to be accessed, as follows:

RS1	RS0	Bit 2 of Control Register A	Register accessed
0	0	0	Data Direction Register A
0	0	1	Port A

and

RS1	RS0	Bit 2 of Control Register B	Register accessed
1	0	0	Data Direction Register B
1	0	1	Port B

Except for bit 2, all bits of each control register deal only with the handshaking lines. Consequently, if the ports do not make use of these handshaking lines, the setup of the PIA is simple. For example, for a PIA addressed as page 03, port A is set up as an input port using the initialization sequence:

ADD	MNE	REG	OP	Comments
PIA0	EQU		0300H	⎫ Assign (hex) addresses to labels
PIA1	EQU		0301H	⎭ (see Fig. 2-32)
	CLR		PIA1	Clear bit 2 of Control Register A
	CLR		PIA0	Data Direction Register A ⟵ 00
	LDA	A	#00000100B	Set bit 2 of A using immediate (#) addressing
	STA	A	PIA1	Set bit 2 of Control Register A

From this point on, port A can be transferred into accumulator A at any time with the one instruction LDA A PIA0.

In similar fashion, port B of this same PIA can be set up as an output port with the initialization sequence:

ADD	MNE	REG	OP	Comments
PIA2	EQU		0302H	Assign (hex) addresses to labels
PIA3	EQU		0303H	
	CLR		PIA3	Clear bit 2 of Control Register B
	LDA	A	#0FFH	A ⟵ FF
	STA	A	PIA2	Data Direction Register B ⟵ FF
	LDA	A	#00000100B	Set bit 2 of A using immediate (#) addressing
	STA	A	PIA3	Set bit 2 of Control Register B

At any subsequent time, data can be moved to port B from accumulator A with the one instruction STA A PIA2.

Setting up the handshake lines of a PIA is complicated by the large number of variations possible, and also because the function of each bit of control register A is not identical to the function of the corresponding bit of control register B. *Automatic* handshaking is possible on port A only if it is used as an input port, as shown in Fig. A4-7a. Likewise, automatic handshaking is possible on port B only if it is used as an output port. This is not to say that handshaking cannot be done if the ports are set up otherwise, but only that *extra* instructions will have to be included solely to handshake.

The contents of the control registers shown in Fig. A4-7a will cause an interrupt to be generated when a negative-going edge is applied to either the CA1 input or the CB1 input, provided that the interrupt output lines ($\overline{IRQA}$ and $\overline{IRQB}$) of the PIA are connected to the $\overline{IRQ}$ input on the CPU chip, as shown in Fig. A4-6. $\overline{IRQA}$ and $\overline{IRQB}$ have open-collector outputs so that they can be tied together with the corresponding outputs of any number of PIAs. Any one of these outputs can then pull the $\overline{IRQ}$ line low, generating an interrupt.

The negative-going edge on either CA1 or CB1 sets bit 7 of the corresponding control register. Incidentally, bits 6 and 7 of the control registers are unaffected by the STA A PIA1 and STA A PIA3 instructions used to initialize these registers, since these bits are "read-only." The interrupt service routine can determine which device interrupted by first executing a TST PIA1 instruction. This will set the N flag in the condition code register if the interrupt occurred on port A owing to a negative-going edge on CA1. Control Register A is being tested by this instruction, and N is set if bit 7 equals 1. A BMI instruction can cause a branch to the routine for this device. Otherwise, a TST PIA3, BMI sequence checks input port B.

Automatic handshaking with input port A set up as in Fig. A4-7a means that CA2 goes high automatically when a negative-going edge occurs on CA1. It also means that bit 7 of control register A is automatically set at this time. Both CA2 and bit 7 of control register A go low again automatically when data is read into the CPU from input port A.

Automatic handshaking of output port B set up as in Fig. A4-7a means

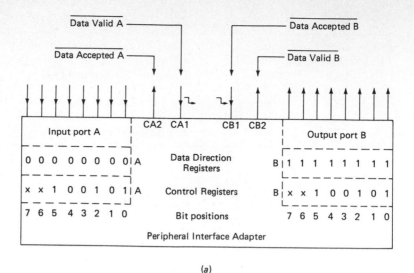

(a)

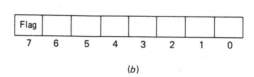

(b)

Figure A4-7. Setup for handshake control of the Peripheral Interface Adapter. (a) Setup for interrupt control and automatic handshaking on both ports; (b) location of handshaking flag input in Control Register A (B), set by a negative-going handshake input on CA1 (CB1) and cleared by reading from input port A (reading from output port B).

Address lines →	A15	A14	A13	A12	A11	A10	A9	A8	Hex addresses				Address lines to detect	
	Binary addresses													
[0]	0	0	0	0	[0]	X	X	00,	01,	02,	03	$\overline{15}$	$\overline{10}$
[0]	0	0	0	[1]	1	X	X	0C,	0D,	0E,	0F	$\overline{15}$	11
[0]	0	0	[1]	0	1	X	X	14,	15,	16,	17	$\overline{15}$	12
[0]	0	[1]	0	0	1	X	X	24,	25,	26,	27	$\overline{15}$	13
[0]	[1]	0	0	0	1	X	X	44,	45,	46,	47	$\overline{15}$	14
[1]	[0]	1	1	1	0	X	X	B8,	B9,	BA,	BB	15	$\overline{14}$
[1]	1	[0]	1	1	0	X	X	D8,	D9,	DA,	DB	15	$\overline{13}$
[1]	1	1	[0]	1	0	X	X	E8,	E9,	EA,	EB	15	$\overline{12}$
[1]	1	1	1	[0]	0	X	X	F0,	F1,	F2,	F3	15	$\overline{11}$
[1]	1	1	1	1	[1]	X	X	FC,	FD,	FE,	FF	15	10

Figure A4-8. Modified page-selection scheme.

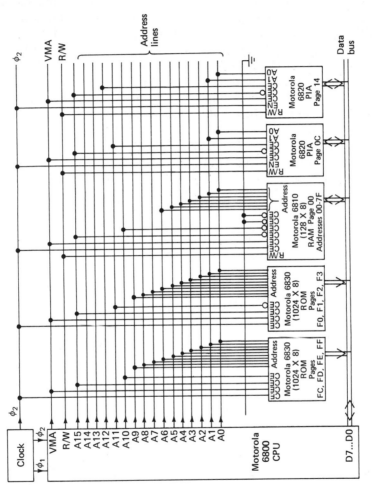

Figure A4-9. Page selection with ROM on page FF and RAM on page 00.

that CB2 goes high automatically when a negative-going edge occurs on CB1 and that bit 7 of control register B is automatically set at this time. However, the handshaking is not quite completely automatic. The "dummy instruction," LDA A PIA2, is needed to clear bit 7 of control register B. Then CB2 goes low again automatically when data is written to output port B from the CPU.

If either port of the PIA is to be used under flag control rather than interrupt control, the interrupt can be disabled by not connecting to the $\overline{\text{IRQA}}$ or $\overline{\text{IRQB}}$ output shown in Fig. A4-6. Alternatively, either of the $\overline{\text{IRQA}}$ and $\overline{\text{IRQB}}$ outputs (or both) can be disabled by initializing bit 0 of the appropriate control register to zero. In either case, bit 7 of each control register can still be tested to determine when an external device handshakes.

Before concluding this appendix, it might be useful to extend the page-selection ideas of Fig. 3-26 to handle Motorola's 1024 × 8 ROM, 128 × 8 RAM, and PIA. To deal with ROM chips which extend over four consecutive pages, address lines A8 and A9 must not be used to distinguish between one chip and another (assuming page selection will be carried out with only two chip enable inputs). The modified page-selection scheme is shown in Fig. A4-8.

The Motorola 6830 (1024 × 8) ROM has four chip enables, each of which can be mask-programmed as either CE or $\overline{\text{CE}}$. The Motorola 6810 (128 × 8) RAM has two CEs and four $\overline{\text{CEs}}$, as shown in Fig. P3-7. The Motorola 6820 PIA has the enabling inputs shown in Fig. A4-6. These considerations lead to the circuit of Fig. A4-9.

APPENDIX A5

RCA COSMAC

The RCA COSMAC* CPU structure and instruction set appears unusual when measured by other microcomputers. Rather than being put off by this unusualness, a designer does well to look further to gauge both the strengths and the weaknesses of the approach. For example, the use of static CMOS technology means that power-standby capability (discussed in Sec. 4-3) can be implemented far more easily than with most other microcomputers. When power fails, it is only necessary to stop the clock and to provide battery backup for the CPU and for CMOS RAM. With the clock stopped, the CPU typically draws only 100 μA, permitting a battery to provide standby capability for a long time.

The CPU has the register structure shown in Fig. A5-1. It consists of an 8-bit "data" register or accumulator (D), a 1-bit "data flag" or carry bit (DF), an interrupt enable flipflop (IE), a register matrix having sixteen 16-bit registers (R0, . . . , RF) which serve as program counters or pointers to memory or

---

* RCA's initial two-chip implementation of the COSMAC CPU is more properly designated by their CDP1801U and CDP1801R part numbers. It is this initial two-chip version which is characterized throughout Chap. 2. In this appendix, we will consider the updated, single-chip COSMAC CPU, designated CDP1802D.

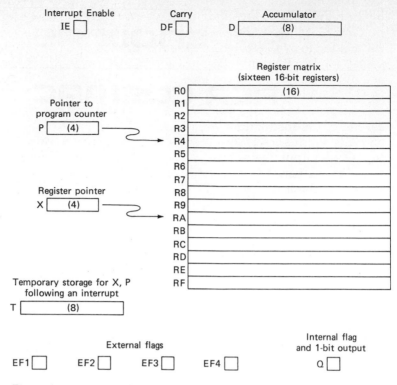

Figure A5-1. RCA COSMAC CPU registers.

scratchpad registers, a 4-bit pointer (P) which selects the register to be used as the program counter, another 4-bit pointer (X) which selects the register to be used as a pointer to an operand in memory, an 8-bit temporary storage register (T) used to hold X and P when an interrupt occurs, four external flags (EF1, . . . , EF4) which are pins on the CPU chip which can be tested directly, and an internal flag (Q) which can be set, cleared, and tested under program control and which also drives an output line from the CPU chip.

The COSMAC instruction set is given in Fig. A5-2. If in some senses the instruction set is less powerful than that of other microcomputers, this is offset to some extent by the *efficiency* of the instruction set. Thus there are only seven 3-byte instructions, whereas over half the instructions are 1-byte instructions. Because certain short *sequences* of instructions are generally useful, an assembler having macro-defining capability would be a definite asset. In fact, RCA's COSMAC assembler includes a variety of macros and other shortcuts built into it.

The 16-bit register associated with some instructions is indicated by the generic label RN. This stands for any of the 16-bit registers R0 through RF in the register matrix. Some instructions use a selected register as a pointer to memory. Thus M(RN) indicates the memory location pointed to by the register RN pointed to by the register field of the instruction. On the other hand, M(RX) indicates the memory location pointed to by the register RX pointed to by the register pointer X. That is, operands in memory are accessed solely with doubly indirect addressing, as defined in Sec. 2-4. When an 8-bit operand is to be accessed in the register matrix, the notation shown in Fig. A5-3 is used.

In order to facilitate operations upon arrays, as discussed in Sec. 2-12, several of the instructions (that is, LDA, LDXA, STXD, OUT, MARK, RET, and DIS) automatically increment or decrement the pointer to memory. The input and output instructions are particularly powerful for moving arrays of data directly between an I/O device and memory, without passing through the accumulator, although the input instruction INP loads the accumulator in addition to the memory location. The terminology I(3) for the operands of these instructions means that 3 bits of the instruction are used to specify the I/O port.

The addition instructions add two 8-bit operands, with or without carry, producing a 9-bit result, with the DF, or carry, bit used to hold the ninth bit. Thus, if a carry results, DF will be set to one. On the other hand, the subtraction instructions subtract two 8-bit operands with or without borrow, and clear the DF bit if a borrow results. For example, if 43 (hex) is subtracted from 42 (hex) without borrow,

$$D \leftarrow FF = 42 - 43 \quad \text{and} \quad DF \leftarrow 0$$

A subtract with borrow instruction on this same data would have made $D \leftarrow FE$ and $DF \leftarrow 0$ if an initial borrow (DF = 0) had existed. Arithmetic operations upon BCD numbers are complicated by the lack of a decimal adjust instruction.

Only the add, subtract, and shift instructions affect the carry bit DF. This is indicated by the $\updownarrow$ symbol in the second to the last column of Fig. A5-2. The last column marks with an ∗ those instructions which have been built into the updated, single-chip (CDP1802D) COSMAC CPU which are not available in the original two-chip (CDP1801U and CDP1801R) COSMAC CPU.

The COSMAC utilizes either present-page or full addressing for branch instructions, permitting branches to be made under most circumstances with 2-byte instructions. Thus RP.0 ← I signifies that the lower 8 bits of the program counter (that is, the register pointed to by P) are to be replaced by the second byte of the instruction. If the software is broken up into a main program and a lot of subroutines, if each of these is relatively short (a good philosophy for generating software without bugs), and if no subroutine is permitted to cross a page boundary (using the techniques discussed in Sec. 2-9), then present-page addressing will suffice for all requirements except jumping to, and returning from, subroutines. Subroutine linkage requires some special handling anyway, and this special handling will deal with full addresses, as will be discussed shortly.

Figure A5-2. RCA COSMAC Instruction Set

Operation	MNE	REG	OP	Description	Bytes	Cycles	DF	Not available in 1801 CPU
Move	GLO	RN		D ⟵ RN.0	1	2	—	
	GHI	RN		D ⟵ RN.1	1	2	—	
	PLO	RN		RN.0 ⟵ D	1	2	—	
	PHI	RN		RN.1 ⟵ D	1	2	—	
	LDN	RN		D ⟵ M(RN) for N ≠ 0	1	2	—	*
	LDA	RN		D ⟵ M(RN); Increment RN	1	2	—	
	STR	RN		M(RN) ⟵ D	1	2	—	
	LDX			D ⟵ M(RX)	1	2	—	
	LDXA			D ⟵ M(RX); Increment RX	1	2	—	*
	STXD			M(RX) ⟵ D; Decrement RX	1	2	—	*
	INP		I(3)	D = M(RX) ⟵ Device I (I ≠ 0)	1	2	—	
	OUT		I(3)	Device I ⟵ M(RX); Increment RX (I ≠ 0)	1	2	—	
Move, immediate	LDI		I(8)	D ⟵ I	2	2	—	
	SEP	RN		P ⟵ N	1	2	—	
	SEX	RN		X ⟵ N	1	2	—	
	SEQ			Q ⟵ 1	1	2	—	*
	REQ			Q ⟵ 0	1	2	—	*
Increment	INC	RN		Increment RN	1	2	—	
	IRX			Increment RX	1	2	—	*
Decrement	DEC	RN		Decrement RN	1	2	—	
Add	ADD			D ⟵ D + M(RX)	1	2	↔	
	ADI		I(8)	D ⟵ D + I	2	2	↔	
Add with carry	ADC			D ⟵ D + M(RX) + DF	1	2	↔	*
	ADCI		I(8)	D ⟵ D + I + DF	2	2	↔	*

Operation	Mnemonic	Imm.	Function	Bytes	Cycles	DF	
Subtract	SM		D ⟵ D − M(RX)	1	2	↔	
	SMI	I(8)	D ⟵ D − I	2	2	↔	*
	SD		D ⟵ M(RX) − D	1	2	↔	
	SDI	I(8)	D ⟵ I − D	2	2	↔	*
Subtract with borrow	SMB		D ⟵ D − M(RX) − $\overline{DF}$	1	2	↔	
	SMBI	I(8)	D ⟵ D − I − $\overline{DF}$	2	2	↔	*
	SDB		D ⟵ M(RX) − D − $\overline{DF}$	1	2	↔	
	SDBI	I(8)	D ⟵ I − D − $\overline{DF}$	2	2	↔	*
AND	AND		D ⟵ D AND M(RX)	1	2	—	
	ANI	I(8)	D ⟵ D AND I	2	2	—	
Exclusive-OR	XOR		D ⟵ D ⊕ M(RX)	1	2	—	
	XRI	I(8)	D ⟵ D ⊕ I	2	2	—	
OR (inclusive)	OR		D ⟵ D OR M(RX)	1	2	—	
	ORI	I(8)	D ⟵ D OR I	2	2	—	
Shift right	SHR		DF ⟵ LSB(D); 0 ⟶ D (shift right)	1	2	↔	*
Ring shift right	RSHR		DF ⟶ D (ring shift right)	1	2	↔	*
Shift left	SHL		DF ⟵ MSB(D); D ⟵ 0 (shift left)	1	2	↔	*
Ring shift left	RSHL		DF ⟶ D (ring shift left)	1	2	↔	*
Save pointers	SAV		M(RX) ⟵ T	1	2	—	
Push pointers onto stack	MARK		T ⟵ X,P; M(R2) ⟵ X,P; X ⟵ P; Decrement R2	1	2	—	*
Return from interrupt	RET		X,P ⟵ M(RX); Set IE; Increment RX	1	2	—	
	DIS		X,P ⟵ M(RX); Clear IE; Increment RX	1	2	—	

(Continues)

Figure A5-2. (Continued)

Operation	MNE	REG	OP	Description	Bytes	Cycles	DF	Not available in 1801 CPU
Idle	IDL			Halt until an interrupt or DMA request occurs	1	2	—	
No operation	NOP			Continue	1	3	—	*
Branch unconditionally	BR		I(8)	RP.0 ← I	2	2	—	
	LBR		I(16)	RP ← I	3	3	—	*
Branch on D	BZ		I(8)	RP.0 ← I if D = 0	2	2	—	
	LBZ		I(16)	RP ← I if D = 0	3	3	—	*
	BNZ		I(8)	RP.0 ← I if D ≠ 0	2	2	—	
	LBNZ		I(16)	RP ← I if D ≠ 0	3	3	—	*
Branch on DF	BDF		I(8)	RP.0 ← I if DF = 1	2	2	—	
	LBDF		I(16)	RP ← I if DF = 1	3	3	—	*
	BNF		I(8)	RP.0 ← I if DF = 0	2	2	—	
	LBNF		I(16)	RP ← I if DF = 0	3	3	—	*
Branch on Q	BQ		I(8)	RP.0 ← I if Q = 1	2	2	—	
	LBQ		I(16)	RP ← I if Q = 1	3	3	—	*
	BNQ		I(8)	RP.0 ← I if Q = 0	2	2	—	
	LBNQ		I(16)	RP ← I if Q = 0	3	3	—	*
Branch on external flags	B1		I(8)	RP.0 ← I if EF1 = 1	2	2	—	*
	BN1		I(8)	RP.0 ← I if EF1 = 0	2	2	—	*
	B2		I(8)	RP.0 ← I if EF2 = 1	2	2	—	*
	BN2		I(8)	RP.0 ← I if EF2 = 0	2	2	—	*
	B3		I(8)	RP.0 ← I if EF3 = 1	2	2	—	
	BN3		I(8)	RP.0 ← I if EF3 = 0	2	2	—	
	B4		I(8)	RP.0 ← I if EF4 = 1	2	2	—	
	BN4		I(8)	RP.0 ← I if EF4 = 0	2	2	—	

Skip unconditionally						
	SKP	Skip over next byte	1	2	—	*
	LSKP	Skip over next two bytes	1	3	—	*
Skip conditionally:						
on D		Skip over next two bytes				
	LSZ	if D = 0	1	3	—	*
	LSNZ	if D ≠ 0	1	3	—	*
on DF	LSDF	if DF = 1	1	3	—	*
	LSNF	if DF = 0	1	3	—	*
on Q	LSQ	if Q = 1	1	3	—	*
	LSNQ	if Q = 0	1	3	—	*
on IE	LSIE	if IE = 1	1	3	—	*

16-bit
register labeling

Register matrix

RO	R0.1	R0.0
R1	R1.1	R1.0
R2	R2.1	R2.0
R3	R3.1	R3.0
R4	R4.1	R4.0
R5	R5.1	R5.0
R6	R6.1	R6.0
R7	R7.1	R7.0
R8	R8.1	R8.0
R9	R9.1	R9.0
RA	RA.1	RA.0
RB	RB.1	RB.0
RC	RC.1	RC.0
RD	RD.1	RD.0
RE	RE.1	RE.0
RF	RF.1	RF.0

Upper bytes   Lower bytes

Figure A5-3. Designation of 8-bit register matrix locations.

The execution time is identical for most COSMAC instructions, as indicated by the "2 cycles" listed for most instructions in Fig. A5-2. Since the clock can operate at any rate up to 3.2 MHz (using 5-V power, or 6.4 MHz using 10-V power), and since each "cycle" is made up of eight clock periods, each 2-cycle instruction is executed in

$$\frac{16}{3.2} = 5 \ \mu s$$

when the COSMAC is powered with 5 V and clocked at its maximum clock rate.

Because the program counter can be located in any one of the sixteen 16-bit registers, subroutines (or an interrupt service routine) can be entered simply by changing which register is the program counter. One possible approach is shown in Fig. A5-4. Initially, register RF is loaded with the entry point SUBR to the subroutine, as in Fig. A5-4a. Incidentally, this 6-byte sequence is the type of thing for which macros are usefully employed. Thus LOD RF SUBR might be defined to load register RF with the full address of SUBR. Then, as shown in Fig. A5-4b, the main program might execute instructions using R3 as the program counter. It can call the subroutine SUBR with the instruction SEP RF. This makes register RF the program counter, and since it has been previously initialized to the address SUBR, the CPU will begin executing subroutine instructions. Note that the fetch cycle for the SEP RF instruction concluded by incrementing R3. Consequently, all the time that the subroutine is being executed, the main program is waiting to be continued by the instruction SEP R3. Exiting from the

ADD	MNE	REG	OP	Comments	Program counter
	.				
	.				
	.				
	LDI		SUBR.0		R3
	PLO	RF			R3
	LDI		SUBR.1		R3
	PHI	RF			R3
	.				
	.				
	.				

(a)

ADD	MNE	REG	OP	Comments		Program counter
	.					R3
	.					R3
	SEP	RF		Jump to subroutine SUBR		R3
NEXT	.			Next instruction	Main	R3
	.				program	R3
	.					R3
	.					R3
	.					R3
	.					
SUBR-1	SEP	R3		Return to main program, leaving SUBR in RF		RF
SUBR	.			Enter subroutine here	Subroutine	RF
	.				SUBR	RF
	.					RF
	.			Instructions to be		RF
	.			executed in subroutine		RF
	.					RF
	.					RF
	.					RF
	BR		SUBR-1	Unconditional branch		RF
	.					
	.					
	.					

(b)

Figure A5-4. *Fast subroutine linkage mechanism. (a) Initialization of pointer in register RF to subroutine SUBR at start-up; (b) subroutine linkage.*

ADD	MNE	REG	OP	Comments		Program counter
	.					R3
	.					R3
	LOD	RF	SUBR	Macro defined to load SUBR into RF	Main	R3
	SEP	RF		Jump to subroutine SUBR	program	R3
NEXT	.					R3
	.					R3
	.					R3
	.					R3
SUBR	.			First instruction of SUBR		RF
	.					RF
	.				Subroutine	RF
	.				SUBR	RF
	.					RF
	.					RF
	SEP	R3		Return		RF

Figure A5-5. *Alternative subroutine linkage mechanism.*

subroutine uses an unconditional branch to the address just before SUBR, followed by the SEP R3 instruction. This leaves register RF containing the address SUBR when the main program is returned to. A subsequent call to SUBR can be made with a SEP RF instruction without any need to reinitialize register RF again.

The preceding approach ties up register RF with the sole function of serving as program counter for one subroutine. Alternatively, the approach of Fig. A5-5 uses register RF as the program counter for *all* subroutines which are called by the main program. Then register RE might be used in the same fashion to execute subroutines called by the subroutines which use RF as program counter. Using registers RF, RE, RD, . . . in this fashion permits the orderly nesting of subroutines to a deep level without using up all the registers just to serve the needs of subroutine linkage.

In developing the software for an instrument of any complexity organized around the COSMAC, the above subroutine linkage mechanisms, while relatively fast, do give rise to potential programming bugs if the designer is not alert as to which register is the program counter at all times. To get around this problem, a stack structure for subroutine linkage can be set up. This structure, plus the automatic use of register R0 for DMA and registers R1 and R2 for interrupts, suggests the dedication of registers R0, . . . , R6 as shown in Fig. A5-6.

Figure A5-6. RCA's Suggested Dedication of Registers

Register	Use
R0	Used automatically during DMA operations as a pointer to memory
R1	Used automatically as the program counter for interrupts
R2	RAM stack pointer
R3	Program counter (under "normal" circumstances)
R4	Program counter for calling all subroutines
R5	Program counter for returning from all subroutines
R6	Top of stack

To call a subroutine starting at an address labeled MAD, the COSMAC assembler will accept the macro instruction

CALL   MAD

This is assembled as shown in Fig. A5-7*b*. If the registers have been initialized at start-up as in Fig. A5-7*a* so that R4 points to the CALSUB subroutine of Fig. A5-7*c*, the execution of this macro will result in the starting address of MAD being loaded into R3, R3 being made the program counter again, and the return address being put on the top of the stack, in register R6. At the completion of the subroutine, execution of the macro

EXIT

will undo what was done by the CALL macro, loading R3 with the return address and making R3 the program counter again.

A side benefit of this subroutine linkage structure is that constants can be passed to a subroutine directly as immediate data, as shown in Fig. A5-8. It is only necessary to follow the CALL macro instruction with the number of

ADD	MNE	REG	OP	Comments	Program counter
	LOD	R1	INT	Load R1 with address of interrupt service routine	R3
	LOD	R2	STKIN	Initialize stack pointer	R3
	LOD	R4	CALSUB	Load R4 with address of CALSUB routine	R3
	LOD	R5	RETURN	Load R5 with address of RETURN routine	R3

(a)

Figure A5-7. Implementing a stack. (a) Use of a LOD macro to initialize registers at start-up; (b) definition of the COSMAC assembler's macro, CALL MAD; (c) the CALSUB subroutine initiated by the CALL macro (17 bytes, 32 cycles); (d) definition of the COSMAC assembler's macro, EXIT; (e) the RETURN subroutine initiated by the EXIT macro (12 bytes, 22 cycles).

ADD	MNE	REG	OP	Comments	Program counter
	SEP	R4			R3
	DC		MAD.1	⎱ "Define constant" directives used	
	DC		MAD.0	⎰ to store the address MAD	

(b)

ADD	MNE	REG	OP	Comments	Program counter
CAL1	SEP	R3		Return to main program	R4
CALSUB	GHI	R6			R4
	STR	R2			R4
	DEC	R2		Move top of stack (R6)	R4
	GLO	R6		out to stack in RAM	R4
	STR	R2			R4
	DEC	R2			R4
	GHI	R3			R4
	PHI	R6		Move program counter in R3	R4
	GLO	R3		to top of stack (R6)	R4
	PLO	R6			R4
	LDA	R6			R4
	PHI	R3		Move subroutine address, pointed	R4
	LDA	R6		to by R6, to R3; increment R6 to	R4
	PLO	R3		return address	R4
	BR		CAL1		R4

(c)

ADD	MNE	REG	OP	Comments	Program counter
	SEP	R5			R3

(d)

ADD	MNE	REG	OP	Comments	Program counter
RET1	SEP	R3		Return to main program	R5
RETURN	GHI	R6			R5
	PHI	R3		Move return address stored in the	R5
	GLO	R6		top of stack (R6) back to main	R5
	PLO	R3		program counter (R3)	R5
	INC	R2		Increment to top of RAM stack	R5
	LDA	R2			R5
	PLO	R6		Move top of RAM stack to	R5
	LDN	R2		top of stack (R6)	R5
	PHI	R6			R5
	BR		RET1		R5

(e)

Figure A5-7. (Continued)

fixed constants which the subroutine expects to have passed to it in this way. Then within the subroutine each

LDA   R6

instruction will use the top of the stack as a pointer to ROM and will move the byte of data to the accumulator. It will also automatically increment the program-counter contents stored in the top of stack. After the subroutine has picked up all the constants passed to it in this way, the top of stack will contain the return address (that is, the address immediately following the last parameter, shown as NEXT in Fig. A5-8a). This method of passing

ADD	MNE	REG	OP	Comments	Program counter
	.				
	.				
	.				
	CALL		MAD	Call multibyte addition subroutine	R3
	DC		3	This "define constant" directive is used to tell MAD to operate upon 3 bytes	
NEXT	.				R3
	.				
	.				

(a)

ADD	MNE	REG	OP	Comments	Program counter
MAD	.				R3
	.				R3
	.				R3
	LDA	R6		Load fixed parameter into D and advance R6 to the return address	R3
	.				R3
	.				R3
	.				R3
	EXIT				R3

(b)

Figure A5-8. Passing a fixed parameter to a subroutine. (a) The CALL macro followed by a parameter to be used by the called subroutine; (b) loading accumulator D with the fixed parameter.

fixed parameters to subroutines is often particularly convenient, since the parameters do not tie up scratchpad registers but can be obtained as needed using 1-byte instructions. Since parameter passing occurs extensively in the software for a microcomputer-based instrument, any efficiency obtained can result in an overall savings in ROM words needed for subroutine linkage compared with the ROM needed for this same purpose in another microcomputer. That is, the savings in parameter passing can offset the ROM used to store the CALSUB and RETURN subroutines of Fig. A5-7. Thus the COSMAC microcomputer has a powerful but slow subroutine linkage mechanism for general use and a fast mechanism requiring more careful use when speed is required.

The minimum configuration circuitry of a COSMAC microcomputer is shown in Fig. A5-9 including CPU and clock in a single chip, RAM, ROM, input port, output port, and interrupt input. In addition, but not shown, is the DMA capability built into the CPU chip and discussed briefly at the end of Sec. 3-8.

The COSMAC saves CPU pins by multiplexing the 16-bit address onto an 8-bit address bus. The ROM shown in Fig. A5-9 includes two features to facilitate putting together a minimum-chip microcomputer configuration. First, it uses the CPU's "TPA" timing pulse to latch up the page portion of the address (using an arbitrary, mask-programmed page address). The

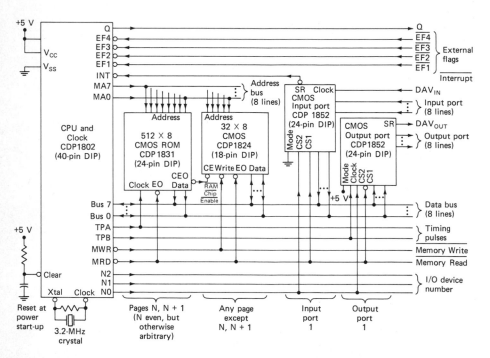

Figure A5-9. RCA COSMAC microcomputer—minimum configuration.

timing for this is shown in Fig. A5-10.   Second, it generates a $\overline{\text{RAM chip}}$ enable output $\overline{\text{CEO}}$ which goes high whenever the ROM chip is selected.   As shown in Fig. A5-9, this signal can be used to enable a RAM chip at all times except when reading from ROM.   This means that the RAM chip shown will be enabled not only for all operations accessing RAM (using any page address except the two consecutive pages mask-programmed into the ROM chip) but also for all I/O instructions.   This is as it should be, since one of the COSMAC's strengths is its ability to move data directly between RAM and I/O ports.

RAM can be easily expanded by using the same $\overline{\text{CEO}}$ output from the

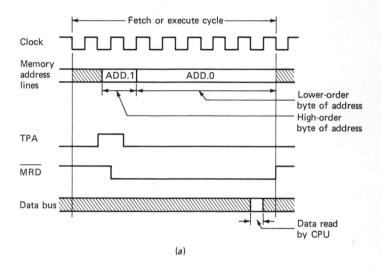

(a)

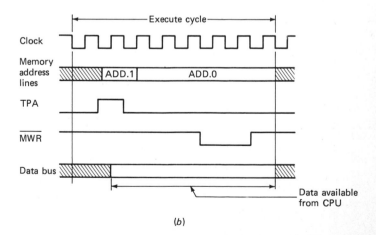

(b)

Figure A5-10.   Memory read-write timing.   (a) Memory read operation; (b) memory write operation.

ROM chip to enable RCA's 128 × 8 CMOS RAM chip or two 256 × 4 CMOS RAM chips. To expand still further (or to use standard ROM, PROM, or EPROM chips) TPA can be used to strobe a separate latch chip which, in turn, can drive a decoder, providing latched and decoded page-selection signals to enable separate pages of memory chips.

The I/O ports shown in Fig. A5-9 use RCA's general-purpose CMOS I/O port chip. The "Mode" input is used to hard-wire the chip as either an input port or an output port. One of the chip select inputs ($\overline{CS2}$) is tied to one of the CPU's N0, N1, or N2 outputs so as to create input ports which respond to INP 1, INP 2, or INP 4 instructions and output ports which respond to OUT 1, OUT 2, or OUT 4 instructions. The number of ports can be expanded by decoding N0, N1, and N2. The other chip select input is enabled in asserted form ($\overline{CS1}$) when the chip is used as an input port and

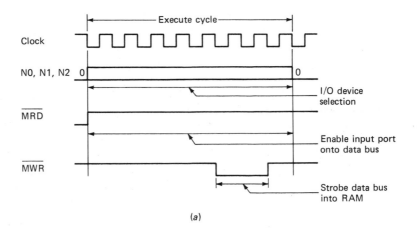

(a)

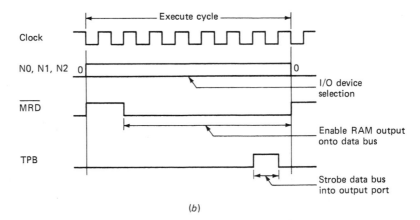

(b)

Figure A5-11. I/O timing. (a) Input port to RAM; (b) RAM to output port.

negated form ($\overline{CS1}$) when used as an output port. Then the $\overline{\text{Memory Read}}$ ($\overline{MRD}$) signal can be used for enabling, for both input and output, with the timing signals shown in Fig. A5-11.

Each input port includes a DAV_{IN} (data valid) handshaking input set up for automatic handshaking, as shown in Fig. A5-9. The input data is latched into the input port by a positive pulse on the DAV_{IN} input. Then, in response to the trailing (falling) edge of the DAV_{IN} pulse, the $\overline{SR}$ output goes low. This $\overline{SR}$ output can be used to provide either interrupt control, by tying it to the CPU's $\overline{INT}$ input (as shown in Fig. A5-9), or flag control by tying it to one of the CPU's four external flag inputs $\overline{EF1}, \ldots, \overline{EF4}$. The $\overline{SR}$ output goes high again automatically when the input port is read. To provide for a *pair* of handshaking lines, the Q output from the CPU can serve as the DAC (data accepted) signal, under program control.

In similar fashion, each output port includes a data valid output DAV_{OUT}. This output goes high on the trailing edge of the TPB timing pulse which strobes the data into the output port. However, it remains high only during the fetch cycle for the next instruction. Consequently, it is useful for strobing the output data into an external device. It is *not* satisfactory, by itself, for handshaking with a device which might not be ready for data.

The CPU chip includes an interesting feature for increasing the clock rate above that obtainable with 5-V power while maintaining TTL compatibility. By tying V_{CC} to 5 V, TTL compatibility on all inputs and outputs is achieved. Then V_{DD} can be raised as high as 15 V to increase the clock rate. Each output can sink 1.5 mA (typically) at 0.4 V, and source 1.6 mA (typically) at 2.5 V. Consequently, even a "worst-case" CPU chip should drive low-power Schottky TTL logic comfortably.

The power start-up circuit of Fig. A5-9 clears P, X, and R0 and *sets* IE. However, interrupts are ignored during the execution of the first instruction. Consequently, to avoid interrupts at start-up, a program must begin with the sequence shown in Fig. A5-12a. The "define constant" (DC #00) assembler directive will be assembled into the 1-byte hex number 00.

ACTUAL ADDRESS	MNE	REG	OP	Comments	Program counter
	ORG		#0000	Start-up begins at page zero, address zero	R0
0000	DIS			} X ⟵ 0; P ⟵ 0; IE ⟵ 0; advance program	R0
0001	DC		#00	} counter to address 0002	
0002	.				R0
	.				
	.				

(a)

Figure A5-12. COSMAC *handling of interrupts.* (a) *Start-up program sequence to disable interrupts;* (b) *enabling interrupts;* (c) *interrupt service routine.*

ADD	MNE	REG	OP	Comments	Program counter
	.				
	.				
	.				
	SEX	R3		X ⟵ 3 (same as P)	R3
	RET			⎫ X ⟵ 3; P ⟵ 3; IE ⟵ 1; advance program	R3
	DC		#33	⎬ counter to NEXT	
NEXT	.			⎭	R3
	.				
	.				

(b)

ADD	MNE	REG	OP	Comments	Program counter
INT-1	RET			X,P ⟵ stack; increment stack pointer; IE ⟵ 1	R1
INT	DEC	R2		Begin service routine; decrement stack pointer	R1
	SAV			Stack ⟵ T	R1
	DEC	R2		Decrement stack pointer	R1
	STXD			Stack ⟵ D; decrement stack pointer	R1
	RSHR			Rotate DF into D	R1
	STR	R2		Stack ⟵ D; (that is, DF)	R1
					R1
	.			⎫ Instructions to service the device	R1
	.			⎬ which caused the interrupt	R1
	.			⎭	R1
	LDA	R2		D ⟵ stack; increment stack pointer	R1
	RSHL			Restore DF	R1
	LDA	R2		D ⟵ stack; increment stack pointer	R1
	SEX	R2		X ⟵ 2	R1
	BR		INT-1	Branch to INT-1	R1

(c)

Figure A5-12. (Continued)

When we are ready to enable interrupts (and assuming register R3 is being used as the program counter), we can execute the sequence shown in Fig. A5-12b. If the $\overline{\text{INT}}$ interrupt input line happens to be already pulled low when this sequence occurs, the CPU will be interrupted immediately. Otherwise the CPU will be interrupted at the completion of any subsequent instruction during which $\overline{\text{INT}}$ is pulled low. In response to the interrupt, the CPU will move X and P to T, set P to 1 and X to 2, and clear IE. The CPU will then begin executing the interrupt service routine whose address has been previously loaded into register R1, as shown in Fig. A5-7a. The interrupt service routine will then take the form shown in Fig. A5-12c, assuming the register usage defined in Fig. A5-6 and the stack structure defined in Fig. A5-7. This service routine stores T, D, and DF upon entry into the service routine and restores them at the end.

APPENDIX A6

ROCKWELL PPS-8

The CPU registers of the Rockwell PPS-8 can be conveniently considered in four groups, as shown in Fig. A6-1. The flag group consists of 1-bit flags (C, Q, BR, SK, AD, EX, IE). C is the normal carry bit, while Q is an intermediate carry used with BCD operations, as discussed in Sec. 7-6.

In order to provide extremely efficient branch instructions, the PPS-8 reserves one bit of most instructions to tell whether or not the *next* instruction is a branch instruction. In this way, a 1-byte instruction can be used to branch to any address on the present (128 address) page while a 2-byte branch instruction will branch anywhere. To handle this, when the assembler sees a branch instruction, it sets the "branch tag" bit of the previous instruction. If the previous instruction does not include a branch tag bit, the assembler automatically inserts a 1-byte instruction which does nothing more than set the branch flag BR. Thus the branch flag is set by one instruction to tell the CPU that the next instruction is a branch. The branch instruction is then interpreted as shown in Fig. A6-2.

Some PPS-8 instructions include a built-in test (for example, "has the automatic incrementing of the pointer associated with this instruction carried the pointer across a page boundary?"), setting the skip flag SK to skip over the next instruction (which would typically be a branch instruction) if

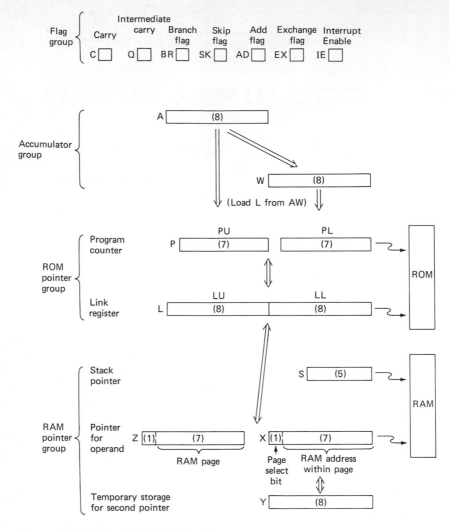

Figure A6-1. Rockwell PPS-8 CPU registers.

the test is passed. This permits an instruction to be used for efficient operations upon arrays by aligning the end of the array at a page boundary. The
same instruction can be used for other purposes and the branch condition ignored if the designer ensures that the incremented pointer will never cross a
page boundary.

   The add flag AD is set by the execution of an add instruction (and
cleared by the following instruction). It is used to link an add instruction
with an immediately following decimal adjust instruction for BCD addition
operations.

   The PPS-8 instruction set includes a variety of instructions to exchange

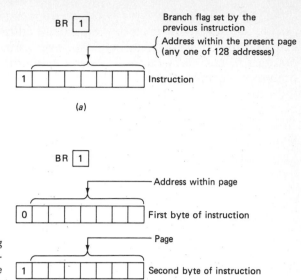

Figure A6-2. Use of branch flag BR to identify a branch instruction. (a) Format of a 1-byte branch instruction; (b) format of a 2-byte branch instruction.

the contents of two registers. Many of these are macros made up of a load instruction followed by a store instruction (which we might expect would leave the same number in both registers). However, a load instruction sets the exchange flag EX so that if it is followed immediately by the store instruction, an exchange is actually carried out. Otherwise the EX flag is cleared.

The interrupt enable flag IE can be set or cleared under program control. It is automatically cleared when an interrupt occurs, disabling further interrupts until IE is set again under program control. In addition, interrupts are disabled whenever the branch flag (BR), the skip flag (SK), the add flag (AD), or the exchange flag (EX) is set. This prevents paired instructions which use any of these flags as a link between them from becoming unpaired (impaired!) by an interrupt.

The accumulator group of registers shown in Fig. A6-1 includes the 8-bit accumulator A together with a temporary register W. Many of the load accumulator instructions move the old contents of the accumulator to W. Then, if the following instruction is a "store accumulator" instruction, the CPU will sense that the exchange flag EX has been set by the load instruction and actually take the operand to be stored from W rather than from A. In addition, a full address can be loaded into the link register L by loading A with the address within the page first, followed by the page. This will result in the page in A and the address within the page in W. The combination can then be moved to L.

The hardware of the PPS-8 microcomputer treats ROM differently from RAM (and both of these differently from I/O chips). Consequently, even though ROM addresses extend upward from page zero, address zero, there is no confusion with the corresponding RAM addresses even though they also extend upward from page zero, address zero. Certain instructions use pointers to communicate with ROM while other instructions use different pointers to communicate with RAM. This distinction between pointers is indicated in Fig. A6-1.

The ROM pointer group of registers shown in Fig. A6-1 includes a 14-bit program counter P and a 16-bit link register L. The program counter is used in the conventional way as a pointer to ROM for the location of the next instruction. The PPS-8 uses ROM pages having 128 addresses rather than the 256 addresses of most other microcomputers. In doing so, it makes available one bit to use in a special way. Thus Fig. A6-2 illustrates how this bit is used to distinguish between a present-page branch instruction and a full-address branch instruction.

The link register L is used as a pointer to ROM for accessing tables and other fixed data. It also serves as the top of the stack for subroutine calls and returns. Thus a subroutine call automatically moves L onto the stack in RAM and then moves P (and the carry bit C) to L. Putting the top of stack in a CPU pointer to ROM provides a feature of the PPS-8 microcomputer not shared by most other microcomputers. As will be discussed in more detail shortly, it means that fixed parameters can be passed to a subroutine as immediate data located in ROM immediately following the subroutine call instruction. The link register is also used as temporary storage for a pointer to RAM. Thus, while no instructions use it as a pointer to RAM, its contents can be exchanged with the contents of the ZX register-pair which is used by instructions as a pointer to RAM.

The RAM pointer group of registers includes the 5-bit stack pointer S and the three 8-bit registers Z, X, and Y. The stack pointer is cleared when power is first turned on. It uses the bottom 32 addresses of RAM on page zero for the stack. It increments the stack pointer automatically after each byte is pushed onto the stack. Conversely, as it pops data off the stack, it automatically decrements the stack pointer and then loads a CPU register from the resulting address pointed to.

Just as for ROM, the PPS-8 uses RAM pages having 128 addresses each. By holding these 7-bit addresses in 8-bit registers, an eighth bit is available to distinguish between indirect page-zero addressing of an operand and indirect full addressing of an operand. Thus, as shown in Fig. A6-1, the register-pair made up of Z and X is the pointer to RAM operands. If the most significant bit of X is a zero, the content of Z is ignored and the operand is addressed on page zero. If this most significant bit of X is a one, the page address of the operand is contained in Z.

The Y register is used as temporary storage for a second pointer having either a page zero address or the page address stored in Z. Alternatively, the Y register is often used as a loop counter. An instruction which automatically decrements the X register can cause the next instruction to be skipped when the content of the X register equals the content of the Y register. By skipping over an instruction which branches back through the loop again, an exit from the loop is obtained.

The PPS-8 instruction set is given in Fig. A6-3. It is all the options on the instructions which make the PPS-8 both powerful and difficult for the newcomer. To give order to these options, Fig. A6-3 describes each instruction in terms of a basic operation, an indication of whether any pointer is incremented or decremented, an indication of whether a skip condition is included, a final exchange or move operation (if any), and a comment code.

A comment code of M indicates that the instruction is actually a macro made up of two instructions which are coupled together with an exchange flag which is set (EX = 1). We generally want to avoid using one of these instructions immediately following an instruction which can skip. If the skip occurs, only the first instruction of the macro is skipped, not the entire macro.

A comment code of N indicates an instruction which does not include a branch tag. Consequently, if one of these instructions is immediately followed by an unconditional branch instruction, the assembler will *automatically* insert the 1-byte set branch flag instruction NOP (which makes BR = 1). Thus, the mnemonic NOP need never appear in a program; it should certainly *never* be used as a "no operation" instruction to bide time since it will cause a branch (misinterpreting the first byte of the following instruction as an address).

The number of cycles given for each instruction can be multiplied by 4 μs to obtain the instruction execution time. The conditional branch instructions list 2,3 cycles. The choice depends upon whether or not the branch address is on the present page, since this case simplifies what is generally a 3-byte 3-cycle instruction into a 2-byte 2-cycle instruction.

The number of bytes required by an instruction is flagged with an * for quite a few instructions. The asterisk indicates an optional feature of the PPS-8 which can be used to reduce the number of bytes needed by some instructions which appear repeatedly throughout a program and which use the same second byte (or second and third bytes) over and over again. For example, an instruction to branch to a specific subroutine may be used many times. The full address can be stored in a "subroutine entry pool" optionally located at specific addresses on page 1 of ROM. In like manner, immediate data which is used many times can be stored in a "literal pool" on page 0 of ROM. For large programs, this feature can provide significant ROM savings. For small programs, the feature can be ignored and pages 0 and 1 of ROM used almost entirely for storing program instructions. In the latter case, only a few addresses must be set aside to handle interrupt service routine addresses for implementing the PPS-8's vectored interrupt capability. In any case, further discussion of these "pools" is beyond the scope of this appendix.

Returning to a discussion of specific instructions listed in Fig. A6-3, note the large number of variations in the load, store, and exchange instructions. These permit especially efficient operations upon arrays. On the

Figure A6-3. Rockwell PPS-8 Instruction Set

Operation	MNE	OP	Basic operation	Increment or decrement pointer	Skip condition	Final operation	Comment code	Bytes	Cycles	Carry
Load A	L		W←A←M(ZX)	—	—	—		1	1	—
	LN		W←A←M(ZX)	Inc. X(7:1)	X = 0	—		1	1	—
	LD		W←A←M(ZX)	Dec. X(7:1)	X = 127	—		1	1	—
	LNXL		W←A←M(ZX)	Inc. X(7:1)	X = 0	ZX ↔ L		1	1	—
	LDXL		W←A←M(ZX)	Dec. X(7:1)	X = 127	ZX ↔ L		1	1	—
	LNCX		W←A←M(ZX)	Inc. X(7:1)	X = 0 or X = Y	ZX ↔ L		1	1	—
	LDCX		W←A←M(ZX)	Dec. X(7:1)	X = 127 or X = Y	ZX ↔ L		1	1	—
	LNXY		W←A←M(ZX)	Inc. X(7:1)	X = 0	X ↔ Y		1	1	—
	LAL		W←A←M(L)	Inc. L	—	—		1	1	—
	LAI	I(8)	A←I	—	—	—		2*	3	—
	IN	I(8)	A←Device I	—	—	—		3*	3	—
	IO4	I(8)	(see text)	—	—	—		2	2	—
	RIS		A←Interrupt status	—	—	—		2	2	—
Store A	S		M(ZX)←A	—	—	—		1	1	—
	SN		M(ZX)←A	Inc. X(7:1)	X = 0	—		1	1	—
	SD		M(ZX)←A	Dec. X(7:1)	X = 127	—		1	1	—
	SNXL		M(ZX)←A	Inc. X(7:1)	X = 0	ZX ↔ L		1	1	—
	SDXL		M(ZX)←A	Dec. X(7:1)	X = 127	ZX ↔ L		1	1	—
	SNCX		M(ZX)←A	Inc. X(7:1)	X = 0 or X = Y	ZX ↔ L		1	1	—
	SDCX		M(ZX)←A	Dec. X(7:1)	X = 127 or X = Y	ZX ↔ L		1	1	—
	SNXY		M(ZX)←A	Inc. X(7:1)	X = 0	X ↔ Y		1	1	—
	OUT	I(8)	Device I←A	—	—	—		2	2	—
Exchange A	X		W←A↔M(ZX)	—	X = 0	—	M	2	2	—
	XN		W←A↔M(ZX)	Inc. X(7:1)	X = 0	—	M	2	2	—
	XD		W←A↔M(ZX)	Dec. X(7:1)	X = 127	—	M	2	2	—
	XNXL		W←A↔M(ZX)	Inc. X(7:1)	X = 0	ZX ↔ L	M	2	2	—

Category	Mnemonic	Imm.	Operation	Pointer adjust	Skip	Transfer	Mod.	Words	Cycles	Notes
Load X,Y,Z	XDXL		W ← A → M(ZX)	Dec. X(7:1)	X = 127	ZX ⟷ L	M	2	2	—
	XNCX		W ← A → M(ZX)	Inc. X(7:1)	X = 0	ZX ⟷ L	M	2	2	—
	XDCX		W ← A → M(ZX)	Dec. X(7:1)	X = 127	ZX ⟷ L	M	2	2	—
	XNXY		W ← A → M(ZX)	Inc. X(7:1)	X = 0	X ⟷ Y	M	2	2	—
	XAX		W ← A → X	—	—	—		1	1	—
	XAY		W ← A → Y	—	—	—		1	1	—
	XAZ		W ← A → Z	—	—	—		1	1	—
	XAL		W ← A → LU	—	—	—		1	1	—
	LX		X ← M(ZX)	—	—	—	N	2*	2	—
	LY		Y ← M(ZX)	—	—	—	N	2*	2	—
	LZ		Z ← M(ZX)	—	—	—	N	2*	2	—
	LXA		X ← A	—	—	—		1	1	—
	LYA		Y ← A	—	—	—		1	1	—
	LZA		Z ← A	—	—	—		1	1	—
	LXI	I(8)	X ← I	—	—	—		3*	3	—
	LYI	I(8)	Y ← I	—	—	—		3*	3	—
	LZI	I(8)	Z ← I	—	—	—		3*	3	—
	LXL		X ← M(L)	Inc. L	—	—		2*	3	—
	LYL		Y ← M(L)	Inc. L	—	—		2*	3	—
	LZL		Z ← M(L)	Inc. L	—	—		2*	3	—
Load LU	LLA		LU ← A	—	—	—	N	1	1	—
Exchange pointers	XY		X ⟷ Y	—	—	—		1	1	—
	XL		ZX ⟷ L	—	—	—		1	1	—
Push onto stack	PSHA		Stack ← A	Inc. S last	S = 31	—		2*	2	—
	PSHX		Stack ← X	Inc. S last	S = 31	—		2*	2	—
	PSHY		Stack ← Y	Inc. S last	S = 31	—		2*	2	—
	PSHZ		Stack ← Z	Inc. S last	S = 31	—		2*	2	—
	PSHL		Stack ← L	Inc. S last	—	L ← AW		1	3	—
Pop from stack	POPA		A ← stack	Dec. S first	S = 31	—		2*	2	—
	POPX		X ← stack	Dec. S first	S = 31	—		2*	2	—
	POPY		Y ← stack	Dec. S first	S = 31	—		2*	2	—
	POPZ		Z ← stack	Dec. S first	S = 31	—		2*	2	—
	POPL		L ← stack	Dec. S first	—	—		1	3	—

(Continues)

Figure A6-3. (Continued)

Operation	MNE	OP	Basic operation	Increment or decrement pointer	Skip condition	Final operation	Comment code	Bytes	Cycles	Carry
Increment or decrement pointer	INCX		—	Inc. X(7:1)	X = 0	—	M	1	1	—
	INCY		—	Inc. Y(7:1)	Y = 0	—		2	2	—
	INXY		—	Inc. X(7:1)	X = 0	X ⟷ Y		1	1	—
	DECX		—	Dec. X(7:1)	X = 127	—		1	1	—
	DECY		—	Dec. Y(7:1)	Y = 127	—	M	2	2	—
	DEXY		—	Dec. X(7:1)	X = 127	X ⟷ Y		1	1	—
Increment A	INCA		A ← A + 1	—	—	—	N	1	1	—
Set carry	SC		C ← 1	—	—	—		1	1	1
Reset carry	RC		C ← 0	—	—	—		1	1	0
Set bit	SB	I(3)	Bit I of M(ZX) ← 1	—	—	—		2*	2	—
Reset bit	RB	I(3)	Bit I of M(ZX) ← 0	—	—	—		2*	2	—
Complement	COM		A ← $\overline{A}$	—	—	—	N	1	1	—
Add	A		A ← A + M(ZX)	—	—	—		1	1	⟷
	ASK		A ← A + M(ZX)	—	C = 1	—		1	1	⟷
	AISK	I(8)	A ← A + I	—	C = 1	—		3*	3	⟷
Add with carry	AC		A ← A + M(ZX) + C	—	—	—		1	1	⟷
	ACSK		A ← A + M(ZX) + C	—	C = 1	—		1	1	⟷
Decimal adjust	DC		A ← A + 66 (hex)	—	—	—	N	1	1	⟷
	DCC		(see text)	—	—	—	N	1	1	⟷

Operation	MNE	OP	Description	Comment code	Bytes	Cycles	Carry
AND	AN		$A \leftarrow A$ AND $M(ZX)$		1	1	—
	ANI	I(8)	$A \leftarrow A$ AND I		3*	3	—
Exclusive-OR	EOR		$A \leftarrow A \oplus M(ZX)$		1	1	—
OR (inclusive)			$A \leftarrow A$ OR $M(ZX)$		1	1	—
Rotate	RAL		C — A (rotate left)	N	1	1	—
	RAR		C — A (rotate right)	N	1	1	—
Move digit	MDL		MSD of $A \leftarrow$ LSD of $A \leftarrow$ MSD of $M(ZX)$	N	1	1	—
	MDR		LSD of $A \leftarrow$ MSD of $A \leftarrow$ LSD of $M(ZX)$	N	1	1	—
Conditional skip	SKZ		Skip next instruction if $A = 0$		1	1	—
	SKNZ		if $A \neq 0$		1	1	—
	SKC		if $C = 1$		1	1	—
	SKNC		if $C = 0$		1	1	—
	SKN		if bit 8 of $A = 1$		1	1	—
	SKP		if bit 8 of $A = 0$		1	1	—
	SKE		if $A = M(ZX)$		1	1	—
Branch, uncond.	B	Label	Branch to labeled address	N	1,2	1,2	—
	BDI	Label	Branch to labeled address; disable interrupts (IE $\leftarrow$ 0)	N	2	2	—
Conditional branch	BZ	Label	Branch to labeled address if $A = 0$	N	2,3	2,3	—
	BNZ	Label	if $A \neq 0$	N	2,3	2,3	—
	BC	Label	if $C = 1$	N	2,3	2,3	—
	BNC	Label	if $C = 0$	N	2,3	2,3	—
	BN	Label	if bit 8 of $A = 1$	N	2,3	2,3	—
	BP	Label	if bit 8 of $A = 0$	N	2,3	2,3	—
	BNE	Label	if $A \neq M(ZX)$	N	2,3	2,3	—
	BBT	I,label	if bit (8-I) of $M(ZX) = 1$	N	2,3	2,3	—
	BBF	I,label	if bit (8-I) of $M(ZX) = 0$	N	2,3	2,3	—
Set branch flag	NOP		BR $\leftarrow$ 1 (this instruction is automatically inserted by assembler, if needed—see text)		1	1	—
Branch to sub.	BL	Label	Stack $\leftarrow$ L $\leftarrow$ C,P; P $\leftarrow$ labeled address		2*	3	—
Return	RT		C,P $\leftarrow$ L $\leftarrow$ stack		1	3	↔
	RSK		C,P $\leftarrow$ L $\leftarrow$ stack; skip over next instruction		1	3	↔
	RTI		C,P $\leftarrow$ L $\leftarrow$ stack; IE $\leftarrow$ 1		1	3	↔

other hand, a designer need not be overwhelmed by all these variations. For programming which has nothing to do with arrays, there is a single instruction to load the accumulator (L), to store it (S), and to exchange it (X).

Those instructions which increment or decrement the pointer X list this as Inc. $X(7:1)$ or Dec. $X(7:1)$. This notation indicates that the most significant bit $X(8)$ remains unchanged by this incrementing or decrementing process. Recall that the most significant bit of the X register distinguishes between page-zero addressing of an operand and full addressing of an operand (using the Z register to supply the page of the operand).

Most instructions which involve data in memory use the contents of the RAM memory location pointed to by the ZX register-pair, as discussed previously. This location is identified as M(ZX) in Fig. A6-3. However, the PPS-8 includes four instructions (LAL, LXL, LYL, and LZL) which use the L register as a pointer to data in ROM. In addition to their use in accessing constants and tables in ROM, these instructions can be used in passing fixed parameters to a subroutine. For example, a subroutine which operates upon two arrays SOURCE and DEST, each of which is LENGTH bytes long, might use the procedure shown in Fig. A6-4 to pass these parameters to the subrou-

ADD	MNE	OP	Comments
	BL	SUBR	Branch to subroutine SUBR
	DW	LENGTH	DW defines LENGTH as a 1-byte constant
	DWA	SOURCE	} DWA defines SOURCE and DEST as
	DWA	DEST	} 2-byte full addresses
NEXT			

(a)

ADD	MNE	OP	Comments
SUBR	LYL		Y ⟵ LENGTH
	LXL		
	LZL		} ZX ⟵ SOURCE
	LAL		
	LAL		} AW ⟵ DEST
	PSHL		L ⟵ AW; stack ⟵ return address
	.		body of subroutine using instructions to
	.		exchange ZX and L so as to access corresponding
	.		elements in two arrays in RAM
	POPL		L ⟵ return address (from stack)
	RT		Return from subroutine to instruction labeled NEXT

(b)

Figure A6-4. *Parameter passing to a subroutine.* (a) *Calling sequence used to pass fixed parameters to a subroutine;* (b) *picking up these parameters in the subroutine.*

tine. It might be interesting to compare both the number of ROM words used and the execution time spent parameter passing in this way with the more direct approach of a microcomputer like the Intel 8080 in which these fixed parameters are loaded as immediate data into CPU registers just prior to calling the subroutine. The PPS-8 compares favorably if the subroutine needs several parameters, but not all at the same time. In this case the subroutine can access each parameter as it is needed, without tying up CPU registers along the way.

Alternatively, parameters can be passed to subroutines directly by loading immediate data into CPU registers before calling a subroutine. The "immediate" instructions LAI, LXI, LYI, and LZI load the A, X, Y, and Z registers with 8 bits of "immediate" data I, included as one of the bytes of the instruction. This is indicated by the notation I(8).

The I/O instructions are listed in Fig. A6-3 as IN and OUT. The second byte of these instructions uses 4 bits to designate one of up to 15 I/O chips, 3 bits to designate one of up to 8 commands to that chip, and one bit to designate input or output. Later in this appendix, we will see how these commands are used in conjunction with the PPS-8 general I/O chip. For this chip and for other more specialized I/O chips (for example, a controller chip for a printer), these commands set up the operating mode (for example, automatic handshaking), read status information, and transfer data. However, the instructions are not actually written into a program as IN or OUT instructions. Rather, the PPS-8 assembler recognizes specific mnemonics for each of the commands appropriate to a specific type of I/O chip. Thus the general I/O chip, called the Parallel Data Controller (PDC), employs four output commands (for example, LBRA, load buffer register A) and four input commands (for example, RSR, read status register).

The operand field of an I/O command having one of these mnemonics is used solely to designate an I/O chip number (between 1 and 15). Chip number 0 is not actually used as such. Rather, this number is reserved to interrogate all I/O chips at once and determine the source of an interrupt. The appropriate instruction, read interrupt status (RIS), is listed in Fig. A6-3.

One other I/O instruction, IO4, is listed in Fig. A6-3. The 8-bit PPS-8 microcomputer is designed to take advantage of any of the I/O chips for the 4-bit PPS-4 microcomputer. The IO4 instruction handles data in 4-bit bytes, as required by PPS-4 chips. The PPS-4 microcomputer permits up to 16 I/O chips to be used, each chip employing up to 16 commands (each of these having its own mnemonic). Consequently the mnemonic IO4 is again not really used as such. Each instruction will perform a bidirectional transfer, with bits 8–5 of the accumulator going out to the I/O chip and bits 4–1 of the accumulator being loaded from the I/O chip.

The push and pop instructions permit CPU registers to be stored on, and restored from, the stack located in addresses 0–31 of RAM. They bypass the link register L, which holds the return address during subroutine execution and thus serves as the top of stack for return addresses.

The PPS-8 decimal adjust instructions operate somewhat differently from the one discussed in Sec. 7-6. Their use is illustrated in Fig. A6-5, which also shows the use of the "complement and add" approach used by the PPS-8 for subtraction.

In addition to rotate instructions, the PPS-8 includes MDL and MDR instructions which can be used to shift multibyte decimal numbers left or right a digit at a time. In these instructions, MSD of A means most significant digit of A.

While the PPS-8 has one instruction for calling a subroutine (BL), it has three instructions for returning. Each of these restores the link register L to the program counter (and the carry bit) as well as the top of stack in RAM to L. In addition, a subroutine can exit to the next instruction or skip over that to the following instruction, as shown in Fig. A6-6. (Another microcomputer might do the analogous thing by setting or clearing the carry bit within the subroutine and then testing it upon return.) The third return instruction RTI is used at the completion of an interrupt service routine to reenable interrupts.

The circuitry of a PPS-8 microcomputer, including clock chip, CPU, RAM, ROM, and I/O ports is shown in Fig. A6-7. The clock generator uses outputs A and $\overline{B}$ to divide each 4-μs clock cycle into four clock phases—ϕ_1, ϕ_2, ϕ_3, and ϕ_4. These clock phases plus two CPU-generated signals—the write/IO select signal (W/IO) and the read inhibit signal (RIH)—define the use of the 8-bit instruction/data bus at all times. They permit the use of the instruction/data bus (I/D8, . . . , I/D1) to read instructions or constants from ROM, to read from or write to RAM, to transfer addresses and commands to I/O chips, and to transfer data to or from I/O chips.

To make use of this specialized bus structure, all the PPS-8 chips include circuitry to decode the timing and control signals. This (and the 17-V power-supply voltage) necessitates the use of a special Bus Interface Circuit chip if it is desirable to use the RAM and ROM chips designed for general use by other manufacturers. The PPS-8 ROM chip includes 16 pages of 128 words per page. It is mask-programmed not only for its data but also for its (16 consecutive) page numbers. By expanding up to eight ROM chips, a PPS-8 microcomputer can make use of all 14-bit addresses (16K words of ROM).

The RAM chip holds two pages (of 128 words per page). A 6-bit chip address is set up by tying each of six address straps high or low. The chip uses dynamic RAM and includes its own refresh circuitry.

When power comes on, the CPU detects the signal on its power-on (PO) input, clears the program counter and stack pointer, and emits a synchronized power-on (SPO) output to all I/O chips. This will include not only the Parallel Data Controllers of Fig. A6-7, but also any special-purpose controllers used in a PPS-8 microcomputer configuration (for example, a floppy-disk controller).

The PPS-8 microcomputer has a built-in priority interrupt structure. A falling edge on the INT0 input has highest priority and cannot be disabled. It is useful for power-failure detection and shutdown. A falling edge on the

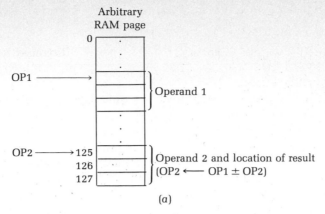

Arbitrary
RAM page

OP1 ⟶ { Operand 1

OP2 ⟶ 125
126 Operand 2 and location of result
127 (OP2 ⟵ OP1 ± OP2)

(a)

ADD	MNE	OP	Comments
	LZI	PAGE	Conventional parameter passing by loading
	LXI	OP1	CPU registers
	LYI	OP2	
	BL	MADD	Branch to subroutine
		(or MSUB)	

(b)

ADD	MNE	OP	Comments
MADD	RC		Reset carry bit initially
MAD1	LNXY		A ⟵ byte of OP1; increment pointer to OP1; X ⟷ Y
	DC		A ⟵ A + 66 (hex)
	AC		A ⟵ A + byte of OP2 + carry
	DCC		Decimal adjust
	SNXY		Byte of OP2 ⟵ A; increment pointer to OP2; skip the next instruction if this pointer has been incremented from 127 to 0; X ⟷ Y
	B	MAD1	Branch to MAD1 for next byte
	RT		Return from subroutine

(c)

ADD	MNE	OP	Comments
MSUB	SC		Set carry bit initially
MSB1	LNXY		A ⟵ byte of OP1; increment pointer to OP1; X ⟷ Y
	COM		Complement A
	AC		A ⟵ A + byte of OP2 + carry
	DCC		Decimal adjust
	SNXY		Byte of OP2 ⟵ A; increment pointer to OP2; skip the next instruction if this pointer has been incremented from 127 to 0; X ⟷ Y
	B	MSB1	Branch back to MSB1 for next byte
	RT		Return from subroutine

(d)

Figure A6-5. Use of decimal adjust instructions. (a) Multibyte operands, with OP2 aligned at the top of a page; (b) calling sequence; (c) multibyte decimal addition subroutine MADD; (d) multibyte decimal subtraction subroutine MSUB.

ADD	MNE	OP	Comments
SUBR			
	.		⎫
	.		⎬ Subroutine
	.		⎭
	.		
	SKC		Skip if carry = 1
	RSK		Return to instruction labeled NEXT
	RT		Return to B ERROR1 instruction

(a)

ADD	MNE	OP	Comments
	.		
	.		
	.		
	BL	SUBR	Branch to SUBR subroutine
	B	ERROR1	Deal with error
NEXT	.		Continue (because no error occurred)
	.		
	.		

(b)

Figure A6-6. Use of alternative subroutine return instructions. (a) Alternative exits from a subroutine; (b) subroutine call followed by a contingent branch to an error routine.

INT1 input will be honored if interrupts are enabled and if INT0 is not pending. It is useful for a real-time clock. When INT2 goes low, it will be honored if interrupts are enabled and if neither INT0 nor INT1 is pending. It is the interrupt input used for servicing I/O chips, each of which has an open-collector output which can pull this input low. Priority among these I/O chips is established by the ACKO/ACKI daisy-chain structure shown in Fig. A6-7, with the I/O chip closest to the CPU having highest priority. However, this priority does not come into play until the interrupt service routine executes a read interrupt status (RIS) instruction. In response to this instruction, the highest-priority I/O chip requesting interrupt service sends its chip number (1–15) and some status information to the CPU's accumulator.

The CPU acknowledges an interrupt on any of its three interrupt inputs by disabling further interrupts (that is, by clearing the interrupt enable flag) from INT1 or INT2. It then executes a subroutine call to an address automatically loaded into the program counter from one of the three pairs of locations on page 1 shown in Fig. A6-8.

The Parallel Data Controller (PDC) is Rockwell's general-purpose I/O chip. It includes two 8-bit I/O ports, each of which has two control lines. All these inputs and outputs are TTL compatible. Each PDC chip includes four address straps for hard-wiring a chip number (from 1 to 15).

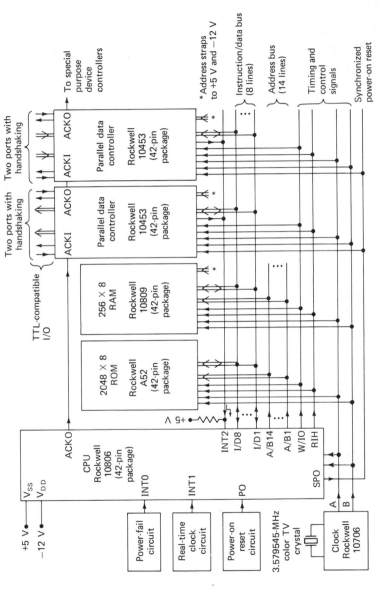

Figure A6-7. Rockwell PPS-8 microcomputer configuration.

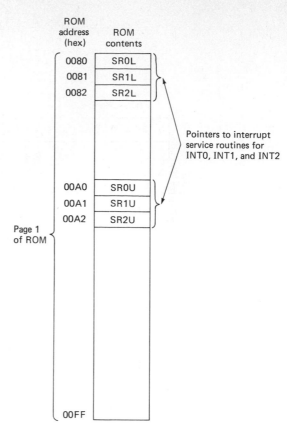

Figure A6-8. Memory map for interrupt vectors.

SR2L = lower 7 bits of address SR2
SR2U = upper 7 bits of address SR2

The two I/O ports A and B are entirely independent, but identical in their capability (except that port A can be set up for use with the PPS-8 DMA controller, discussed in Sec. 3-8). Each port can be set up in any one of eight different modes. When used for input, the port's input data can be latched into a register by a transition on one of the control lines, or it can remain unlatched. In either case, the two control lines both serve as interrupt inputs. As an output port, one of the control lines can be set up to provide a strobe pulse (lasting one clock cycle) to latch the data into a device connected to the output port. The other control line then serves as an independent interrupt input. Alternatively, the two control lines associated with the output port can both serve as independent interrupt inputs.

Each port can also be set up with four input lines and four output lines. The input data can be latched or unlatched and the output data can be generated with or without a strobe pulse.

Finally, each port can be set up for handshaking. When used for input

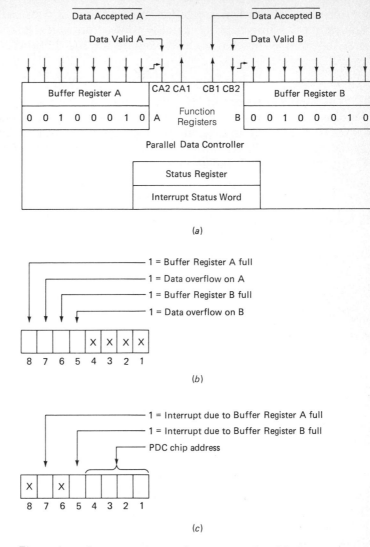

Figure A6-9. *Input ports set up for automatic handshaking.* (a) PDC *configuration and required Function Register contents;* (b) *meaning of Status Register bits;* (c) *meaning of Interrupt Status Word.*

ports as in Fig. A6-9a, the PDC latches the data into Buffer Register A on the rising edge of the CA2 control line (Data Valid, A). At the same time, it sets bit 8 of the Status Register (as indicated in Fig. A6-9b), generates an interrupt, and makes the CA1 control line (Data Accepted, A) go high.

In response to the interrupt, the CPU executes a read interrupt status (RIS) instruction which reads the word shown in Fig. A6-9c into the accumulator. This provides the interrupt service routine with the chip address for this chip and also an indication of whether port A or port B interrupted. Assuming the interrupting Parallel Data Controller has a chip address of 3, the service routine can next execute the instruction

RSR 3

to "read status register" in I/O chip number 3. The content of this register is shown in Fig. A6-9*b*. It permits the CPU to check for data overflow by a device trying to load in a second byte of data before the first byte has been accepted by the CPU (without a proper handshake having taken place). Assuming all is well, the service routine can then execute the instruction

RBRA 3

to "read buffer register A" from I/O chip number 3. This not only reads the input port into the accumulator, but also drives the CA1 control line low automatically and clears the bits corresponding to port A in the Status Register and the Interrupt Status Word. Thus the handshaking is completely automatic.

Port B is used in exactly the same way, with the RBRB 3 instruction used to read in from Buffer Register B. The two ports are initially set up as handshaking input ports by loading the accumulator with the immediate data

00100010

and then executing the instructions

LFRA 3

and

LFRB 3

to "load function register A (B)" of I/O chip number 3 with this mode-setting data.

The two ports of a Parallel Data Controller having chip number 4 are set up as *handshaking output ports* by loading the accumulator with the immediate data

00010110

and then executing the instructions

LFRA 4

and

LFRB 4

This setup is illustrated in Fig. A6-10*a*.

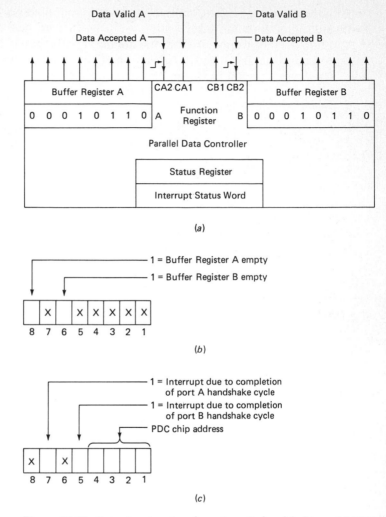

Figure A6-10. Output ports set up for automatic handshaking. (a) PDC
configuration and required Function Register contents; (b) meaning
of Status Register bits; (c) meaning of Interrupt Status Word.

Data is transferred from the accumulator to each output port with

LBRA 4

and

LBRB 4

load buffer register A (B) instructions. This automatically clears the Status

Register bit for the port (shown in Fig. A6-10b) and also sets the Data Valid handshaking output line high.

When the output port is read, the device signals this by raising the Data Accepted handshaking input. This automatically drives the Data Valid line low. However, it is not until the device completes the handshake by lowering the Data Accepted input again that an interrupt is generated. The interrupt service routine need not actually read the Status Register (Fig. A6-10b), since in this mode, it gets all the information available in the Interrupt Status Word, loaded from the interrupting I/O chip by a read interrupt status (RIS) instruction.

It is not necessary that both ports of a Parallel Data Controller be set up either as inputs or as outputs. By setting up one port as in Fig. A6-9 and the other as in Fig. A6-10, a PDC can be used to provide both a handshaking input port and a handshaking output port.

The implementation of direct memory access capability is beyond the scope of this appendix. However, it should be pointed out that some of the optional capability of the Parallel Data Controller not used here permits DMA to be implemented for up to eight channels easily and flexibly using no extra chips beyond the necessary PDC chips for input and output and the DMA chip discussed in Sec. 3-8.

INDEX